Coastal California

John A Vlahides
Tullan Spitz

Contents

North Coast
p41

San Francisco
Bay Area
p81

Central Coast
p116

Los Angeles
p146

San Diego
Area
p176

Lonely Planet books provide independent advice. Lonely Planet does not accept advertising in guidebooks, nor do we accept payment in exchange for listing or endorsing any place or business. Lonely Planet writers do not accept discounts or payments in exchange for positive coverage of any sort.

Destination: Coastal California

Timothy Leary called it the 'nose-cone of the rocket.' Indeed no state in America evokes as much mystique or lore. And no part of the state better lives up to its reputation than Coastal California.

It's impossible to overstate the majesty of the spectacular scenery. Along the North Coast, sun dapples through the canopy of towering redwoods, illuminating deep-green mosses and spiky ferns beneath the tallest trees in the world. Barking and braying sea lions and elephant seals laze upon craggy rock formations jutting out of the Pacific; beneath them sea cucumbers, orange starfish and white anemones cling to the rocks, despite the relentlessly pounding surf. Stand on a bluff in winter and see pods of migrating whales breach offshore, as eagles, falcons and vultures circle overhead. In the south the wide sandy beaches and chiseled bodies of sexy surfers, made famous in movies and television, exceed expectations.

And remember that the state's cultural centers also lie along the Pacific. Though known for their man-made environments – superb restaurants, top-notch hotels, world-class museums, great shopping and happening nightlife – San Francisco, Los Angeles and San Diego all hold lesser-known natural treasures along their coastlines. You need only know where to look.

RICHARD CUMMINS

All roads lead to the water in Coastal California, but there's more here than just the ocean. Watch birds fill the sky at **Tolowa Dunes State Park** (p44) and see whales breach from the bluffs at **Mendocino Headlands State Park** (p69). Climb the spiral staircase inside the **Point Arena Lighthouse** (p74) or scream your lungs out riding the vintage rollercoasters at the **Santa Cruz Beach Boardwalk** (p113). Gasp at the extravagance of **Hearst Castle** (p131) and swoon for James Dean at **Griffith Park** (p159). Or simply revisit a lost world of trans-Atlantic opulence aboard the **Queen Mary** (p170).

JUDY BELLAH

Enjoy spectacular views from the historic **Point Reyes Lighthouse** (p85)

Get active – or just laze around – on the beaches of **Santa Barbara** (p138)

BRENT WINEBRENNER

Take holiday snaps of a quintessential **Big Sur** (p127) landmark, the 1932 Bixby Bridge

JOHN E

DAVID TOMLINSON

Remember to stop and enjoy the view along the dramatic coastline of the **17-Mile-Drive** (p124)

STEPHEN SAKS

Discover the rugged wilderness of
the **Channel Islands National Park** (p144)

Watch wild seals basking in the sun on the
beaches near downtown **La Jolla** (p199)

BRENT WINEBRENNER

DAVID PE

Watch the sun set after a long day of hiking in the **Santa Monica Mountains** (p162)

Stop and smell the flowers in the **Mendocino Coast Botanical Gardens** (p66)

LEE FOSTER

MARK & AUDREY GIBSON

Drive beneath towering redwoods along the **Avenue of the Giants** (p63)

GREG GAWLOWSKI

Imagine a land of dinosaurs in the prehistoric-looking **Fern Canyon** (p50)

LEE FOSTER

Saddle up and explore ancient forests in the **Redwood National Park** (p50)

Stroll beneath the world's tallest trees in **Redwood National Park** (p50)

KRAIG LIEB

Take a step back in time at **Balboa Park** (p180)

ANTHONY PIDGEON

Ride the solar-powered ferris wheel and the vintage-1920s carousel at **Santa Monica Pier** (p165)

RICHARD CUR

JOHN ELK III

Gaze at the graceful jellyfish in **Monterey Bay Aquarium** (p121)

Drive or cycle across a San Francisco icon, the Art-Deco **Golden Gate Bridge** (p100)

GREG GAWL

Getting Started

Advance planning ensures a good trip. Remember that California is huge, and it takes time to get around. To some places you can take the train or bus, but to reach the coast's many remote sights, you'll need a car. Once you're out of the major cities it's easy to navigate, and your biggest problem will be keeping your eyes focused on the road and not on the beautiful scenery. If you've got kids with you, fret not: there's plenty for them to do. And despite the proliferation of high-cost lodging along the coast, budget travelers will find deals along the way.

WHEN TO GO

Coastal California is a great place to visit year-round. Most visitors arrive between June and September, crowding major tourist attractions and causing significant spikes in room rates, even at motels. If you come in summer, try to travel midweek, when crowds are thinner and rates cheaper.

Expect summertime fog anywhere north of Santa Barbara. It gets chilly, but it never gets cold. (However, if you crave July heat, you'll have to head inland to escape the fog.) Though it rains in winter, the coast never freezes, and the hills turn green. In spring they're dotted with wildflowers before summertime droughts turn them gold again. During the spring and fall, the ubiquitous coastal fog clears, providing the greatest opportunity to see the famous coastal vistas. Indian summer stretches from September through October.

See Climate Charts (p207) for more information.

You can enjoy hiking, canoeing, rafting and other warm-weather outdoor activities in summer, spring and fall; swimming is only comfortable at the height of summer in Northern California and from around May to October in Southern California, though surfers and divers hit the waters year-round in wet suits. Winter is whale-watching season, when gray whales migrate down the coast from Alaska.

COSTS

The cost of travel in California depends largely on the degree of comfort you require. The main expenses are transportation, accommodations, food and drink, and sightseeing. If you're traveling with children or want to keep your costs down, always ask about discounts.

The easiest and most comfortable way to see California is by car. Rental rates range between $120 and $250 a week; insurance costs $15 to $35, depending on the coverage selected. For more information on transportation, see p216.

Lodging costs run highest between Memorial Day (late May) and Labor Day (early September). Basic motels start at $50 a night and top

---

DON'T LEAVE HOME WITHOUT...

- A sweater...and expect to wear it, especially up north
- A raincoat between November and April.
- Sun hat, water bottle and sunglasses, all essential items
- Games for long car rides, especially if you have kids
- A bathing suit...and pack it in your carry-on bag. If your luggage gets lost, at least you'll be able to take a swim upon arrival and forget your worries.

out at $130. Mid-range accommodations cost $100 to $200, and up to $900 for luxurious top-end resorts. B&Bs range between $100 and $300. Also see Accommodations (p204).

If you don't insist on sit-down meals, you need not spend much money on food. Eat at simple, hole-in-the-wall restaurants. If you want a more substantial meal, lunch is cheaper than dinner. Remember to add tax and a 15% to 20% tip. Plan on $10 to $30 per meal; ask for children's menus too.

Many museums have an admission-free day or evening once a week. Entrance to national parks and historic sites costs $4 to $20 per vehicle and is good for multiple entries over seven days.

PRE-DEPARTURE READING

HOW MUCH?

Motel rooms in northern California $50-110

Dinner for two in San Francisco $30-60+

Movie ticket to feature film $9

Local phone calls 35-50¢

Small cup of coffee $1.25

Southern California would not exist as it does today without water. Marc Reisner's *Cadillac Desert: The American West and Its Disappearing Water* examines in lively prose the contentious, sometimes violent, water wars that gave rise to modern California.

In *The White Album,* Joan Didion pens many fine essays capturing the essence of contemporary California culture, from an architectural critique of the Governor's Mansion that Reagan built, to the psychology of driving Los Angeles' freeways.

For a frothy taste of San Francisco in 1978, the serial-style *Tales of the City,* by Armistead Maupin, collars the reader as he follows the lives of several colorful, fictional characters, gay and straight. Its short chapters make it ideal for reading on the plane, and you'll want to rush to the sights mentioned in the text.

If you've never read any novels by John Steinbeck, you must do so before visiting Coastal California. Pick up *Cannery Row,* particularly if you plan to visit Monterey. Travel back to a time when California's first capital was populated by adventurers and hooligans, heroes and whores. In Steinbeck's classic tale, you'll come to appreciate the humanity and holiness in all of them. *East of Eden* takes place in nearby Salinas, and is an epic family drama as well as a study of archetypes and opposites. Best of all, when you arrive in the area, you'll immediately recognize the landscape and sites Steinbeck so deftly describes in both texts.

LONELY PLANET INDEX

Gallon of unleaded gasoline $2.20

Liter of bottled water 95¢

Bottle of beer in a bar $2-4

Souvenir T-shirt $10

Burrito $3-5

INTERNET RESOURCES

Hunt down bargain airfares, book hotels, check on weather conditions or chat with locals and other travelers about the best places to visit – or avoid – on the World Wide Web.

Start with the Lonely Planet website (www.lonelyplanet.com). You'll find succinct summaries and the Thorn Tree bulletin board, where you can ask questions before you go or dispense advice when you get back.

Other recommendations:

California Department of Tourism (www.gocalif.com) Links to all visitors bureaus throughout the state.

California State Government (www.ca.gov) Links to general information, history, culture, doing business and environmental protection.

California State Parks (www.parks.ca.gov) Indispensable site for history, information and reservations at all state parks.

Caltrans (www.dot.ca.gov) For questions about driving in California, including trip planning, map assistance, highway and weather conditions.

National Park Service (www.nps.gov) Provides information on every national park, historic site and monument.

National Weather Service (www.wrh.noaa.gov) Extensive climate data, including forecasts, radar, weather records and satellite images.

TOP TENS
MUST-SEE MOVIES

Pre-departure planning and dreaming can sometimes best be done at home, in a comfy chair, with a bowl of popcorn in one hand and a remote control in the other. Head to your local video store for these films, from classics to cheese.

- *Sunset Boulevard* (1950)
  Director: Billy Wilder
- *Rebel Without a Cause* (1955)
  Director: Nicholas Ray
- *Vertigo* (1958)
  Director: Alfred Hitchcock
- *Some Like It Hot* (1959)
  Director: Billy Wilder
- *The Birds* (1963)
  Director: Alfred Hitchcock

- *Chinatown* (1974)
  Director: Roman Polanski
- *The Times of Harvey Milk* (1984)
  Director: Rob Epstein
- *The Lost Boys* (1987)
  Director: Joel Schumacher
- *The Player* (1992)
  Director: Robert Altman
- *American Beauty* (1999)
  Director: Sam Mendes

TOP READS

Immerse yourself in the culture of California, past and present, by picking up a good book. There's no better way to get a sense of place.

- *The Maltese Falcon* (1930)
  Dashiell Hammett
- *The Day of the Locust* (1939)
  Nathanael West
- *Cannery Row* (1945)
  John Steinbeck
- *Baghdad by the Bay* (1949)
  Herb Caen
- *Dharma Bums* (1958)
  Jack Kerouac

- *The Electric Kool-Aid Acid Test* (1968)
  Ken Kesey
- *The Joy Luck Club* (1989)
  Amy Tan
- *The Woman Warrior* (1998)
  Maxine Hong Kingston
- *Less than Zero* (1985)
  Bret Easton Ellis
- *A Heartbreaking Work of Staggering Genius* (2001) Dave Eggers

FESTIVALS & EVENTS

Californians love a good party. From street fairs to regattas, there are festivals all year long. The following list is our top 10; for a more extensive list of major festivals, see p209.

- Tournament of Roses Parade
  (January)
- Chinese New Year
  (February)
- San Francisco International Film Festival
  (April)
- Kinetic Sculpture Race
  (May)
- Bay to Breakers
  (May)

- San Francisco Gay Pride
  (June)
- Carmel Bach Festival
  (July)
- Annual US Open Sandcastle Competition
  (July)
- Monterey Jazz Festival
  (September)
- Christmas Boat Parade
  (December)

Itineraries

CLASSIC ROUTES

THE GRAND TOUR: OREGON TO MEXICO   One Month

If you've dreamed of seeing the entire California coast, one month provides just enough time to get a sense of place. Linger wherever you like, but don't stay too long, lest one month become three. Remember, there are 1100 miles of coastline between Oregon and Mexico. This outline tour leads you to the major sights – the woods, the beaches and the cities – but still offers lots of flexibility.

Find a home base in or around **Crescent City** (p46) to start. It's a great jumping-off point for exploring the **Smith River National Recreation Area** (p46) and **Jedediah Smith Redwoods State Park** (p45). Just south of here the scenery and fishing are terrific around **Klamath** (p49), which is just north of **Redwood National Park** (p50), home to some of the world's tallest, most magnificent trees. If you've never seen tidepools, visit **Patrick's Point State Park** (p52) and stay in **Trinidad** (p52). **Eureka** (p55) has good food and lots to do nearby. Hikers should plan to trek the **Lost Coast** (p61). Victoriana aficionados should not miss **Ferndale** (p59). Hike the largest contiguous redwood forest in the world at **Humboldt Redwoods State Park** (p63); drive the **Avenue of the Giants** (p63) and make it a point to see the Dyerville Giant.

Say goodbye to the redwoods and move your home base to Mendocino County, either to **Fort Bragg** (p66) or **Mendocino** (p68), depending on your bank roll. Witness geological time at **Jug Handle State Reserve** (p68) or **Van Damme State Park** (p72). Lighthouse lovers should climb **Point Arena Lighthouse** (p74). Set up house in **Anchor Bay** (p74) or **Sea Ranch** (p75), or camp around **Salt Point State Park** (p76) or **Sonoma Coast State Beach** (p76). When it's time to move on, pick a spot in Marin County: **Olema** (p86) and **Point Reyes Station** (p83) have comfy B&Bs. Don't miss **Point Reyes National Seashore** (p85). City lovers will be relieved to spot the **Golden Gate Bridge** (p100). Eat like royalty in **San Francisco** (p104) or avoid the city altogether and head to **Half Moon Bay** (p110). Kids dig **Santa Cruz** (p111); they also love running around the **Monterey Bay Aquarium** (p121). If you don't have kids with you, splurge in **Big Sur** (p127) at a luxury lodge or camp beneath the stars. Drop your jaw at **Hearst Castle** (p131) and pull yourself together in **San Luis Obispo** (p134). Head to **Santa Barbara** (p138) and shop 'til you drop; eat well, too. Hike the **Santa Ynez Mountains** (p141) or sail to **Channel Islands National Park** (p144). Burn lots of fuel in **Los Angeles** (p146); take the kids aboard the **Queen Mary** (p170), to **Disneyland** (p152), or surfing and kayaking around **Laguna Beach** (p173). Ride the ferry to **Catalina Island** (p169). Set up camp in **San Diego** (p176) and see **Balboa Park** (p180). Finish your journey with a day trip to **Tijuana** (p193).

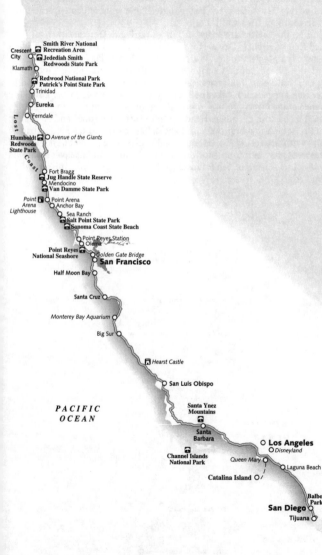

Smith River National
Recreation Area
Crescent
City
Jedediah Smith
Redwoods State Park
Klamath
Redwood National Park
Patrick's Point State Park
Trinidad
Eureka
Ferndale
Lost
Humboldt
Redwoods
State Park
Avenue of the Giants
Coast
Fort Bragg
Jug Handle State Reserve
Mendocino
Van Damme State Park
Point
Arena
Lighthouse
Point Arena
Anchor Bay
Sea Ranch
Salt Point State Park
Sonoma Coast State Beach
Point Reyes Station
Olema
Point Reyes
National Seashore
Golden Gate Bridge
San Francisco
Half Moon Bay
Santa Cruz
Monterey Bay Aquarium
Big Sur
Hearst Castle
San Luis Obispo
PACIFIC
OCEAN
Santa Ynez
Mountains
Santa
Barbara
Channel Islands
National Park
Los Angeles
Disneyland
Queen Mary
Laguna Beach
Catalina Island
Balboa
Park
San Diego
Tijuana

Coastal California's
major attractions
stretch along the
coastline from
border to border
and our Grand Tour
features them all.
You'll need at least
a month to do the
trip justice, but
you could easily
spend three...

THE REDWOOD HIGHWAY

Two Weeks

The tallest trees in the world grow along the North Coast of California. To see the giant redwoods, start in **San Francisco** (p91) and make a loop. Head north on Hwy 101, the Redwood Highway, all the way to the far north on day one, then slowly work your way back on Hwy 1, along the Pacific. Alternatively do this route in reverse and make the return trip in one day. Hwy 101 is the faster route. Time your return trip carefully, and avoid Bay Area traffic.

Cross the **Golden Gate Bridge** (p100) and drive to **Crescent City** (p46); stay a couple of nights. Drive Howland Hill Rd or walk in **Jedediah Smith Redwoods State Park** (p45). Watch birds at **Tolowa Dunes State Park** (p44) and then head south to tour **Redwood National Park** (p50). Outdoorsy types should stay in **Klamath** (p49), but after a few nights in the woods, city folk appreciate **Eureka** (p55) and Victorian **Ferndale** (p59). Drive the **Avenue of the Giants** (p63) and go hiking. Stay the night near **Garberville** (p63) or back in Ferndale. Head south to **Fort Bragg** (p66) and **Mendocino** (p68). Book a few nights around **Anchor Bay** (p74) and take a day trip to **Salt Point State Park** (p76). Spend a night or two near **Point Reyes National Seashore** (p85) and loop south on Hwy 1 around **Mt Tamalpais State Park** (p88). Leave time in **San Francisco** (p91) to see sights you missed when you arrived.

Strolling under California's famous redwoods is the highlight of this two-week nature-lovers' trip, with many chances to hike, bike or simply wander through wilderness along the way.

CENTRAL COAST PEAKS, WAVES & TOWNS   One Week

Along the Central Coast, the Coastal Range lords over sophisticated seaside cities. If you like a mix of outdoor activities, cultural tours, shopping and eating, this trip is for you.

Start your week in **San Luis Obispo** (p134), where you can get your bearings by doing a little sightseeing. If you're feeling athletic, rent a bicycle and squeeze in a cardio workout before you have dinner. The next day, pull on your hiking boots, carry lots of water and climb to the summit of beautiful Bishop's Peak; be sure to scramble to the top for the spectacular vista (this is a strenuous hike). The next day, let your muscles rest and spend the day combing the sand at **Avila Beach** (p136) or **Pismo Beach** (p136), where you can indulge in some clam chowder for lunch. After a couple of nights in San Luis Obispo, you'll be ready to head south to **Santa Barbara** (p138). If you're still sore, stay in town and shop, visit one of the fine museums or hit the zoo. Strong-legged hikers ready for another round should hit the **Santa Ynez Mountains** (p141). If it's too hot on the mountain, consider surfing at **Leadbetter Beach** (p141), or simply spread a blanket out on the sand on **West Beach** (p141) with the kids or **Butterfly Beach** (p141) with your sweetheart. If you prefer campgrounds to hotels, spend only one night in Santa Barbara, then board the boat for **Channel Islands National Park** (p144), where you can spend several days exploring the islands. Alternatively, you can splurge and fly there for the afternoon. After your return to the mainland, stop in **Malibu** (p163) to surf, or hike the **Santa Monica Mountains** (p162).

If you've only got a week, don't try to squeeze in too much. Focus on one area, such as the Central Coast, and kick back, relax and enjoy the best mountains, beaches and towns on offer.

TAILORED TRIPS

TAKE ME OUT TO THE BALLGAME   One Week

California has five major-league baseball teams: the San Francisco Giants, the Oakland A's, the Anaheim Angels, the Los Angeles Dodgers and the San Diego Padres. If you time your visit right, you'll be able to watch all five teams play a home game. Before you book your flights or rent a car, check Major League Baseball's website (www.mlb.com); it links to all five teams' game schedules and has information on ticket purchase.

Stay a couple of nights in **San Francisco** (p91). From downtown you can walk to Pac Bell Park to see the Giants play; the next night, ride BART to see the A's play at the Coliseum (don't drive in the Bay Area if you don't have to). When it's time to go to **Los Angeles** (p146), you can rent a car or save six to 12 hours' drive time by flying instead. Rent a car in LA (don't arrive during rush hour) to get to the Dodgers Stadium. **San Diego** (p176) and its new Petco Park is two hours south of LA; **Anaheim** (p152) and Edison Field lies within 30 minutes south of Downtown LA.

BRUSH UP ON YOUR HISTORY   Four Days

Start in Monterey at the the **Monterey State Historic Park** (p122) and discover the former capital of Alta California. See the Custom House, where Commodore Sloat raised the American flag in 1846. Tour the adobe houses and various museums, making certain to see the gardens as well. On day two, drive half an hour to **San Juan Bautista** (p114) and visit the mission and fort, stopping at the blacksmith's shop and to tour the Castro-Breen Adobe. After lunch, drive 4½ hours south via Hwy 101 to **Santa Barbara** (p138); spend the night. Begin day three by exploring **El Presidio de Santa Barbara** (p140). After lunch, head to the hills and **Chumash Painted Cave**

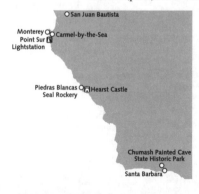

State Historic Park (p138) to see the pictographs; they're the oldest record of human habitation along the California coast. Spend day four driving back up the coast along Hwy 1 to Monterey, making a stop at **Hearst Castle** (p131), or continue all the way to **Carmel-by-the-Sea** (p124), where you can tour the mission before having dinner. Kids might get bored; if you bring them along, be sure to visit places such as the **Monterey Bay Aquarium** (p121), **Santa Barbara Zoo** (p140), **Piedras Blancas Elephant Seal Rookery** (p130) and **Point Sur Lightstation** (p128) along the coast.

The Authors

JOHN A VLAHIDES

Coordinating Author, North Coast & San Francisco Bay Area

A native New Yorker, John now lives in San Francisco, where he spends his free time touring the coast of California by motorcycle, sunning on the sand beneath the Golden Gate Bridge and skiing the Sierra Nevada. John studied cooking in Paris, then worked as a luxury-hotel concierge and earned membership in *Les Clefs d'Or*, the international union of the world's top concierges. Independent travel writer and author of a monthly advice column on ethics and etiquette for *Genre* magazine, John also sings with the San Francisco Symphony Chorus.

My Coastal California

Before I began researching this book I'd always loved the North Coast, so I was thrilled to have a reason to spend time there, especially along the Smith River (p46), one of America's last undammed waterways. I can't wait to go back and trek the Lost Coast (p61), but until I do I'm happy to hike the coast near my home town San Francisco (p81), particularly at the Marin Headlands (p89) and Mt Tamalpais (p88). Come winter, I'm going to head up to Redwood National Park (p50) during the rainy season to hike in the silence beneath the canopy of trees when nobody is there – Northern California woods are magical in the rain. One more tip: if you can, travel to Coastal California in May, while everything is still green and vast fields of wildflowers bloom a rainbow of colors.

TULLAN SPITZ

Coastal California Outdoors, Central Coast, Los Angeles Area & San Diego Area

Tullan spent 10 years in San Francisco, exploring Northern California and the Central Coast on hikes and bike tours. Formerly a Lonely Planet editor, Tullan co-authored the publisher's *Cycling USA: West Coast*. She now works at Oregon Public Broadcasting and lives in Portland, Oregon, with her husband Andrew and stepson Nick.

CONTRIBUTING AUTHOR

Dirk Sutro wrote the Architecture section of The Culture chapter. He is also the author of the *San Diego Architecture* guidebook and *West Coast Wave: New California Houses*, the architecture critic for the *Los Angeles Times*, San Diego edition, and a contributor to *Architecture* and *Landscape Architecture*. He once lived in a beachy mobile home, and now resides in a cutesy little tract house in Encinitas with his wife Sally and daughters Hannah and Semira.

Snapshot

The world looks to California for drama of all kinds, from TV and movies to celebrity gossip, so it should come as no surprise that, in 2003, the state made worldwide headlines when Arnold Schwarzenegger won the governor's seat in a highly contentious recall election that ousted former Democratic Governor Gray Davis from power. Davis had ridden high on the wave of good times in the late 1990s, but when the state's economy fell apart, so did his popularity.

No place in America was more affected by the year-2000 demise of the dot-coms and subsequent plunge of world markets than California, the nation's wealthiest state and the world's fifth-largest economy. The same year brought rolling blackouts to California's recently deregulated electricity market, and the state had to buy its energy on the spot market, day by day, at ridiculously inflated prices. Consumers' bills doubled overnight. Governor Davis, forced into a corner, negotiated expensive long-term contracts. Then, after the contracts had been signed, allegations emerged that power generators had created an artificial energy crisis by pulling electricity off the state's grid in a bid to drive up prices. The companies went bust and the money vanished.

Interestingly enough, at the beginning of the crisis, when President George W Bush was asked if he would help California, he said California got itself into this mess, California could get itself out. Despite ties to failed energy giant Enron, one of the principal players in the power crisis, the White House has since remained mum about the matter, shifting the nation's focus to overseas wars, away from domestic problems such as California's energy woes.

In November 2002, Davis won a second four-year term, but Republican malcontents forced an October 2003 recall election on the grounds of 'malfeasance,' blaming the governor for the $40 billion budget deficit. Citizens were angry at Davis' bad habit of favoring big-money special interests – and Republicans played on it. Arnold Schwarzenegger entered the race and won on a balanced-budget and anti-special-interest platform, despite receiving hefty campaign donations. But this is a state that loves its celebrities. Californians will always forgive an action hero more easily than a state bureaucrat.

After the election, Schwarzenegger faced the challenge of balancing the budget without cutting spending on healthcare or education, and without increasing taxes. The state legislature, dominated by Democrats, had to override contention with the new Republican governor, lest they seemed uncooperative and eventually found themselves voted out of office. California politics is no easy game.

Lots of companies have left the state, fed up by the high cost of doing business in California. The population is split about this. Some feel that the only hope for California's future is to woo giant corporations, build nuclear power plants, allow off-shore drilling for oil – whatever it takes to create jobs fast. Others are happy that the 'carpetbaggers' have left, believing that the state's resources are overtaxed as it is and that slow growth will best serve the state's long-term economic interests.

But this is California, land of new ideas, and the mostly optimistic citizenry will find a way to come out ahead. In the meantime locals and visitors alike are rediscovering inexpensive ways to have fun for free. Fortunately no one needs look far, particularly along the coast.

FAST FACTS

California's population, 2000: 35.6 million

Projected population, 2025: 50 million

Median age, California: 33.3 years

Median age, US: 35.3 years

Median household income, California, 2001: $47,262

Median household income, US, 2001: $42,228

Total percentage of Americans who live in California: 12%

History

PREHISTORIC TIMES

It's generally accepted that the first people in the Americas came from east Asia, over a land bridge to Alaska across what is now the Bering Strait. The first immigrants were probably nomadic hunters following large game animals. Among the earliest known inhabitants of North America were the makers of stone tools found near Clovis, New Mexico, which have been dated to around 11,000 years ago.

The most spectacular artifact left behind by California's early inhabitants is their rock art, dating from 500 to 3000 years ago. Many of the sites are closed to the public in the interest of preservation, but you can visit Chumash Painted Cave State Historic Park (p138), near Santa Barbara.

NATIVE CALIFORNIANS

Archaeological evidence paints a clear picture of the Indians at the time of European contact. The native peoples of California belonged to more than 20 language groups with around 100 dialects. They lived in small groups, often migrating with the seasons from the coast up to the mountains.

Acorn meal was their dietary staple, supplemented by small game, such as rabbits and deer, and fish and shellfish along the coast. Other plants were used for food and the fiber used in making baskets and clothing. California Indians used earthenware pots, fish nets, bows, arrows and spears with chipped stone points, but their most developed craft was basket making. They wove baskets with local grasses and plant fibers and decorated them with attractive geometric designs. Some were so tightly woven that they would hold water. You can see some of the native plants used in basket weaving at the authentic reproduction Sumêg Village (p52) at Patrick's Point State Park.

Coastal and inland peoples traded, but generally they didn't interact much, partly because they spoke different languages. Conflict was almost nonexistent. California Indians had neither a warrior class nor a tradition of warfare – at least not until the Europeans arrived.

EUROPEAN DISCOVERY

Following the conquest of Mexico in the early 16th century, the Spanish turned their attention toward exploring the edges of their new empire. There was much speculation about a golden island beyond Mexico's western coast, and California was actually named (before it was explored), after a mythical island in a Spanish novel. The precise etymology of the name 'California' has never been convincingly established, though there is now wide consensus that it derives from 'Calafia,' the novel's heroine queen, who ruled a race of gold-rich black Amazons.

In 1542 the Spanish crown engaged Juan Rodríguez Cabrillo, a Portuguese explorer and retired conquistador, to lead an expedition up the West Coast to find the fabled land. He was also charged with finding the equally mythical Strait of Anian, an imagined sea route between the Pacific and the Atlantic.

If you're wondering what happened to California's Native American population, find definitive answers in *Handbook of North American Indians*, edited by Robert Heizer; California is covered in Volume 8. Also pick up *The Ohlone Way: Indian Life in the San Francisco-Monterey Bay Area*, by Malcolm Margolin.

20,000–15,000 BC	1542
The Americas' early inhabitants arrive from Asia and groups eventually settle in California	Spanish navigator Juan Rodríguez Cabrillo and his crew are the first Europeans to sight mainland California

When Cabrillo sailed into San Diego, he and his crew became the first Europeans to see mainland California. The ships sat out a storm in the harbor, then sailed northward. They made a stop at the Channel Islands where, in 1543, Cabrillo fell ill, died and was buried. The expedition continued as far as Oregon, but returned with no evidence of a sea route to the Atlantic, a city of gold or islands of spice. The unimpressed Spanish authorities forgot about California for the next 50 years.

The English pirate Sir Francis Drake sailed up the California coast in 1579. He missed the entrance to San Francisco Bay, but pulled in near Point Reyes (p85) – at what is now Drakes Bay – to repair his ship, which was bursting with the weight of plundered Spanish silver. He claimed the land for Queen Elizabeth, named it Nova Albion (New England) and left for other adventures.

For more detailed information, see the websites of the California Historical Society (www.californiahistory .net), the San Francisco Historical Society (www.sfhistory.org) and the San Diego Historical Society (www.sandiego history.org).

THE MISSION PERIOD

Around the 1760s, as Russian ships came to California's coast in search of sea-otter pelts, and British trappers and explorers were spreading throughout the West, the Spanish king grew worried that they might pose a threat to Spain's claim. Conveniently for the king, the Catholic Church was anxious to start missionary work among the native peoples, so the two got together and developed Catholic missions inside military forts (presidios). The Indian converts would live in the missions, learn trade and agricultural skills, and ultimately establish pueblos, or small Spanish towns.

Ostensibly, the purpose of the presidios was to protect the missions and deter foreign intruders. In fact, these garrisons created more threats than they deterred, as the soldiers aroused hostility by raiding the Indian camps to rape and kidnap women. Not only were the presidios militarily weak, but their weakness was well known to Russia and Britain and did nothing to strengthen Spain's claims to California.

The mission period was an abject failure. The Spanish population remained small; the missions achieved little more than mere survival; foreign intruders were not greatly deterred; and more Indians died than were converted. Well worth a detour, head inland for a visit to Mission San Juan Bautista (p114).

One of the first travelers to record his impressions of California, Richard Henry Dana visited the state in 1835 during the Mexican Rancho period. He recounts his thoughts in *Two Years Before the Mast*. It's a good read and is widely available. Dana Point, south of LA, is named after the author.

THE 19TH CENTURY

Mexico gained independence from Spain in 1821, and many of the new nation's people looked to California to satisfy their thirst for private land. By the mid-1830s the missions had been secularized, with a series of governors doling out hundreds of free land grants. This process gave birth to the rancho system. The new landowners were called rancheros or Californios; they prospered quickly and became the social, cultural and political fulcrums of California. The average rancho was 16,000 acres in size and largely given over to livestock to supply the trade in hide and tallow.

American explorers, trappers, traders, whalers, settlers and opportunists showed increasing interest in California, seizing on prospects that the Californios ignored. Some of the Americans who started businesses converted to Catholicism, married locals and assimilated into Californio society. One American, Richard Henry Dana, author of *Two Years Before the Mast* (1840), worked on a ship in the hide trade in the 1830s and

1769	1821
Spain attempts to settle California by establishing the first Catholic mission, Mission San Diego de Alcalá	Mexico gains independence from Spain, and California falls under Mexican rule

wrote disparagingly of Californians as 'an idle and thriftless people who can make nothing for themselves.'

Impressed by California's potential wealth and hoping to fulfill the promise of Manifest Destiny (the imperialist doctrine to extend US borders from coast to coast), US president Andrew Jackson sent an emissary to offer the financially strapped Mexican government $500,000 for California. Though American settlers were by then showing up by the hundreds, especially in Northern California, Jackson's emissary was tersely rejected.

In 1836 Texas had seceded from Mexico and declared itself an independent republic. When the US annexed Texas in 1845, Mexico broke off diplomatic relations and ordered all foreigners without proper papers to be deported from California. Outraged Northern California settlers revolted, captured the nearest Mexican official and, supported by a company of US soldiers led by Captain John C Frémont, declared California's independence from Mexico in June 1846 by raising their 'Bear Flag' over the town of Sonoma. The Bear Flag Republic existed for all of one month. (The banner lives on, however, as the California state flag.)

Meanwhile, the US had declared war on Mexico following the dispute over Texas, which provided the US all the justification it needed to invade Mexico. By July, US naval units occupied every port on the California coast, including the then-capital Monterey.

When US troops captured Mexico City in September 1847, putting an end to the war, the Mexican government had little choice but to cede much of its northern territory to the US. The Treaty of Guadalupe Hidalgo, signed on February 2, 1848, turned over California, Arizona and New Mexico to the US. Only two years later, California was admitted as the 31st state of the United States. (An interesting detail of this treaty guarantees the rights of Mexican citizens living in areas taken over by the US. Many Mexicans feel that this provision still entitles them to live and work in those states, regardless of their country of birth.)

'San Francisco made more money speculating on silver than Nevada did mining it: huge mansions sprouted on Nob Hill, and California businessmen became renowned for their unscrupulous audacity'

THE GOLD RUSH

By an amazing coincidence, gold was discovered several days before the signing of the treaty and quickly transformed the newest American outpost. The population surged from 15,000 to 90,000 over the course of a year between 1848 and 1849.

The growth and wealth stimulated every aspect of life, from agriculture and banking, to construction and journalism. But mining ruined the land. Hills were stripped bare, erosion wiped out vegetation, streams silted up and mercury washed down rivers into San Francisco Bay. San Francisco itself became a hotbed of gambling, prostitution, drink and chicanery, giving rise to the Barbary Coast, whose last vestiges live today in the strip joints along Broadway in North Beach (p95).

California experienced a second boom with the discovery of the Comstock silver lode (1860), though the lode was actually beyond the Sierra Crest in what would soon become Nevada. Exploiting it required deep-mining techniques, which necessitated companies, stocks, trading and speculation. San Francisco made more money speculating on silver than Nevada did mining it: huge mansions sprouted on Nob Hill (p95), and California businessmen became renowned for their unscrupulous audacity.

1848	1850
Gold is discovered in California and the population jumps from 15,000 to 90,000	California becomes the 31st state of the United States of America

THE RAILROAD & AGRICULTURE

The transcontinental railroad shortened the trip from New York to San Francisco from two months to five days, opening up markets on both coasts. Tracks were laid simultaneously from the east and the west, converging in Utah in 1869.

By the 1870s speculation had raised land prices to levels no farmer or immigrant could afford, the railroad brought in products that undersold the goods made in California, and some 15,000 Chinese laborers – no longer needed for rail construction – flooded the labor market. A period of unrest ensued, which culminated in anti-Chinese laws and a reformed state constitution in 1879.

Los Angeles was not connected to the transcontinental railroad until 1876, when the Southern Pacific Railroad (SP) laid tracks from San Francisco to the fledgling city. The SP monopoly was broken in 1887, when the Atchinson, Topeka & Santa Fe Railroad Company (AT&SF) laid tracks linking LA across the Arizona desert to the East Coast. The competition greatly reduced the cost of transport and led to more diverse development across the state, particularly in Southern California and the San Joaquin Valley. The lower fares spurred the so-called 'boom of the '80s,' a major real estate boom lasting from 1886 to 1888. More than 120,000 migrants, mostly from the Midwest, came to Southern California, settling in the 25 new towns laid out by AT&SF in the eastern part of Los Angeles County.

Much of the land granted to the railroads was sold in big lots to speculators who also acquired, with the help of corrupt politicians and administrators, a lot of the farm land that was released for new settlement. A major share of the state's agricultural land thus became consolidated as large holdings in the hands of a few city-based landlords, establishing the pattern (which continues to this day) of industrial-scale 'agribusiness' rather than small family farms. These big businesses were well placed to provide the substantial investment and the political connections required to bring irrigation water to the farmland. They also established an ongoing need for cheap farm labor.

In the absence of coal, iron ore or abundant water, heavy industry developed slowly, although the 1892 discovery of oil in the Los Angeles area stimulated the development of petroleum processing and chemical industries.

THE 20TH CENTURY

The population, wealth and importance of California increased dramatically throughout the 20th century. The great San Francisco earthquake and fire of 1906 decimated the city, but it was barely a hiccup in the state's development. The revolutionary years in Mexico, from 1910 to 1921, caused a huge influx of immigrants from south of the border, re-establishing Latino communities that had been smothered by American dominance. The Panama Canal, completed in 1914, made shipping feasible between the East Coast and West Coast.

The Great Depression saw another wave of immigrants, this time from the impoverished prairie states of the Dust Bowl. Outbreaks of social and labor unrest led to a rapid growth of the Democratic party in California.

DID YOU KNOW?

San Francisco's first cable car started running along Clay St on August 1, 1873.

Five days a week for half a century, Herb Caen wrote a column in the *San Francisco Chronicle*. Read his collected musings in *Baghdad by the Bay*. With pith and panache he paints an everyday portrait of San Francisco during the second half of the 20th century.

1869	1873
The transcontinental railroad shortens the New York to San Francisco trip from two months to five days	Levi Strauss & Co receives a patent for its hard-wearing denim pants (or blue jeans)

Some of the Depression-era public works projects had lasting benefits, from San Francisco's Bay Bridge to the restoration of mission buildings.

WWII had a major impact on California. Women were co-opted into war work and proved themselves in a range of traditionally male jobs; visit the Rosie the Riveter Monument (p102). Anti-Asian sentiments resurfaced, many Japanese-Americans were interned, and more Mexicans crossed the border to fill labor shortages. Many of the service people who passed through California liked the place so much that they returned to settle after the war. In the 1940s the population grew by 53% (reaching 10.6 million in 1950), and during the 1950s by 49% (reaching 15.9 million in 1960).

Before you visit Monterey, pick up a copy of John Steinbeck's *Cannery Row* and learn what life on the waterfront was like before the cannery closed and the tourist shops took over.

SOCIAL CHANGE

Unconstrained by tradition, California has long been a leader in new attitudes and social movements. As early as the 1930s, Hollywood was promoting fashions and fads for the middle classes, even as strikes and social unrest rocked San Francisco and author John Steinbeck articulated a new concern for the welfare and worth of working-class people.

During the affluent post-war years of the 1950s, the 'Beat' movement in San Francisco's North Beach (p95) railed against the banality and conformity of suburban life, instead choosing North Beach coffeehouses for jazz, poetry and pot. When the postwar baby boomers hit their late teens, many took up where the Beat generation left off, heeding Tim Leary's counsel to 'turn on, tune in, drop out.' Their revolt climaxed in San Francisco's Haight district (p95) during the 1967 'Summer of Love.' Sex, drugs and rock and roll ruled the day.

Jack Kerouac's autobiographical *Dharma Bums* explores the transformative power of relationships, and the paradoxes of spiritual awakening and middle-class values in late '50s California.

Laying the foundation for social revolution, the '60s yielded gay liberation, which started in New York in 1969, but exploded in San Francisco in the '70s. Today San Francisco remains the most exuberantly gay city in the world. To visit the thriving community, stroll through the Castro district (p95).

In the late 1980s and '90s, California catapulted to the forefront of the healthy lifestyle, with more aerobics classes and self-actualization workshops than you could shake a totem at. In-line skating, snowboarding and mountain biking rose to fame in California. Be careful what you laugh at. From pet rocks to soy burgers, California's flavor of the month will probably be next year's world trend.

TECHNOLOGY

California has led the world in computer technology. In the 1950s, Stanford University in Palo Alto needed to raise money to finance postwar growth, so it built Stanford Industrial Park, leasing space to high-tech companies that might benefit the university. Hewlett-Packard, Lockheed and General Electric moved in, forming what is now considered the germ cell of Silicon Valley. In 1971 Intel invented the microchip, and in 1976 Apple invented the first personal computer.

The Oscar-winning documentary *The Times of Harvey Milk* (1983) tells the story of San Francisco's first openly gay city supervisor who, on a dark day in 1978, was shot to death in his City Hall office.

Digital technology reinvented our world view. But in the fat years of the 1990s, companies jumped on the dot-com bandwagon. Many reaped huge overnight profits, fueled by misplaced optimism, only to crash with equal velocity at the turn of the millennium. The future remains to be seen, but one thing is certain: California will lead the way.

1908	**1976**
Los Angeles produces its first full-length movie – the 'industry' is born	The first personal computer, the Apple I, is designed in Silicon Valley.

The Culture

The rest of America marvels at California, never quite sure how to categorize it. It's best not to try, since the state is forever reinventing itself. Remember, this is the place that gave the world both hippies *and* Ronald Reagan.

REGIONAL IDENTITY

With over 1100 miles of coastline, it's helpful to think of California as two states: Northern California and Southern California. In fact there is a movement, however small, to divide the state. Culturally it makes sense, but economically it's perhaps not the best thing to do because the north has the natural resources (ie water) and the south has the money. The idea has never gone before voters, maybe because nobody can agree on where to draw the line between north and south.

In the extreme northern section of the state, several neighboring counties in Oregon and California want to establish the 'State of Jefferson,' claiming that they're ignored by their respective state capitals. Since 1941 they have lobbied for their cause, but ask average Californians if they've heard of the movement and nearly all will say no. This aptly demonstrates the vast cultural differences – and the lack of mutual awareness – from one region to the next. Unlike in, say, tiny Rhode Island, Californians in one part of the state are often oblivious of the local problems and concerns at the other end of the state.

In any case, believe everything you've ever heard about Californians – so long as you realize that the stereotypes are most always exaggerated. Sure, valley girls snap chewing gum in the shopping malls east of Los Angeles, blond surfer boys shout 'Dude!' across San Diego beaches, and tree huggers toke on joints in the North Coast woods, but all in all, it's hard to peg the population, so bear in mind that the following exploration of identity addresses general trends, not hard-and-fast rules.

Woodsy types live in the north. Think flannel shirts and hunting caps. There aren't a lot of people – and there's not a lot of money floating around. Christian-fundamentalist radio stations broadcast on several strong frequencies. (Along Hwy 101 in Humboldt County, look for the redwood-burl sculptor whose sign outside reads, 'Carving for Christ.') On the other end of the spectrum, you'll also find some of the state's most progressive liberals in the north (in Arcata, some border on fanaticism). If you see a beat-up old diesel Mercedes-Benz chugging along the highway, chances are that it's running on bio-diesel, possibly even spent french fry grease. There's a lot of ingenuity in these parts.

In the Bay Area, the politics are liberal and the people open-minded, with a strong live-and-let-live ethic. In Marin, there's a tremendous sense of civic pride that borders on narcissism. San Francisco is something of a melting pot, but there aren't a lot of lower-income people since rents are so high.

Los Angeles has greater racial tension – possibly because it's more diverse than San Francisco – but it's likely the unease reflects the disparity between the haves and have-nots. Whatever the case, it's hard to generalize about LA, but one thing is for sure: everybody drives. You're nothing – and nowhere – without a car.

Between Los Angeles and San Diego in Orange County ('beyond the orange curtain'), George W Bush is welcomed with open arms at $1000-a-plate Republican fundraising dinners. Many people live in gated

For more information on the 'State of Jefferson' cause, see www.jeffersonstate.com.

communities and have limited tolerance for (or exposure to) outsiders. The conservative politics extend to San Diego, perhaps because of the large number of navy people who live there, but extreme-right-wing fundamentalists are few and far between. This is California, after all, not the Bible Belt.

LIFESTYLE

Residents along California's coastline appreciate what they have and don't take it for granted. Maybe it's because a large number of people in California grew up somewhere else and came here for the temperate climate, expansive world view and freedom to live however they want. So just as it's impossible to generalize about what type of people live on the California coast, it's equally difficult to qualify *how* people live. The unifying theme is a love of the outdoors.

Perhaps that's why Frank Lloyd Wright built so many homes in the Los Angeles area. In his designs he sought to bring the outdoors inside, with vast panes of glass opening up to patios that connected to other parts of the home. It's a recurring theme in modern California architecture (for more on coastal architecture, see p26), particularly in Southern California where many people have swimming pools (almost nobody on the coast north of Santa Barbara has a pool; it's too cold).

People spend a lot of time outdoors, which explains why most residents consider themselves environmental-conservationists. But disagreements persist about how to conserve the coast. Ongoing legal battles rage over where private property ends and public land begins. Coastwalk (www.coastwalk.org), populist defender of the coast, makes an annual pilgrimage from Oregon to Mexico to raise public awareness that there is no continuous footpath along the Pacific. Private communities like Sea Ranch (p75) have been forced in recent years to provide access to all.

Coastal communities depend heavily on tourism, and even in the Far North, where the standard of lodging and dining isn't as high as elsewhere along the coast, you'll still get a friendly reception. People are pleasant – sometimes to a fault. In fact, in polite society everyone is so determined to get along that it can be hard to find out what somebody really thinks. This increases the further south you go. Political correctness thrives along the coast. Sometimes it's annoying. If you stick around one of the larger metropolitan areas for a while, you'll inevitably exchange telephone numbers with a person who expresses interest in seeing you again. In most parts of the world that means, 'Call me.' Not in California. It's just a nicety. Often the other person never calls, and if you make an attempt, you may never hear back.

Some might say that you're 'codependent' for holding expectations of your new friend. Self-help-group jargon has thoroughly and completely infiltrated the daily language of Coastal Californians. For example, the word 'issue' is constantly bandied about; generally this is the polite way to refer to someone else's problems without implying that the person has…well, problems. It's all about getting along and being nice.

This all flies out the window on an extended middle finger on the state's always-busy freeways. Road rage has become a serious problem. If you plan to do any driving whatsoever, before you put the key in the ignition, take a deep breath and meditate on remaining calm throughout your journey. Expect to encounter self-righteous, irrational, angry people who won't hesitate to cut you off, then flip you off. Factor it in, and let it go. Such barbarism occurs mostly inland and around major cities. Take heart: it's not the norm.

'A large number of people in California grew up somewhere else and came here for the temperate climate, expansive world view and freedom to live how-ever they want'

Despite its problems, California is a very civilized place, especially along the coast. The ocean has a mellowing effect on everyone. You'll enjoy a great trip, and you'll meet lots of nice people. Promise.

POPULATION

California ranks as the most populous state in the US. It's also one of the fastest growing, posting increases of more than 5 million residents between 1990 and 2000.

DID YOU KNOW?

California is known as the Golden State, its official colors are blue and gold, its capital is Sacramento and the state flower is the California poppy.

The state's racial makeup continues to shift. Hispanic, Latino and Asian populations steadily increase, while Caucasians (non-Hispanic) post a decline. The US census of 2000 found the following racial breakdown: Caucasian (non-Hispanic; 46.7%, 15.82 million), Hispanic & Latino (32.4%, 10.97 million), African American (7.4%, 2.5 million), Asian & Pacific Islander (11.6%, 4.36 million) and American Indian (1.9%, 627,000).

California is an amazingly diverse society. In 2002 nearly one in four residents was foreign-born, and approximately 30% of America's total immigrant population lived in California. Of these, Mexicans compose the largest group, followed by those from the Philippines, El Salvador, Vietnam, China, Korea, India, UK, Canada and Germany (in that order). California also has large populations of Iranians and Armenians.

Most immigrants live in urban areas and bring their cultures and languages with them, creating richly textured neighborhoods and districts, particularly in Los Angeles, where most just-off-the-boat immigrants live.

As you work your way southward along the coast from Oregon, you'll notice that population densities steadily increase, maxing out in the Bay Area and dropping off again south of San Francisco. Between Monterey and San Luis Obispo, few people live on the water. It's too remote, and the region often gets isolated by closures of unstable Hwy 1. Greater Los Angeles sprawls along the coast toward San Diego in a continuous string of suburbs, small cities and incorporated towns, interrupted by occasional long stretches of beach.

ARCHITECTURE

Not counting Catalina Island, oil drilling rigs, and Hawaiian islands, Coastal California represents the western frontier of American architecture. From Frank Lloyd Wright to roller coasters to radical houses, the coast has buildings that epitomize the state's reputation as a mecca for artists and dreamers. Exemplary designs are found from Crescent City, near the Oregon border, all the way south to Tijuana.

Coastal lighthouses date from a maritime era before urbanization by automobile, and represent California's insecure adolescent penchant for imported design styles. Crescent City's 1856 Battery Point Lighthouse (p47), at the foot of A Street, is a simple New England saltbox. Six miles offshore lies a more intriguing specimen: St George Reef Lighthouse, built of granite blocks at a cost of $700,000 after 150 passengers lost their lives when the steamer Brother Johnathan ran aground on the reef in 1865. Other notable lighthouses are the 1909 Point Cabrillo (p69) near Mendocino, and San Diego's 1855 Point Loma Lighthouse (p195).

Painted lady Victorians sashay through all of California's major cities, but one of the sexiest is up north in Eureka. When it comes to wedding cake flourishes, Eastern influences and obsessive craftsmanship such as carved columns and leaded glass, Eureka's Carson Mansion (p55), built 1884–86, is the equal of San Diego's 1887 Villa Montezuma and dozens of done-up Ladies in San Francisco.

If your coastal tour consists mainly of a visit to San Francisco (p91), you can still relish some architectural treats. A prominent example is the 1972 TransAmerica Pyramid, visible from most anywhere in the area and an icon among West Coast high-rises. Architect William Pereira hoped that his innovative tapered design would provide natural light and fresh air to its occupants. Near the San Francisco waterfront, also don't miss these gems:

- **Palace of Fine Arts** Bernard Maybeck's 1915 building, on Baker St at Beach St, designed for the Panama-Pacific Exposition.
- **Ghirardelli Square** A complex of shops and restaurants designed in the early 1960s by Wurster, Bernardi & Emmons, around the original brick chocolate factory, with outdoor spaces and landscape by Lawrence Halprin.
- **2800 block of Pacific Avenue** A few blocks from the Bay, including homes by important Bay Area architects Gardiner Dailey, William Wurster, Joseph Esherick, Willis Polk and Ernest Coxhead.
- **Vedanta Society** This 1905 mansion, on the corner of Filbert & Webster Sts, is headquarters for the Hindu sect. It's a hookah-pipeful of Far East combined with Wild West Victorian, crowned by cream-puff towers.
- **National Maritime Museum** On Beech St, just west of Polk Street, a rare 1939 West Coast example of ocean liner-inspired Streamline Moderne, designed by William Mooser Sr and his son Jr.

Down the coast, the foggy, craggy coastline has inspired lots of powerful architecture. Carmel has the most romantic of California's missions. Mission San Carlos Borroméo de Carmelo (p126), designed in Mexican Provincial Baroque style, has weathered stone walls, towers, gorgeous garden courtyards and a beautiful mission church.

Also in Carmel is the spectacular Frank Lloyd Wright–designed Walker house. Crafted from stone, it steps down a slope west of Scenic Drive at Martin St, fronting Monterey Bay. Another building associated with a regional writer is poet Robinson Jeffers' rustic stone Tor House and Hawk Tower (p126).

Further down the coast, Santa Maria's Hi-Way Drive In, at 3085 Santa Maria Way, is among the best of America's remaining drive-in movie theaters – from a 1950s high of more than 4000, less than 1000 remain.

In Santa Barbara, enjoy the romantic Spanish revival courthouse (p139), the Mission (p139) and the University California Santa Barbara (UCSB) campus, with buildings by Charles Moore. UCSB's art history library houses plans and drawings by important California architects.

Los Angeles, some say, is the global epicenter of experimental architecture. The 1949–51 Wayfarers' Chapel (p169) was designed by Lloyd Wright (Frank's son) as a meditation place for travelers and a memorial to scientist-philosopher Emanuel Swedenborg. It's a wondrous place, crafted almost entirely of glass.

In Santa Monica, architect Frank Gehry's 1978 home, on the corner of Washington Avenue and 22nd St, is the 'laboratory' where Gehry's radical ideas first found expression. He encased the original Dutch Colonial within new construction, using raw materials such as plywood and chain-link fence. Gehry went on to design world-renowned buildings, including the Guggenheim Museum in Spain, and LA's own Disney Concert Hall. Gehry's 1985–91 headquarters for ad agency Chiat/Day on Main St features gigantic binoculars by artist Claes Oldenburg.

California's many piers are essential public design features in their communities. The Santa Monica Pier (p165) is one of the flashiest, bearing an amusement park with rides that fly you above the Pacific.

'From Frank Lloyd Wright to roller coasters to radical houses, the coast has buildings that epitomize the state's reputation as a mecca for artists and dreamers'

The 1919–21 Horatio West Court apartments at 140 Hollister Ave, Ocean Park is one of the best examples of architect Irving Gill's revolutionary modernism.

Venice was an odd experiment, replicating its namesake canal community in Italy. At 326 Indiana Ave, one of the most famous and visible homes was designed by architect Brian Murphy in 1989 for actor Dennis Hopper. It greets visitors with a cold wall of corrugated metal.

In San Diego, the missions provided an undeniable architectural influence. Stop at Oceanside's 1798 Mission San Luis Rey de Francia at 4050 Mission Ave – it's less crowded but at least as awe-inspiring as the San Diego mission near Qualcomm Stadium.

Also see the boathouses at 726–32 Third Ave, Encinitas, built in 1925. A few blocks south, at Coast Highway and K Street, are Self Realization Fellowship's ashram and meditation garden (p198), designed under the supervision of spiritual leader Paramahansa Yogananda. To the east of the railroad tracks at 959 Cornish Dr is a grand 1923 Egyptian Revival house.

In design-savvy Solana Beach, a few miles south, drive (and shop!) is the Cedros Design District (p199). It's a mix of old warehouses and quonset huts (including the Belly Up Tavern), with contemporary buildings including architect Rob Quigley's transit station. Along the Coast Highway, at 437 Hwy 1010, is architect Tom McCabe's 1992 BeachWalk. See if you can spy facades that resemble the faces of a flirting couple.

In La Jolla, UC San Diego has dozens of stunning buildings, including the upside-down looking Theodore (Dr Seuss) Geisel Library (p202), designed by William Pereira, with a subtle underground addition by Gunnar Birkerts. The 1965 Salk Institute (p202), designed by Louis Kahn, is the one San Diego building known to design buffs worldwide. Experience its power as you stand in the courtyard at sunset.

La Jolla also has several important Irving Gill buildings, including the concrete 1912 Woman's Club (p200). Across the street, architects Robert Venturi and Denise Scott Brown re-created Gill's 1915 Scripps residence as part of their remodeling of the Museum of Contemporary Art (p201).

Pioneering LA architect RM Schindler's only San Diego design is the 1923 El Pueblo Rivera courtyard apartments at 230–48 Gravilla St.

Near downtown San Diego's waterfront, there are several must-sees:

- **Santa Fe Depot** Mission Revival-style 1915 building on Broadway at Kettner Blvd, designed by Bakewell and Brown.
- **Martin Luther King Jr Promenade** A long, narrow public park along Harbor Drive, designed in 1993 across from the Arthur Erickson–designed San Diego Convention Center.
- **Beaumont Building** Architect Rob Quigley's own live-work 1985 building at 434 W Cedar St, just east of the grand County Administration Center (1936), designed by Richard Requa, Sam Hamill, Louis Gill (Irving's nephew) and William Templeton Johnson.
- **Little Italy** (p185) Centered along India Street, a mix of original buildings and new stand-outs including the LIND project (2001), at Kettner Blvd and Cedar Street, designed by several leading San Diego architects.
- **Balboa Park** (p179) A few blocks inland from San Diego Bay, where leading architects led by Bertram Goodhue and Richard Requa mustered to create spectacular displays for expos in 1915 and 1935.

Lastly, hop the San Diego Trolley from downtown to San Ysidro, and walk across the border for shopping, dining and checking out design in Tijuana, where the latest spectacle is a metallic Border Arch.

Dirk Sutro compiled our Architecture section, and has written several publications on the subject. Keen building buffs can see more of his work in the publications, *West Coast Wave: New California Houses* and *San Diego Architecture from Mission to Modern: Guide to the Buildings, Planning, People, and Spaces That Shape the Region.*

Environment

THE LAND

The third-largest state after Alaska and Texas, California covers about 156,000 sq miles, making it larger than Great Britain or Italy. The state's northern edge lies at about the same latitude as Boston or Rome, and the southern edge at the same latitude as Savannah in Georgia, or Tel Aviv, Israel.

The Coast Range runs along most of California's coastline, its western side plunging straight into the Pacific and its eastern side rolling gently toward the Central Valley. San Francisco Bay divides the range roughly in half. Three-quarters of the way down the state, the Coast Range is joined to the Sierra Nevada (along California's eastern border) by a series of mountains called the Transverse Ranges. These mountains, mostly around 5000ft high, divide the state into Southern and Northern California. To the south, the Los Angeles Basin directly fronts the ocean, bordered by a series of mountains that extend into Mexico. San Diego, on the edge of this plateau 120 miles south of LA, lies right on the border with Mexico.

California sits on one of the world's major earthquake fault zones, on the edge of two plates: the Pacific Plate, which consists of the Pacific ocean floor and much of the coastline, and the North American Plate, which covers all of North America and part of the Atlantic ocean floor. The primary boundary between the two is the infamous San Andreas Fault, which runs for 650 miles and has spawned numerous smaller faults. Walk the Earthquake Trail at Point Reyes (p85) for an up-close lesson in plate tectonics.

Earthquakes are common, although most are too small or too remote to be detected without sensors. In fact, small earthquakes are a good sign. The plates should move at a rate of about 1 inch per year. When they don't, the energy stores up, eventually resulting in large-scale quakes.

For more information about earthquake activity, see the US Geological Survey website (http://earthquake.usgs.gov). This government body collects and stores data on all earthquakes in the United States.

WILDLIFE
Animals

Spend even one day along the coast and you're likely to spot some sort of pinniped, be it an elephant or harbor seal, California sea lion or sea otter. See them frolic along the Central Coast, at either Point Lobos State Reserve (p126) near Carmel, Point Piedras Blancas just north of Hearst Castle (p131), or on the Channel Islands (p144) off Santa Barbara. The Año Nuevo State Reserve (p111) on the San Francisco Peninsula is the largest elephant-seal breeding ground in the world. And right in San Francisco proper, you can watch sea lions up close at Pier 39 (p98).

Between December and March, people come from far and wide to see gray whales breach offshore on their annual southward migration. Get a good view at Point Reyes (p85). Pods of bottle-nosed dolphins and porpoises swim close to shore year-round from Morro Bay (p132) to Mexico.

Many bird species migrate along the Pacific Flyway, one of the four principle migration routes in North America, and there's a changing roster of birds overhead depending on the season. There are great places everywhere on the coast to hunker down with a pair of binoculars, but stellar standouts include Lake Earl (p44), Humboldt Bay National Wildlife Refuge (p59), Arcata Marsh (p54), and Audubon Canyon Ranch (p87).

Year-round residents include gulls, grebes, terns, cormorants, sandpipers and little sanderlings that chase receding waves along the shore, looking for critters in the freshly turned sand.

Monarch butterflies are beautiful orange creatures that follow remarkable migration patterns in search of milkweed, their only source of food. They spend winter in California by the tens of thousand, mostly on the Central Coast, notably in Pismo Beach (p136), Pacific Grove (p121) and San Simeon (p130).

The Audubon Society (www.audubon.org) prints a number of field guides on birds, plants, animals and weather. They're small enough to carry in a purse and useful for answering questions about California's natural environment.

Plants

Coastal ecosystems range from drenched to parched. The northern end of the Coast Range supports stands of coast redwoods (*Sequoia sempervirens*), towering giants with spongy red bark, flat needles and olive-size cones that rely on fog as their primary water source. On the lush forest floor beneath them, look for sword ferns, redwood sorrel and deep-green mosses. Because they're both so tall, it's easy to confuse redwoods with Douglas fir trees; determine which is which by examining their bark. The redwood has fibrous, reddish-brown bark that spirals up the trunk in thick, sinewy lines. The bark of the Douglas fir isn't as red and looks like a jigsaw puzzle.

Along the Central Coast, the Monterey cypress and Monterey pine have thick, rough, grayish bark; long, reaching branches growing in clusters from the top of the trunk; and long needles. Depending where they stand, they're sometimes contorted by the coast's frequent and powerful wind. They too derive much water from the billowing fog.

Southern California, by comparison, is a much more arid region. Look for live oak, with holly-like evergreen leaves and fuzzy acorns; aromatic California laurel, with long slender leaves that turn purple; and manzanita, tree-like shrubs with intensely red bark and small berries.

And throughout the state, both on the coast and inland, the hills turn green in winter, not summer. Because it almost never freezes, as soon as the autumn and winter rains arrive, the dried-out brown grasses spring to life with new growth. Wildflowers pop up as early as February. Along the coast look for little purple wild irises until June. And everywhere look for oak trees: California has 20 native species of them.

The Torrey pine, a species adapted to sparse rainfall and sandy, stony soils, is extremely rare. Look for them near San Diego and on Santa Rosa Island, which is part of Channel Islands National Park (p144).

Endangered Species

The coastline of California – indeed, much of the state – has been drastically altered by development. Imagine almost all of the land along the Pacific between the Oregon border and Santa Cruz covered with stands of giant redwoods. Today only 4.5% of them remain. They provide an important habitat: in recent years scientists have discovered that the complexity of these forests matches that of the tropical rainforests.

Near Ferndale (p59), the most famous casualty of logging in recent years, the spotted owl has been protected in the Headwaters Forest Reserve, but it's rarely open to the public.

To learn more about the history of the timber wars in the Headwaters Forest Reserve, visit www.headwaters forest.org.

California condors, giant birds weighing up to 20lb with a wingspan of 9ft, have all but disappeared, and conservationists are working hard to save them. Stop by Wild Animal Park (p202) near San Diego for a look at them.

All along the coast at state beaches, you're likely to hear about the threatened Western snowy plover, tiny birds that nest in the sand. They scare easily. When threatened by dune buggies or joggers, they take off, leaving their eggs, which burn in the sun. The Monterey Bay Aquarium (p121) is working to restore their habitat by rescuing abandoned eggs and pairing the chicks with adult males, who raise the young.

Introduced Species

Unfortunately, California has been overrun by introduced species. Ice plant, the ropy green groundcover with purple and white flowers that creeps over beach dunes, came originally from South Africa. During construction of the railroads in the 19th century, fast-growing eucalyptus trees were imported from Australia to make railroad ties, but the wood proved poor and split when driven through with a stake. The trees now grow like weeds, fueling summertime wildfires with their flammable, explosive seed capsules. Even snails come from far away, brought to California in the 1850s from France to produce escargots. Now they're everywhere.

NATIONAL PARKS

The National Parks Service protects spectacular stretches of coastline in California. Established in 1968, Redwood National Park (p50) covers 112,000 acres in a patchwork of public and private lands. Unlike the state's more famous inland parks, Sequoia and Yosemite, which were established in 1890, there simply wasn't enough land in the redwoods to delineate a big block. These forests were hotly contested, with loggers itching to get their hands on the valuable lumber. By making them national parks, the federal government sought to protect a disappearing habitat at a crucial time. In fact, logging on adjacent hillsides continues to threaten the park's health, since erosion fills stream beds and causes landslides. Take heart: logging interests in surrounding forests cooperate with the NPS.

Further down the coast the NPS oversees the Golden Gate National Recreation Area (GGNRA; see p88), also an assemblage of lands abutting state parks. Among its sights: Muir Woods (p89), Alcatraz Island (p94) and San Francisco's Ocean Beach (p100).

Off the shore of Santa Barbara, Channel Islands National Park (p144) is largely undeveloped. The islands are prized for their rich marine life and aquatic environments. Unlike other national parks in California, they receive few visitors because of their remote locations: to reach them requires a long boat ride on choppy seas, though you can fly the 30 miles to Santa Rosa Island for day or overnight trips. No bridge connects them to the mainland. The islands support several species of plant and animal, including the rare Torrey pine. From the shore on a rare day without fog or mist, look at the islands and see if you can spot splashes of yellow from the many coreopsis flowers.

For more information about protected areas, see the National Parks Service website (www.nps.gov) and the California State Parks website (www.parks.ca.gov).

ENVIRONMENTAL ISSUES

California's development has come at the expense of the environment. Pollution from mining washes into waterways that find their way to the ocean, polluting wetlands along the Pacific Flyway. Tons of particulate matter spews into the air from automobile and diesel emissions, contributing to asthma in children in urban areas. The ocean is overfished, land is disappearing beneath asphalt and landfills, and tankers leak oil off the coast.

But the news isn't all bad. Californians maintain a high awareness of environmental matters and often vote for preservation, especially in

For more information about environmental issues in Coastal California, contact the Sierra Club (www.sierraclub.org), America's oldest, largest and most effective environmental group.

Northern California, land of the left. Take San Francisco for example. The city plans to recycle *all* of its trash by the year 2020. Indeed, it has already instituted city-wide composting of perishable organic matter. The city's residents also overwhelmingly voted to fund construction of solar power plants that will produce 50 *megawatts* of electricity – and that's just to start.

Along the coast air pollution isn't that bad, due in large part to the prevailing westerly winds that blow in clean air off the ocean. But travel inland, particularly in the LA Basin, and the air takes on a thick haze, obscuring vistas and creating health hazards. Fortunately California leads the nation in emissions control.

Of equal concern is water. There never seems to be enough to satisfy demand by coastal cities and inland farms. Most of it comes from the Sierra Nevada Mountains, in the eastern part of the state, but global warming and droughts both affect winter snowpack. If it rains in the Sierra – or doesn't snow at all – there's nothing to melt into the reservoirs that supply inland farms and coastal cities. Fortunately the citizenry has learned how to conserve. And you will too: expect a low-flow showerhead in your hotel room.

Coastal California Outdoors

Although people have flocked to this vast state for a number of reasons, from finding gold to finding fame, most count natural beauty as one of the most important jewels in the state's crown. California's coastal region has countless destinations to explore by foot, bike, kayak and surfboard. And then there's the undersea region, a playground for divers. Volumes have been written on outdoor activities in California; this chapter gives you a glimpse of what's on offer, and will hopefully whet your appetite for adventure.

HIKING

Hiking is one of the most fulfilling activities for a nature lover. Moving at a natural pace, unaided by machinery, as close as possible to the landscape, the hiker sees, hears and smells so much more than a motorist and cyclist. Hikers, especially those who tread lightly, are treated to regular glimpses of wildlife. In Coastal California you can spot anything from mountain lions to lizards. The observant hiker will be treated to an array of wildflowers from April to August, some so small and precious they are nearly invisible, and others so large and flamboyant they are almost unbelievable. Many are fragrant – from sweet to spicy. The National Audubon Society's *Field Guide to Wildflowers, Western Region* is an excellent guide to the region. Before heading off, always be prepared with water, sunscreen, bug repellent and a map. Remember that we're all guests in the wild, and follow the adage: 'Take only pictures, leave only footprints.'

Some highly recommended literary gems that cover California's awe-inspiring scenery are *Unfolding Beauty: Celebrating California's Landscapes*, edited by Terry Beers (Heyday Books, 2000); and *Natural State: A Literary Anthology of California Nature Writing*, edited by Steven Gilbar (University of California Press, 1998).

WHAT'S TO LOVE OUTDOORS

- Hiking beneath towering ancient redwoods in **Redwood National Park** (p50)
- Whale-watching from the westernmost tip of **Point Reyes** (p85)
- Driving the **Avenue of the Giants** (p63)
- Climbing the 'ecological staircase' at **Jug Handle State Reserve** (p68)
- Canoeing with the current up the Big River tidal estuary in **Mendocino** (p68)
- Tidepooling at **Salt Point State Park** (p76)
- Kayaking the mouth of the **Gualala River** (p75) or **Humboldt Bay** (p55), near Eureka
- Floating down the **Russian River** (p77) from Forestville to Guerneville in a canoe
- Beachcombing by the thundering surf at **Sonoma Coast State Beach** (p76)
- Climbing the spiral stairs up the 10-story **Point Arena Lighthouse** (p74) – the only lighthouse in California visitors can ascend
- Backpacking the **Lost Coast** (p61) on a three-day journey along 24 miles of pristine coastal California wilderness
- Walking across the **Golden Gate Bridge** (p100)
- Standing in the **Marin Headlands** (p89), looking at the Golden Gate Bridge as the fog rolls in, obscuring the roadway but not the tops of the towers
- Riding the ferry to Sausalito on **San Francisco Bay** (p90)
- Mountain biking the trails of **Mt Tamalpais** (p88)

Redwood National Park

Redwoods are a symbol of California, and no trip to the state would be complete without a reverent walk amid these ancient trees, the tallest in the world and seen only here. These majestic giants can live more than 2000 years, and the largest recorded is about 350ft tall and 22ft in diameter at the base. Created in 1968, the Redwood National Park (p50) encompasses three state parks, and there are many excellent hiking opportunities here.

Point Reyes National Seashore

Come in winter or spring and the hillsides will be a brilliant green; visit in summer and they will be golden. Either way the views are exquisite at Point Reyes National Seashore (p85). Try the 3.5-mile Tomales Point Trail through the Tule Elk State Reserve for vistas of the Pacific, Tomales Bay and the graceful, big-horned elk.

San Francisco Bay Area

So far, more than 200 miles of the planned 400-mile **San Francisco Bay Trail** (☎ 510-464-7900; http:\\baytrail.abag.ca.gov) have been completed. This amazing trail, a recreational corridor which will connect the area's nine counties, includes such diverse spots for walking as the Golden Gate Bridge and the San Francisco Bay National Wildlife Refuge. Maps are available by calling or visiting the website.

San Luis Obispo

The prominent hills you see around San Luis Obispo (p134) are the Nine Sisters. Ascend one of the many switchbacks of the tallest volcanic peak, Bishop's Peak, for glorious views.

Los Angeles

You can hike for miles in the country's largest urban park, the Santa Monica Mountains National Recreation Area (p162), amid oak woodlands and other Mediterranean environments, but you'll have to share the park with mountain lions and other wildlife. Another fine choice is heading to the Hollywood Hills (p159).

San Diego

Visit La Jolla's Torrey Pines State Reserve (p202) to see the last remaining *Pinus torreyana* on the mainland.

DIVING & SNORKELING

Offshore and unseen are California's many aquatic environments, explored by divers and snorkelers. Visit Salt Point State Park (p76), the state's first underwater park.

Environmentalists and egalitarians alike will want to know about Coastwalk (☎ 800-550-6584; www.coastwalk.org), a 20-year-old organization dedicated to completing the California Coastal Trail, a continuous trail along the state's entire length; protecting the natural environment; and providing public access. Contact the group to find out about access and guided hikes.

MOUNT TAM

The name Mt Tamalpais (tam-uhl-*pie*-uhs) comes from the Coast Miwok *tamal páyis* meaning 'coast mountain.' The dramatic profile of this mountain, etched by its East Peak (2571ft) and West Peak (2560ft), is a beloved symbol of Bay Area residents. You could live here all your life and never tire of the mountain's many trails and vistas. For trail choices and information on place names, pick up a copy of the excellent topographical trail map, *A Rambler's Guide to the Trails of Mt Tamalpais and the Marin Headlands*, published by **Olmstead & Bros Map Co** (☎ 510-658-6534; PO Box 5351, Berkeley, CA 94705) and available at many bookstores.

With excellent outfitters, Monterey and Carmel Bays (p122) are popular for their healthy kelp. A much-loved spot is Point Lobos (p126).

BICYCLING

California is the bicycle tourist's heaven. It offers amazing scenery; intense, challenging riding; numerous campgrounds and B&Bs; and gourmet delights to satisfy any appetite. Almost year-round the weather is welcoming, so there's no end to the fun.

The best way to discover good day rides or tours in an area is to head to a bike shop and talk to staff and patrons. Bike shops often sell locally produced maps geared specifically to cyclists too. Local bicycle coalitions are also a wealth of information:

East Bay (☎ 510-433-7433; www.ebbc.org)
Los Angeles (☎ 213-629-2142; http://labikecoalition.org)
San Diego (☎ 858-487-6063; www.sdcbc.org)
San Francisco (☎ 415-431-2453; www.sfbike.org)
San Luis Obispo (☎ 805-541-4076; www.slobikelane.com)
Santa Barbara (☎ 805-568-3046; www.sbbike.org)

Books are another good source of route information, but check the publication date and keep in mind that two of California's important Ds – development and disaster – ensure that change is the only constant for roads and routes.

Stellar maps of California cycling routes include those by **Krebs Cycle Products** (www.krebscycleproducts.com; PO Box 7337, Santa Cruz, CA 95061) and the *Pacific Coast Route* by **Adventure Cycling** (☎ 406-721-1776; PO Box 8308, Missoula, MT, 59807).

Day Rides

There are many great day rides throughout the state. One of the best (and most accessible) is the Mt Tam Loop. This 35-mile ride takes you counterclockwise around Mt Tamalpais, starting and ending at the Larkspur Ferry terminal (with service to San Francisco). Views from Fairfax Bolinas Rd are amazing – and well-earned. (For route, see Lonely Planet's *Cycling West Coast USA* or Krebs Cycle Products' *North San Francisco Bay & Wine Country Bicycle Touring Map*.)

Tours

Bike touring in California is for the hearty. Be prepared for hills, wind, heat, cold and, in places, traffic. The following suggestions are two favorite routes. Always tour with a good bike map.

BAY AREA–WINE COUNTRY–RUSSIAN RIVER

There are numerous routes from the San Francisco Bay Area north into wine country and beyond. Ferries and buses accommodate bikes, enabling cyclists to get beyond the city before beginning to ride. Krebs' *North San Francisco Bay & Wine Country* map covers the area. One excellent trip is to ferry from San Francisco to Vallejo and cycle out through the Napa Valley on the Silverado Trail, sampling wine along the way and visiting charming Calistoga and Healdsburg. Head to Guerneville (p77) for swimming in the Russian River, and then continue out to Fort Ross (p76), a historic Russian fort, on the coast. Return via Jenner and Bodega Bay (p77) – famed spot of the filming of Alfred Hitchcock's *The Birds* – and take the coast all the way back through Marin (p89). Or return inland to Petaluma and catch the bus back to the city.

The ocean and coastal habitat have been greatly impacted by human contact, from pollution to overfishing. To learn about the health of the oceans and coasts – and the environmental dangers facing them – log onto the Ocean Conservancy (www.oceanconservancy.org) or the Pew Oceans Commission (www.pewoceans.org). For advice on making sustainable seafood choices, check out Monterey Bay Aquarium's Seafood Watch program (www.mbayaq.org/cr/seafoodwatch.asp).

SAN FRANCISCO TO SAN LUIS OBISPO

The California coast is a rite of passage for some bike tourists, but not everyone has time to cover the entire state. Take a week or 10 days to propel yourself some 235 miles south from San Francisco, up and down the major hills and around the curves and twists of Hwy 1. Camp in Big Sur (p127), visit Hearst Castle (p131) and enjoy the urban delights at your destination, San Luis Obispo (p134), from where you can return via Amtrak. (Use Adventure Cycling's *California Coast Section 2* map or Lonely Planet's *Cycling West Coast USA* guide.)

SURFING

'Ever since pioneer surfer George Freeth was brought from Hawaii as a tourist attraction, people have been discovering and rediscovering the joy of California's waves'

Ever since pioneer surfer George Freeth was brought from Hawaii to Redondo Beach as a tourist attraction, people have been discovering and rediscovering the joy of California's waves from atop surfboards. ₊

Like cyclists, surfers can benefit from good sport-specific maps. Plan a coastal adventure using maps produced by the **Surf Report** (☎ 714-496-5922; www.surfmaps.net). The maps, which detail surf breaks and provide information on seasonal weather and water temperature, are sold county by county, or in a Southern California set ($40). Also useful is Bank Wright's book *Surfing California*.

Enlightened surfers may also want to check out **Surfrider** (☎ 949-492-8170; http://surfrider.org; PO Box 6010, San Clemente, CA 92674), a non-profit organization that strives to protect the coastal environment.

For more information on surfing, see Coastal San Diego (p189).

SEA KAYAKING

The California coast's many bays and estuaries provide endless opportunities for paddlers of the seafaring kind.

Monterey (p118) is practically unbeatable for sea kayaking, where you can frolic amid wildlife and kelp. There are adventures appropriate for people with all skill levels.

The Channel Islands National Park (p144) is perhaps the most remote choice for kayakers. Plan ahead to have Island Packers (p145) transport you and your kayak to one of these islands where you can paddle all day and camp overnight.

In San Diego's La Jolla (p201), sea kayakers have the chance to explore spooky caves carved out of the coast.

Food & Drink

California's food and drink compare with the world's finest, and many great trends began here. North America's only indigenous beer-brewing style originates in California. San Francisco, not Seattle, gave rise to the current coffee culture. The organic-food industry is booming throughout the state. Tying it all together, San Francisco and Los Angeles play off each other, ever-expanding the genre of California cuisine.

STAPLES & SPECIALITIES

The Golden State provides almost all of America's tomatoes, artichokes, most of its lettuce and cabbage, and nearly everything else that comes from the earth. You name it, California grows it. Residents love produce. The single most common way to eat vegetables is in salad. Served with a crusty loaf of freshly baked bread, it's a classic Californian meal.

Salad was once thought of as 'rabbit food' by many a Yankee. Men of Illinois saw men of California eating salads and called them gay (remember 'real men don't eat quiche'?). Thirty years and 300,000 coronary bypass surgeries later, the rest of America has followed suit – if only with iceberg lettuce (also grown here). In California, where ripe avocados, fresh fruits and crunchy nuts originate, there's always something unusual thrown into the salad bowl.

With 1100 miles of coastline, innumerable rivers and streams, it's no wonder Californians love fish. Fishing is not only a huge industry, but a tremendously popular sport. As you travel the coast from spring through fall, you'll see salmon on every restaurant menu, much of it locally caught. (Try it cooked traditionally, on a cedar plank; it's delicious.) In the Far North, pick up salmon jerky to nibble on in the car. Oysters, too, are very popular. Though most indigenous species have been decimated or vanished altogether, look for oyster farms, like Johnson's on Point Reyes (p85).

Some people associate California with vegetarianism, but many locals are actually great lovers of meat. For years the paradigm for beef was corn-fed cattle from the Midwest. In California, however, a reverse trend is in progress. Better restaurants now serve grass-fed beef, produced from cattle that range freely, without dietary or hormonal supplements. Not only does it improve the meat's texture and flavor, but it's more environmentally friendly, since cattle aren't forced to consume a crop that requires vast amounts of water, fuel and electricity to grow and process into feed. But corn is federally subsidized, which makes it cheap; it also causes the animals to grow faster, reducing costs for farmers and eventually consumers.

Still, 'organic' meats and produce have taken off in California among savvy food lovers and environmentalists alike. This is ironic since California's giant agribusiness companies produce huge amounts of genetically modified foods in the Central Valley. The cognoscenti won't buy it. Top chefs now insist on organics, claiming that they're not only environmentally safer, but they simply taste better.

As you drive through Half Moon Bay (p110) and other coastal agricultural regions, stop at the mom-and-pop farmstands and buy whatever is in season; about half of them sell organically grown items. See if you can't taste the difference.

For information and links to all things edible, see www.foodreference.com.

DRINKS

DID YOU KNOW?

California produces more than 17 million gallons of wine annually.

Californians love wine, and ever since Stag's Leap cabernet sauvignon and Chateau Montelena chardonnay (both from the Napa Valley) beat French rivals in 1976 at the Paris Tasting – the 'World Cup of Wine' – California has basked in the glow of international attention for its excellent vintages. From Mendocino to Santa Barbara, head inland just a few miles, and you'll find yourself in some of the world's greatest wine-growing regions. Check out the Anderson Valley (p72) in the north and the hills above Santa Barbara (p138) in the south.

Unlike in France, locally made wine is expensive – and many prefer to drink beer. During the gold rush, men wanted lager but couldn't brew it in the temperate San Francisco climate. Instead they devised a way to brew lager as one would brew ale, at higher temperatures. The result: steam beer.

Steam beer is the only indigenous American beer. All of it is made by hand in smallish breweries. Anchor Steam in San Francisco is the original steam brewer. Today, various ales have grown in popularity. Again, stop in the Anderson Valley (p72) or at any of the microbreweries listed in the destination chapters.

For more information on Californian wine, see the definitive website (www.wineinstitute.org) for local viticulture.

In cafés – which are everywhere – people love strong coffee. Don't be ashamed to wrinkle your nose at pale brown water. Most baristas respect mud drinkers. In roadside diners, expect weak brews.

On the nonalcoholic front many vintners have started bottling their unfermented wine-grape juice. Look for it on restaurant menus and at better non-chain food stores.

CELEBRATIONS

Holidays are feast days, usually spent at home. For Thanksgiving Day and Christmas Day, roast turkey always appears on the table, but lately many California residents – in classic form – have sought new, non-traditional ways to cook them. Starting in late October, food sections of local newspapers brim with alternative recipes for preparing holiday turkeys. (The latest craze is to brine the fowl in salt water before roasting, resulting in a succulent, flavorful, juicy bird.)

On other holidays, such as Independence Day and Labor Day, everybody has a BBQ, cooking everything from hot dogs and steaks, to salmon and vegie burgers over an open fire. Unlike in most regions of America, you can safely plan a BBQ months in advance without worrying that it's going to rain. Barely a drop falls between May and November.

Working your way southward along the Pacific, keep your eyes open for harvest festivals. Most occur between spring and fall, but look for them any time of year. They're uproarious, wacky, lighthearted and loaded with good things to eat. Before you hit the road, check with local visitors centers to see if your trip will coincide with a festival like the Mendocino Crab and Wine Days (p70) in January.

WHERE TO EAT & DRINK

As for choosing one restaurant over another, whenever possible pick one where the chef is also the owner. It makes all the difference in consistency and quality.

California-Cuisine Restaurant

There is no such thing as a typical California-cuisine restaurant. You can't pigeonhole the style. It may draw its primary influences from Europe, or maybe Asia. There are no rules, except that the food is extremely fresh.

minimally processed and perfectly prepared. For sauces, chefs generally rely on flavor-packed reductions of stocks rather than fat-enriched gravies.

Steak House
Despite their reputation, Californians eat a lot of meat. From north to south, steak houses are a constant on the state's food scene. Patrons come for cold gin and rare beef. The dining room is candlelit; in the separate full bar, there's a TV showing the ball game.

Seafood House
California seafood restaurants serve fish in an egalitarian atmosphere of conviviality. The tradition is as old as the Gold Rush. Virtually anywhere a wharf juts out to sea, you'll find a California seafood house.

Bar & Grill
It's just what the name says. At its simplest, it's a sawdust saloon that cooks a limited menu on its small grill. At the other end are fabulous places to eat a steak and drink one-too-many martinis without having to worry about talking too loudly. Like the steak house and the seafood house, the bar and grill is an unpretentious place. They serve lots of meat and have full bars, as well as a good selection of beers.

Quick Eats
Virtually all grocery stores sell to-go food, usually sandwiches, but sometimes freshly roasted chickens, sushi, salads, deli meats and cheeses. In the destination chapters, most 'Eating' sections begin with the location of farmers' markets and indie grocery stores, both great places to grab food on the fly. If you want to eat in a sit-down restaurant but have to get out quickly, tell your waiter as soon as you sit down.

VEGETARIANS & VEGANS
California may have more vegetarians and vegans per capita than any other state, but outside the Bay Area and Greater Los Angeles, strictly vegetarian restaurants are few and far between. Take heart: vegetarians may go to virtually any proper sit-down restaurant in California and order a satisfying meal from the regular menu. Sometimes as much as 60% of the offerings will be vegetarian. This is especially true of Chinese and Indian restaurants, both of which are plentiful. Western-style restaurants have obligatory vegetarian-pasta dishes, salads, portobello mushrooms in season, baked squashes and eggplant (aubergine), pilafs, and pies. Dishes of steamed mixed vegetables dressed with olive oil or an emulsion sauce are popular, and people do astonishing things with tofu. Even many Mexican restaurants will offer vegetarian dishes, a thing unheard of in Mexico – just make sure they didn't use lard in the beans. Along the North Coast (p41) and in Santa Cruz (p111) you'll do very well. Ravens in Mendocino (p71) and Green's in San Francisco (p104) stand out for stellar, white-tablecloth dining; here you'll find no health food, no hippie food, just top-notch cookery without animal products.

'California may have more vegetarians and vegans per capita than any other state'

WHINING & DINING
If you're traveling with kids, you'll be happy to know that most restaurants will be happy to see you. Always ask for a children's menu; it's sometimes printed on a take-home coloring book or placemat. There are also loads of mid-range places where Mom and Dad can enjoy a good bottle of wine and the kids can have ice-cream sundae.

High-end restaurants don't like kids. Meals in such places last two hours or more, too long to expect little ones to sit without squirming or screaming. Unless they're exceptionally well-behaved, properly dressed, and old enough to appreciate the meal, don't bring children to nice restaurants without first calling to inquire if it's appropriate (also see Children on p206).

HABITS & CUSTOMS

Restaurants in California serve lunch between 11:30am and 2:30pm, and dinner between 5:30pm and 10pm. If a restaurant accepts reservations, book a table. Most people eat dinner between 6pm and 8pm. Lots of residents regularly eat out, and restaurants in metropolitan areas get crowded, even on Wednesdays.

If you're not sure what to wear, choose a pressed long-sleeved collared shirt and tuck it into an attractive pair of pants with a good pair of shoes and belt. Add some product to your hair, and voilà! You're a local. If you're still uncertain about dress codes, call the restaurant.

The average Californian eats one good-sized meal a day, usually at dinner. Lunch is more casual than dinner. Many people snack throughout the day.

General table manners are fairly intuitive – don't chew with your mouth open, speak in a loud voice or behave in a rude manner, and you'll be OK. Wait until everyone is served before starting to eat. If you choose to offer food to someone else at the table, simply cut off a small piece and transfer it with the fork to the other's plate. Table servers are politely addressed as 'waiter' or 'waitress,' or possibly 'sir,' but never by shouting, 'Hey, buddy!' or 'Come here!' At better restaurants, *you* must ask for the bill.

Smoking is illegal in restaurants. If you're in someone's home who smokes, wait until all have finished eating, then ask permission of your host and the others at the table. If anyone objects, it's common practice to go outside or into another room.

DID YOU KNOW?

Some chichi joints up and down the coast no longer simply charge a corkage fee; they're levying a tax on birthday cake 'cuttage' as well. Birthday well-wishers are surprised to find that they're being charged to cut the celebratory cake. Even if it's already cut! Perhaps in the future they'll charge a lightage fee for igniting the candles. And then a blowage fee. Call ahead and ask.

North Coast

Welcome to the land of timber wars, spotted owls, flannel shirts, RVs and Christian rock. The antithesis of Southern California in almost every way, the often chilly and damp North Coast is marked by a rugged coastline of craggy cliffs and foggy coves. (Think Hitchcock films, not *Baywatch*.) Extending southward from the Oregon border all the way to the San Francisco Bay Area, the most sparsely populated coastal counties are those at the top of the state: Del Norte (pronounced del-*nort*, not del-*nor*-tay) and Humboldt, which are often considered part of the Pacific Northwest. There are no real freeways here, and if you wear a bikini at the beach you'll freeze. As you work your way south on Hwy 101, you'll more often pass through dense forest than along the ocean. The water is nearby but hard to reach because of the rough terrain and lack of roads over the ridgeline of the unstable coastal range. The wooded landscape yields to lagoons and marshes, then to the small city of Eureka, but within 30 minutes you're back in the woods driving past elk and towering redwoods. It's not until you get south of the Lost Coast, the most rugged stretch of the state's coastline, that Hwy 1 begins, allowing you to drive along the Pacific's edge down the winding coast road. As you pass through Mendocino and Sonoma counties, pickup trucks with gun racks will give way to luxury sedans with babies on board, and you'll start to sense you're nearing civilization. But even just north of San Francisco, when you're at the coast, you'll feel a world away from society.

HIGHLIGHTS

- Hiking the prehistoric landscape of **Fern Canyon** (p50) at Prairie Creek Redwoods State Park

- Driving beneath towering redwoods along the **Avenue of the Giants** (p63)

- Whale-watching from the bluffs at **Mendocino Headlands State Park** (p69)

- Rafting in the **Smith River National Recreation Area** (p46)

- Trekking the spectacular hills of the **Lost Coast** (p61)

- Canoeing with the rising tide up **Big River** (p42) in Mendocino

- Bird-watching in **Humboldt Bay National Wildlife Refuge** (p59)

- Strolling beneath the world's tallest trees in **Redwood National Park** (p50)

- Walking through pygmy forests and along the San Andreas Fault at **Salt Point State Park** (p76)

- Climbing the **Point Arena Lighthouse** (p74) for jaw-dropping views

★ Smith River National Recreation Area

★ Fern Canyon

★ Redwood National Park

★ Humboldt Bay National Wildlife Refuge

★ Avenue of the Giants

★ Lost Coast

★ Mendocino Headlands State Park
★ Big River

★ Point Arena Lighthouse

★ Salt Point State Park

Climate

Foggy in summer and rainy in winter, the North Coast's climate better resembles the weather in Seattle than San Diego. If you turn on the local TV or radio news, you'll no doubt hear the weatherman's mantra: 'morning low clouds and fog clearing to the coast by midday.' The sunniest weather comes in spring and fall, generally April and May, and September and October. Warm beach days don't come often. Barring the occasional heat wave, expect daytime temperatures along the coast in the 60s to low 70s in summer, and 40s to 50s in winter. The rainy season lasts from November through early April, and the further north you go, the more it rains. It never freezes or snows directly along the coast. Inland weather is a different story, where the highest peaks of the Coast Range can get many feet of snow in winter, and summertime valley temperatures often reach the 90s.

National & State Parks

Much of the California coast is privately held, but public lands make a patchwork extending from Oregon to Mexico. You'll find groves of ancient and towering trees, open grass prairies dotted with oaks, ecosystems as complex as rainforests, and drop-dead vistas from bluffs high above the sea. Most notable along the North Coast are the **Redwood National and State Parks** (see boxed text below), covering over 112,000 acres of beaches and forests extending from Crescent City almost to Eureka.

All along the North Coast lie state beaches with wonderful geological or man-made features, like tidepools rich with anemones, starfish, and sea cucumbers. To see the critters up close, try **MacKerricher State Park** (p65), just north of Fort Bragg, or **Patrick's Point State Park** (p52), just north of Eureka, where there's also an authentic reconstructed Indian village. At **Jug Handle State Reserve** (p68) you can hike an ecological 'staircase,' which reveals five wave-cut terraces that evolved over half a million years, each showing what the one below will look like in another 100,000 years.

Even in populous California, there are still wilderness areas along the coast, most notably the **King Range National Conservation Area** (p62) and the **Sinkyone Wilderness State Park** (p62), more commonly known as the Lost Coast, where the rugged and crumbling mountains prevented construction of a coastal highway. Almost everywhere along the coast it's impossible to drive for more than a few minutes without coming upon public coastal access, be it a beach, a hiking trail along a cliff, or a historical sight. For comprehensive information on state parks, visit the California State Parks website at www.parks.ca.gov. For details about national parks, visit www.nps.gov.

Getting There & Around

Most every place on the coast lies along US Highway 101 or California Highway 1, so the easiest and most efficient way to see the North Coast is by car. Rent one in a metropolitan area where there's competition, and you'll save money. If you're flying to the region, book a flight to San Francisco or Oakland (p80), and stay the night to get your bearings. From here, you can drive to Marin County in a few minutes, or Crescent City in seven hours. Though Greyhound buses serve the region, once you get north of the Bay Area, stops are few and far between, and you'll wind up renting a car anyway to get where you're going. Despite its name, Amtrak's *Coast Starlight*, the train connecting Los Angeles and Portland, Oregon, cuts inland north of San Francisco and travels through the Central Valley, not along the coast. Stick to flying and driving.

REDWOOD NATIONAL & STATE PARKS

A patchwork of public lands jointly administered by the state and federal governments, Redwood National and State Parks are actually a string of parks, starting in the north at **Jedediah Smith Redwoods** (p45) and continuing south to **Del Norte Coast Redwoods** (p48), **Prairie Creek Redwoods** (p50) and finally **Redwood National Park** (p50). Federal land fills in the gaps between the state parks, and the ensemble bears the name Redwood National and State Parks. Together they have been declared an International Biosphere Reserve and a World Heritage Site.

UPPER NORTH COAST

☎ 707

Few visitors to California ever venture north of Mendocino and beyond the 'redwood curtain.' You'll have plenty of room to roam: you won't hit any traffic jams, and depending on when you come, you won't see many people. But you will see trees. Lots of them. So much of the coastal drive passes through forested areas that you can lose perspective on where you are and forget that you're by the ocean. Though it's magical beneath the canopy of trees, take the time to stop at pullouts along the road for an overview: a long shot of the rocky coast, the wildflower-studded prairie lands and dense woods through which you're driving. You'll marvel at the scale of it all.

PELICAN STATE BEACH

Little more than a wide strip of sand, never-crowded **Pelican State Beach** (☎ 464-6101, ext 5151) occupies five acres of coastline just south of the Oregon border. Coming from

the north, pull off of Hwy 101 immediately past the state agricultural inspection station. The parking area is a small patch of grass, and there are no facilities. It's a great beach for kite flying; pick one up at the gift shop just north of the state line.

Pitch a tent by the ocean (no windbreaks) at **Clifford Kamph Memorial Park** (☎ 464-7230; www.co.del-norte.ca.us; 15100 Hwy 101; sites $5), where RVs aren't allowed. **Sea Escape** (☎ 487-7333; www.seaescape.us; 15370 Hwy 101 N; s/d $85/95), set just back from the ocean, has clean motel-style suites with kitchens. Stay on the beach at secluded **Casa Rubio** (☎ 487-4313; www.casarubio.com; r $78-158), where three of the four ocean-view inn rooms have kitchens. Down the street, the **Nautical** (☎ 487-5006; 16850 Hwy 101 N; dishes $13-22; ☾ dinner Tue-Sun) has spectacular sunset views and serves seafood and roasted meats on white tablecloths; make a reservation.

Six miles south of Pelican State Beach, the town of **Smith River** needs a paint job, but the pretty **White Rose Mansion Inn** (☎ 487-9260; www.whiterosemansion.com; 1495 Fred Haight Dr; r $118-175) has comfortable B&B rooms in a Victorian farmhouse surrounded by mature gardens.

TOLOWA DUNES STATE PARK & LAKE EARL WILDLIFE AREA

Ten miles south, via Hwy 101 and Lake Earl Dr, the **park and wildlife area** (☎ 464-6101, ext 5112; ☾ sunrise-sunset) encompass about 10,000 acres of terrain, including wetlands, dunes, meadows, wooded hillsides and two lakes, **Lake Earl** and **Lake Tolowa**, which are connected by a narrow waterway. Everywhere there are birds, over 250 species of them. This is a major stopping point along the Pacific flyway for rare geese, ducks, swans and many other species. Listen for their chorus of resonant, low warbles and high-pitched whistles. On land look for coyotes and deer, while out at sea you can spot whales, harbor seals and sea lions. If you like to fish, catch cutthroat trout in the lakes. There are 20 miles of hiking and horseback trails, most of them level and sandy. Tread lightly on the fragile lands. In summer inquire about guided walks. The best wetlands trails lie at the northern portion of the park, where a delicate balance exists between freshwater and marine habitats. Pick up information from the Crescent City–Del Norte County Chamber of Commerce or the Redwood

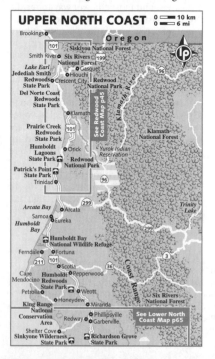

UPPER NORTH COAST 0—10 km 0—6 mi

National and State Parks office in Crescent City (p46). Come in spring and early summer, while everything is still green and lush. In winter it's very wet, and in fall very dry.

The park and wildlife area is split into a patchwork of public and private lands administered by two state agencies: California State Parks and the Department of Fish and Game (DFG); it's hard to tell where one area begins and another ends. The DFG focuses on single-species management, hunting and fishing, while the State Parks' focus is on eco-diversity and recreation. Thus, you might be hiking a vast expanse of gorgeous and pristine dunes, with peerless views of mountains and sea, when out of nowhere you'll hear a shotgun in the woods or whining all-terrain vehicles on the wave slope below. But take heart: there are strict regulations limiting where and when you can hunt or drive, and trails are clearly marked.

There are two primitive **campgrounds** (sites $7): a walk-in environmental campground (no water) and an equestrian campsite (non-potable well water). Both are first-come, first-served. Register at Jedediah Smith or Del Norte Coast Redwoods State Park campgrounds. Bring firewood, and be prepared for mosquitoes in late spring and early summer.

JEDEDIAH SMITH REDWOODS STATE PARK

The northernmost of California's redwood parks, **Jedediah Smith** (vehicle day-use fee $4) sits 18 miles south of Pelican State Beach (via Hwys 101 and 197 south to 199 east) and 10 miles east of Crescent City (via Hwy 101 north to 197 east). The stands of trees are so dense that there are few trails through the middle of the park. However, the outstanding 11-mile **Howland Hill scenic drive** cuts through otherwise inaccessible areas (take Hwy 199 to South Fork Rd; turn right after crossing two bridges). It's a rough gravel road, impassable for RVs and graded only once in spring, but for those who can't easily hike, this is the best way to see the forest up close.

As you drive along Hwy 199, you'll see brown wooden signs with yellow lettering announcing the names of groves. Pull over. There's rarely a trail, but canyon overlooks

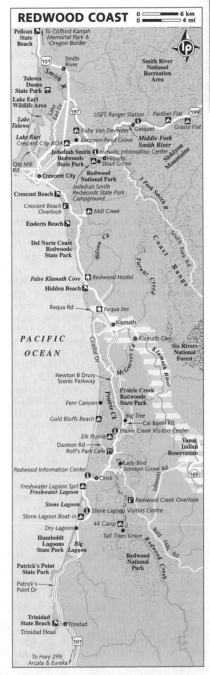

REDWOOD COAST

provide glimpses of the forest's density and lush diversity. Stop for a stroll through the **Simpson-Reed Grove**.

If it's foggy at the coast it's probably sunny and warm here. There's a swimming hole and picnic area near the main park entrance, off Hwy 199, about 5 miles east of Hwy 101. An easy half-mile nature trail, departing from the far side of the campground, crosses the Smith River via a summer-only footbridge, taking you to **Stout Grove**, the park's most famous redwood stand. The **visitors center** (☎ 464-5101, ext 5113; 🕑 Wed-Mon May-Sep) sells hiking maps and nature guides. If you wade in the river, be careful in spring when currents are swift and the water cold.

The popular **campground** (summer reservations ☎ 800-444-7275; www.reserveamerica.com; sites $12) sits beneath towering trees beside the Smith River. There are hot showers and, in summer, lots of people.

Just east of the campground, the **Hiouchi Information Center** (☎ 464-6101, ext 5064; 🕑 9am-5pm, mid-Jun–mid-Sep) stocks maps and books. Families can borrow free activity backpacks stuffed with projects for kids. When the park's two visitors centers are closed, go to Redwood National and State Parks Headquarters (see opposite) in Crescent City.

A mile east of the park in Hiouchi, rent inner tubes, inflatable kayaks and mountain bikes at **Lunker Fish Trips** (☎ 458-4704, 800-248-4704; 2590 Hwy 199); they also lead fishing and wilderness trips. **Hiouchi Motel** (☎ 458-3041, 866-446-8244; www.hiouchi.com; 2097 Hwy 199; s/d $60/65) has straightforward motel rooms, good for those wanting to spend time on the river. Across the street, the **Hiouchi Hamlet RV Resort** (☎ 458-3321, 800-722-9468; tent/RV sites $15/20) also has a small market; pick up supplies and fishing licenses.

CRESCENT CITY
pop 8800
On a crescent-shaped bay, Crescent City is the first sizable town you'll hit driving south – there's not another one until you reach Arcata. Like the rest of the North Coast, it's often foggy in summer, and cold and wet in winter, with 75in of annual rainfall.

Though founded in 1853 as a seaport and supply center for inland gold mines, Crescent City has few old buildings: half

---

DETOUR TO SMITH RIVER NATIONAL RECREATION AREA

West of Jedediah Smith Redwoods State Park, the Smith River, the state's last remaining undammed waterway, runs right beside Hwy 199. Originating high in the Siskiyou Mountains, its serpentine course cuts through deep canyons beneath thick forests of fir and madrona. Chinook salmon and steelhead trout annually migrate up its clear waters. Camp, hike, raft and kayak, but if you want to fish, check regulations. Stop by the **Six Rivers National Recreation Area Headquarters** (☎ 457-3131; 10600 Hwy 199, Gasquet) to get your bearings. Pick up pamphlets here for the **Darlingtonia Trail** and **Myrtle Creek Botanical Area**, both easy jaunts into the woods where you can see rare plants and learn about the area's geology. **Patrick Creek Lodge** (☎ 457-3323; www.patrickcreeklodge.com; s $41-52, d $52-86; lunch $5-10, dinner $15-22), a 1926 log-cabin-style roadhouse, serves three surprisingly good meals a day; they also have simple accommodations upstairs and six motel units in an adjacent building.

---

the town was destroyed by a tsunami (tidal wave) in 1964 (see boxed text on p48), a defining event that has curiously become a point of civic pride, as evidenced by the tsunami-logo flags decorating downtown lampposts. Completely rebuilt, it lacks 19th-century charm, but has a certain '60s-kitsch appeal, with many structures of utilitarian design colored avocado, pink, and white. The local economy depends heavily on fishing (especially for shrimp and crab) and on the Pelican Bay maximum security prison, just north of town.

Orientation & Information
As you approach town from the north or south, Hwy 101 splits into two parallel one-way streets, with southbound traffic on L St and northbound on M St. To see the major sights, turn west on Front St toward the lighthouse and stop at the **Crescent City–Del Norte County Chamber of Commerce** (☎ 464-3174, 800-343-8300; www.northerncalifornia.net; 1001 Front St; 🕑 9am-6pm Mon-Fri year-round, 9am-5pm Sat summer only). Crescent City's tiny downtown

commercial area is centered along 3rd St. **Redwood National and State Parks Headquarters** (☎ 464-6101; 1111 2nd St, cnr K St; ☺ 9am-5pm) has on-staff rangers and information about all four parks under its jurisdiction.

Sights & Activities

The 1856 **Battery Point Lighthouse** (☎ 464-3089), at the south end of A St, still operates on a tiny, rocky island that you can easily walk to at low tide. From April to September, tour the **museum** (tours $2), but hours vary depending on tides and weather. Phone for tour schedules, or check the bulletin board in the parking lot.

Six miles offshore near the California–Oregon border, the **St George Reef Lighthouse** (☎ 464-8299; www.stgeorgereeflighthouse.us) is visible from the mainland only on clear days. You can't get there by boat, but you can take a helicopter for $150, which includes a one-hour tour.

The **Del Norte Historical Society Museum** (☎ 464-3922; 577 H St, at 6th St; admission $2; ☺ 10am-4pm Mon-Sat May-Sep), inside a 1926 jailhouse, has collections of local Native American artifacts and minor historical exhibits on Del Norte's pioneer past, the '64 tsunami and a giant Fresnel lens from the St George Reef Lighthouse.

Skip the Ocean World aquarium on Hwy 101, with its small tanks and gift-shop atmosphere; instead stop by the **North Coast Marine Mammal Center** (☎ 465-6265; 424 Howe Dr; admission by donation; ☺ 10am-5pm), just east of Battery Point, where injured seals, sea lions, and dolphins recuperate after being rescued.

Howe Drive Park (Howe Dr, btwn B & H Sts) has a great harborside beach for little ones, with no big waves to worry parents. There are also picnic tables and a bicycle trail. Further east on Howe Dr, near J St, you'll come to **Kidtown** (admission free), with slides and swings and a make-believe castle for kids to play on. For a scenic drive, head north on Pebble Beach Dr, which ends at **Point St George**, where you can walk through grassy dunes and watch birds.

Visitors can see the manufacture of cheese at the **Rumiano Cheese Company** (☎ 465-1535; cnr 9th & E Sts; ☺ 8am-5pm Mon-Fri summer, hrs vary winter). There's a tasting room, where fresh hot curds sell out quickly between 11am and 2pm.

On weekend evenings, there's glow-in-the-dark bowling at **Tsunami Lanes** (☎ 464-4323; 760 L St). If you like surfing, rent a board at **Noll Surf & Skate** (☎ 465-4400; 275 L St).

Sleeping

Because most people stop here for only one night while traveling between San Francisco and Portland, motels tend to be a little overpriced.

Crescent Beach Motel (☎ 464-5436; www.crescent beachmotel.com; 1455 Hwy 101 S; s/d $77/85) Just south of town, the Crescent Beach has simple, plain rooms, but the unobstructed ocean views can't be beat.

Anchor Beach Inn (☎ 464-2600; www.anchorbeach inn.com; 880 Hwy 101 S; s/d $79/98) If you want amenities like a refrigerator, microwave, DSL line and soundproof walls, this motel has the most up-to-date rooms.

Curly Redwood Lodge (☎ 464-2137; www.curlyred woodlodge.com; 701 Hwy 101 S; r $40/61 winter/summer) Aficionados of '50s-modern love this motel, whose rooms are paneled with the lumber of a single giant curly redwood, but the place needs upgrades like thicker carpeting and door seals.

The county operates two reservable **campgrounds** (☎ 464-7230; sites $10) just outside town: **Florence Keller Park** (3400 Cunningham Lane) has 50 sites in a beautiful redwood grove (take Hwy 101 north to Elk Valley Cross Rd and follow the signs); and **Ruby Van Deventer Park** (4705 N Bank Rd) has 18 sites along the Smith River, off Hwy 197.

Lighthouse Cove B&B (☎ 465-6565; 215 South A St; r $145) There's one suite at the ocean's edge with spectacular views.

Cottage by the Sea (☎ 464-9068, 464-4890, 877-642-2254; 205 South A St; www.waterfrontvacation.net; ste with kitchen $135) Next door to the lighthouse is this sparkling-clean cottage lovingly decorated with too many pillows on the bed. It's by the sea but has no view.

Castle Island Getaway (☎ 465-5102; www.castle islandgetaway.com; 1830 Murphy Ave; r $85-125) Two blocks from the ocean, this getaway has three rooms (reservations required) in a private home run by an urbane innkeeper; the upstairs suite has the most space.

At press time a new resort hotel called the **Hampton Inn** (foot of A St) was under construction. Officials insist it will be great, but Lonely Planet makes no promises until we've seen it ourselves.

Eating & Drinking

Java Hut (☎ 465-4439; 437 Hwy 101 N; ⊙ 5am-10pm) It's almost impossible to get strong coffee on the North Coast, but you'll find the good stuff here.

Good Harvest Cafe (☎ 465-6028; 700 Northcrest Dr, cnr Hwy 101; dishes $3-8; ⊙ breakfast & lunch) The Good Harvest serves the best breakfast in town; it also offers homemade soups, smoothies, sandwiches and great salads for lunch, with lots of vegetarian options.

Glen's Restaurant and Bakery (☎ 464-2914; 722 3rd St; dishes under $10; ⊙ 5am-6:30pm Tue-Sat) An old-school diner, Glen's Restaurant and Bakery serves all the standards, plus its own fresh baked goods.

Thai House (☎ 464-2427; 105 N St; dishes $8-11; ⊙ lunch & dinner) Behind Safeway, Thai House serves surprisingly authentic Thai and Vietnamese cooking, with a few Chinese dishes as well.

Beachcomber Restaurant (☎ 464-2205; 1400 Hwy 101 S; dishes $12-18; ⊙ dinner, closed Wed) If you want a fish dinner, try the Beachcomber, with full ocean views (arrive before sunset), vinyl booths and straightforward preparations of fish and meat. Try the parmesan halibut, or save money by ordering a 'small dinner' for $7 to $11.

Surfside Grill & Brewery (☎ 464-7962; 400 Front St; dishes $7-11; ⊙ 11am-10pm) Serving microbrews, burgers and sandwiches, this cavernous eatery is the place to be on Friday evenings, when you can get drunk and nobody will notice you shouting.

Getting There & Around

North of town, tiny **Crescent City airport** (CEC; ☎ 464-5750) is served by **United Express** (☎ 800-241-6522). You can rent a car at **Hertz** (☎ 464-5750, 800-654-3131) by reservation only.

The **Greyhound bus station** (☎ 464-2807; 500 E Harding Ave) lies just east of Northcrest Dr, about a mile north of the downtown area via Hwy 101 N. **Redwood Coast Transit** (☎ 464-9314) serves the Crescent City area.

DEL NORTE COAST REDWOODS STATE PARK

Marked by steep canyons and dense woods, about half of the park's 6400 acres (vehicle day-use fee $4) are virgin redwood forest, crisscrossed by over 15 miles of hiking trails. Pick up maps and information and inquire about guided walks at the Redwood National and State Parks Headquarters in Crescent City (p46) or at the Redwood Information Center (p50) in Orick.

At the park's north end, watch the surf pound at **Crescent Beach**, just south of Crescent City via Enderts Beach Rd. Continue up the hill to the **Crescent Beach Overlook** and picnic area for whale-watching (November to December and March to April). Hike via the Crescent Beach Trail (or via the Coastal Trail from the south) to **Enderts Beach** for magnificent tidepools at low tide (tread lightly and obey posted regulations).

Tall trees cling precipitously to canyon walls that drop to the rocky, timber-strewn coastline, and it's almost impossible to get

---

CRESCENT CITY'S GREAT TSUNAMI

On March 28, 1964, most of downtown Crescent City was destroyed by a great tsunami (tidal wave). At 3:36am, a giant earthquake occurred on the north shore of Prince William Sound in Alaska. Measuring 9.2 on the Richter scale, the quake was the most severe ever recorded in North America. The first of the ensuing giant ocean swells reached Crescent City only a few hours later.

Officials warned the sheriff's office, and at 7:08am evacuation of the waterfront began. The waves arrived an hour later. The first two were small, only about 13ft above the tide line, and many rejoiced, thinking the worst had passed. Then a very eerie thing happened: the water receded until the bay was emptied, leaving boats that had been anchored offshore sitting in the mud. Frigid water surged in, rising all the way up to 5th St, knocking buildings off their foundations, carrying away cars, trucks and anything else in its path. By the time the fourth and final wave receded, 29 blocks of town were destroyed, with more that 300 buildings displaced. Five gasoline storage tanks exploded. Eleven people died, three of whom were never found.

Many old-timers are still remembered for their heroic acts during and after the waves, helping to save their neighbors and later rebuild the town. Today the contemporary little downtown shopping center that replaced many of the destroyed buildings bears an unusual but appropriate name – Tsunami Landing.

to the water, except via the gorgeous but steep **Damnation Trail** or **Footsteps Rock Trail**. If you don't want to hike, head south to **Wilson Beach/False Klamath Cove**, where you can picnic and stretch your legs on the sand. Two miles further south, **Hidden Beach** has great tidepools.

Sleeping

HI Redwood Hostel (☎ 482-8265, 800-909-4776; www.norcalhostels.org; 14480 Hwy 101; dm/r $16/42; ❤ call for check-in hours, closed Dec-Feb except for groups) When you approach the rambling 1908 farmhouse on its bluff overlooking False Klamath Cove, you'll know you're somewhere special. Reserve well in advance. Greyhound buses stop outside.

Mill Creek Campground (summer reservations ☎ 800-444-7275; www.reserveamerica.com; sites $15) Mill Creek has hot showers and 145 sites in a redwood grove, 2 miles east of Hwy 101, 7 miles south of Crescent City.

KLAMATH

pop 1420

It's easy to drive past tiny Klamath, the southernmost unincorporated town in Del Norte county. The most noticeable landmark from the highway is the Klamath River Bridge at the southern end of town, where golden California bears stand sentry. Pull off Hwy 101 to Klamath Rd, the main street. There's not much here but water and trees, making it an excellent base for outdoor adventures. For information or to learn about August's **Salmon Festival**, contact the **Klamath Chamber of Commerce** (☎ 800-200-2335; www.klamathcc.org). For hiking maps, stop by the Redwood National and State Parks Headquarters (p47) in Crescent City or the Redwood Information Center (p50) in Orick.

Sights & Activities

The mouth of the **Klamath River** is a dramatic sight. For the best views, head north of town to Requa Rd and the **Klamath River Overlook**, and picnic on high bluffs above driftwood-strewn beaches. On a clear day, this is one of the most spectacular viewpoints on the North Coast. For a good hike, head north along the coastal trail. Have an entire beach to yourself by hiking to **Hidden Beach**; access the trail at the north end of Motel Trees (see this page).

Just south of the river, on Hwy 101, follow signs for the scenic coastal drive, a narrow, winding country road (unsuitable for RVs and trailers) atop extremely high cliffs over the ocean. Come when it's not foggy, and mind your driving. Though technically in Redwood National Park, it's so close to Klamath that you should see it while still up north.

It's hard to miss the giant statues of Paul Bunyan and Babe the Blue Ox towering over the parking lot at the **Trees of Mystery** (☎ 482-2251, 800-638-3389; 15500 Hwy 101; adult/child $17/10; ❤ 8am-7pm Jun-Aug, 9am-4pm Sep-May), a shameless tourist trap with a gondola running through the redwood canopy, hardly worth the price of admission. However, the **End of the Trail Museum**, tucked behind the gift shop, has an outstanding collection of Native American arts and artifacts, and it's free.

Sleeping & Eating

You'll get more for your lodging dollar in woodsy Klamath than in suburban Crescent City, but there aren't nearly as many places to eat or grocery shop, and there's nothing to do at night except play cards. You'll find a market and simple diner on the main street in town.

Historic Requa Inn (☎ 482-1425, 866-800-8777; www.requainn.com; 451 Requa Rd; r summer $79-120) By far the best place to stay in Klamath (if not the entire county), this 1914 inn sits atop the bank of the river, and many of the small but comfortable country-style rooms have river views. Guests eat breakfast and dinner in a dining room overlooking the estuary. There's a large common area, where you can read or play board games by the fire. The dining room is sometimes open to the public.

Ravenwood Motel (☎ 482-5911, 866-520-9875; perryemery@aol.com; 131 Klamath Blvd; r/ste with kitchen $58/95) The spotlessly clean rooms are individually decorated with furnishings you'd expect in an urban hotel, not a small-town motel. Mattresses are firm, and sheets have high thread counts. Outside there are BBQ grills.

Motel Trees (☎ 482-3152, 800-848-2982; 15495 Hwy 101 S; r from $50) Opposite Trees of Mystery, this motel has standard-issue rooms and some theme rooms.

Woodland Villa Cabins (☎ 482-2081, 888-866-2466; www.klamathusa.com; 15870 Hwy 101; cabins $60-130) Rent simply furnished cottages here; some have kitchens and can sleep eight. There's also a small market on-site.

Camp Marigold (☎ 482-3585, 800-621-8513; 16101 Hwy 101; tent/RV site $10/15, cabin $48) You can rent a freestanding vacation cabin here. The small pine-paneled rooms need upgrading, but they're OK for brief stays. Skip the overpriced lodge rooms.

Forest Cafe (☎ 482-5585; dishes $5-17; ⌾ 7:30am-9pm summer, closed Tue & Wed winter) Adjacent to the Motel Trees, this cavernous family-style restaurant serves up straightforward American cooking.

PRAIRIE CREEK REDWOODS STATE PARK

Famous for its virgin redwood forests and unspoiled coastline, this 14,000-acre section of Redwood National and State Parks has over 70 miles of hiking trails and spectacular scenic drives. Pick up maps and information and sit by the river-rock fireplace at **Prairie Creek Visitors Center** (☎ 464-6101, ext 5300; ⌾ 9am-5pm Mar-Oct, 10am-4pm Nov-Feb). Kids love the taxidermy dioramas with their push-button light-up displays. Outside, elk roam grassy flats.

Sights & Activities

The 8-mile **Newton B Drury Scenic Parkway** runs parallel to Hwy 101, passing through untouched ancient redwood forests. It's worth the short detour off the freeway to view the magnificence of these trees from your car. Numerous trails branch off from roadside pullouts. If you're depressed by the overall destruction of redwood forests, stop at the **Ah-Pah Interpretive Trail** and stroll the recently reforested logging road: you'll be surprised how quickly the forest grows back and inspired by humankind's ingenuity.

Other scenic drives include the 3-mile-long **Cal Barrel Rd**, which intersects the parkway just north of the visitors center. Further south, take Davison Rd to **Gold Bluffs**. Turn west at Rolf's Park Cafe and Motel (see opposite) south of the park in Orick, and double back north along a some-times-rough gravel road for 3.5 miles over the coastal hills to the **fee station** (per vehicle $4), then head up the coast to **Gold Bluffs Beach**, where you can picnic or camp. One mile ahead, park and take an easy half-mile trail to prehistoric-looking **Fern Canyon**, and see 60ft-high fern-covered canyon walls.

There are 28 hiking and mountain biking trails through the park, from simple to strenuous. If you're tight on time or have mobility impairments, stop at **Big Tree**, an easy 100-yard walk from the parking area. Several other short nature trails start near the visitors center, including the Five-Minute Trail, Revelation Trail, Nature Trail and Elk Prairie Trail. Notable treks include the 11.5-mile **Coastal Trail** and 3.5-mile **South Fork–Rhododendron–Brown Creek Loop**, particularly beautiful in spring when rhododendrons and wildflowers bloom. Approach from the Brown Creek to South Fork direction – unless you like tramping uphill.

Sleeping & Eating

There are no motel rooms or cabins; if you want to sleep here, pitch a tent in the campgrounds at the southern end of the park.

Elk Prairie Campground (summer reservations ☎ 800-444-7275; www.reserveamerica.com; sites summer/winter $15/12) Elk roam this popular campground, where you can sleep under redwoods or at the prairie's edge. Has hot showers and some hike-in sites.

Gold Bluffs Beach (no reservations; sites $14) This campground sits between 100ft cliffs and wide-open ocean, but there are some windbreaks and solar-heated showers. Look for sites up the cliff under the trees.

REDWOOD NATIONAL PARK

Redwood National Park is the southernmost member of the Redwood National and State Parks. This is where you'll find the world's tallest tree (aptly named 'Tall Tree') and the Redwood Creek watershed, the place of great controversy in the years preceding the park's establishment in 1968. The small town of **Orick** (population 650), at the southern tip of the park, is little more than a few storefronts and salmon-jerky stands.

Orientation & Information

Unlike most national parks, there are no fees and no highway entrance stations at Redwood National Park, so it's imperative to pick up the free official map either at park headquarters (p47) in Crescent City or at the **Redwood Information Center** (☎ 464-6101, ext 5265; www.nps.gov/redw; Hwy 101; ⌾ 9am-5pm) in Orick, where there's a 12-minute introductory video. You can also pick up a free permit to visit Tall Trees Grove (see opposite). For in-depth redwood ecology, buy the excellent official parks handbook ($7.50).

COAST REDWOODS: THE TALLEST TREES ON EARTH

Though they covered most of the northern hemisphere millions of years ago, redwood trees now grow only in China and two areas of California. Coast redwoods *(Sequoia sempervirens)* are found in a narrow, 450 mile-long strip along California's Pacific coast between Big Sur and southern Oregon. They can live for 2200 years, grow to 367.8ft tall (the tallest tree ever recorded) and achieve a diameter of 22ft at the base, with bark up to 12in thick.

The structure of coast redwoods has been compared to a nail standing on its head. Unlike most trees, coast redwoods have no deep taproot and their root system is shallow in relation to their height – only 10ft to 13ft deep and spreading out 60ft to 80ft around the tree. The trees sometimes fall due to wind, but they are very flexible and usually sway in the wind as if they're dancing.

What gives these majestic giants their namesake color? It's the redwoods' high tannin content, which also makes their wood and bark resistant to insects and disease. The thick, spongy bark also has a high moisture content, enabling the ancient trees to survive many naturally occurring forest fires.

Coast redwoods are the only conifers in the world that can reproduce not only by seed cones, which grow to about the size of an olive at the ends of branches, but also by sprouting from their parents' roots and stumps, using the established root systems. Often you'll see a circle of redwoods standing in a forest, sometimes around a wide crater; this 'fairy ring' is made up of offspring that sprouted from one parent tree, which may have deteriorated into humus long ago. Burls, the large bumpy tissue growths on trunks and fallen logs, are a third method of reproduction.

Today only 4% of the North Coast's original two million acres of ancient redwood forests remain standing. Almost half of these old-growth forests are protected in Redwood National and State Parks.

Sights & Activities

Once you've gotten your bearings, drive 2 miles up Bald Hills Rd, off Hwy 101, to **Lady Bird Johnson Grove**, one of the park's most beautiful groves, reached via a gentle 1-mile loop trail. Look for the signed turn-off south of Rolf's Park Cafe and Motel (see this page). Continue another 5 miles to **Redwood Creek Overlook**. Atop the ridgeline at 2100ft elevation, you'll see over the trees and the entire watershed – provided it's not foggy. Just past the overlook lies the gated turn-off for the **Tall Trees Grove**, location of several of the world's tallest trees. Rangers issue only 50 vehicle permits per day, but they rarely run out. Pick one up, along with the gate-lock combination, from the information center (see opposite) in Orick or the park headquarters (p47) in Crescent City. Allow four hours round-trip, which includes a 6-mile trip down a rough dirt road (speed limit 15mph) and a steep 1.3-mile one-way hike which descends 800ft to the grove.

Several longer hikes include the awe-inspiring **Redwood Creek Trail**, which also reaches Tall Trees Grove. You'll need a free backcountry permit to hike and camp along this trail, accessible only from Memorial Day to Labor Day, when summer footbridges are up. Otherwise, there's no way to cross the creek.

You can also come on horseback; call **Redwood Trails** (☎ 488-3895). There's primitive camping in the park; inquire at visitors centers.

Sleeping & Eating

Rolf's Park Cafe and Motel (☎ 488-3841; Hwy 101 at Davison Rd; r $55; breakfast & lunch $7-12, dinner $10-22; ⏲ 9am-8pm, closed Oct-Mar) Rolf's stands out for its fine stick-to-your-ribs European-country cooking. Specializing in wild game and German dishes, they also serve grilled fish and can accommodate vegetarians. You won't leave hungry. They also rent adequate motel rooms with two double beds.

HUMBOLDT LAGOONS STATE PARK

A series of lagoons stretching for 8 miles between land and sea, this is an excellent coastal spot for bird-watching and an important marshland for several species of plant and animal. The **Stone Lagoon visitors center** (☎ 488-2041; Hwy 101; ⏲ 10am-3pm Jun-Sep) opens when they have volunteers. **Freshwater Lagoon** sits within Redwood National Park boundaries to the north of the state park. Picnic at the north end of **Stone Lagoon**, which also has two **campgrounds**, one with boat-in access only. Hike along the **Coastal Trail**, which passes through the park, but beware: in winter Stone Lagoon sometimes breaches its ocean barrier. Further south, **Big Lagoon County Park** has a swimming beach (beware the currents) and picnic area.

PATRICK'S POINT STATE PARK

Coastal bluffs jut out to sea at 640-acre **Patrick's Point** (☎ 677-3570; 4150 Patrick's Point Dr; day-use $4), where forests yield to meadows, and sandy beaches abut rocky headlands. Stroll scenic overlooks, climb giant rock formations, watch whales breach, gaze into tidepools, or listen to barking sea lions and singing birds from this manicured park.

Sumêg, an authentic reproduction of a Yurok village, has hand-hewn redwood buildings where Native Americans gather for traditional ceremonies. In the adjacent native plant garden you'll find species used for making traditional baskets and medicines.

On **Agate Beach** look for stray bits of jade and sea-polished agate. Follow signs to tidepools; tread lightly and obey regulations. The 2-mile **Rim Trail**, a former Yurok trail around the bluffs, circles the point with access to huge rocky outcroppings. Make it a point to climb **Wedding Rock**, one of the most romantic spots in the park. Other nature trails lead around unusual rock formations like **Ceremonial Rock** and **Lookout Rock**.

The park has three **campgrounds** (summer reservations ☎ 800-444-7275; www.reserveamerica.com; sites summer/winter $15/12; ☽ Penn Creek & Abalone May-Sep 15, Agate Beach year-round), all well-tended and attractive, with coin-operated hot showers. Penn Creek and Abalone campgrounds are more sheltered than Agate Beach.

TRINIDAD

pop 400

Six miles south of Patrick's Point, the spiffy town of Trinidad gained its name when Spanish sea captains arrived on Trinity Sunday in 1775 and named the area La Santisima Trinidad (the Holy Trinity). It didn't boom, though, until the 1850s, when it became an important port for miners. Schooners from San Francisco brought supplies for inland gold fields, and carried back lumber from the North Coast. Today tourism and fishing keep the economy going.

Orientation & Information

Trinidad is a small town, and it's easy to get your bearings. Approach from the north via Patrick's Point Dr or Hwy 101 (exit at Trinidad) to the intersection of Main St, and Patrick's Point Dr (which becomes Scenic Dr further south). To reach town, take Main St.

The **Trinidad Chamber of Commerce** (☎ 667-1610; www.trinidadcalif.com) provides tourist information on the web, but doesn't have a visitors center. There's an **information kiosk** (cnr Patrick's Point Dr & Main St), just west of the freeway. Pick up the pamphlet *Discover Trinidad*, which has an excellent map. The annual **Trinidad Fish Festival** happens in June; it's one of the few times the lighthouse opens to visitors.

Sights & Activities

The **Trinidad Memorial Lighthouse** (cnr Trinity & Edwards Sts), a replica of an 1871 lighthouse, sits on a bluff at the end of the commercial district, overlooking the bay. Half a block inland, **Trinidad Museum** (☎ 677-3883; 529B Trinity St; ☽ noon-3pm Fri-Sun May-Sep) has exhibits on the area's natural and human history.

HSU Telonicher Marine Laboratory (☎ 826-3671; Ewing St, near cnr of Edwards St; admission free; ☽ 9am-5pm Mon-Fri year-round, 10am-5pm Sat & Sun during school year) has a touch tank, several aquariums (look for the giant Pacific octopus), an enormous whale jaw and a three-dimensional map of the ocean floor.

The free town map from the information kiosk shows several great hiking trails, most notably the **Trinidad Head Trail**, which affords superb coastal views. It's also good for whale-watching (November to April). Walk along an exceptionally beautiful cove at **Trinidad State Beach**; take Main St and bear right at Stagecoach, then make the second left (the first is a picnic area) into the small lot.

Scenic Dr twists south along coastal bluffs, passing tiny coves with views back toward the bay. After 2 miles, it leads to the long, broad expanses of **Luffenholtz Beach** (accessible via the staircase) and **Moonstone Beach**, one of the few white-sand beaches along the North Coast not littered with giant driftwood. Further south it becomes Clam Beach County Park, but Scenic Dr ends sooner, forcing you onto Hwy 101 to reach the county park.

Trinidad is famous for its fishing. Arrange a trip through **Salty's Surf and Tackle Tours** (☎ 677-0300; 332 Main St) or **Trinidad Bay Charters** (☎ 839-4743, 800-839-4744; www.trinidadbay charters.net). The harbor is at the bottom of Edwards St, at the foot of Trinidad head. A five-hour trip costs about $65.

Surfing isn't terribly safe here – leave that for Crescent City.

North Coast Adventures (☎ 677-3124; www.north coastadventures.com; 2hrs/day $50/90) gives sea- and river-kayaking lessons and guided eco-trips around the North Coast.

Sleeping

Most of the area's lodging is north of town on Patrick's Point Dr.

Trinidad Bay B&B (☎ 677-0840; www.trinidad baybnb.com; 560 Edwards St; r $130-180) Right in town, this tidy four-room B&B sits atop a bluff overlooking the harbor.

Trinidad Inn (☎ 677-3349; www.trinidadinn.com; 1170 Patrick's Point Dr; r $65-85, with kitchen plus $10) Rooms are sparklingly clean and nicely decorated at this up-market clapboard motel under tall trees.

Bishop Pine Lodge (☎ 677-3314; www.bishop pinelodge.com; 1481 Patrick's Point Dr; cottages $80-105, with kitchen plus $10) A summer camp atmosphere prevails at Bishop Pine, where you can rent freestanding redwood cottages in a grassy meadow; expect woodsy charm and retro furniture.

View Crest Lodge (☎ 677-3393; www.viewcrest lodge.com; 3415 Patrick's Point Dr; tent/RV sites $16/20, 1-bedroom cottages $85-115) On a hill above the ocean, some of the well-maintained, modern cottages have views and Jacuzzis; most have kitchens. There's also a good campground.

Emerald Forest (☎ 677-3554; www.cabinsinthe redwoods.com; 753 Patrick's Point Dr; tent/RV sites $20/26, cottages $95-120) Has shady campsites and friendly proprietors, but the cottages are nothing special. There's a market on-site.

Lost Whale Inn (☎ 677-3425; www.lostwhale inn.com; 3452 Patrick's Point Dr; r summer $170-200, winter $140-170) If you like B&Bs, this gabled inn sits perched on a grassy cliff and has jaw-dropping views out to sea; furnishings are modern and comfortable, and children are welcome.

Turtle Rocks Oceanfront Inn (☎ 677-3707; www .turtlerocksinn.com; 3392 Patrick's Point Dr; r summer/winter $195/130) Next door to the Lost Whale, Turtle Rocks Inn has spacious, modern rooms with glass-paneled decks and ocean views.

Eating

Larrupin' Cafe (☎ 677-0230; 1658 Patrick's Point Dr; dishes $18-22; Ⓨ dinner Thu-Mon) Trinidad's best-known and best-loved restaurant serves consistently great mesquite-grilled seafood and meat in a sophisticated, unpretentious country house; make reservations.

Moonstone Grill (☎ 677-1616; Moonstone Beach; dishes $18-26; Ⓨ dinner Wed-Sun) Moonstone's contemporary menu features fresh seafood and top-quality steaks, served in an austere, white-tablecloth dining room overlooking vast Moonstone Beach. Make reservations, and come before sunset.

Seascape Restaurant (☎ 677-3762; Trinidad Harbor; breakfast & lunch $8-10, dinner $11-22; Ⓨ 7am-10pm summer, 7am-8:30pm winter) Sit in a vinyl booth and watch fishermen from the Seascape, which serves good breakfasts and standard seafood dishes.

Trinidad Bay Eatery (☎ 677-3777; cnr Parker & Trinity Sts; dishes $5-10; Ⓨ 7am-8pm summer, 7am-3pm winter) serves diner food and big breakfasts.

ARCATA

pop 16,500

Sixteen miles south of Trinidad, Arcata was founded in 1850 by the Union Timber Company. Originally called Union Town it was a base for the nearby lumber camps. In the late 1850s Bret Harte worked here as a journalist; the town became the setting for some of his gold rush–era stories. Today Humboldt State University (HSU) has redefined Arcata as a college town.

The aesthetic is decidedly scruffy, and posses of harmless, excitable students roam downtown on weekend evenings. But on the plaza, keep your distance from the ragtag junkie punks. Arcata prides itself on its go-it-alone far-left politics. Indeed, the City Council passed an ordinance in April 2003 outlawing voluntary compliance with the USA Patriot Act. If you like to argue politics, you're going to love it here.

Orientation

Roads run on a grid, with numbered streets traveling east–west and lettered streets north–south. G and H Sts run north and south (respectively) to HSU and Hwy 101. The plaza is bordered by G and H and 8th and 9th Sts. Eureka lies 5 miles south on Hwy 101. Alternatively take Samoa Blvd to Hwy 255 for a scenic route around Arcata Bay.

Information

Arcata Chamber of Commerce & Visitors Center
(☎ 822-3619; www.arcatachamber.com; 1635 Heindon Rd; ☺ 9am-5pm) Two miles north of town, off Giuntoli Lane on the west side of Hwy 101. Sits inside the California Welcome Center and provides both local and statewide visitor information. Pick up the free fold-out *Official Map Guide to Arcata*.

Bureau of Land Management (BLM; ☎ 825-2300; 1695 Heindon Rd) Has information on the Lost Coast and King Range National Conservation Area.

Humboldt Internet (☎ 825-4638; 750 16th St; $2 per hr; ☺ 10am-1:30pm & 3:30-5pm Mon-Fri) Has Internet access on PCs.

Kinko's (☎ 822-8712; 1618 G St; $0.20 per min; ☺ 7am-11pm Mon-Fri, 9am-6pm Sat & Sun) Uses Macs and PCs.

Northtown Books (☎ 822-2384; 957 H St) Carries new books, periodicals, travel maps and guides.

Tin Can Mailman (☎ 822-1307; 1000 H St) Excellent bookstore with hard-to-find books. Sells used volumes on two floors.

Sights & Activities

Several downtown historic buildings cluster around **Arcata Plaza**. The large 1857 **Jacoby's Storehouse** (cnr H & 8th Sts) is a National Historic Landmark, as is the 1915 **Hotel Arcata** (cnr G & 9th Sts). The vintage 1914 **Minor Theatre** (1013 10th St) screens films. The 1854 **Phillips House Historical Museum** (☎ 822-4722; cnr 7th & Union Sts; admission by donation; ☺ 2-4pm Sun & by appointment) has guided tours.

At the east end of 11th and 14th Sts, **Redwood Park** has beautiful redwood trees and picnic areas. Adjoining the park is the sizable **Arcata Community Forest**, a 575-acre old-growth forest crisscrossed by 10 miles of trails, with dirt paths and paved roads good for hikers and mountain bikers.

On the shores of Humboldt Bay, the **Arcata Marsh & Wildlife Sanctuary** has 5 miles of walking trails and outstanding bird watching. The **Redwood Coast Audubon Society** (☎ 826-7031; donation welcome) offers guided walks every Saturday at 8:30am, rain or shine, from the parking lot at the south end of I St. Friends of Arcata Marsh give guided tours every Saturday at 2pm starting from the **Arcata Marsh Interpretive Center** (☎ 826-2359; 600 South G St; tours free; ☺ 9am-5pm).

Humboldt State University (HSU; ☎ 826-3011), which takes up most of the northeast side of town, is Arcata's current raison d'être. The HSU **Natural History Museum** (☎ 866-4479; 1315 G St; adult/child $2/1; ☺ 10am-5pm Tue-Sat) has fossils, live regional animals, a beehive, tidepool tank, and tsunami and seismic displays. **Center activities** (☎ 826-3357), on the 2nd floor of the University Center, beside the clock tower, sponsors activities, workshops, group outings, and sporting-gear rentals and sales; non-students welcome.

If you're at all bohemian, you must visit **Finnish Country Sauna & Tubs** (☎ 822-2228; cnr 5th & J Sts; ☺ noon-10pm Sun-Thu), where you can sip chai tea and read foreign newspapers by the fire or outside in the meditative garden, then rent a private open-air redwood hot tub ($7.65 per half-hour) or sweat in one of two saunas. Book a tub before you arrive, especially on weekends.

Take a drop-in yoga class at **Community Yoga** (☎ 440-2111; 890 G St; classes $5-10).

Rent a bike (or get one serviced) at **Revolution Bicycle** (☎ 822-2562; 1360 G St) or **Life Cycle Bike Shop** (☎ 822-7755; 1593 G St).

Arcata's most famous event is the **Kinetic Sculpture Race** (☎ 845-1717; www.kinetic sculpturerace.org) on Memorial Day weekend, when people on self-propelled contraptions travel 38 miles from Arcata to Ferndale. The **Arcata Bay Oyster Festival** (☎ 822-4500) and **Bebop and Brew** (☎ 826-2267; www.bebopandbrew .com) happen every June. The **North Country Fair** (☎ 822-5320) comes in September.

Sleeping & Eating

Fairwinds Motel (☎ 822-4824; fax 822-0568; 1674 G St; r $55-65) This standard-issue motel sits at the north end of town, walking distance from the plaza. There are more motels further north, on suburban Giuntoli Lane.

Hotel Arcata (☎ 826-0217, 800-344-1221; 708 9th St; r $70-85, ste $125-140) Anchoring the plaza, the renovated 1915 brick Hotel Arcata has high ceilings and comfortable, albeit small, rooms. Rates include continental breakfast.

Lady Anne B&B (☎ 822-2797; 902 14th St; r $90-115) It's a short walk to town from this 1888 mansion, whose clean and comfortable rooms are full of Victorian bric-a-brac.

Wildflower Cafe & Bakery (☎ 822-0360; 1604 G St; dishes $5-9; ☺ 8am-8pm) Arcata's long-time top choice for vegetarians, the Wildflower serves delicious pancakes and frittatas, and excellent organic salads and crepes.

Jambalaya (☎ 822-4766; 915 H St; dishes $13-20; ☺ dinner Tue-Sat) Seafood is the specialty here, but you'll also find roasted chicken and grilled steaks at this lively eatery. Try the oysters. Make reservations for weekends.

Folie Douce (☎ 822-1042; 1551 G St; dishes $16-26; ☯ dinner Tue-Sun) Arcata's best restaurant has a short but highly inventive contemporary menu, featuring roasted meats and pizzas from a wood-fired oven. The wine list is excellent. Make reservations.

On the plaza, **Tomo Japanese Restaurant** (☎ 822-1414; 708 9th St; lunch $8-11, dinner $14-17; ☯ lunch Mon-Fri, dinner daily) prepares the area's most popular sushi; **Abruzzi** (☎ 826-2345; 791 8th St; dishes $12-20; ☯ 5:30-9:30pm) serves stylized pastas and Italian specialties; and **Plaza Grill** (☎ 826-0860; 791 8th St; dishes $13-20; ☯ 5-11pm), a dressed-down steak-house, also has a huge bar.

Wildberries Marketplace (☎ 822-0095; 747 13th St; ☯ 7am-11pm) sells natural foods and has a great deli, bakery and juice bar. Outside Wildberries, there's also a **farmers market** (☯ 3-6pm Tue Jun-Oct), a great stop for self-caterers and foodies. For weekend shopping, visit the **farmers market** (☯ 9am-1pm Sat Apr-Nov) at Arcata Plaza.

EUREKA
pop 25,600

Six miles south of Arcata, Eureka hugs the shores of Humboldt Bay, the state's largest bay and seaport north of San Francisco. As you drive into the city on Hwy 101, Eureka may not impress. But if you venture into Old Town, just a couple of blocks away, you'll see well-preserved Victorians, several museums and a refurbished waterfront. There's a thriving community of artists here: you'll see lots of photographs, paintings and sculpture in restaurants, bars and other public spaces. Unfortunately it's an early-to-bed town, and the sidewalks roll up by 9pm.

Orientation

Most streets lie on a grid, with numbered streets crossing lettered streets. The free Eureka Visitors Map shows walking tours and scenic drives focusing on architecture and history. Old Town, along 2nd and 3rd Sts from C St to M St, was once Eureka's down-and-out area, but has been refurbished into a pedestrian district of shops, art galleries, cafés and restaurants. The F St Plaza and Boardwalk runs along the waterfront at the foot of F St.

Information

Eureka–Humboldt County Convention & Visitors Bureau (☎ 443-5097, 800-346-3482; 1034 2nd St; ☯ 9am-noon & 1-5pm Mon-Fri) Has maps, brochures and friendly, well-informed staff.
Eureka Chamber of Commerce (☎ 442-3738, 800-356-6381; 2112 Broadway; ☯ 8:30am-5pm Mon-Fri, 10am-4pm Sat & Sun) South on Hwy 101. Also has visitor information and maps.
Going Places (☎ 443-4145; 328 2nd St) Travel-oriented bookstore. One of several excellent bookstores in Old Town.
Pride Enterprises Tours (☎ 445-2117, 800-400-1849) Ray Hillman, local historian and founder, leads outstanding tours.
Six Rivers National Forest Headquarters (☎ 442-1721; 1330 Bayshore Way; ☯ 8am-4:30pm Mon-Fri) Has maps and information about the forest.

Sights & Activities

Eureka has many fine Victorian houses, the most famous the ornate **Carson Mansion** (134 M St) 1880s home of lumber baron William Carson. It took 100 men a full year to build it. Today it's the private Ingomar Club for men, and is not open to the public. The pink house at 202 M St, opposite Carson Mansion, is an 1884 Queen Anne Victorian designed by the same architects and built as a wedding gift for Carson's eldest son.

The incredible **Blue Ox Millworks & Historic Park** (☯ 444-3437, 800-248-4259; www.blueoxmill.com; at the bay end of X St; adult/child $7.50/3.50; ☯ 9am-4pm Mon-Sat) uses antique tools and mills to produce authentic gingerbread trim and other decoration for Victorian buildings. This is one of few places in the world where you can see this; a one-hour self-guided tour takes you through the entire mill and other historical buildings, including a blacksmith shop and recreated 19th-century skid camp. Kids love the oxen.

Board a **Humboldt Bay Harbor Cruise** (☎ 445-1910; 75min narrated cruise adult/child $12.50/6.50; ☯ departures Tue-Sun May-Oct) on the MV *Madaket*, the oldest passenger vessel in continuous use in the USA, and learn about the history of Humboldt Bay. Launched in 1910, the *Madaket* ferried workers to the lumber mills and passengers around the bay until the Samoa Bridge was built in 1972. Phone for reservations, location and schedules.

Visitors can spend a day on the bay with **Hum-Boats Sail, Canoe & Kayak Center** (☎ 443-5157; www.humboats.com; Startare Dr, at Woodley Island Marina), which rents out kayaks and sailboats.

EUREKA

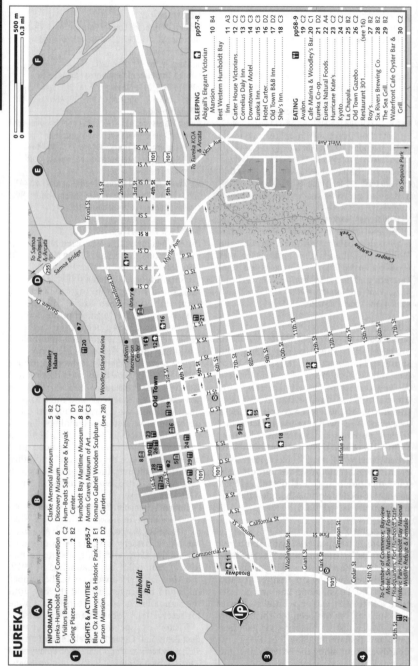

0   500 m
0   0.3 mi

INFORMATION
Eureka-Humboldt County Convention & Visitors Bureau.................................1 C2
Going Places.................................2 B2

SIGHTS & ACTIVITIES   pp55-7
Blue Ox Millworks & Historic Park....3 E1
Carson Mansion.............................4 D2
Clarke Memorial Museum.................5 B2
Discovery Museum..........................6 C2
Hum-Boats Sail, Canoe & Kayak Center...7 D1
Humboldt Bay Maritime Museum....8 B2
Morris Graves Museum of Art..........9 C3
Romano Gabriel Wooden Sculpture Garden.....................................(see 28)

SLEEPING 🏠   pp57-8
Abigail's Elegant Victorian Mansion.....................................10 B4
Best Western Humboldt Bay Inn..11 A3
Carter House Victorians................12 C2
Cornelius Daly Inn.......................13 C3
Downtowner Motel......................14 C3
Eureka Inn.................................15 C3
Hotel Carter..............................16 D2
Old Town B&B Inn......................17 D2
Ship's Inn.................................18 C3

EATING 🍴   pp58-9
Avalon......................................19 C2
Cafe Marina & Woodley's Bar.......20 C1
Eureka Co-op.............................21 D2
Eureka Natural Foods...................22 A4
Hurricane Kate's.........................23 C2
Kyoto.......................................24 C2
La Chapala.................................25 B2
Old Town Gazebo........................26 C2
Restaurant 301.......................(see 16)
Roy's..27 B2
Six Rivers Brewing Co...................28 B2
The Sea Grill..............................29 B2
Waterfront Cafe Oyster Bar & Grill......................................30 C2

They also have lessons and tours, ecotours, a water taxi, sailboat charters, sunset sails and full-moon kayak rides.

A relic of Eureka's recent past, the **Romano Gabriel Wooden Sculpture Garden** (315 2nd St), is enclosed by a glass case, just off the sidewalk between D and E Sts. For 30 years the brightly painted folk art in Gabriel's front yard delighted locals. After he died in 1977, the city moved the collection here to preserve it.

The **Clarke Memorial Museum** (☎ 443-1947; 240 E St; admission by donation; ☽ noon-4pm Tue-Sat), in the former 1912 Bank of Eureka building, has Native American artifacts and thousands of items relating to early Humboldt County history.

Also in Old Town are the small **Humboldt Bay Maritime Museum** (☎ 444-9440; 423 1st St; admission free; ☽ noon-4pm daily) and the **Discovery Museum** (☎ 443-9694; 517 3rd St; admission $3; ☽ 10am-4pm Tue-Sat, noon-4pm Sun), a hands-on museum for kids.

Across Hwy 101, the **Morris Graves Museum of Art** (☎ 442-0278, events ☎ 442-9054; 636 F St; admission by donation; ☽ noon-5pm Wed-Sun) has six galleries with rotating exhibitions of California artists inside a three-story, 1904 Carnegie library, the state's first public library. They also host Saturday evening live jazz, dance and spoken-word performances (September to May).

Fort Humboldt State Historic Park (☎ 445-6567; 3431 Fort Ave; admission free; ☽ 9am-5pm) lies off Broadway, on the south side of town; turn inland onto Highland Ave to reach the entrance. The fort was established in 1853 on a high bluff overlooking Humboldt Bay. Outdoor exhibits show how giant redwoods were felled and dragged to mills. Take a steam engine ride on the 3rd Saturday of the month, May through September.

Sequoia Park (☎ 442-6552; 3414 W St; admission by donation; ☽ 10am-7pm Tue-Sun May-Sep, 10am-5pm Oct-Apr), in a 77-acre old-growth redwood grove, has bicycle and hiking trails, a duck pond, children's playground, picnic areas and a small nonprofit zoo.

Festivals & Events

Annual celebrations include the **Redwood Coast Dixieland Jazz Festival** and the **Rhododendron Festival**, both in April. Summer concerts are held at the F St Pier. **Blues by the Bay** in July presents outdoor waterfront concerts. **First Saturday Night Arts Alive!** makes a progressive tour of galleries the first Saturday of every month. The **Kinetic Sculpture Race** from Arcata to Ferndale passes through Eureka. For details, contact the chamber of commerce or visitors bureau (p55).

Sleeping

Eureka makes a good base for exploring the nearby shoreline and national and state parks. Room rates run high in midsummer; you can sometimes find better deals in Arcata (p54).

MOTELS

Dozens of motels line Hwy 101. Save money by staying south of the city center on the suburban strip.

Best Western Humboldt Bay Inn (☎ 443-2234, 800-521-6996; www.humboldtbayinn.com; 232 W 5th St; summer/winter r $110/85; ☒) This luxury motel has firm mattresses, thick carpeting, DVD players, DSL lines, robes, microwaves and refrigerators. Request a remodeled room.

Bayview Motel (☎ 442-1673, 866-725-6813; www.bayviewmotel.com; 2844 Fairfield St; r summer/winter $80/67) South of town near the mall, the upscale Bayview has spotless rooms with many extras, including refrigerators and patios overlooking Humboldt Bay. Suites have fireplaces and Jacuzzis.

Downtowner Motel (☎ 443-5061, 800-862-4906; 424 8th St; r $55; ☒) Rooms are quiet and spacious, but they need upgrading.

B&BS

Old Town B&B Inn (☎ 443-5235, 888-508-5235; www.oldtownbnb.com; 1521 3rd St; r $120-140) Built in 1871, this B&B has four cozy rooms at the edge of Old Town.

Ship's Inn (☎ 443-7583, 877-443-7583; www.travelbygenie.com; 821 D St; r $100-150) Three spacious rooms with modern furnishings and some antiques are available at this inn, five blocks from Old Town.

Cornelius Daly Inn (☎ 445-3638, 800-321-9656; www.dalyinn.com; 1125 H St; r $90-160) This impeccably maintained 1905 colonial revival mansion has rooms individually decorated with turn-of-the-20th-century European and American antiques. Downstairs the four guest parlors are trimmed with rare woods; outside there are some century-old flowering trees.

Abigail's Elegant Victorian Mansion (☎ 444-3144; www.eureka-california.com; 1406 C St; r $95-195) Inside this National Historic Landmark that's practically a Victorian living-history museum, the innkeepers lavish guests with warm hospitality, including a ride around Eureka in vintage 1920s automobiles.

Carter House Victorians (☎ 444-8067, 800-404-1390; www.carterhouse.com; r $190-360, cottages $500) Operated by the Hotel Carter, you won't find a more luxurious B&B room anywhere in town. Stay in one of three sumptuously decorated side-by-side houses: a single-level 1900 house, a honeymoon-hideaway cottage, and a replica of an 1880s San Francisco mansion which the owner built himself, entirely by hand (the craftsmanship is astounding). Unlike at other B&Bs, you won't see the innkeeper unless you so desire. Guests take breakfast in their rooms or at the adjacent hotel's understated and elegant restaurant.

HOTELS

Eureka Inn (☎ 442-6441, 800-862-4906; fax 442-0637; www.eurekainn.com; 518 7th St; r $130-300; 🐾) Once the Redwood Empire's grandest hotel, this 1922 Tudor-style property is on the National Register of Historic Places. Though it needs a fluff job, it retains its charm, if not its glory. Guest rooms are comfortable, with some large suites good for families. Ask for one of the renovated rooms.

Hotel Carter (☎ 444-8067, 800-404-1390; www.carterhouse.com; 301 L St; r $140-210, ste $250-325) Hotel Carter bears the standard for North Coast luxury lodging. Recently constructed in period style, it's a Victorian lookalike without the drafty windows. All rooms have top-quality linens and modern amenities; suites have in-room whirlpools and marble fireplaces. Rates include full made-to-order breakfast, plus wine and hors d'oeuvres each evening.

Eating

La Chapala (☎ 443-9514; 201 2nd St; dishes $5.50-13.50; 🕙 11am-9pm) For good Mexican food, head to family-owned La Chapala, where the margaritas are strong and the flan homemade.

Six Rivers Brewing Co (☎ 268-3893; 325 2nd St; pub grub $5-10, dishes $8-16; 🕙 11am-10pm) A place where beer is as important as the food, Six Rivers serves surprisingly good seafood and grill fare, especially the fish and chips.

Waterfront Cafe Oyster Bar & Grill (☎ 443-9190; 102 F St; dishes $8-16; 🕙 9am-9pm) A simple menu of seafood and sandwiches features here – try the fish burger.

Cafe Marina & Woodley's Bar (☎ 443-2233; 601 Startare Dr; dishes $10-16; 🕙 lunch & dinner) Across from Old Town in the Woodley Island Marina, this café serves pretty good American preparations of seafood with great dockside views of the small-craft harbor.

The Sea Grill (☎ 443-7187; 316 E St; dishes $15-20; 🕙 lunch Tue-Fri, dinner Mon-Sat) Serves seafood and steaks in a casually elegant dining room with thick carpeting and well-spaced tables. The mahogany bar came round Cape Horn in the 1880s.

Roy's (☎ 442-4574; 218 D St; dishes $12-19; 🕙 dinner Tue-Sat) If Eureka still had Mafia, they'd eat pasta at Roy's. The five-cheese ravioli and the balsamic vinaigrette are delicious, but avoid more complicated dishes.

Hurricane Kate's (☎ 444-1405; 511 2nd St; dishes $12-20; 🕙 lunch & dinner Tue-Sat) Loud, bustling and self-consciously hip, Hurricane Kate's pumps out eclectic, tapas-style dishes and roasted meats and wood-fired pizzas.

Kyoto (☎ 443-7777; 320 F St; dishes $15-25; 🕙 dinner Wed-Sat) Great care goes into every plate at tiny Kyoto, where the chef-owner uses organic ingredients to prepare beautiful sushi and more unusual dishes, like broiled sake-marinated deep-sea cod and lobster-salad hand rolls. Service is knowledgeable and attentive. Make reservations.

Avalon (☎ 445-0500; cnr 3rd & G Sts; dishes $18-26; 🕙 dinner Tue-Sat) Sophisticated yet accessible, Avalon's diverse California menu features everything from foie gras to hamburgers. Come in jeans or jacket and tie. Don't fill up on the crusty homemade bread: leave room for chocolate soufflé.

Restaurant 301 (☎ 444-8062; 301 L St; breakfast $10, dinner $18-28; 🕙 breakfast & dinner) Eureka's most understatedly elegant and romantic dining room, Restaurant 301's contemporary menu uses produce from its own organic garden (tours available). Try the excellent three-course prix-fixe meal. The wine list is exquisite. Restaurant 301 also serves Eureka's best breakfast.

Pick up groceries at **Eureka Natural Foods** (☎ 442-6325; 1626 Broadway) or **Eureka Co-op** (☎ 443-6027; cnr 5th & L Sts). Also check out the

farmers market (Old Town Gazebo, cnr 2nd & F Sts; ☺ 10am-1pm Tue Jun-Oct). You'll find cafés and sandwiches in Old Town.

SAMOA PENINSULA

The windswept 7 mile-long, half-mile-wide Samoa Peninsula is the north spit of Humboldt Bay, which supposedly resembles Pago Pago Harbor, on the island of Samoa (except for the lumber mill). The shoreline road is a backdoor route between the towns of Eureka and Arcata. Reach the beach by walking west through the dunes.

At the southern end of the peninsula, **Samoa Dunes Recreation Area** (☎ 825-2300; ☺ sunrise-sunset) is a popular spot for picnicking and fishing. To spot wildlife, head to **Mad River Slough & Dune**; from Arcata, take Samoa Blvd west 3 miles, then turn right at Young St, the Manila turn-off. Continue to the community center parking lot, from where a trail passes mudflats, salt marsh and tidal channels. Over 200 species of bird can be seen here around the year: migrating waterfowl in spring and fall, songbirds in spring and summer, shorebirds in fall and winter, and abundant wading birds year-round.

The 475-acre **Lanphere Dunes Preserve** protects one of the finest examples of dune succession on the entire Pacific coast. These undisturbed sand dunes can reach heights of over 80ft. Because the environment is fragile, access is by guided tour only. A couple of miles south of Lanphere Dunes, the 100-acre **Manila Dunes Recreation Area** (☎ 445-3309) is open to the public, with access from Peninsula Dr.

Friends of the Dunes (☎ 444-1397; www.friends ofthedunes.org) leads 2½-hour rain-or-shine Saturday walks through Lanphere Dunes and Manila Dunes. Call for schedules or check the website.

Samoa Airport B&B (☎ 445-0765; www.north coast.com/airbb; 900 New Navy Base Rd; r $80-105) has utilitarian rooms inside a refurbished military house which is beside a runway dating from WWII, when the now-private Eureka Municipal Airport was a US Navy blimp base.

Samoa Cookhouse (☎ 442-1659; off Samoa Blvd; dishes $8-13; ☺ breakfast, lunch & dinner), the West's last surviving lumber-camp cookhouse, serves all-you-can-eat family-style meals at long tables with checkered tablecloths. It's great for families (kids eat half price). It's also worth stopping by the little museum.

HUMBOLDT BAY NATIONAL WILDLIFE REFUGE

The **refuge** (☎ 733-5406, ☺ sunrise-sunset) protects wetlands habitat for more than 200 species of birds migrating annually on the Pacific flyway. Peak season for most waterbirds and raptors runs from September to March, while the season for black brant geese and migratory shorebirds runs mid-March to late April. Gulls, terns, cormorants, pelicans, egrets and herons come year-round. Look for harbor seals offshore; bring binoculars. If it's open, drive out on South Jetty Rd to the mouth of Humboldt Bay.

Pick up a map at the **visitors center** (☎ 733-5406; 1020 Ranch Rd; ☺ 7am-4pm Mon-Sat). It highlights two 30-minute walks on interpretive trails. Turn west from Hwy 101 at the Hookton Rd exit, about 11 miles south of Eureka.

Overlooking the refuge, **Southport Landing** (☎ 733-5915; www.northcoast.com/southprt/; 444 Phelan Rd, Loleta; r $100-$165) has gorgeous views. This 1890 early colonial revival mansion has five charming country-style rooms with very comfortable mattresses, and a redwood ballroom on the 3rd floor where you can play billiards.

FERNDALE

pop 1400

Ferndale, 20 miles south of Eureka, has preserved its Victorian architecture so well, the town is listed as a State and National Historical Landmark. Stroll Main St and poke your head into art galleries, antiquarian bookstores, quaint emporiums and soda fountains. Though it relies heavily on tourism, the town has refreshingly managed to avoid becoming a tourist trap.

The **Ferndale Chamber of Commerce** (☎ 786-4477; www.victorianferndale.org) prints a map and visitors guide, available around town.

Sights & Activities

As Ferndale settlers grew wealthy from dairy farming, some built ornate mansions known as 'butterfat palaces.' The **Gingerbread Mansion** (400 Berding St), an 1898 Queen Anne–Eastlake, is the most photographed building in town. The **Shaw House** (703 Main St) was the first permanent structure built in Ferndale; the town's founder, Seth Shaw, started constructing the gabled Carpenter Gothic in 1854, though it was not completed until after his death in 1872. Called 'Fern Dale' for the 6ft-tall ferns that grew here, it housed the settlement's first post office, of which Shaw was the postmaster – hence the town's name, Ferndale. The 1866 **Fern Cottage** (☎ 786-4835; Centerville Rd), west of town, is open by appointment.

The **Ferndale Museum** (☎ 786-4466; Shaw & 3rd Sts; admission by donation; call for hr) is jam-packed with historical artifacts.

Nearby, the **Kinetic Sculpture Museum** (☎ 834-0529; 580 Main St; 10am-5pm Mon-Sat, noon-4pm Sun) houses fanciful, astounding kinetic sculptures used in the annual races.

At 110-acre **Russ Park**, half a mile from downtown via Bluff St, take short tramps through fields of wildflowers, past ponds, redwood groves and eucalyptus trees.

Festivals & Events

Look for: the famous **Kinetic Sculpture Race** and the **Tour of the Unknown Coast** bicycle race in May; the **Scandinavian Mid-Summer Festival** with folk dancing and feasting in June; the **Humboldt County Fair** in mid-August; **Victorian Village Oktoberfest & Harvest Day**; and elaborate Christmas celebrations. Contact the chamber of commerce for details (p59).

Sleeping

Victorian Inn (☎ 786-4949; www.a-victorian-inn.com; 400 Ocean Ave; r $85-150) The bright and sunny rooms inside this 1890 two-story former bank are comfortably furnished with thick carpeting, good linen and antiques.

Hotel Ivanhoe (☎ 786-9000; www.hotel-ivanhoe .com; 315 Main St; r $95-145) Ferndale's oldest hostelry opened in 1875 and survived several fires. Now it has four antique-laden rooms and an Old West–style 2nd-floor porch where you can drink morning coffee.

Shaw House (☎ 786-9958, 800-557-7429; fax 786-9758; www.shawhouse.com; 703 Main St; r $85-185) California's oldest B&B is also Ferndale's first grand home. Lots of the original detail work remains, including painted wood ceilings. This is the best in town for overall value and charm.

Gingerbread Mansion Inn (☎ 786-4000, 800-952-4136; www.gingerbread-mansion.com; 400 Berding St; r & ste $150-385) An American icon in the world of B&Bs, the Gingerbread's luxurious rooms are decked out with high-end Victorian furnishings. Rates include afternoon tea and evening turndown.

There are several other good bets:

Collingwood Inn B&B (☎ 786-9219, 800-469-1632; 831 Main St; r $110-205) Inside the historic Hart House, which has four elegant Victorian-style guest rooms and gracious hospitality.

Stewart Inn & Gallery (☎ 786-9687; 1099 Van Ness Ave; r $115-135) An 1895 creek-side farmhouse, which has two rooms filled with original artwork

Grandmother's House (☎ 786-9704; 861 Howard St, off Main St; r $75) Child-friendly place in a modest 1901 Queen Anne beside pastoral fields.

Francis Creek Inn (☎ 786-9611; 577 Main St; r $60-70) Has four plain motel-style rooms

Ferndale Laundromat & Motel (☎ 786-9471; 632 Main St; units $50) Has two units, each with two bedrooms, kitchen and private bathroom.

Eating

Inexpensive bakeries, cafés and some old-fashioned lunch counters line Main St.

Ferndale Meat Co (☎ 786-4501; 376 Main St; sandwiches $5; 8am-5pm) Makes sandwiches heavy with cheeses and smoked meats.

Curley's Grill (☎ 786-9696; 400 Ocean Ave; dishes $6-18; 11:30am-9pm daily, from 8am Sat & Sun) Curley's serves everything from steak sandwiches and meatloaf to braised lamb shank and niçoise salad. It's inconsistent, but when you hit it right, it's great. The beer and wine lists are outstanding.

Hotel Ivanhoe (☎ 786-9000; 315 Main St; dishes $10-20; dinner Wed-Sun) The Ivanhoe serves Italian-American food and prime rib on weekends in a quiet dining room with cloth napkins. The pub here is mellower than the raucous bar at Curley's.

Entertainment

Ferndale Repertory Theatre (☎ 786-5483; 447 Main St) Presents productions year-round; if you're in town, don't miss it.

Shopping

Golden Gait Mercantile (☎ 786-4891; 421 Main St) You can lose hours browsing shelves of yesteryear's goods at the Golden Gait.

Hobart Gallery (☎ 786-9259; 393 Main St) This gallery shows and sells unusual mixed-media art.

Silva's (☎ 786-4425; 400 Ocean Ave) You'll find gorgeous jewelry at Silva's in the lobby of the Victorian Inn.

SCOTIA
pop 1200

Established in 1887, Scotia is a rarity in modern times: it's one of the last 'company towns' in California, entirely owned and operated by the Pacific Lumber Company (Palco), which runs the world's largest redwood lumber mill. The **Scotia Museum & Visitors Center** (☎ 764-2222; www.palco.com; cnr Main & Bridge Sts; ⓧ 8am-4:30pm Mon-Fri summer) is at the south end of town.

As you drive Hwy 101 and see what appears to be a never-ending forest of redwood, understand that this 'forest' sometimes consists of trees only a few rows deep, a carefully crafted illusion. To see the reality of modern-day clear-cutting, head west of Rio Dell (one town north of Scotia) on Bear River Ridge Rd. In spots it looks like a tornado struck.

If you're under 40 or not 'clean-cut,' you'll certainly get suspicious looks in right-wing Scotia. You might get the feeling you're being watched: it's not unusual for security to keep an eye on strangers in Scotia.

For a free summertime self-guided tour of the **mill** (ⓧ 7:30-10:30am, 11:30am-2pm Mon-Fri), stop by the museum to pick up your tour permit; the rest of the year, pick one up at the guardhouse at the mill entrance. Give yourself an hour to see everything from giant trees being debarked through to their metempsychosis into board lumber. There's also a **fisheries exhibit**.

There's no compelling reason to linger, but if you want to, the **Scotia Inn** (☎ 764-5683, 888-764-2248; www.scotiainn.com; 100 Main St; r/ste from $110/165) is a fairly comfortable inn. Drop by the Scotia Inn's steak-and-potato **pub** (dishes $8-18) or antique-furnished **Redwood Dining Room** (dishes $17-26) for game cuisine and an extensive wine list.

Hoby's Market (105 Main St) sells hot deli sandwiches, fresh salads and general provisions. Otherwise there are several motels and diners in Rio Dell, across the river bridge from Scotia.

LOST COAST

California's 'Lost Coast' extends from where Hwy 1 cuts inland, north of Westport, up to around Ferndale. It became 'lost' when the state's highway system bypassed the region early in the 20th century. The steep, rugged King Range rises to over 4000ft less than 3 miles from the coast, with near-vertical cliffs plunging into the sea. High rainfall (over 100in per year) causes frequent landslides. Hwy 1 was thus routed inland and, in time, legislation was passed to protect the region from development.

Today, the Lost Coast is one of California's most pristine coastal areas. The central and southern portions fall respectively within the King Range National Conservation Area and Sinkyone Wilderness State Park. The area north of the King Range is more accessible, but the scenery not as consistently dramatic.

In fall there's a good chance of clear, if somewhat cool, weather. Wildflowers bloom April through May, and California gray whales migrate off the coast from November to May. The warmest (and driest) months are June to August. Be warned, though, that the weather can quickly change.

Information
The only sizable community on the Lost Coast is Shelter Cove, an isolated unincorporated town 25 miles west of Garberville. Though there are several one-horse rural settlements (eg Petrolia and Honeydew), the area is a patchwork of government-owned land and private property. When driving the winding back roads, take it easy, especially in fog. Pull over to let people pass. Watch out for ticks; Lyme disease is common. And don't jump any fences or otherwise trespass, especially in October at harvest time; this is pot-growing country, and some won't hesitate to fire a shotgun your direction. Locals rush to say that nearby Cape Mendocino is the westernmost point in the contiguous US. It's not. That honor belongs to Cape Alava, Washington.

Shelter Cove
pop 400

Surrounded by the King Range National Conservation Area, remote Shelter Cove lies on a large south-facing cove at Point Delgada. It's little more than a tiny seaside subdivision with an airstrip in the middle; indeed, many visitors are private pilots. By car there's one route: a 23-mile-long paved but narrow road winding west over the mountains from Redway, near Garberville;

it's a good 45 minute drive. Cell phones don't work here. If you want to disappear, this is a good place to go.

The **Shelter Cove Motor Inn** (☎ 986-7521, 888-570-9676; www.sheltercovemotorinn.com; 205 Wave Dr; r $88-120) has unobstructed ocean views and clean albeit charmless rooms. Downstairs is the **Lost Coast Coffee Company** (☎ 986-7888).

The well-maintained modern rooms at the **Oceanfront Inn & Lighthouse** (☎ 986-7002; www.oceanfrontinnca.com; 10 Seal Court; r $125-145, ste $145-175) have microwaves, refrigerators and private balconies overlooking the sea; suites have full kitchens.

Slightly inland lodgings include the small apartments at **Shelter Cove Beachcomber Inn** (☎ 986-7551, 800-718-4789; 412 Machi Rd; r $55-95) and the plain rooms at **Marina Motel** (☎ 986-7595; 533 Machi Rd; r $85).

Northern California Properties (☎ 986-7346; 101 Lower Pacific Dr) rents vacation properties.

The excellent **Cove Restaurant** (☎ 986-1197; 10 Seal Court; dishes $6-19; ☽ 11:30am-9pm Thu-Sun, closed Jan) has something for everyone, from vegetarian stir-fry to New York steak. Eat with friendly locals at **Mario's** (☎ 986-1401; 533 Machi Rd; breakfast $5-9, dinner $10-18; ☽ breakfast & dinner Jun-Aug, hrs vary Sep-May) and take in views of the cove while dining on omelettes at breakfast and simple preparations of fresh fish, pasta and meat at dinner.

King Range National Conservation Area

Covering 35 miles of virgin coastline, with ridge after ridge of steep mountainous terrain plunging almost vertically into the surf, this 60,000-acre wilderness has its highest point at namesake King's Peak (4087ft).

About 9 miles east of Shelter Cove in Whitethorn, the **Bureau of Land Management** (BLM; ☎ 986-5400, 825-2300; 768 Shelter Cove Rd; ☽ 8:30am-4:30pm Memorial Day-Labor Day, 8am-4:30pm Mon-Fri Sep-May) has maps and directions for hiking trails and campsites; they're posted outside after hours. Information is also available from the BLM office in Arcata (p54), which administers the conservation area.

The best way to see the Lost Coast is to hike. The **Lost Coast Trail** follows 24 miles of coastline from the Mattole Campground on the north end, near Petrolia, to Black Sands Beach at Shelter Cove on the south end. The prevailing northerly winds make it best to hike the trail from north to south; plan on trekking three or four days. For information on backpacker shuttle services to trailheads, call the BLM or contact **Lost Coast Trail Transport Services** (☎ 986-9909; roxanne@saber.net).

Trail highlights include an abandoned lighthouse at Punta Gorda, remnants of old shipwrecks, tidepools and abundant marine and coastal wildlife including sea lions, seals and more than 300 bird species. The trail is mostly level, passing along beaches and over rocky outcrops; consult tide tables as some outcroppings are passable only at low tide.

A good day hike along the northern stretch of the Lost Coast Trail starts at the Mattole Campground trailhead and travels 3 miles south along the coast to the Punta Gorda lighthouse. Reach the Mattole Campground at the ocean end of Lighthouse Rd, 4 miles from the intersection with Mattole Rd, southeast of Petrolia.

Wailaki and Nadelos both have developed **campgrounds** (sites $5-7). There are also four other campgrounds scattered across the range, plus multiple primitive walk-in sites. For camping outside developed campgrounds, you'll need a free campfire permit, available from BLM offices.

Sinkyone Wilderness State Park

Named for the Sinkyone Indians who once inhabited the area, this 7367-acre wilderness extends south of Shelter Cove along pristine coastline. The **Lost Coast Trail** continues for another 22 miles, from Whale Gulch to Usal Beach Campground, taking at least three days to hike. Near the north end of the park, the **Needle Rock Ranch** (☎ 986-7711) serves as a remote visitors center where you can register for a campsite and get maps and trail guides. (It's also the only source for potable water.)

To get to Needle Rock, drive west from Garberville and Redway on Briceland Rd 21 miles through Whitethorn to Four Corners. Turn left (south) and continue another 3.5 miles down a very rugged road to the ranch house; it takes about 1½ hours. There's also road access to Usal Beach Campground at the south end of the park from Hwy 1. North of Westport, unpaved County Rd 431 takes off from the highway at milepost 90.88 and travels 6 miles up the coast to the campground. These roads are not maintained during rainy months and quickly become impassable; to get through you'd need a 4WD and a chainsaw. Seriously.

North of the King Range

You can reach the northern section of the Lost Coast year-round via the paved but narrow and winding Mattole Rd. It takes three hours to navigate the 68 miles from Ferndale in the north, out to the coast at Cape Mendocino and then inland again to Humboldt Redwoods State Park and Hwy 101. Don't expect redwood forests: the vegetation here is mostly grassland and pasture. It's beautiful in spots, but there aren't many places to stop.

You'll pass through two tiny settlements. **Petrolia** is the site of California's first oil well, which sits capped-off on private property. Check out the cemetery instead. There's a store but no gas here, and the locals dislike outsiders. At **Honeydew** there's a **gas station** (🕑 9am-5pm) at the Honeydew post office/market/hangout. The locals here are friendly, but there's nothing to do but sit on the front porch of the store. The drive is enjoyable (though stressful for nervous drivers), but the wild, spectacular scenery of the Lost Coast lies further south in more remote regions.

HUMBOLDT REDWOODS STATE PARK & AVENUE OF THE GIANTS

California's largest redwood park, **Humboldt Redwoods State Park** (☎ 946-2409) covers more than 53,000 acres – 17,000 of which are old-growth – and contains some of the world's most magnificent trees.

When you see the **Avenue of the Giants** road sign on Hwy 101, exit and take this incredible 32-mile scenic drive, which runs parallel to the highway. You'll find free driving guides at the roadside signboards at both the avenue's northern entrance, a few miles south of Scotia at Pepperwood, and its southern entrance, 6 miles north of Garberville, near Phillipsville; there are also several access points off Hwy 101.

Just south of Weott, a volunteer-staffed **visitors center** (☎ 946-2263; 🕑 9am-5pm summer, 10am-4pm winter) shows videos and sells excellent field guides, hiking maps and books. Don't bypass its small but excellent **museum** housing the historic 1917 'Travel Log.'

The primeval **Rockefeller Forest**, about 4.5 miles west of the avenue via Mattole Rd, appears just as it did over a century ago. Today it's the largest contiguous old-growth redwood forest anywhere. In

Founders Grove, just north of the visitors center, **Dyerville Giant** was knocked over in 1991 by another falling tree. A walk along the gargantuan 370ft length, with its wide trunk towering above, helps you appreciate how huge these ancient trees are.

Elsewhere the park has more than 100 miles of trails for hiking, mountain biking and horseback riding. Easy walks include the short nature trails in Founders Grove and Rockefeller Forest and the **Drury-Chaney Loop Trail** (with fresh berry picking in summer). More challenging treks include the popular **Grasshopper Peak Trail**, starting south of the visitors center, which climbs to the fire lookout at 3379ft.

Unless you want to **camp** (☎ 800-444-7275; www.reserveamerica.com; sites $14), the only place worth spending the night is the **Miranda Gardens Resort** (☎ 943-3011; www.mirandagardens.com; 6766 Ave of the Giants, Miranda; r $65-175; 🐾). Rooms are in cozy cottages; many have kitchens and redwood paneling, and some have fireplaces. There's also a children's playground. Across the street there's a pizza parlor.

GARBERVILLE & REDWAY

Garberville pop 1800 / Redway pop 1200

Garberville and its sister Redway (2 miles west of Hwy 101) became famous in the 1970s for sinsemilla (potent, seedless marijuana) grown in the surrounding hills after feds chased the growers out of Santa Cruz County. Aging hippies and pot-farmer wannabes still roam Redwood Dr, the main drag. Garberville is the region's primary commercial center.

The **Garberville–Redway Area Chamber of Commerce** (☎ 923-2613, 800-923-2613; www.garberville.org; 773 Redwood Dr, Garberville; 🕑 10am-5pm Mon-Fri, plus 11am-3pm Sat summer) has information and pamphlets. To learn what's really going on, tune in to Redwood Community Radio (KMUD 91.1FM).

Reggae on the River (☎ 923-4583; www.reggaeontheriver.com) draws huge crowds in August for a three-day-long festival. Tickets ($150) sell out well in advance.

Other annual events include the **Avenue of the Giants Marathon** in May; the **Harley Davidson Redwood Run** and **Garberville Rodeo** in June; a **Shakespeare Festival** in August; the **Hemp Fest** every November; and **Winter Arts Fair** in mid-December. Contact the chamber of commerce for details.

Sleeping

For cheap lodging, try **Humboldt Redwoods** (☎ 923-2451; 987 Redwood Dr, Garberville; r $55-80) or **Sherwood Forest** (☎ 923-2721; www.sherwoodforest motel.com; 814 Redwood Dr; r $55-80; 🐾).

Best Western Humboldt House Inn (☎ 923-2771, 800-528-1234; 701 Redwood Dr, Garberville; r $99) The best motel in town, this place has good beds, upgraded furnishings, refrigerators and coffeemakers.

Benbow Inn (☎ 923-2124, 800-355-3301; www.ben bowinn.com; 445 Lake Benbow Dr; r $120-245, cottages $325) The Redwood Empire's first luxury destination resort stands as a monument to 1920s rustic elegance. Guest rooms have top-quality mattresses, triple-sheeted beds and attractive furnishings. The excellent **dining room** (breakfast & lunch $10-15, dinner $15-30) serves European–American cuisine. Guests enjoy complimentary afternoon tea and evening hors d'oeuvres.

Eating

Woodrose Cafe (☎ 923-3191; 911 Redwood Dr; dishes $6-12) Garberville's best-loved restaurant cooks delicious egg breakfasts and the town's best lunches, with good sandwiches and organic salads.

Calico's Deli & Pasta (☎ 923-2253; 808 Redwood Dr, Garberville; dishes $5-10; ☾ 11am-9pm) Stop by Calico's for a plate of house-made pasta or a sandwich.

Mateel Cafe (☎ 923-2030; 3342-3344 Redwood Dr, Redway; lunch $7-11, dinner $16-22; ☾ 11:30am-9pm Mon-Fri, 2:30-9pm Sat) Serves steaks, chops, stone-baked pizzas and organic salads.

707 Restaurant (☎ 923-7007; 773 Redwood Dr; dishes $15-24; ☾ dinner Tue-Sun) The flavors are bold and inventive at Garberville's only contemporary California restaurant. Try the coconut prawns.

Alternatively, head to the **Eel River Cafe** (☎ 923-3783; 801 Redwood Dr, Garberville; dishes under $10) for blueberry pancakes or the **House of Burgess** (☎ 923-3817; 747 Redwood Dr, Garberville; dishes under $10) for great biscuits and gravy.

Drinking

Sicilito's (☎ 923-2814; 445 Conger St; ☾ 11:30am-10pm) Popular for microbrews and frat-boy food.

Riverwood Inn & El Rio Mexican Restaurant (☎ 943-3333; 2828 Ave of the Giants, Phillipsville) Hear live blues, folk and rock at this long-standing roadhouse near Garberville that serves strong drinks and pretty good food.

Getting There & Around

Greyhound buses stop at 432 Church St, off Redwood Dr.

RICHARDSON GROVE STATE PARK

Seven miles south of Garberville, bisected by the Eel River, **Richardson Grove** (☎ 247-3318; Hwy 101; vehicle day-use fee $4) occupies 1400 acres of virgin redwood forest. Many trees are over 1000 years old and more than 300ft tall. The **visitors center** (☎ 247-3318; ☾ 9am-2pm) sells nature books and gifts. It's inside the 1930s Richardson Grove Lodge, which has a roaring fireplace in cold weather.

The park has three **campgrounds** (summer reservations ☎ 800-444-7275; www.reserveamerica.com; sites $14) with hot showers; some sites open year-round.

LOWER NORTH COAST

☎ 707

The famous Hwy 1 (or Pacific Coast Hwy) snakes its way along the Lower North Coast until it turns inland to Leggett. Highlights include lonely, windswept Fort Ross, artsy Mendocino village and, of course, the rugged beauty of the coastline itself.

LEGGETT

pop 200

The tiny town of Leggett marks the end of the ancient redwood forests and the beginning of Hwy 1. There's not much here but a gas station, market and pizza joint.

The 1000-acre **Standish-Hickey State Recreation Area** (☎ 925-6482; 69350 Hwy 101; admission per vehicle $4), 1.5 miles north of town, has picnic areas, swimming holes and hiking trails in virgin redwood forest. Riverside **campgrounds** (☎ 800-444-7275; www.reserveamerica.com; sites $14) with hot showers are open year-round; in summer phone for reservations. Avoid sites close to the highway.

Chandelier Drive-Thru Tree Park (☎ 925-6363; Drive-Thru Tree Rd; admission per vehicle $3; ☾ 8am-dusk) has 200 acres of virgin redwood forest with picnic areas and nature walks. And yes, there's a giant redwood tree with a square hole carved out, which cars can drive through. Only in America.

Redwoods River Resort (☎ 925-6249; www.red woodriverresort.com; 75000 Hwy 101; tent/RV sites $18/28, cabins $74-99, lodge r $69-115) offers a variety of lodgings, good for families who like to meet other families.

Greyhound buses stop opposite the Standish-Hickey reserve at **Price's Peg House** (☎ 925-6444; 69501 Hwy 101; ☷ 8am-9pm), a small grocery store and deli.

WESTPORT

pop 200

The first coastal hamlet south of the Lost Coast, Westport feels like a sleepy frontier settlement. An important turn-of-the-20th-century shipping port, it once had the longest logging chute in California. Today, there's very little here except for romantic, windswept beaches and abundant peace and quiet.

One-and-a-half miles north of town, **Westport-Union Landing State Beach** (☎ 937-5804; sites $14) extends 3 miles on coastal bluffs over churning seas. It's mostly a primitive campground, but a rough hiking trail passes tidepools and streams, accessible only at low tide.

The **Lost Coast Lodge** (☎ 964-5584; www.lostcoast inn.com; 38921 N Hwy 1; r $70-90) has simple rooms and a sleepy bar downstairs.

Howard Creek Ranch (☎ 964-6725; www.howard creekranch.com; 40501 N Hwy 1; r $75-125, ste $105-160) occupies 60 acres of forest and farmland abutting the wilderness. Accommodations are in the 1880s farmhouse or the carriage barn, with unusual redwood rooms, expertly handcrafted by the owner. Rates include a delicious full breakfast. It's a place for hiking boots, not high heels.

DeHaven Valley Farm (☎ 961-1660, 877-334-2836; www.dehaven-valley-farm.com; 39247 N Hwy 1; B&B r $90-120, cottages $140-145) is a secluded 1875 Victorian manor house on 20 acres, with clean, comfortable, albeit simple rooms. It's a great place to unwind. Staff also serve excellent dinners from Wednesday to Sunday.

If you want to rent a house, consider the two-bedroom 1832 **Westport House** (☎ 937-4007; per night $200, 2-night minimum), which overlooks the pounding surf.

MACKERRICHER STATE PARK

Around 12 miles to the south of Westport, **MacKerricher State Park** (☎ 964-9112) preserves 9 miles of pristine rugged coastline with rocky headlands, sandy beaches, dunes and tidepools. Bring your camera.

LOWER NORTH COAST

The **visitors center** (☎ 964-9112; ☷ 11am-3pm Sat & Sun, 10am-6pm summer) sits next to the reconstructed whale skeleton at the park entrance. Hike the gentle coastal trail along dark-sand beaches and see rare and endangered plant species (tread lightly). **Lake Cleone**, a 30-acre freshwater lake, gets stocked with trout. At nearby **Laguna Point**, an interpretive boardwalk overlooks harbor seals and, from about December to April, migrating whales.

The **Ricochet Ridge Ranch** (☎ 964-7669; 24201 N Hwy 1) offers horseback riding trips for all levels through the redwoods or along the beach. The guides are great and the horses top quality. A 90-minute ride costs $40.

The popular park **campgrounds** (reservations ☎ 800-444-2725; www.reserveamerica.com; sites $16), nestled in pine forest, have hot showers and potable water. Ten more semi-secluded **walk-in sites** (sites $14), just 50 yards from the parking area, are first-come, first-served.

Cleone Gardens (☎ 964-2788, 800-400-2189; www.cleonegardensinn.com; 24600 N Hwy 1; r $86-112) is a cross between an inn and a motel. Some rooms have fireplaces and decks overlooking the property's five lovely landscaped acres.

NORTH COAST

FORT BRAGG
pop 7025

Far less touristy than its charming neighbor Mendocino, Fort Bragg makes an excellent, albeit more homely, base for exploring the area's spectacular coast. Established in 1857, the fort was named for Colonel Braxton Bragg and abandoned a decade later. In 1885, a lumber company opened a mill and constructed the California Western Railroad – later nicknamed the 'Skunk Train' – to haul giant redwoods out of the forest. The last of the North Coast sawmills closed here in 2002, and the town relies increasingly on tourism for revenue.

Orientation & Information

Most everything in town lies on or near Main St, a 2-mile stretch of Hwy 1. Numerous shops, a movie theater and post office are on Franklin St, which runs parallel one block east. Fort Bragg's wharf district, with its fishing-boat docks and seafood restaurants, lies at Noyo Harbor, at the mouth of the Noyo River, at the south end of town. The access road is just north of Hwy 20.

The **Fort Bragg–Mendocino Coast Chamber of Commerce** (☎ 961-6300; www.mendocinocoast.com; 332 N Main St; ☿ 9am-5pm Mon-Fri, 9am-3pm Sat) has a wealth of information about Fort Bragg, Mendocino and surrounds. For high-speed Internet access, visit **Seal of Approval** (☎ 964-7099; 260 N Main St; $1.50 per 10min; ☿ 8am-6pm Mon-Thu, 8am-8pm Fri & Sat).

Sights & Activities

Fort Bragg's pride and joy, the vintage **Skunk Train** (☎ 964-6371, 800-777-5865; www.skunktrain.com; adult/child $35/17), got its nickname in 1925 when passenger service began, using stinky gas-powered steam engines. Today, the historic steam and diesel locomotives are odorless, making runs between Fort Bragg and Northspur (the halfway point between Fort Bragg and Willits) through redwood-forested mountains and along rivers, crossing 30 bridges and passing through two deep mountain tunnels. The depot is at the foot of Laurel St, one block west of Main St, in the center of town.

The **Guest House Museum** (☎ 964-4251; 343 N Main St; admission $2; ☿ 10am-4pm Tue-Sun summer, 11am-4pm Wed-Sun winter), a majestic 1892 Victorian house, displays historical photos and relics of Fort Bragg's logging history. Literally and figuratively on the other side of the street, **Triangle Tattoo & Museum** (☎ 964-8814; 356B N Main St; ☿ noon-7pm) shows tattoo artifacts and art. The co-op gallery **Northcoast Artists** (☎ 964-8266; 362 N Main St) shows mixed media by area artists. Antique shops and bookstores line **Franklin St**, one block east.

Once the city dump, **Glass Beach** is named for the sea-polished glass found lying on the sand at low tide. Take the short headlands trail from Elm St, off Main St, and don't walk barefoot. The nearby **North Coast Brewing Co** (☎ 964-2739; 455 N Main St) offers brewery tours Monday to Saturday; call for times.

A number of small boats at Noyo Harbor offer coastal and **whale-watching cruises** and deep-sea **fishing trips**. You can sometimes buy fish right off the boats. **Noyo Pacific Outfitters** (☎ 961-0559; www.noyopacific.com; 32400 North Harbor Dr) rents out kayaks and guides snorkeling and abalone diving trips.

One of northern California's hidden gems, the **Mendocino Coast Botanical Gardens** (☎ 964-4352; 18220 N Hwy 1; adult/child $6/3; ☿ 9am-5pm Mar-Oct, 9am-4pm Nov-Feb) displays native flora along serpentine paths on 47 acres of seafront land and coastal bluffs south of town. The main trails are wheelchair accessible.

Festivals & Events

The **Fort Bragg Whale Festival**, the third weekend in March, has microbrewed-beer tasting, a crafts fair and whale-watching trips. The **Rhododendron Show** falls in late April to early May.

The **World's Largest Salmon BBQ** is held in Noyo Harbor on the Saturday closest to 4th of July. **Paul Bunyan Days** celebrates California's logging history with a logging show, square dancing, parade and arts fair on Labor Day weekend.

Sleeping

Fort Bragg generally has cheaper rooms than nearby Mendocino. Rates drop significantly in winter. Skip the properties flanking the Noyo River Bridge (particularly the overpriced one on the west side): the state is rebuilding the bridge and there'll be construction noise through mid-2005. Whenever possible, book in advance.

MOTELS

Colombi Motel (☎ 964-5773; 647 Oak St; r $45-50) In Fort Bragg's barrio, this motel has clean rooms with kitchens, and is next door to a laundromat; check in at the deli across the street.

Hi Sea Inn (☎ 964-5929; 1201 N Main St; r $79-109) Of the four oceanfront motels north of downtown, this is the best because it doesn't pretend to be more than it is: a straightforward motel with spectacular views.

There are lots of motels on the suburban strip south of downtown. The **Coast Motel** (☎ 964-2852; www.coastmotelfortbragg.com; 18661 Hwy 1; r $48-75; 🐾), just south of Hwy 20, has some of the cheapest rooms in town. The 65-room **Seabird Lodge** (☎ 964-4731, 800-345-0022; www.seabirdlodge.com; 191 South St; r $83-110; 🐾) has a heated indoor pool and standard-issue rooms set back from the road.

B&BS

Weller House Inn (☎ 964-4415, 877-893-5537; www.wellerhouse.com; 524 Stewart St; r $95-170) The individually decorated rooms in this beautifully restored 1886 Victorian have down comforters, good mattresses and fine linens. The reconstructed water tower is the tallest structure in town – and has a hot tub up top. Guests enjoy breakfast in the 900-sq-ft redwood ballroom.

Grey Whale Inn (☎ 964-0640, 800-382-7244; www.greywhaleinn.com; 615 N Main St; r $110-182, ste $192) Fort Bragg's original hospital, the comfortable Grey Whale Inn, has huge rooms, high ceilings and big windows. The penthouse suites have sweeping views.

Rendezvous Inn (☎ 964-8142, 800-491-8142; www.rendezvousinn.com; 647 N Main St; r $110) The spartan rooms at the Rendezvous have few amenities, but Fort Bragg's best chef cooks breakfast (see Eating & Drinking this page).

Lodge at Noyo River (☎ 964-8045, 800-628-1126; www.noyolodge.com; 500 Casa del Norte Dr; r $95-175) Overlooking Noyo Harbor, the lodge has spacious rooms in a 19th-century lumber baron's house, and seven modern suites with oversized soaking tubs.

Other recommendations:

Avalon House (☎ 964-5555; www.theavalonhouse.com; 561 Stewart St; r $85-155) Across the street from Weller House Inn, with well-furnished rooms in a 1905 Craftsman-style home

Colonial (☎ 964-1384; www.colonialinnfortbragg.com; 533 E First St; r $99-154)

Old Stewart House (☎ 961-0775, 800-287-8392; www.oldstewarthouseinn.com; 511 Stewart St; r $120-145) Has a cozy downstairs parlor

Eating & Drinking

Eggheads (☎ 964-5005; 326 N Main St; dishes $8-13; 🕑 7am-2pm Thu-Tue) For breakfast, Eggheads can't be beat. There are 50 varieties of omelettes, some made with locally caught Dungeness crab. They also serve great sandwiches and burgers.

Cafe One (☎ 964-3309; 753 N Main St; dishes $6-14; 🕑 breakfast & lunch daily, dinner Fri-Sat) Everything's organic at this café, which prepares excellent egg dishes, beautiful salads and sandwiches. Though vegie-friendly, they also serve meat.

Rendezvous Inn (☎ 964-8142; 647 N Main St; dishes $16-23; 🕑 dinner Wed-Sun) Rustic elegance meets urban sophistication at Fort Bragg's best restaurant, which serves expertly prepared, down-to-earth provincial French cooking in a redwood-paneled Craftsman-style house. Make a reservation.

Mendo Bistro (☎ 964-4974; 301 N Main St; dishes $10-19; 🕑 dinner) Upstairs in the Company Store building, lively Mendo Bistro serves good crab cakes, grilled steaks, roasted chicken and house-made pasta. Great for groups with diverse tastes. Request a window table.

North Coast Brewing Co (☎ 964-3400; 444 N Main St; lunch $10, dinner $8-17; 🕑 lunch & dinner) Down a pint of microbrew and munch on killer garlic fries at North Coast; they also serve sandwiches and steaks.

Sharon's by the Sea (☎ 962-0680; 32096 N Harbor Dr; lunch $5-16, dinner $10-22; 🕑 lunch & dinner) At touristy Noyo Harbor, Sharon's serves the best food, and you can sit outside.

For light meals, **Headlands Coffeehouse** (☎ 964-1987; 120 E Laurel St; dishes $4-8; 🕑 7am-10pm), just east of Main St, is the town's best café. For pizza and beer go to **Piaci Pub & Pizzeria** (☎ 961-1133; 120 W Redwood Ave; 🕑 dinner).

Skip the overpriced Wharf Restaurant & Lounge (unless you're with your grandparents). Instead head next door to unpretentious **Cap'n Flint's** (☎ 964-9447; 32250 N Harbor Dr; dishes $7-12; 🕑 11am-9pm) and eat the same fish and chips for less money.

For the best groceries, head to **Harvest Market** (☎ 964-7000; Hwy 1 & Hwy 20; 🕑 5am-11pm). There's also a **farmers market** (cnr Laurel & Franklin Sts; 🕑 3:30-6pm Wed late-May–Oct).

Down local microbrews or throw back shots at mellow **North Coast Brewing Company** (☎ 964-3400; 444 N Main St) or the **Old Coast Hotel** (☎ 961-4488; 101 N Franklin St).

Entertainment

Caspar Inn (☎ 964-5565; 14957 Caspar Rd; cover $5-8, free Wed; ☺ live entertainment Wed-Sat) About 5 miles south of Fort Bragg off Hwy 1, this inn has live local rock, R&B, world beat and open-mic nights. It's always worth the drive.

Headlands Coffeehouse (☎ 964-1987; 120 E Laurel St) Presents live music – jazz to classical – seven nights a week and Sunday afternoons.

Footlighters Little Theater (☎ 964-3806; 248 E Laurel St) Presents 1890s-style musicals, comedy and melodrama on Wednesday and Saturday evenings in summer.

Opera Fresca (937-3646, 888-826-7372; www.operafresca.com) performs fully staged operas at various venues; while the **Gloriana Opera Company** (☎ 964-7469; www.gloriana.org; 721 N Franklin St) stages operettas and musicals.

Shopping

Fort Bragg has good shopping on Franklin St and Main St. Musicians and photographers must see **Fiddles & Cameras** (☎ 964 -7370; 400 N Main), an old-fashioned specialty emporium. The **Bookstore** (☎ 964-6559; 223 E Redwood Ave) specializes in used fiction and sells inexpensive art. **Bragg About Books** (☎ 964-7634; 319 N Franklin) carries antiquarian books.

Getting Around

Mendocino Transit Authority (MTA; ☎ 462-1422, 800-696-4682) operates a county-wide bus service; the No 5 'BraggAbout' bus operates between Noyo Harbor and Elm St, north of downtown, but the route doesn't always parallel Main St (Hwy 1).

Fort Bragg Cyclery (☎ 964-3509; 579 S Franklin St) rents out bicycles.

JUG HANDLE STATE RESERVE

Halfway between Mendocino and Fort Bragg, Jug Handle preserves an 'ecological staircase' that you can see on a 5-mile (round-trip) **self-guided nature trail**. Five wave-cut terraces ascend in steps from the seashore, each about 100ft and 100,000 years removed from the one before it. Each terrace has its own distinct geology and vegetation; on one level is a pygmy forest,

similar to the better-known one at Van Damme State Park (p72), 8 miles south. Stroll the headlands, watch for whales, or lounge on the sandy beach. Pick up trail guides from the parking lot. They detail the geology, flora and fauna you'll find along the way. It's easy to miss the park entrance; look carefully for the turn-off from Hwy 1 just north of Caspar.

Jug Handle Creek Farm & Nature Center (☎ 964-4630; http://jughandle.creek.org; Hwy 1; r $22-30) offers the chance to participate in local habitat restoration or simply learn about native plant species at this non-profit 39-acre farm, which also has three cabins and seven hostel rooms in a 19th-century farmhouse for overnight guests. If you stay, you must donate one hour's work, or pay to opt out. Book early.

Annie's Jughandle Beach B&B Inn (☎ 964-1415, 800-964-9957; www.jughandle.com; Hwy 1; r & ste $120-230), opposite the reserve, has cheery rooms inside an 1880s farmhouse furnished with antiques; some have Jacuzzis and fireplaces. Expect a big Southern-style breakfast.

MENDOCINO

pop 1000

Perched atop high bluffs on a peninsula jutting out to sea, magical Mendocino was built as a lumber-mill town by transplanted New Englanders in the 1850s. The mills shut down in the 1930s, and the town faltered until it was rediscovered by artists in the 1950s. Today it's populated by culturally savvy, politically aware, well-traveled citizens who welcome visitors, but eschew corporate interlopers – don't look for a Big Mac or try to use your cell phone.

The entire town, with its meticulously restored Cape Cod and Victorian buildings, is listed on the National Register of Historic Places. So many tourists come for the galleries, restaurants and B&Bs that, on summer weekends, Mendocino seems a parody of itself, earning it the nickname 'Spendocino.' To avoid the crowds, come midweek or in the off-season, when the mood is more tranquil – and the prices more reasonable.

Information

Check out www.gomendo.com, or drop by the **Ford House Visitors Center & Museum** (☎ 937-5397; 735 Main St; admission $1; ☺ 11am-4pm) for maps, books and information about Mendocino and nearby state parks, and to

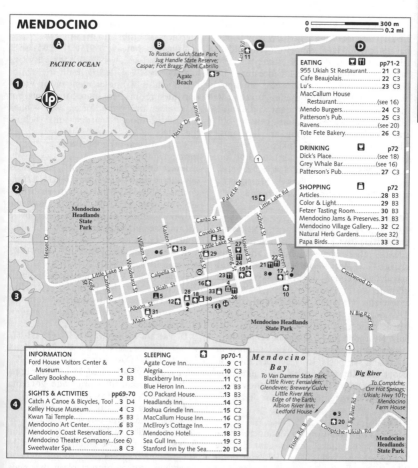

MENDOCINO

0 —————— 300 m
0 —————— 0.2 mi

A — **B** — **C** — **D**

PACIFIC OCEAN

To Russian Gulch State Park;
Jug Handle State Reserve;
Caspar; Fort Bragg; Point Cabrillo

Agate Beach

Mendocino Headlands State Park

Mendocino Headlands State Park

Mendocino Bay

To Van Damme State Park;
Little River; Fensalden;
Glendeven; Brewery Gulch;
Little River Inn;
Edge of the Earth;
Albion River Inn;
Ledford House

Big River

To Comptche;
Orr Hot Springs;
Ukiah; Hwy 101;
Mendocino
Farm House

Mendocino Headlands State Park

see the natural and cultural history exhibits. Look across Main St to see one of the town's signature water towers.

Gallery Bookshop (☎ 937-2665; 319 Kasten St) carries history, travel and children's books.

Sights

The **Kelley House Museum** (☎ 937-5791; 45007 Albion St; admission $2; ◷ 1-4pm Jun-Sep, 1-4pm Fri-Mon Oct-May), inside an 1861 home, has a research library and displays about the area. Peer inside the 1852 **Kwan Tai Temple** (45160 Albion St) to see the old Chinese altar.

The restored 1909 **Point Cabrillo Lighthouse** (☎ 937-0816; www.pointcabrillo.org; Point Cabrillo Dr; admission free; ◷ 11am-4pm Fri-Mon Mar-Oct) stands on a 300-acre wildlife preserve north of

town, midway between Russian Gulch and Caspar Beach. Inquire about guided walks from May to September.

Activities

Mendocino Headlands State Park, surrounding the village, is crisscrossed by trails, with walks overlooking bluffs and rocky coves. On weekends, check with the visitors center about free **spring wildflower walks**. December to March there are **whale-watching walks**; also ask about guided history walks.

Choose from over 200 art classes at the **Mendocino Art Center** (☎ 937-5818, 800-653-3328; www.mendocinoartcenter.org; 45200 Little Lake St; ◷ 10am-5pm), which presents exhibitions, arts-and-crafts fairs and live theater.

Catch A Canoe & Bicycles, Too! (☎ 937-0273, 800-320-2453; Comptche-Ukiah Rd, just off Hwy 1) rents out kayaks and outrigger canoes for self-guided trips up the 8 mile-long Big River tidal estuary, the longest undeveloped estuary in Northern California. There are no highways or buildings, only beaches, forests, salt marshes, streambeds, abundant wildlife and historic logging sites, including century-old train trestles, wooden pilings and log dams. They also rent mountain bikes.

Soak in a private or communal hot tub at **Sweetwater Spa** (☎ 937-4140, 800-300-4140; www.sweetwaterspa.com; 955 Ukiah St; ☺ daily, call for hours), where you can also get a massage.

Festivals & Events

Late January to early February the **Mendocino Crab & Wine Days** has wine tasting, cooking classes, and whale-watching and crab cruises. The **Mendocino Whale Festival** is held the first weekend in March and has wine and chowder tasting, whale-watching walks and musicians. **Mendocino Music Festival** (☎ 937-4041; www.mendocinomusic.com) presents chamber music concerts on the headlands in mid-July. **Mendocino Wine & Mushroom Festival**, held in early November, has guided mushroom tours and symposia. In December, the **Mendocino Coast Christmas Festival** has candlelight inn tours and music. Check with the visitors center or www.gomendo.com for details.

Sleeping

Most accommodations in Mendocino have peaked roofs, picket fences, cabbage-rose wallpaper and lace curtains. If you don't like Victorian B&Bs, you may be out of luck. Fort Bragg's lodgings are more affordable, if less charming (see p66).

Mendocino Coast Reservations (☎ 937-5033, 800-262-7801; www.mendocinovacations.com; 1000 Main St; ☺ 9am-5pm) books vacation homes, cottages and B&Bs.

Sweetwater Spa & Inn (☎ 937-4076, 800-300-4140; 44840 Main St; www.sweetwaterspa.com; r & cottages $125-200) owns a variety of accommodations, both in town and nearby. Rates include spa privileges.

IN TOWN

Blackberry Inn (☎ 937-5281; www.mendocinomotel .com; 44951 Larkin Rd; r $115-170) Above town on a grassy hill, this inn looks like a row of Old West storefronts. Many of the cozy and quiet Americana rooms have wood-burning fireplaces, spa tubs and ocean views.

Mendocino Hotel (☎ 937-0511, 800-548-0513; www.mendocinohotel.com; 45080 Main St; r with/without bathroom from $120/95, ste $275) Built in 1878 as Mendocino's first hotel, many of the Victorian guest rooms here share bathrooms. For more amenities – and thicker walls – book one of the modern garden suites behind the hotel.

There are several good B&Bs in the historic downtown area.

Joshua Grindle Inn (☎ 937-4143, 800-474-6353; www.joshgrin.com; 44800 Little Lake Rd; r $130-245) Mendocino's oldest B&B has uncluttered, bright, airy rooms in an 1869 house, a weathered redwood saltbox cottage and a water tower. All include fine bath amenities, robes and gourmet breakfast.

MacCallum House Inn (☎ 937-0289, 800-609-0492; www.maccallumhouse.com; 45020 Albion St; r $120-295) Stay in an 1882 Victorian refurbished barn with rough-hewn beams, or a freestanding garden cottage. Rooms are very comfortable with modern amenities and antique furnishings.

CO Packard House (☎ 937-2677, 888-453-2677; www.packardhouse.com; 45170 Little Lake Rd; r $175-215) Mendocino's most discreetly elegant B&B. Immaculately decorated in contemporary style, with beautiful fabrics and gorgeous limestone-tiled bathrooms.

Agate Cove Inn (☎ 937-0551, 800-527-3111; www.agatecove.com; 11201 Lansing St; r $130-260, ocean-view cottages $180-290) On a spectacular bluff overlooking the sea and surrounded by 100-year-old cypress trees, rooms and cottages have down comforters, feather beds, CD players and VCRs – with no Victorian froufrou.

Stanford Inn by the Sea (☎ 937-5615, 800-331-8884; www.stanfordinn.com; cnr Hwy 1 & Comptche Ukiah Rd; r $245-295; ▢ ▣) At Mendocino's best inn, the plush rooms have wood-burning fireplaces, fine art, stereos and top-quality mattresses with fine linen; outside there's a small organic farm, produce from which is served in the restaurant. All this plus a giant solarium with swimming pool and hot tub, canoe rentals, llamas, sumptuous breakfasts and a warm welcome for pets.

Other recommendations:

Sea Gull Inn (☎ 937-5204, 888-937-5204; 44960 Albion St; r $55-165) Have breakfast delivered to your door at Mendocino's best-value lodging.

McElroy's Cottage Inn (☎ 937-1734, 888-262-3576; www.mcelroysinn.com; 998 Main St; r $70-115) An early 1900s Craftsman-style home with simple, clean rooms.

Blue Heron Inn (☎ 937-4323; www.theblueheron.com; 390 Kasten St; r $95-115) Spartan rooms with luxurious bed linen.

Headlands Inn (☎ 937-4431; www.headlandsinn.com; cnr Albion & Howard Sts; r $110-205) Another with picket fence and lace curtains.

Alegria (☎ 937-5150, 800-780-7905; www.oceanfrontmagic.com; 44781 Main St; r $189-259) Every room has an ocean view, deck and fireplace.

OUT OF TOWN

Russian Gulch State Park (☎ 800-444-7275; www.reserveamerica.com; sites $14) Two miles north of town, this state park has a shady campground with hot showers, a beach and rocky headlands.

There are also several good inns outside town.

Fensalden (☎ 937-4042; www.fensalden.com; 33810 Navarro Ridge Rd, Albion; r $130-165, bungalow $225) Seven miles south on 20 grassy acres, the comfortable rooms at this 1880s stagecoach stop are furnished with period antiques. Ask about the bungalow, which has a full kitchen and sleeps six.

Other recommendations:

Mendocino Farmhouse (☎ 937-0241, 800-475-1536; www.mendocinofarmhouse.com; Olson Lane, off Comptche-Ukiah Rd; r $115-145)

Glendeven (☎ 937-0083, 800-822-4536; www.glendeven.com; 8205 N Hwy 1; r $135-235)

Brewery Gulch (☎ 937-4752, 800-578-4454; www.brewerygulchinn.com; 9401 N Hwy 1; r $175-260)

Eating

IN TOWN

It's hard to eat in town without spending a lot of money. At dinner, try the MacCallum House bar (see this page) or Patterson's Pub (see p72) for cheaper eats.

Tote Fete Bakery (☎ 937-3383; 10450 Lansing St; sandwiches $5-7) Perfect for a quick bite or to stock picnic baskets; there's a garden out back.

Lu's (45013 Ukiah St; snacks $5-8; 🕑 11:30am-5:30pm) Pick up a delicious organic vegetarian burrito from this tiny freestanding shack.

Mendo Burgers (☎ 937-1111; 10483 Lansing St; dishes $5; 🕑 11am-5pm) Behind the Mendocino Bakery & Cafe, Mendo Burgers serves both meat and vegie burgers at an old-fashioned lunch counter.

Reservations are recommended for all restaurants listed in this section.

Cafe Beaujolais (☎ 937-5614; 961 Ukiah St; dishes $22-28; 🕑 dinner) In a refurbished 1896 house, Mendocino's pioneer California-cuisine restaurant serves innovative, refined and inspired cooking. The kitchen uses only organic meats and produce.

Ravens (☎ 937-5615; cnr Hwy 1 & Comptche Ukiah Rd; breakfast $8-13, dinner $14-28; 🕑 breakfast & dinner) Haute contemporary cuisine meets vegetarianism at the Ravens in the Stanford Inn by the Sea, where produce comes from its own organic gardens. There's everything from sea-palm strudel to pizza. Fantastic breakfasts, too.

MacCallum House Restaurant (☎ 937-0289; 45020 Albion St; breakfast $10, bar menu $6-12, dinner $20-32; 🕑 breakfast & dinner) Sit on the veranda or by the river-rock fireplace for a romantic dinner of duck, gnocchi, lamb, steak or fish. The chef-owner uses only all-organic ingredients. The evening bar menu is one of Mendocino's few bargains. Come for breakfast, too.

955 Ukiah St Restaurant (☎ 937-1955; 955 Ukiah St; dishes $15-25; 🕑 dinner Wed-Sun) For consistently good seafood and steaks, this restaurant serves dinners in a casual, inviting dining room.

OUT OF TOWN

Little River Inn (☎ 937-5942, 888-466-5683; Hwy 1, Little River; www.littleriverinn.com; r $110-280; lunch $8-14, dinner $19-28; 🕑 breakfast, lunch & dinner) Three miles south of Mendocino, enjoy unhurried hospitality at Little River; the spacious garden-view restaurant features uncomplicated American cooking like crab cakes, grilled salmon and filet mignon. It's also a first-rate resort with ocean-view rooms and wood-burning fireplaces.

Edge of the Earth (☎ 937-1970; Hwy 1, Little River; dishes $18-24; 🕑 dinner Thu-Sun) Across the road from the Little River Inn, behind the post office, this eatery overlooks the ocean and serves seafood and organic vegetarian food in a nine-table dining room.

The food is as good as the view at two spots in Albion, 7 miles south of Mendocino. There's **Albion River Inn** (☎ 937-1919, 800-479-7944; www.albionriverinn.com; N Hwy 1, Albion; r $200-$310; dishes $16-26), which also rents ultra-luxurious ocean-view rooms; and the **Ledford House** (☎ 937-0282; 3000 N Hwy 1, Albion;

bistro meals $15-18; regular dishes $22-28), which has a moderately priced 'bistro menu' in addition to regular entrees – try the cassoulet.

Drinking

Have cocktails at the **Mendocino Hotel** (see p70) or the **Grey Whale Bar** at the MacCallum House Restaurant (see p71). Locals do shots 'til 2am at **Dick's Place** (☎ 937-5643; 45080 Main St) and drink beer till midnight at **Patterson's Pub** (☎ 937-4782; 10485 Lansing St), an Irish bar with a great bar menu.

Entertainment

Mendocino Theatre Company (☎ 937-4477; www .1mtc.org; 45200 Little Lake St) This local company performs at the Mendocino Art Center.

Shopping

Mendocino Village Gallery (☎ 937-4999; 45084 Little Lake St) showcases paintings by local artists; in the same building, Natural Herb Gardens sells aromatherapy and massage oils.

Articles (☎ 937-3891; 611 Albion St; ☺ closed Wed) Peruse handmade crafts and cards inside an old water tower you can ascend.

If you like stained glass, check out **Color & Light** (☎ 937-1003; 10525 Ford St; ☺ closed Tue-Thu). **Papa Birds** (☎ 937-2730; 45040 Albion St) has birdhouses and all things avian.

The fantastic **Mendocino Jams & Preserves** (☎ 937-1037; 440 Main St) offers tastings; try the ketchup. Sample wines at **Fetzer Tasting Room** (☎ 937-6190; 45070 Main St; ☺ 10am-6pm).

Getting There & Around

The **Mendocino Transit Authority** (MTA; ☎ 462-1422, 800-696-4682) operates a county-wide bus service.

VAN DAMME STATE PARK

Two miles south in Little River, **Van Damme State Park** (☎ 937-5804; Hwy 1; day-use fee $4) is best known for its **pygmy forest**, where acidic soil and an impenetrable layer of hardpan below the surface create a natural bonsai forest with decades-old trees growing only a few feet high. A raised wheelchair-accessible boardwalk provides easy access to the forest.

To get there, turn east from Hwy 1 onto Little River Airport Rd, a half-mile south of the Van Damme State Park entrance, and go 3 miles. Or you can hike up from the campground on the 3.5-mile **Fern Canyon**

Scenic Trail, which crosses back and forth over Little River. The **visitors center** (☎ 937-4016; ☺ 10am-4pm daily summer, Sat & Sun only winter) has nature exhibits, videos and interpretive programs; a half-hour marsh loop trail starts nearby. For sea-cave kayaking tours ($45) and kayak rentals ($20), contact **Lost Coast Kayaking** (☎ 937-2434).

HIGHWAY 128 & ANDERSON VALLEY

If you're in a hurry or grow weary of curvy Hwy 1 and the coast's chilly weather, cut inland to Hwy 101 and continue south via Hwy 128, 10 miles south of Mendocino; it's more winding than Hwy 1, but after 60 miles, you'll reach the freeway. Along the rural route, you'll pass through woods, vineyards, orchards, pastureland and oak-dotted prairies. In summer it's always warmer here than at the ocean. Most come for the wineries, but also enjoy great hiking, cycling, fishing, canoeing and kayaking. Tiny **Boonville** (population 700) and **Philo** (population 400) are the valley's principal towns.

Information

For information contact the **Anderson Valley Chamber of Commerce** (☎ 895-2379; www.anderson valleychamber.com).

Sights & Activities

Two miles east of Hwy 1, the road reaches **Navarro Redwoods State Park** (☎ 895-3141) and continues for 11 miles under the canopy of second-growth redwoods before emerging in the Anderson Valley. Look for the giant stumps from which new growth sprouts, and see how the forest repairs itself a century after being devastated by logging. Six miles after the junction with Hwy 1, stop at the Paul M Demmick campground for picnicking (bring your own water), swimming, and fishing along the Navarro River, which runs hardest in winter and spring.

Hendy Woods State Park (☎ 937-5804, reservations 800-444-7275; www.reserveamerica.com; sites/cabins $12/20), bordered by the Navarro River, just off Hwy 128 on Philo-Greenwood Rd, has hiking trails, two small virgin redwood groves, picnic areas and a forested campground with hot showers. It's often warmer here than at Navarro Redwoods.

Most of the valley's dozen or so small **wineries** (www.avwines.com) are outside Philo.

Many are family-owned and offer tastings; some offer tours. **Navarro Vineyards** (☎ 895-3686; 5601 Hwy 128; ☯ tastings 10am-6pm) makes outstanding wines, particularly pinot noir and Riesling, but some are pricey. **Husch Vineyards** (☎ 800-554-8724; 4400 Hwy 128; ☯ tastings 10am-6pm summer, 10am-5pm rest of year) has good, affordable vintages.

The **Anderson Valley Historical Society Museum** (☎ 895-3207; 12340 Hwy 128, Boonville), inside a little red schoolhouse on Hwy 128 just west of Boonville, has historical photos and artifacts. **Anderson Valley Brewing Co** (☎ 895-2337; 17700 Hwy 153; tours free), just east of the crossroads at Hwy 128, crafts award-winning beers in a Bavarian-style brewhouse. Tours leave at 1:30pm and 4pm; call to confirm.

Take a cooking class with some of Wine Country's best chefs at the **Apple Farm** (☎ 895-2461; 18501 Greenwood Rd, Philo). They also rent cottages in the orchards for $200.

Festivals & Events
The annual celebrations include the **Boonville Beer Festival**, **California Wool & Fiber Festival** and **Pinot Noir Festival**, all in May, followed by the **Wild Iris Folk Festival** in early June.

Sleeping & Eating
Philo Pottery Inn (☎ 895-3069; www.philopotteryinn.com; 8550 Hwy 128; r $110-165) Made of unfinished redwood inside and out, this cozy B&B has comfy rooms and well-tended gardens.

Boonville Hotel (☎ 895-2210; www.boonvillehotel.com; 14040 Hwy 128; r $95-200) Decorated in contemporary American-country style with seagrass flooring, pastel colors and fine linen, rooms are small but very comfortable.

Outside of town, **Sheepdung Estates** (☎ 894-5322; www.sheepdung.com) has modern cottages on wide-open ranch lands.

Anderson Valley Inn (☎ 895-3325; www.avinn.com; 8480 Hwy 128, Philo; r $55) This inn has simple motel rooms at budget prices.

Buckhorn Saloon (☎ 895-3369; 14081 Hwy 128; lunch $7-10, dinner $11-16; ☯ 11am-9pm daily, Thu-Mon winter) The Buckhorn serves grill food to accompany its many beers on tap. Sometimes they host live music.

Boonville Hotel (☎ 895-2210; www.boonvillehotel.com; 14040 Hwy 128; dishes $18-25; ☯ dinner Thu-Mon, bar 3pm-late daily) This stylized roadhouse serves a well-executed menu of contemporary American cooking. Try the rib-eye or the wild salmon. Make reservations.

> **BOONTLING**
>
> Boonville is linguistically famous. 'Boontling' developed here around the turn of the 20th century, when Boonville was a pretty remote place. Locals used the dialect to *shark* (stump) outsiders and amuse themselves. You may hear *codgie kimmies* (old men) asking for a *horn of zeese* (a cup of coffee) or some *bahl gorms* (good food) while you're in town. If you're lucky, you may spot the tow truck called Boont Region De-arkin' Moshe (literally, Anderson Valley Un-wrecking Machine).

A **farmers market** (☯ 9:45am-noon Sat May-Oct) assembles outside the Boonville Hotel. Shop for natural foods at the **Boont Berry Farm** (☎ 895-3576; 13981 Hwy 128), which has a good deli and bakery.

ELK
pop 250

Tiny Elk sits atop a bluff overlooking giant, mesmerizing rock formations jutting out of the Pacific. At the south end of town, **Greenwood State Beach** (☎ 877-3458) has picnic tables and a path down the cliff to the beach where Greenwood Creek meets the sea. Elk's **visitors center** (☎ 11am-1pm Sat & Sun mid-Mar–Oct) has exhibits on the town's logging past. **Force 10** (☎ 877-3505; 6143 Hwy 1) guides ocean kayaking; two-hour trips cost $95.

Several upmarket B&Bs take advantage of the views – and tourists, by charging outrageous sums for lodging. The most reasonably priced place in town, **Griffin House** (☎ 877-3422; www.griffinn.com; 5910 S Hwy 1; cottages $98-198) doesn't pretend to be more than it is – an unpretentious cluster of comfortable, if plain, beachside cottages. Next door **Greenwood Pier Inn** (☎ 877-9997; www.greenwoodpierinn.com; 5928 S Hwy 1; r $130-$275), run by aging hippies, has cottages set along a meandering garden path. Also consider **Sandpiper House** (☎ 877-3587, 800-894-9016; www.sandpiperhouse.com; 5520 S Hwy 1; r $155-260).

If you want to break open your piggie bank, **Elk Cove Inn** (☎ 877-3321, 800-275-2967; www.elkcoveinn.com; 6300 S Hwy 1; r $190-250, cottages/ste $275/325) has drop-dead views, 400-thread-count sheets, friendly staff and a spa. The 1915 Craftsman-style **Harbor House Inn** (☎ 877-3203, 800-720-7474; www.theharborhouseinn.com; 5600 S

Hwy 1; r & cottages $295-440) includes breakfast and a delicious four-course dinner.

If you can't sleep cheap, at least you can eat well for relatively little. **Queenie's Roadhouse Cafe** (☎ 877-3285; 6061 S Hwy 1; dishes $6-9; ✆ breakfast & lunch Thu-Mon) serves great omelettes, scrambles, salads and sandwiches. At **Bridget Dolan's** (☎ 877-1820; 5910 S Hwy 1; dishes $9-17), a dressed-down pub, you'll find straight-shooting food like lasagna and salad, pot pies, and bangers and mash.

South of Elk, hidden on 92 acres above the ocean, exquisite **Victorian Gardens** (☎ 882-3606; 14409 S Hwy 1, Manchester; r $160-250; dinner for two $150; ✆ dinner Thu-Sun) serves a five-course classical-Italian set menu, paired with superb wines, in the dining room of a rambling 1904 farmhouse, to no more than several couples a night. The Italian-born innkeeper prepares dinner; his gracious and charming wife serves. They don't need the money; it's a labor of love. Reservations essential. The four guest rooms are beautifully appointed.

POINT ARENA
pop 400

A former fishing village, Point Arena gets its name from the nearby windswept point where a lighthouse has stood for more than a century. Well worth a visit, **Point Arena Lighthouse** (☎ 882-2777; www.pointarenalighthouse.com; adult/child $5/1; ✆ 10am-4:30pm summer, 10am-3:30pm winter) stands 10 stories high, 2 miles north of town. It's the only lighthouse in California you can ascend. Check in at the museum, then climb the 145 steps to the top and see the Fresnel lens and the jaw-dropping view.

You can rent one of the former US Coast Guard three-bedroom homes next to the lighthouse. Contact **Point Arena Lighthouse Keepers** (☎ 882-2777, 877-725-4448; www.pointarenalighthouse.com; houses $175-190).

A mile west of town at Arena Cove, you'll find the **Arena Cove Restaurant** (790 Port Dr; lunch $9-12, dinner $12-20; ✆ 11am-9pm), a fairly good restaurant overlooking an ugly pier; and the **Wharf Master's Inn** (☎ 882-3171, 800-932-4031; www.wharfmasters.com; 785 Port Rd; r $95-175), a cluster of small, modern inn buildings on a hill overlooking the cove.

Downtown, on Hwy 1, there's a good burrito shop, several cafés and a nothing-special motel. **Carlini's Cafe** (☎ 882-2942; 206 Main St; dishes $5-8; ✆ breakfast & lunch Thu-Tue) serves the town's best breakfast and lunch.

Make it a point to stop by **Point Arena Bakery** (☎ 882-3770; 213 Main St; ✆ 7:30am-noonish Wed-Sun), which makes bread and pastries as good as any in San Francisco; they close when they sell out. If you're here in the evening, the **Arena Cinema** (☎ 882-3456; 214 Main St) shows mainstream, foreign and art films in a beautifully restored movie house.

ANCHOR BAY
pop 500

Between Point Arena and Anchor Bay, Hwy 1 passes by secluded beaches that are hard to find but worth the effort. Locals call this part of the coast the 'banana belt': in summer it can be warm and sunny while in nearby Mendocino and Bodega Bay it's foggy and cold. There's not much in quiet Anchor Bay except for several inns and a tiny shopping center.

Seven miles north of town, pull off Hwy 1 at mile-marker 11.41 for **Schooner Gulch** (☎ 937-5804; no services). A trail through the trees leads into a forest, then down the cliffs to a wide sandy beach with tidepools. If you bear right at the fork in the trail, you'll reach **Bowling Ball Beach**, the next beach north, where at low tide you'll see rows and rows of large round rocks resembling bowling balls – but you have to come at low tide.

There's no better grocer within 50 miles than the **Anchor Bay Store** (☎ 884-4245; Hwy 1; ✆ 8am-8pm Mon-Sat, 8am-7pm Sun). Next door, there's a rice-and-beans Mexican joint and a fairly good fish-and-french-fries restaurant.

Anchor Bay makes an excellent jumping-off point for exploring the surrounding coast.

Mar Vista Cottages (☎ 884-3522, 877-855-3522; www.marvistamendocino.com; 35101 S Hwy 1; 1-bedroom cottages $140-170, 2-bedroom cottages $180-200) has 12 cozy, modest and spotlessly clean 1930s vacation cottages with old-fashioned kitchens and sumptuously comfortable beds. On the 9-acre grounds are BBQs, a redwood soaking tub, picnic areas and an organic vegetable garden (grazing encouraged). Across the road is a great beach. Families and dogs welcome.

North Coast Country Inn (☎ 884-4537, 800-959-4537; www.northcoastcountryinn.com; 34591 S Hwy 1; r $175-215), perched on a hillside beneath towering trees, is surrounded by impeccably maintained gardens. Six spacious, well-appointed American country style rooms have fireplaces as well as books, board games and private entrances. Full breakfast and a hot tub sweeten the deal.

GUALALA

pop 585

The small coastal settlement of Gualala (pronounced wah-*lah*-luh) began as a lumber-mill town in the 1860s. Today it serves mostly as a commercial center for locals as well as vacationers renting homes in nearby Sea Ranch. Stop by **Dolphin Arts Gallery** (☎ 884-3896; 39225 Hwy 1; 10am-5pm Wed-Mon, noon-4pm Tue) for maps and limited information; it's hidden behind the 19th-century Gualala Hotel. The **Redwood Coast Chamber of Commerce** (☎ 884-1080, 800-778-5252; www.redwoodcoastchamber.com) has information on local businesses.

Sights & Activities

Inland along Old State Rd, at the south end of town, the **Gualala Arts Center** (☎ 884-1138; 9am-4pm Mon-Fri, noon-4pm Sat & Sun) has changing gallery exhibitions and organizes the annual **Art in the Redwoods Festival** on the 3rd weekend in August. Further along Old State Rd, you can camp at the attractive **Gualala River Redwood Park** (☎ 884-3533; day-use $6, tent sites $15, RV sites $32-38; Memorial Day-Labor Day).

The 195-acre **Gualala Point Regional Park** (☎ 785-2377, camping reservations 565-2267; 42401 Hwy 1; day-use sites $16), about a mile south of town, has hiking trails through woods and meadows along the coast and up the Gualala River. Stop by the visitors center for information.

In summer a spit of sand forms at the mouth of the Gualala River, cutting it off from the ocean and turning it into a warm-water lake, perfect for kayaking. **Adventure Rents** (☎ 884-4386, 888-881-4386; www.adventurerents.com) rents out canoes and kayaks and provides instruction; advanced boaters can rent ocean kayaks.

Sleeping & Eating

There are several restaurants, motels and ocean-view inns on the main drag, but they're overpriced for what they offer, with one notable exception.

The Gualala Hotel (☎ 884-3441, 888-482-5252; www.thegualalahotel.com; 39301 S Hwy 1; r $70-105) This century-old hotel has simple accommodations. Some rooms share bathrooms

and the mattresses are soft, but the owners continue to make upgrades. Rates are reasonable, especially for rooms above the saloon (light sleepers beware). There's also a good restaurant for lunch and dinner.

St Orres Inn (☎ 884-3303; www.saintorres.com; 36601 Hwy 1; B&B $80-95, cottages $110-250) Famous for its unusual architecture, there's no place like St Orres, just north of town. The main hotel has dramatic rough-hewn timbers and Russian-looking copper domes. Outside, on the property's 90 acres, handcrafted cottages range from rustic to fairly luxurious. The inn's fine **dining room** (reservations ☎ 884-3335; dishes $40; dinner) serves creative, inspired California cuisine in one of the coast's most romantic rooms.

SEA RANCH

Just south of Gualala, the giant upmarket subdivision of Sea Ranch sprawls along the coast for almost 10 miles. There are strict zoning laws, and houses are constructed of weathered, exposed wood only. It's entirely residential – mostly vacation homes – and except for a post office and small store, there's no real commercial area. If you need gasoline, you've got to go to Gualala.

Public through-ways onto many private beaches have been mandated by law, after years of litigation against the ranch corporation. Hiking trails lead from sign-posted roadside parking lots to the sea, and along the tops of the bluffs. The **Stengel Beach trail** (at Hwy 1 mile-marker 53.96) has a staircase to the beach; **Walk-On Beach** (milemarker 56.53) provides wheelchair access. Don't trespass on adjacent lands. For details on hiking, including maps, contact the **Sea Ranch Association** (☎ 785-2444; www.tsra.org).

Sea Ranch Lodge (☎ 785-2371, 800-732-7262; www.searanchlodge.com; 60 Sea Walk Dr; r with breakfast $205-395), a marvel of forward-thinking '60s-modern California architecture, has spacious, luxurious rooms, many with dramatic views over the bluffs to the sea; some have hot tubs and fireplaces. The very fine contemporary restaurant serves three meals; there's also a bar. Golf packages available.

North of the lodge, Sea Ranch's iconic non-denominational **chapel** stands on the inland side of Hwy 1.

If you want to rent a house in Sea Ranch, contact **Rams Head Realty** (☎ 785-2427, 800-785-3455; www.ramshead-realty.com).

SALT POINT STATE PARK

Craggy cliffs of sandstone drop from open prairies into the sea at 6000-acre **Salt Point State Park** (☎ 847-3221; vehicle day-use fee $4). Hiking trails crisscross windswept grasslands and wooded hills, connecting pygmy forests and coastal coves rich with tidepools. Bisected by the San Andreas fault, the composition of rock on the east side of the park is vastly different than on the west side. Notice the geology as you move about. Near Gerstle Cove, look for *tafonis* (formations of honeycombed sandstone).

For drop-dead views of the pristine coastline, walk out to the viewing platform overlooking **Sentinel Rock**; it's a short stroll from Fisk Cove's parking lot, at the northern end of the park. Just south of here, **Stump Beach** has picnic areas with firepits and stairs to the beach. Further south still, look for seals lazing on the rocks at **Gerstle Cove Marine Reserve**, one of California's first underwater parks; tread lightly at its tidepools, and don't lift the rocks, since even a glimpse of sunlight can kill the small critters underneath.

If you're here in April or May, check out **Kruse Rhododendron State Reserve**. Growing abundantly in the filtered light of the redwood forest, the rhododendrons reach heights of 30ft or more, with a magnificent display of pink blossoms in spring; to get here turn east from Hwy 1 onto Kruse Ranch Rd, then follow signs.

Two campgrounds, **Woodside** and **Gerstle Cove** (☎ reservations 800-444-7275; www.reserveamerica .com; sites $12), both sign-posted from Hwy 1, have campsites under Monterey pines with cold running water, but no showers. Walk-in **environmental campsites** (sites $10) are about a half-mile from the parking area, on the east side of Woodside campground.

FORT ROSS STATE HISTORIC PARK

In March 1812, a group of 25 Russians and 80 native Alaskans (including members of the Kodiak and Aleutian tribes) arrived here, near the site of a Kashaya Pomo Indian village, and began to build a wooden fort. The southernmost outpost of the 19th-century Russian fur trade on America's Pacific coast, Fort Ross was established as a base for sea-otter hunting operations, for growing wheat and other crops to supply Russian settlements in Alaska, and for trade

with Alta California ('Upper California,' the name given by the Spanish). The Russians dedicated the fort in August 1812, but occupied it only until 1842. After severely depleting the sea-otter population and the relative failure of agricultural production, they abandoned it.

Today you can see an accurate reconstruction of the Russian fort at **Fort Ross State Historic Park** (☎ 847-3286; 19005 Hwy 1; admission per vehicle $4; ☯ 10am-4:30pm), 2 miles south of Salt Point. Most of the original buildings were sold, dismantled and carried away to Sutter's Fort in California's Central Valley during the gold rush.

The **visitors center** (☎ 847-3437) has historical displays and an excellent bookshop with volumes on Californian history, nature and Russian-American history. Ask about hiking to the old Russian cemetery and orchard.

On **Living History Day**, the last Saturday in July, costumed volunteers bring the fort's history to life; have a look at the website (www.parks.ca.gov) for other frequently held special events in the area, or call the visitors center.

Stay in a rustic cottage with fireplace, or a former dairy barn at **Stillwater Cove Ranch** (☎ 847-3227; 22555 Hwy 1; r $50-90, bunkhouse $155), around 3 miles north of Fort Ross and just across from the ocean. Once a boys' school and working ranch, accommodations are comfortable, if a little plain. There are no TVs, food or in-room phones available, but there are some kitchens. The bunkhouse sleeps eight.

Reef Campground (☎ 847-3286; sites $10; ☯ Apr-Nov), within the park, about 2 miles south of the fort off Hwy 1, has first-come, first-served campsites (cold running water, flush toilets, no showers) tucked into a sheltered seaside gully. Three miles north of the fort, **Stillwater Cove Regional Park** (☎ 847-3245; reservations 565-2267; 22455 N Hwy 1; sites $16) has campsites, hot showers and hiking trails under Monterey pines.

SONOMA COAST STATE BEACH

Stretching for 17 miles from Vista Trail to Bodega Head, **Sonoma Coast State Beach** (☎ 875-3483) is actually a series of beaches separated by rocky outcroppings and headlands. Some are tiny and tucked away in little coves, while others stretch far and wide.

The Pacific Coast Highway owes some of its fame to this strip of coastline. As you drive southward from Fort Ross, it's hard to keep your eyes on the road, so beautiful is the view. Plan to stop for pictures, provided it's not foggy. And always pull all the way over to allow non-sightseers to pass you. As you head south, you'll pass parking lots for the various beaches.

Vista Trail, 2 miles south of Fort Ross, has a paved wheelchair-accessible path atop the bluffs; it overlooks Russian Gulch. As you approach Jenner on Hwy 1, you'll come to spectacular overlooks and parking areas for access to the mouth of the Russian River. Other noteworthy stops include Goat Rock, which has resident harbor seals; Shell Beach, great for tidepooling and beachcombing; Duncan's Landing, where timber ships once moored; sandy Portuguese and Schoolhouse Beaches; 2-mile-long Salmon Creek Beach; and Bodega Dunes. Coastal hiking trails connect nearly all of the beaches.

At the more-or-less halfway point, **Jenner** has several noteworthy places to sleep.

There's everything from seaside cottages to river-view guest rooms at the **Jenner Inn & Cottages** (☎ 865-2377, 800-732-2377; www.jennerinn.com; Hwy 1; r & cottages $88-278), which occupies several buildings throughout town. Rates include breakfast. There's also a wine bar and fireside lounge.

There are several ocean-view cottages and fairly comfortable rooms at **River's End** (☎ 865-2484; www.rivers-end.com; 11048 Hwy 1; r $95-120, cabins $120-180), which also has a good **restaurant** (lunch $10-20, dinner $23-28; ☺ Thu-Mon). There's also a small full bar.

Inland on Willow Creek Rd, on the southern side of the Russian River, are two first-come, first-served environmental campgrounds, **Willow Creek** and **Pomo Canyon** (sites $10). Willow Creek has no water; Pomo Canyon has cold water. Both are open from April to November.

BEWARE TREACHEROUS SURF

The Sonoma Coast beaches are not swimming beaches; it's often unsafe even to wade. Never turn your back on the ocean, stay above the high-tide line, and watch children closely.

DETOUR TO GUERNEVILLE

To escape the summertime fog, head 13 miles inland on Hwy 116 to Guerneville (population 2440), a lively little summer resort town on the banks of the Russian River, popular with young couples, motorcyclists, and gay men and lesbians (who call it 'groinville'). There's a four-block-long main street (River Rd) lined with shops, cafés and restaurants. It teems with people on weekends. North of town, picnic and hike in **Armstrong Woods**, a virgin stand of redwoods. Float downriver in a canoe from **Burke's Canoes** (☎ 887-1222; www.burkescanoetrips.com; 8600 River Rd, Forestville; canoe rental $42); they'll shuttle you back once you're done. If you're gay and want to sip cocktails, head to sexy **Fife's Guest Ranch** (☎ 869-0656, 800-734-3371; www.fifes.com; 16467 River Rd), where there's no charge to use the pool (adults only). Guerneville quiets way down in winter. For information, contact the **Russian River Chamber of Commerce** (☎ 869-9000, 877-644-9001; www.russianriver.com).

BODEGA BAY
pop 950

An hour south of Gualala lies the harbor-side village of Bodega Bay. Despite the many shops, restaurants and inns for tourists, fishing remains the town's principal industry.

Originally inhabited by Pomo Indians, the bay takes its name from Juan Francisco de la Bodega y Quadra, captain of the Spanish sloop *Sonora*, which entered the bay in 1775. But it wasn't settled until the early-19th century when Russians established wheat farms for their fur-trapping empire that stretched from Alaska all the way to Fort Ross. The Russians pulled out of the area in 1842, and American settlers moved in.

Today Hwy 1 runs along the east side of Bodega Bay. On the west side, a peninsula resembling a crooked finger juts out to sea, delimiting Bodega Harbor. At the peninsula's tip, Bodega Head rises 265ft above sea level. To get there (and to see the open ocean), head west from Hwy 1 onto Eastshore Rd, then turn right at the stop sign onto Bay Flat Rd. It's a great place for whale-watching.

The **Sonoma Coast Visitors Information Center** (☎ 875-3866; www.bodegabay.com; 850 Hwy 1;

HITCHCOCK'S BODEGA BAY
by Ryan Ver Berkmoes

Alfred Hitchcock often looked to Northern California for film locations. He liked the fog-shrouded, moody coast and its proximity to his country retreat in the Santa Cruz Mountains. It's easy to visit many sights made famous in his movies.

An otherwise unremarkable stop on a remarkable stretch of Hwy 1, Bodega Bay has an enduring claim to fame as the setting for Hitchcock's *The Birds*. Although special effects radically altered the actual layout of the town, you can get a good feel for the bay and its western shore, supposed site of Mitch Brenner's (Rod Taylor) farm. The Tides Restaurant, where much avian-caused havoc occurs, is still there but has been transmogrified since 1962 into a vast tourist-processing plant, no longer the charming seaside restaurant the movie portrays. But venture 5 miles inland of Bodega Bay to the tiny town of Bodega, and you'll find two *Birds* icons: the schoolhouse and the church. Both stand as they did in the film, and if you see a crow overhead, you may feel the hair rise on your neck.

Coincidentally, right after production of *The Birds* began, a real-life bird attack occurred in Capitola, a sleepy seaside town south of Santa Cruz. Thousands of seagulls ran amok, destroying property, attacking people and making a stinking mess.

🕑 10am-6pm Mon-Thu, 10am-8pm Fri & Sat, 11am-7pm Sun), opposite the Tides Wharf complex, provides information for the Bodega Bay area north to Fort Ross.

The **Bodega Bay Fishermen's Festival** in April is the big event of the year, drawing thousands of visitors; activities include the blessing of the fleet, a flamboyant parade of decorated vessels, an arts-and-crafts fair, kite-flying, feasting and more fun. The great **crab feed** happens in February or March.

Activities
Landlubbers enjoy **hiking** above the crashing surf at **Bodega Head**, where there are several good trails, including a 3.75-mile trail to the Bodega Dunes Campground and a 2.2-mile trek to Salmon Creek Ranch. They don't call it 'Blow-dega Head' for nothing: bring a kite. **Candy & Kites** (☎ 875-3777; 1415 Hwy 1) sells single-line and dual-line varieties.

Ride on horseback along the beach and Salmon Creek with stock from **Chanslor Stables** (☎ 875-3333; 2660 Hwy 1); trail rides cost $25 to $50. On the oceanfront, **Bodega Harbour Golf Links** (☎ 875-3538; www.bodegaharbourgolf .com), an 18-hole Scottish-style golf course designed by Robert Trent Jones Jr, has greens fees of $45 to $75 (without cart).

Bodega Bay Surf Shack (☎ 875-3944; 1400 Hwy 1) rents out surfboards, boogie boards, windsurfing gear, sea kayaks, bicycles and wet suits, and also offers surfing lessons.

Bodega Bay Kayak (☎ 875-8899; 1580 Eastshore Rd) rents out kayaks and guides coastal tours. **Bodega Bay Pro Dive** (☎ 875-3054; 1275 Hwy 1) teaches diving, rents out gear and guides trips.

Make reservations in advance for **sportfishing** charters and, between December and April, **whale-watching** cruises; these trips are popular. **Wil's Fishing Adventures** (☎ 875-2323; 1580 Eastshore Rd) and the **Bodega Bay Sport Fishing Center** (☎ 875-3344; 1500 Bay Flat Rd), beside the Sandpiper Cafe, organize harbor cruises, fishing trips and whale-watching excursions. Bait, tackle and fishing licenses are available at the Bodega Bay Sport Fishing Center or at the **Boathouse** (☎ 875-3495; 1445 Hwy 1), which also schedules fishing trips and serves fish and chips to the locals.

See Sonoma Coast State Beach (p76) for more activities in the area.

Sleeping & Eating
Bodega Harbor Inn (☎ 875-3594; www.bodegaharbor inn.com; 1345 Bodega Ave; r $60-115) A half-block uphill from Hwy 1, this clapboard inn has the most affordable motel rooms in town. Clean and modest, they're furnished with real and faux antiques. Ask about their vacation properties.

Chanslor Guest Ranch (☎ 875-2721; www.chanslor ranch.com; 2660 Hwy 1; r $100-150) A mile north of town, this working horse ranch has two private rooms with kitchenettes.

Bodega Bay Lodge & Spa (☎ 875-3525, 800-368-2468; www.bodegabaylodge.com; 103 Hwy 1; r $210-285; 🐾) You can't do better in Bodega Bay for luxury amenities and excellent service. Many of the well-kept, up-to-date rooms overlook marshland and dunes to the sea beyond. Other features include fireplaces, ocean-view swimming pool, golf course, whirlpool, sauna, spa and fitness center.

Bodega Dunes Campground (☎ 800-444-7275; www.reserveamerica.com; sites $16) has high sand dunes and hot showers. Another 5 miles further north, year-round **Wright's Beach Campground** (reservations ☎ 800-444-7275; www.reserveamerica.com; sites $14) has popular beachside sites without much privacy. **Sonoma County Regional Park** (information ☎ 875-3540, reservations 565-2267; sites $16) operates **Doran Park** (201 Doran Beach Rd) and **Westside Regional Park** (2400 Westshore Rd), both with beaches, hot showers, fishing and boat ramps.

For seafood by the docks, **Tides Wharf & Restaurant** (☎ 875-3652; 835 Hwy 1; breakfast $6-12, lunch $11-21, dinner $15-23) and **Lucas Wharf Restaurant & Bar** (☎ 875-3522; 595 Hwy 1; dishes $14-22; ☯ lunch & dinner) both have views and similar menus of clam chowder, fried fish and coleslaw. Although Tides boasts a great fish market, Lucas Wharf feels less like a factory and has a take-out deli.

Sandpiper Dockside Cafe & Restaurant (☎ 875-2278; 1410 Bay Flat Rd; dishes $12-19) Smaller than Tides Wharf and Lucas Wharf, and cheaper too, this café is more popular with locals; they serve fresh seafood and have a great view of the pier, the marina and the bay. To get there, turn seaward from Hwy 1 onto Eastshore Rd and go straight at the stop sign to the marina.

Duck Club (☎ 875-3525; breakfast $8-12, dinner $18-28; ☯ breakfast & dinner) At the Bodega Bay Lodge, the town's most fashionable and attractive restaurant serves very fine French-inspired California cuisine with a view of Bodega Head. Make reservations.

Bay View Restaurant (☎ 875-2751; Inn at the Tides, 800 Hwy 1; dishes $18-30; ☯ dinner Wed-Sat) In addition to prime steaks, the chef prepares fish he handpicks from the docks across the street. There's also a full bar.

SANTA ROSA
pop 147,595

Driving between San Francisco and the upper North Coast, you can save time by traveling inland on Hwy 101, which will bring you through Santa Rosa (population 147,595), the Wine Country's largest city and Sonoma's county seat. There's a bustling downtown, with a number of good restaurants and places to stay. It's also a good jumping-off point for jaunts to vineyards.

You'll know you're near when you see brake lights on Hwy 101. From 7am until 7pm you're almost sure to hit traffic; at rush hour it slows to a crawl. In summer it's very hot here, with temperatures often reaching the upper 90s, while at the coast it can be 30 degrees cooler. Hwy 101 is the major north–south route through the city; Hwy 12 runs east–west.

In July the old-fashioned **Sonoma County Fair** (☎ 545-4200; www.sonomacountyfair.com) takes place at the fairgrounds on Bennett Valley Rd.

Orientation & Information
The main shopping district is along 4th St, which abruptly ends at Hwy 101 but re-emerges on the other side in the historic Railway Square area. There are a number of downtown parking lots with free parking for the first 1½ hours.

The **Santa Rosa Visitors Bureau** (☎ 577-8674, 800-404-7673; 9 4th St; ☯ 9am-5pm Mon-Fri, 10am-3pm Sat & Sun) is in the railroad depot on the west side of Hwy 101, a few blocks from downtown (take the downtown Santa Rosa exit off Hwy 12 or Hwy 101).

Sights & Activities
Pioneering horticulturist Luther Burbank (1849–1926) developed many of his hybrid plant and tree species at his 19th-century Greek Revival home in Santa Rosa, which is now open as the **Luther Burbank Home & Gardens** (☎ 524-5445; www.lutherburbank.org; cnr Santa Rosa & Sonoma Aves; admission free; ☯ 8am-5pm). The extensive gardens are open to the public. The house and adjacent **Carriage Museum** (admission $3; ☯ 10am-4pm Tue-Sun Apr-Oct) have displays on Burbank's life and work.

You can see exhibits on the life and work of long-time Santa Rosa resident Charles Schulz at the **Charles M Schulz Museum** (☎ 579-4452; www.charlesmschulzmuseum.org; 2301 Hardies Lane; admission $8; ☯ noon-5:30pm Mon & Wed-Fri, 10am-5:30pm Sat & Sun). Schulz is famous for introducing the world to Snoopy and Charlie Brown. Down the street, **Snoopy's Gallery** (☎ 546-3385; 1667 W Steele Lane; admission free; ☯ 10am-6pm) shows a terrific collection of Peanuts paraphernalia. It's 2.5 miles north of downtown.

Next door, the **Redwood Empire Ice Arena** (☎ 546-7147; admission including skates $9), formerly owned and deeply loved by Charles Schulz, is open to the public most afternoons (call for hours).

Sleeping & Eating

Best Western Garden Inn (☎ 546-4031, 800-938-4774; www.thegardeninn.com; 1500 Santa Rosa Ave; r $75-99; ⛽) There are several motels on Santa Rosa Ave. Of the lot, this one has the cleanest, best-maintained rooms.

Hotel La Rose (☎ 579-3200, 800-527-6738; www .hotellarose.com; 308 Wilson St; r/ste $214/264; ℗) If you want to stay in a historic hotel, this 1907 building has attractive, very comfortable rooms right on Railroad Sq.

Vintners Inn (☎ 575-7350; www.vintnersinn.com; 4350 Barnes Rd, near River Rd; r $210-315) North of town, surrounded by vineyards, rooms at this luxurious inn have king beds and private garden-view patios. Breakfast included. The on-site restaurant **John Ash & Co** (☎ 527-7687; dishes $16-27; ☯ lunch & dinner), one of Sonoma's best, serves contemporary Euro-California cuisine in a casually elegant dining room.

There are lots of places to eat and drink downtown along 4th St.

Cantina (☎ 523-3663; 500 4th St; dishes $5-8) For margaritas and Mexican, the Cantina caters to a khakis crowd. Come on Tuesdays for $2 margaritas and 25¢ tacos.

Creekside Bistro (☎ 575-8839; 2800 4th St; breakfast & lunch $5-8, dinner $17-21; ☯ breakfast & lunch daily, dinner Wed-Sun) East of downtown in an old tavern, the Creekside serves all-American daytime meals, and French bistro fare in the evening.

Annapurna (☎ 579-8471; 535 Ross St; dishes under $12) For something different, this place off Mendocino Ave prepares delicate curries, stews and other fragrant Indian and Nepalese dishes, many vegetarian.

Lisa Hemenway's Bistro (☎ 526-5111; 1612 Terrace Way; lunch $8-16, dinner $13-29; ☯ lunch & dinner Tue-Sat) Serves an eclectic variety of stylized classic American cooking as well as examples of contemporary Eurasian-California cuisine in a casual white-tablecloth dining room. Ask about to-go lunch boxes.

La Gare (☎ 528-4355; 208 Wilson St; dishes $14-20; ☯ dinner Wed-Sun) If you're tired of contemporary cooking, La Gare prepares delicious, straightforward, classic French dishes, like escargots and beef bourguignon, in a romantic dining room at Railroad Sq.

Mixx (☎ 573-1344; 135 4th St at Davis St; lunch $9-13, dinner $20-28; ☯ lunch & dinner Mon-Sat) Also near the square, Mixx has an eclectic California menu and an extensive wine list.

Getting There & Away

Golden Gate Transit (☎ 541-2000, 415-923-2000) has daily buses (Nos 72, 74, 76 and 80) between San Francisco and Santa Rosa ($6.60, two hours). The 72 is fastest and 80 the slowest.

Sonoma County Transit (☎ 576-7433, 800-345-7433) runs several local bus routes around Sonoma Valley. **Greyhound** (☎ 800-231-2222) runs buses from San Francisco to Santa Rosa and points north along Hwy 101.

San Francisco & the Bay Area

The mighty Pacific reigns supreme over the man-made environment of the Bay Area. Along the coastline the steep, unstable hills prevent overbuilding of the cliffs and block the inland urban and suburban sprawl from view; the only indication that they're near is the light pollution they emit, obscuring the night sky's constellations. Prevailing westerly winds keep the air crisp and clean.

At the coast, summers remain cool because of the insistent fog hovering offshore; in winter it never freezes. Year-round there's little more than a 30°F spread. It's a different story inland, where you're safe wearing Bermudas and sneakers in July, but in coastal communities such as San Francisco, don't risk it. Indeed, if you were to look inside the bags and backpacks that locals carry, you'd inevitably find outerwear, ready to be thrown on at a moment's notice. In the winter, the fog gives way to rain, and temperatures both inland and at the coast remain a near-constant 50°F.

Visitors flock to San Francisco in droves for the spectacular scenery, outdoor activities and urban scene. In the course of one day, you can hike or mountain bike the rolling hills of Marin County, visit a major museum or the chic boutiques in downtown San Francisco, then spend the afternoon windsurfing or sailing on the bay. And once you're ready for dinner, there's no shortage of terrific dining. Whatever your pleasure, the Bay Area has it all.

HIGHLIGHTS

- Watching whales breach and sea lions frolic from the tip of **Point Reyes** (p85)

- Gazing down onto the Golden Gate Bridge from **Battery Spencer** (p89)

- Strolling atop rocky cliffs to the **Point Bonita Lighthouse** (p89) on Marin Headlands

- Spying on snowy egrets and blue herons in their treetop nests at the **Audubon Canyon Ranch** (p87)

- Catching sweeping views from atop **Mt Tamalpais** (p88)

- Motoring across San Francisco Bay in a ferryboat to **Sausalito** (p91)

- Touring the windswept island prison of **Alcatraz** (p94)

- Hiking in **Big Basin Redwood State Park** (p111)

- Visiting the elephant seals of **Año Nuevo State Reserve** (p111)

- Detouring to **Mission San Juan Bautista** (p114)

NORTH OF THE BAY

☎ 415

The rugged Sonoma Coast gives way to gentle rolling hills in Marin (muh-*rin*), the county just north of San Francisco, known for alternative living, left-leaning politics and redwood hot tubs. As you work your way south on Hwy 1 toward San Francisco, you'll no longer be winding along high bluffs as in Sonoma; instead you'll be nearly at water level, at sight line with blue herons and snowy egrets digging for worms in tidal mudflats. Marin's most prominent coastal feature, Point Reyes National Seashore, juts out to sea on a 71,000-acre triangular peninsula. As you drive past its eastern side, along Tomales Bay on Hwy 1, know that you're at the San Andreas fault, the end of the North American plate, on the very edge of the continent. Further south, before reaching the Golden Gate, you'll skirt Mt Tamalpais, the highest peak in this stretch of the Coastal Range.

SAN RAFAEL

pop 54,800

San Rafael grew up around its mission and is named for St Raphael, the angel of healing. In 1817 the mission was but an outpost for the San Francisco Mission Dolores, and served primarily as a sanatorium for Indians from across the bay who had fallen ill from diseases imported by white men; they came here to heal. The outpost became its own mission in 1822.

Today Hwy 101 bisects San Rafael. Shops, restaurants and cafés line 4th St, the city's main drag; follow it west into Sir Francis Drake Blvd, and you'll eventually reach the Point Reyes Lighthouse. For information, contact the **Marin County Convention & Visitors Bureau** (☎ 499-5000; www.visitmarin.org; 1013 Larkspur Landing Circle, Larkspur) or the **San Rafael Chamber of Commerce** (☎ 454-4163; www.sanrafael.org; 817 Mission Ave, San Rafael).

You can tour the 1949 replica of the original **Mission San Rafael Arcángel** (☎ 454-8141; 1104 5th Ave; museum ⊗ 11am-4pm).

Designed by Frank Lloyd Wright, the **Marin County Civic Center** (☎ 472-3500) stands elegantly on the hills directly east of Hwy 101; exit at N San Pedro Rd, 2 miles to the north of San Rafael. The 2nd-floor **gift shop** (⊗ 10am-4pm Mon-Fri) carries Wright-inspired items and local literature. Docent-led **tours** (☎ 499-6646) begin here at 10:30am Wednesday. The center hosts concerts and events, including the **Marin County Fair** each July and a **farmers market** every Thursday and Sunday morning.

Stop at **China Camp State Park** (☎ 456-0766), where you can picnic or take a short hike by the eastern shores of the San Francisco Bay. The park sprang up around the remains of a Chinese fishing village, one of many shrimp-fishing encampments once prevalent around the bay. There's a small, old-fashioned lunch counter here, too. From Hwy 101, take the N San Pedro Rd exit and head 3 miles east.

If you want to stay the night, **Panama Hotel** (☎ 457-3993; www.panamahotel.com; 4 Bayview St; r $75-160) has B&B rooms in a quiet residential area; staff also operate a good neighborhood **restaurant** (⊗ lunch Sun-Fri, dinner Tue-Sun).

Golden Gate Transit (☎ 923-2000) buses operate between San Francisco and the San Rafael Transit Center at 3rd and Hetherton Sts. Some buses take bicycles across the Golden Gate Bridge; call for details.

POINT REYES STATION

Though relatively small and surrounded by dairy farms and ranch lands, Point Reyes Station is the hub of West Marin, thanks to the railroad, which ran here until 1933. In the 1960s, artists moved in. Today there's a short main drag with shops, galleries, eateries and a saloon.

For information about the area, contact the **West Marin Chamber of Commerce** (☎ 663-9232; www.pointreyes.org), which also has extensive lodging listings. Pick up books at **Point Reyes Books** (☎ 663-1542; 11315 Hwy 1).

The only budget accommodations are at the hostel at nearby Point Reyes National Seashore (p86). Otherwise there are many medium-to-high-end cottages and B&Bs in the area.

In town, consider the **Holly Tree Inn** (☎ 663-1554; www.hollytreeinn.com; Silverhills Rd; r $130-180, cottages $190-250), which has attractive, well-kept B&B rooms and cozy cottages – ask about the one standing in Tomales Bay.

Pick up local cheeses and organic produce at **Tomales Bay Foods and Cowgirl Creamery** (☎ 663-9335; 80 4th St).

SAN FRANCISCO & THE BAY AREA

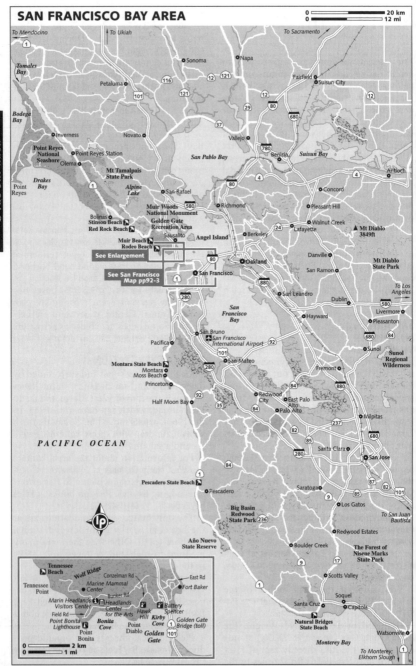

Run by friendly locals and good cooks, the **Pine Cone Diner** (☎ 663-1536; 60 4th St; dishes $5-11; ☺ breakfast & lunch) serves eggs, sandwiches, salads and vegetarian dishes at an old-fashioned lunch counter.

The **Station House Cafe** (☎ 663-1515; 11180 Shoreline Hwy; dishes $7-20; ☺ breakfast, lunch & dinner), long the best restaurant in town, seems lately to be resting on its laurels, but you'll still find very good modern and traditional American cooking; there's an outdoor garden too.

Call the **Dance Palace Community Center** (☎ 663-1075; 503 B St) for current happenings, including movies and live music.

The 1906 **Old Western Saloon** (☎ 663-1661; cnr Main & 2nd Sts) serves drinks every night and hosts live bands on weekends.

Hwy 1, also called Shoreline Hwy, slows to 25mph and becomes Main St through town. **Golden Gate Transit** (☎ 923-2000), in conjunction with the **West Marin Stagecoach** (☎ 526-3239), serves Point Reyes Station, via San Anselmo, from the San Rafael Transit Center; call for schedules.

POINT REYES NATIONAL SEASHORE

Covering 110 sq miles of pristine ocean beaches, vast grasslands and wind-tousled ridges, Point Reyes juts out to sea on a giant peninsula. It's home to 37 species of land animals and a dozen marine animals; nearly half of North America's bird species have been spotted here. Be sure to bring warm clothing, as even the sunniest of days can turn cold and windy.

Orientation & Information

Tomales Bay separates the northern section of the peninsula from the mainland. Sir Francis Drake Blvd crosses Hwy 1 in Olema and heads northward along Tomales Bay, through Inverness, before turning west and south toward the lighthouse. Pierce Point Rd cuts northward from Sir Francis Drake Blvd toward the northernmost tip.

See nature exhibits and pick up maps and information at the **Bear Valley Visitors Center** (☎ 663-1092; www.nps.gov/pore; Bear Valley Rd; ☺ 9am-5pm Mon-Fri, 8am-5pm Sat & Sun), near Olema, which also serves as park headquarters. Ask about ranger-led walks. There are two additional visitors centers: at the Point Reyes Lighthouse (see Sights & Activities this page) and the **Ken Patrick Center** (☎ 669-1250; ☺ 10am-5pm Sat, Sun & holidays) at Drakes Beach.

Sights & Activities

To see firsthand the force of the 1906 San Francisco earthquake (whose epicenter lies here), hike the **Earthquake Trail** from park headquarters at Bear Valley, and view a 16ft gap between the two halves of a once-connected fence line. A 1-mile loop trail leads from the visitors center to **Kule Loklo**, a reproduction of a Miwok village.

Limantour Rd, off Bear Valley Rd about 1 mile north of the Bear Valley Visitors Center, leads to the Point Reyes Hostel and to **Limantour Beach**. At the beach there's a trail running along narrow Limantour Spit, separating Estero de Limantour (Limantour estuary) from the ocean. The **Inverness Ridge Trail** heads from Limantour Rd up to 1282ft Mt Vision, which has spectacular views of the entire national seashore. You can drive almost to the top of Mt Vision from Sir Francis Drake Blvd.

About 2 miles past Inverness, Pierce Point Rd splits off to the right from Sir Francis Drake Blvd. Follow the signs to reach two good swimming holes; **Marshall Beach** requires a mile-long hike from the parking area, but you can drive right to **Hearts Desire Beach**, which lies within **Tomales Bay State Park**, a 2000-acre park abutting Point Reyes, on the east side of the Inverness Ridge. Take the 1-mile **Jepson Trail** to reach one of California's last remaining forests. Along the bay, much of which is tidal marsh, you'll spot a wide variety of birds. Bring binoculars.

Pierce Point Rd continues along the huge windswept sand dunes at **Abbotts Lagoon**, full of peeping killdeer and other shorebirds. Park at Pierce Point Ranch for the trailhead for the 4.7-mile **Tomales Point Trail** along high bluffs through the **Tule Elk State Reserve**. The elk are stunning, especially the males with their giant antlers, but don't get too close; these are wild animals. From Tomales Point, look for Bodega Bay to the north.

The **Point Reyes Lighthouse** (☎ 669-1534; ☺ 10am-4:30pm Thu-Mon) lies at the very end of Sir Francis Drake Blvd. With its wild terrain and ferocious winds, it feels like the end of the earth. For **whale-watching**, this is one of coastal California's best spots. The lighthouse sits below the headlands, at the bottom of 310 steps. Bring your camera.

Nearby **Chimney Rock** makes an excellent short hike, especially in spring, when wildflowers bloom. A viewing area lets you spy on the park's **elephant seal colony**.

SAN FRANCISCO & THE BAY AREA

SAN FRANCISCO
& THE BAY AREA

Because Point Reyes juts so far out to sea, spectacular **North Beach** and **South Beach** get pounded by thundering waves. If you visit either, keep back from the water's edge. Don't swim! And never turn your back on the sea. Rogue waves crash on shore without warning, and people have drowned here.

On weekends during good weather, from late December through mid-April, the road to Chimney Rock and the lighthouse is closed to private vehicles. Instead, take a shuttle ($4) from **Drakes Beach**, a safe place to wade or swim.

Sleeping & Eating

There are no inns or B&Bs west of Inverness Ridge. By staying in Inverness, Olema or Point Reyes Station, you'll be right at park boundaries.

The only non-camping lodging in the park, the **Point Reyes Youth Hostel** (☎ 663-8811; dm $16), just off Limantour Rd, lies in a secluded valley 2 miles from the ocean and is surrounded by hiking trails.

Point Reyes has four hike-in **backcountry campgrounds** (☎ 663-1092; sites $12) with pit toilets, untreated water and picnic tables (no wood fires). *Permits are required*; reserve at the Bear Valley Visitors Center or by calling ☎ 663-8054. Each of the remote camps requires a 2- to 6-mile hike.

Johnson's Drakes Bay Oysters (☎ 669-1149; ☯ 8am-4:30pm) sells cheap, fresh, farm-raised oysters. Look for the sign halfway from Inverness to the Point Reyes Lighthouse.

INVERNESS

The last outpost on your journey westward onto Point Reyes, Inverness lies in the woods along the west shore of Tomales Bay. Several great beaches are only a short drive north. From Hwy 1, Sir Francis Drake Blvd leads straight to Inverness.

Blue Waters Kayaking Tours & Rentals (☎ 669-2600; 12938 Sir Francis Drake Blvd), at the Golden Hinde Inn, offers various Tomales Bay cruises. Alternatively, you can rent a kayak ($30 for two hours, $50 per day) and paddle around secluded beaches and rocky crevices on your own; no experience necessary. There's also a kids' kayaking camp.

Manka's Inverness Lodge (☎ 669-1034; r $185-285, cabins $315-465) perfectly blends rusticity and luxury. Built in 1917 as a hunting and fishing lodge, most rooms have plaid-wool

accents, wood-burning fireplaces and beds made of raw cypress branches dressed with down comforters and feather pillows. The outstanding **restaurant** (☯ Thu-Mon) serves a prix-fixe menu ($58) of local game and wild fish, roasted over an open fire.

Ten Inverness Way (☎ 669-1648; www.teninverness way.com; 10 Inverness Way; r $135-180), a 1904 Craftsman-style house, has rooms with queen beds. There's a large common area with fireplace, and outside are lovely gardens and a private hot tub.

Rooms are in modern A-frame cottages at **Inverness Valley Inn** (☎ 669-7250; 13275 Sir Francis Drake Blvd; r $115-130; 🐾), which stands on 15 acres. Tennis courts and hot tub are available.

Sit outside or in at **Priscilla's Pizza** (☎ 669-1244; Sir Francis Drake Blvd; pizzas from $6), which is right in town; salads and sandwiches are also on offer.

OLEMA

In the 1860s Olema was West Marin's biggest settlement. Stagecoaches from San Rafael stopped here, and there were *six* saloons. In 1875, when the railroad went to Point Reyes Station instead of Olema, the town's importance began to fade. In 1906 it gained dubious distinction as the epicenter of the Great Quake. Today it's the entry point for most visitors to Point Reyes National Seashore. The town lies near the junction of Hwy 1 and Sir Francis Drake Blvd.

Come for a meal and you may well want to stay the night at the **Olema Inn** (☎ 663-9559; www.theolemainn.com; cnr Sir Francis Drake Blvd & Hwy 1; r $125-165), which has simple but well-appointed rooms; downstairs, the **dining room** (☯ lunch Fri-Sun, dinner Wed-Mon) serves fine New American cooking that is consistently good.

BOLINAS

Bolinas is famous for its directional sign disappearing from Hwy 1. Residents of this sleepy beachside community successfully waged a campaign to save the town from development – and from tourists. The highway department finally agreed to leave Bolinas to its own devices and no longer puts up the road sign.

The townspeople tolerate tourists, and many even welcome them, but nothing angers locals more than speeding drivers. The narrow road into town dead-ends, and if you drive too fast, you'll reach the end of the street and likely come face-to-face with an aged, finger-wagging hippie, yelling at you through your car window. Really. (And surfers, if you don't control your board, you may get a punch in the nose.)

Since the 1970s Bolinas has been home to the original Niman Ranch. Fine restaurants nationwide clamor for the company's beef, pork and lamb, raised on sustainable lands with natural feed and without the use of growth hormones.

Sights & Activities
For a town so plainly unexcited about tourism, Bolinas has several tourist-ready shops and attractions.

Bolinas Museum (☎ 868-0330; 48 Wharf Rd; ⓨ 1-5pm Fri, noon-5pm Sat & Sun) has exhibits on the region's history and hangs shows by local artists.

There are tidepools along 2 miles of coastline at **Agate Beach**, around the end of Duxbury Point. The **Point Reyes Bird Observatory** (☎ 868-1221; www.prbo.org; ⓨ 9am-5pm), off Mesa Rd west of town, has bird-banding and netting demonstrations, guided walks, a visitors center and a nature trail; call for activity schedules and dates.

Beyond the observatory is the Palomarin parking lot and access to various walking trails, including the easy (and popular) 2½-mile trail to small but pretty **Bass Lake** and, a mile ahead, **Alamere Falls**; it's another 1½ miles to **Wildcat Beach**.

Sleeping & Eating
Smiley's Schooner Saloon & Hotel (☎ 868-1311; 41 Wharf Rd; r $69-79) Though there are spartan motel-style rooms available at Smiley's, most people come for the 1851 saloon, popular with salty dogs and grizzled deadheads. On weekends it hosts live bands.

Blue Heron Inn (☎ 868-1102; www.blueheron-bolinas .com; 11 Wharf Rd; r $125; dishes $17-23) There are two B&B rooms at the Blue Heron; the menu at the little **dinner house** (ⓨ Thu-Mon) downstairs changes nightly, but always includes Niman Ranch meats.

Thomas' White House Inn (☎ 868-0279; www .thomaswhitehouseinn.com; 118 Kale Rd; r $100-110) Located in a residential area, this pleasant inn offers bed and breakfast on a bluff above Duxbury Reef.

Coast Cafe (☎ 868-2298; Wharf Rd; dishes $6-16; ⓨ breakfast, lunch & dinner) It's hard to beat the Coast Cafe for all-around good food, including huge salads, local fish and meats, and lots of options for vegetarians.

Getting There & Away
Nine miles south of Olema, turn right (west) onto Olema–Bolinas Rd (remember, there's no sign saying 'Bolinas') and follow it into town, where the road ends.

STINSON BEACH
Six miles south of Bolinas, Stinson Beach flanks Hwy 1 with densely packed shops, eateries and B&Bs. Three-mile-long **Stinson Beach** is a popular surf spot, but swim only from late May to mid-September when lifeguards are on duty and conditions safer; for weather conditions, call ☎ 868-1922.

About 1 mile south of Stinson Beach is **Red Rock Beach**. It's a popular clothing-optional beach and attracts smaller crowds, since it's a steep hike down from Hwy 1.

About 3½ miles north of town on Hwy 1, you can climb the hiking trails at **Audubon Canyon Ranch** (☎ 868-9244; www.egret.org; donation requested; ⓨ 10am-4pm Sat & Sun mid-Mar–mid-Jul) to view nests of great blue herons and snowy egrets. The ranch supplies binoculars; from the hills you can watch birds feed in the mudflats of **Bolinas Lagoon** at low tide.

If you want to stay, check out the **Stinson Beach Motel** (☎ 868-1712; www.stinsonbeachmotel .com; 3416 Hwy 1; r $85-200). **Sandpiper Motel** (☎ 868-1632; 1 Marine Way; r $115-195) has several cottages with kitchens.

For meals, try the **Sand Dollar Restaurant** (☎ 868-0434; 3458 Hwy 1) or the **Parkside Cafe** (☎ 868-1272; 43 Arenal Ave).

MUIR BEACH
The turn-off to Muir Beach from Hwy 1 is marked by the longest row of mailboxes on the North Coast. It's a quiet little town with a good beach. To its north there are superb views up and down the coast from the **Muir Beach Overlook**; during WWII, soldiers kept watch from the surrounding concrete lookouts for invading Japanese ships.

The Tudor-style **Pelican Inn** (☎ 383-6000; www.pelicaninn.com; 10 Pacific Way; r from $200) has B&B rooms right out of an English manor house. The **restaurant** (dishes $11-20; ⓨ lunch & dinner) serves classic Anglo-Saxon dishes such as

SAN FRANCISCO & THE BAY AREA

cottage pie and bangers and mash at lunch, and prime rib and Yorkshire pudding at dinner. The bar serves stout and sherry.

The Buddhist retreat **Green Gulch Farm & Zen Center** (☎ 383-3134; www.sfzc.com; 1601 Shoreline Hwy) sits in a valley above Muir Beach. The center's octagonal Japanese-style **Lindisfarne Guest House** (s/d from $75/125) offers a quiet overnight stay with buffet-style vegetarian meals.

MOUNT TAMALPAIS STATE PARK

Lording over Marin County, Mt Tamalpais (Mt Tam) has breathtaking views of ocean, bay and hills. When at her 2571ft summit, you'll feel far away from civilization – even though you're within an hour's drive of one of California's major metropolitan areas.

Mt Tamalpais State Park was formed in 1930, partly from land donated by Congressman William Kent (who also donated the land that became Muir Woods National Monument). The park's 6300 acres are home to deer, foxes, bobcats and many miles of hiking and biking trails.

Mt Tam has been a sacred place to the coastal Miwok Indians for thousands of years, but by the late 19th century, white San Franciscans were escaping the bustle of the city with all-day outings on the mountain. Indeed, in 1896 the 'world's crookedest railroad' (281 turns) was built between Mill Valley and the summit. Though it closed in 1930, **Old Railroad Grade** is today one of Mt Tam's most popular and scenic hiking and biking paths.

Information

Pick up a $1 trail map at park headquarters at **Pantoll Station** (☎ 388-2070; www.parks.ca.gov; 801 Panoramic Hwy; ☒ 8am-4pm Thu-Sun, 8am-7pm Sat & Sun; 'til sunset in summer), which also has parking and a campground.

Sights

From Pantoll Station, drive 4.2 miles to **East Peak Summit**; take Pantoll Rd and then panoramic Ridgecrest Blvd to the top. Parking costs $2; a 10-minute hike leads to the mountain top and the best views.

The state park's natural-stone, 4000-seat **Mountain Theater** (☎ 383-1100) hosts the annual 'Mountain Play' series on six Sundays in early summer. Free **astronomy programs** (☎ 455-5370) take place here in summer around the new moon.

Hiking & Biking

From Pantoll Station, the **Steep Ravine Trail** follows a wooded creek to the coast (about 2.1 miles each way). For a longer hike, veer right (northwest) after 1.5 miles onto the **Dipsea Trail**, which meanders through the trees for a mile before ending at Stinson Beach. Grab lunch, then walk north through town and follow signs for the **Matt Davis Trail**, which leads 2.7 miles back to Pantoll Station. The trail continues beyond Pantoll, wrapping around the mountain, providing superb views.

The **Cataract Trail** runs along Cataract Creek from the end of Pantoll Rd; it's about 3 miles to Alpine Lake. The last mile descends beside spectacular Cataract Falls.

For information on mountain-biking routes and rules at Mt Tam, be sure to check with park headquarters. The **Marin County Bike Coalition** (☎ 456-3469; www.marinbike.org) prints an excellent map of biking routes.

Getting There & Away

From Muir Beach, take Shoreline Hwy (Hwy 1) south, then turn left on Panoramic Hwy and follow signs to Mt Tam. From Stinson Beach, Panoramic Hwy climbs through the park to Pantoll Station, Mill Valley and Hwy 101.

GOLDEN GATE NATIONAL RECREATION AREA (GGNRA)

More than twice the size of San Francisco, the GGNRA is the largest urban park in the world. It extends on both sides of the Golden Gate and covers 75,000 acres, including 28 miles of coastline. Administered by the National Park Service (NPS), it's really a patchwork of lands, bordered by private property and other parks (ie Point Reyes and Mt Tam).

Much of the land belonged to the military. As the armed forces moved out, the Bay Area's politically aware citizens kept developers away by insisting the land remain in the public domain, proving that Bay Area activism, often scorned by other Americans, makes a difference – at least in its own world, if not beyond.

It's hard to pin down where the GGNRA begins and ends, but simply put, if you're in a park around the Golden Gate (with the notable exception of Mt Tamalpais), then you're probably in the GGNRA. Muir Woods, the

SAN FRANCISCO & THE BAY AREA

Marin Headlands, Alcatraz, Fort Point and San Francisco's Presidio all fall within its jurisdiction. For individual sights, look for them by name in the following pages. The southernmost grid of the GGNRA lies at Half Moon Bay's northern shore.

For information on the GGNRA, contact the **National Park Service** (☎ 561-4700; www.nps.gov /goga); there are two visitors centers, one in San Francisco's Presidio (p100) and one in the Marin Headlands (see below).

MUIR WOODS NATIONAL MONUMENT

In 1907 Congressman and naturalist William Kent donated to the federal government the forest now called **Muir Woods** (☎ 388-2595; www.nps.gov/muwo; day-use fee $4; ☽ 8am-sunset, to 5pm winter) to protect it from loggers. President Theodore Roosevelt made the site a national monument in 1908, and at the urging of Kent, named the grove in honor of John Muir, naturalist and founder of the Sierra Club.

Surrounded by Mt Tamalpais State Park, Muir Woods is the closest redwood stand to San Francisco. It can get crowded, especially on weekends. To avoid crowds, come midweek, early in the morning or late in the afternoon, when there are fewer tour buses. (Better yet, come in the rain.) Even at busy times, a short hike is worth the effort, with huge trees and stunning vistas.

Hiking

An easy walk is the 1-mile **Main Trail Loop**, leading alongside Redwood Creek to the 1000-year-old trees at Cathedral Grove; it returns via **Bohemian Grove**, where the tallest tree in the park stands 254ft high. The **Dipsea Trail** leads 2 miles to the top of aptly named Cardiac Hill.

You can also walk down Mt Tamalpais into Muir Woods by following trails from the Panoramic Hwy (such as the **Bootjack Trail** from the Bootjack picnic area) or from Mt Tamalpais' Pantoll Station campground (via the **Ben Johnson Trail**).

MARIN HEADLANDS

The rugged and rolling Marin Headlands stand at the north end of the Golden Gate Bridge. Several hilltop forts and bunkers remain from a century of US military occupation. Today they're preserved in the GGNRA; beneath them look for hidden coves, hiking and biking trails, and some isolated campgrounds.

Get a map at the **GGNRA Visitors Center** (☎ 561-4700; www.nps.gov/goga; ☽ 9:30am-4:30pm) in the old church of Bunker Rd, near Fort Barry. Follow signs from Conzelman Rd.

Sights

Look down upon the Golden Gate Bridge from **Battery Spencer** (Map p84). Thousands of migrating birds of prey soar along the cliffs from late summer to early fall at **Hawk Hill** (Map p84), about 2 miles up Conzelman Rd.

Follow the signs to **Point Bonita Lighthouse** (Map p84; ☎ 331-1540; ☽ 12:30-3:30pm Sat-Mon); from the small parking area (limited spaces), it's a breathtaking half-mile walk to a tunnel through rocks and a swinging bridge over the crashing surf, above which stands the lighthouse. Exhibits inside tell the story of the lightkeeper and the history of the San Francisco coast.

Near the visitors center, above Rodeo Lagoon, the **Marine Mammal Center** (Map p84; ☎ 289-7325; admission free; ☽ 10am-4pm) rehabilitates injured, sick and orphaned sea mammals before releasing them into the wild.

In Fort Barry, also near the visitors center, the **Headlands Center for the Arts** (Map p84; ☎ 331-2787; www.headlands.org) is inside a refurbished barracks converted into artists' work spaces and conference facilities, and hosts speakers, performances and events.

Hiking & Biking

From **Rodeo Beach**, at the end of Bunker Rd, the **Coastal Trail** meanders 3½ miles inland, past abandoned military bunkers, to the **Tennessee Valley Trail**. It then continues 6 miles along the blustery headlands all the way to Muir Beach.

If you want to mountain-bike over bumping, winding trails, the headlands has some excellent routes. Try to end (or begin) the trip with an exhilarating ride across the Golden Gate Bridge.

For a good 12-mile loop, take the **Coastal Trail** west from the fork of Conzelman and McCullough Rds, bumping and winding down to Bunker Rd where it meets **Bobcat Trail**; Bobcat Trail joins **Marincello Trail** and descends steeply into the Tennessee Valley parking area. The **Old Springs Trail** and the **Miwok Trail** take you back to Bunker Rd

SAN FRANCISCO & THE BAY AREA

WHY IS IT SO FOGGY?

When the summer sun's rays warm the air over the chilly Pacific, fog forms and hovers offshore; to grasp how it moves inland requires an understanding of California geography. The vast agricultural region in the state's interior, the Central Valley, is ringed by mountains. Think of it as a giant bathtub. The only substantial sea-level break in these mountains occurs at the Golden Gate, to the west, which happens to be the direction from which prevailing winds blow. As the inland valley heats up and the warm air rises, it creates a deficit of air at surface level, generating wind that gets sucked through the only opening it can find: the Golden Gate. It happens fast, and it's unpredictable. Gusty wind is the only indication that the fog is about to roll in. But it's inconsistent: there can be fog at the beaches south of the Golden Gate and sun a mile to the north. Hills block fog – especially at times of high atmospheric pressure, as often happens in summer. Because of this, weather forecasters speak of the Bay Area's 'microclimates.' In July it's not uncommon for inland areas to reach 100°F, while the mercury at the coast barely reaches 70°F. But as the locals say, if you don't like the weather, just wait a minute.

---

more gently than the Bobcat Trail, though it's impossible to avoid at least a couple of hefty climbs on this ride.

Sleeping

If you want to spend the night, there's only one place: the secluded **Marin Headlands Hostel** (☎ 331-2777; dm $18). For details about camping, check with the visitors center or log onto their website.

Getting There & Away

From southbound Hwy 101, take the exit *immediately* before the Golden Gate Bridge (it's marked 'Sausalito,' but it's the *second* Sausalito exit from Hwy 101 south); turn west up the hill into the headlands. From the south, cross the bridge and take the second exit, marked 'Alexander Ave,' then fork left, crossing under the highway and, right before the entrance to the bridge on-ramp, head

west up the hill. Stop at pullouts along the way on Conzelman Rd, which snakes up into the hills, where it eventually forks: Conzelman Rd continues west (left), becoming a steep, one-lane road clinging to the cliff as it descends to Point Bonita (there it continues to Rodeo Beach and Fort Barry); McCullough Rd, to the right at the fork, heads inland, joining Bunker Rd toward Rodeo Beach.

On Sundays and holidays, **MUNI** (☎ 673-6864; www.sfmuni.com) operates bus No 76 from the CalTrain depot in San Francisco, which goes to Fort Barry and Rodeo Beach.

SAUSALITO

pop 7825

Picturesque Sausalito lies on a south-facing bay east of the Golden Gate Bridge. Bridgeway Blvd, its primary street, teems with tourists on weekends, who come for the up-market shops and galleries and the gorgeous views of Angel Island and San Francisco. In summer it's also warmer here than in San Francisco. Bicyclists ride over the Golden Gate Bridge for lunch and return to San Francisco via the ferry. Kayakers like the protected bay.

Humboldt Park and the ferry terminal mark the town center. The **Sausalito Visitors Center** (☎ 332-0505; www.sausalito.org; 780 Bridgeway Blvd; ☉ 11:30am-4pm Tue-Sun) provides information; there's an **information kiosk** (☎ 331-1093) at the ferry terminal.

Sights & Activities

Make it a point to see the Army Corps of Engineers' **Bay Model Visitors Center** (☎ 332-3871; www.baymodel.org; 2100 Bridgeway Blvd; admission free; ☉ 9am-4pm Tue-Sat), a 1.5-acre scaled model of the San Francisco Bay and river-delta region; self-guided tours take you over and around it as the water flows.

Just under the north tower of the distinctive Golden Gate Bridge there are fine examples of early-20th-century whitewashed military buildings stand preserved on 335-acre **Fort Baker**.

The NPS hasn't figured out what to do with it yet, but at East Fort Baker, the **Bay Area Discovery Museum** (☎ 487-4398; admission $7; ☉ 9am-4pm Tue-Fri, 10am-5pm Sat & Sun) has hands-on exhibits for children, including an underwater sea tunnel, ceramics studio and science lab.

Rent a kayak from **Sea Trek** (☎ 488-1000, 332-4465; www.seatrekkayak.com); rentals start at $15 per hour, and staff also lead tours.

Except for restaurants, the town shuts down when the last ferry leaves.

Sleeping & Eating

Hotel Sausalito (☎ 332-4155; www.hotelsausalito.com; 16 El Portal St; r from $145) If you want to stay, this 1915 hotel has comfortable rooms across from the ferry terminal.

Alta Mira Hotel (☎ 332-1350; 125 Bulkley Ave; r $95-220) The hilltop Alta Mira has magnificent views and a good restaurant and bar.

Casa Madrona (☎ 332-0502, 800-288-0502; www .casamadrona.rockresorts.com; 801 Bridgeway; r from $255) Guests enjoy Sausalito's most plush rooms and a very fine restaurant.

Sushi Ran (☎ 332-3620; 107 Caledonia St; dishes $4-15) The always-packed Sushi Ran has some of the best sushi in the Bay Area. Really. There's a wine and sake bar next door.

If you don't want to wait for a table at Sushi Ran, **Ara Wan** (☎ 332-0882; 47 Caledonia St; dishes $10) serves good Thai food.

Getting There & Away

By car from San Francisco, cross the Golden Gate Bridge and take the Alexander Ave exit (at the end of the bridge) and follow the signs. Parking is difficult.

The ferry is the fun way to get to Sausalito. Golden Gate Transit operates the **Golden Gate Ferry** (☎ 923-2000; www.goldengateferry.org) to and from the San Francisco Ferry Building (one way $5.60); it also operates buses. The **Blue & Gold Fleet** (☎ 773-1188; www.blueandgold fleet.com) sails from Pier 41 at Fisherman's Wharf in San Francisco (one way $7.25). Bikes ride free on both.

SAN FRANCISCO

☎ 415 / pop 791,600

California's first city rose to fame with the 1849 gold rush. Though the mines went bust shortly thereafter, it's easy to see why people stuck around. The hospitable climate and access to inland rivers make it an exceptional port. Today the tremendous natural beauty and urban sophistication appeal to sports people and aesthetes alike, who come from around the world to play by the bay.

ORIENTATION

Compact San Francisco sits at the tip of a 30-mile-long peninsula and measures roughly seven-by-seven miles. To the west lies the Pacific, to the east the San Francisco Bay, which is fed by rivers originating 150 miles east in the Sierra Nevada Mountains. The gap between the tip of the peninsula and the southern tip of Marin County is called the Golden Gate, site of the bridge by the same name. The only major break in the Coast Range, it's where the city's famous fog pours through in summer.

Parks, beaches, tourist attractions and open spaces line the city's coastline. Counterclockwise, from east to west, the Embarcadero, Fisherman's Wharf, the Marina, the Presidio and Ocean Beach fan out along the bay from the Financial District in downtown. At the foot of Market St, the city's main artery, commuter ferries run from the Ferry Building; cruise ships dock to its north, and visitors from far and wide come to buy souvenirs at neighboring Fisherman's Wharf. Kids fly kites along Marina Green, joggers run the hills of the Presidio, and beachcombers build sandcastles at Ocean Beach. But along the bay on the southeastern side, the once-thriving shipyards and ports stand in disrepair. Overshadowed by the busy Port of Oakland, which lies across the bay near the mainland's rail lines, the San Francisco port appeals only to urban-decay buffs who enjoy photographing broken windows and rusty winches; otherwise there's little here for visitors.

To locate numbered piers, from the Ferry Building even-numbered piers extend southward, and odd-numbered piers northward.

The city can be roughly divided into three sections. Downtown resembles a slice of pie, its edges delimited by Van Ness Ave and Market St, with the rounded edge being the waterfront. Its major neighborhoods include the Financial District, North Beach, Chinatown, Union Square, Nob Hill, Russian Hill and Fisherman's Wharf.

The area south of Market St is aptly called South of Market (SoMa); it's the upwardly mobile warehouse district and bleeds into the Mission District, a predominantly Latino area.

The largest area lies west of Van Ness Ave and extends to the Pacific Ocean, encompassing many neighborhoods of interest to

SAN FRANCISCO & THE BAY AREA

visitors, including the very posh Marina and Pacific Heights; Japantown; the Castro (the city's primary gay center); and the Haight District (of 1960s fame). Also in this area are three of the city's best parks – the Presidio, Lincoln Park and Golden Gate Park.

INFORMATION
Bookstores

A Clean Well-Lighted Place for Books (Map pp96-7; ☎ 441-6670; 601 Van Ness Ave, near Civic Center) Regularly hosts readings.

A Different Light Bookstore (Map p106; ☎ 431-0891; 489 Castro St) Stocks gay-interest books and magazines.

Books Inc. (Map p106; ☎ 864-6777; 2275 Market St, The Castro) Carries general interest titles.

Get Lost (Map pp96-7; ☎ 437-0529; 1825 Market St) Specializes in travel books and maps.

Rizzoli Bookstore (Map pp96-7; ☎ 984-0225; 117 Post St, near Union Square) Stocks elegant art and design books.

Stacey's (Map pp96-7; ☎ 421-4687; 581 Market St) The biggest downtown indie bookstore; carries just about everything.

Emergency
Police, ambulance, fire brigade (☎ 911)

Internet Access

Cafe.com (Map pp96-7; ☎ 922-5322; 970 Market St; $7 per hr) Drink coffee and check email here; there's a 30-minute minimum.

Comp USA (Map pp96-7; ☎ 391-9778; 750 Market St) Free web access.

SAN FRANCISCO

INFORMATION	
California Pacific Medical Center..	1 D2
McLaren Lodge..........................	2 C3
San Francisco General Hospital.....	3 E4

SIGHTS & ACTIVITIES	pp94-102
California Academy of Sciences....	4 B3
California Palace of the Legion of Honor......	5 A3
Camera Obscura..........................	(see 6)
Cliff House..................................	6 A3
Conservatory of Flowers...............	7 C3
Fort Point National Historic Site...	8 B2
Japanese Tea Garden...................	9 B3
Skates on Haight..........................	10 C4
Strybing Arboretum & Botanical Gardens............	11 B4
Sutro Baths.................................	(see 6)

SLEEPING	pp103-4
Seal Rock Inn..............................	12 A3

EATING	pp104-7
Beach Chalet................................	13 A4
Ramp...	14 E4
Thep Phanom..............................	15 D3
Waterfront Restaurant & Cafe......	16 E2

ENTERTAINMENT	p107
Teatro Zinzani.............................	17 E2

SHOPPING	p108
Amoeba Records.........................	(see 10)

Main Library (Map pp96-7; ☎ 557-4400; cnr Larkin & Grove Sts, near Civic Center BART & MUNI stations) Eight first-come, first-served 'express' terminals on 1st floor, available for 15 minutes. Library staff can provide information on Internet cafés, as can staff at the visitors center.
Quetzal (Map pp96-7; ☎ 683-4181; 1234 Polk St; $10 per hr) No minimum here; also serves good food.

Internet Resources

Bay Guardian (www.sfbg.com) Features primers on politics and local events.
National Weather Service (www.wrh.noaa.gov/Monterey)
SF Gate (www.sfgate.com) Mainstream news and listings; operated by the *Chronicle*.
SF Station (www.sfstation.com) Best indie site for cultural events and goings-on.
SF Weekly (www.sfweekly.com)

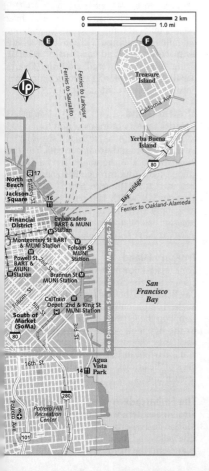

Media

San Francisco has two major dailies, the *San Francisco Chronicle* (owned by the Hearst Corp) and the *Examiner*. Neither is particularly good. The *Chronicle* (nicknamed 'the *Comical*') runs topical, mainstream stories and comes out in the morning; the Sunday edition has the 'Datebook', one of the city's best entertainment resources. The *Examiner*, the newspaper that started the Spanish-American War, remains fascinated with the lurid and sensational; pick it up free in boxes around town.

The city has two great weekly papers, the *San Francisco Bay Guardian* and the *SF Weekly*. The former is independently owned and carries the torch for liberal San Francisco politics. The *SF Weekly*, also liberal, is owned by an out-of-town corporation. Both have excellent events listings, in-depth articles and intelligent writing.

The *Bay Area Reporter* (the BAR) and the *Bay Times* are free gay papers distributed in the Castro and the surrounding neighborhoods.

For an excellent selection of international papers, head to **Harold's International Newsstand** (Map pp96-7; ☎ 441-2665; 454 Geary St; ☾ 7am-11pm) near Union Square. **Café de la Presse** (Map pp96-7; ☎ 398-2680; 352 Grant Ave at Bush St; ☾ 7am-10pm) carries most European papers and magazines; they've got a great café to boot.

Medical Services

In an emergency dial ☎ 911. Most hospitals have emergency rooms. Check the *Yellow Pages* for the nearest locations.
California Pacific Medical Center (Map pp92-3; ☎ 600-3333; 2333 Buchanan St, near Sacramento St) If you can arrive under your own power, this is the most civilized hospital emergency room.
San Francisco General Hospital (Map pp92-3; ☎ 206-8000; 1001 Potrero Ave, enter the ER from 23rd St) For severe trauma, go directly to the best trauma unit in the city – if not the country – but it's full of the destitute and delinquent, and you can wait hours.
Walgreen's The Castro (Map p106; ☎ 861-3136; 498 Castro St); The Marina (Map pp98-9; ☎ 931-6417; 3201 Divisadero St) 24hr pharmacy.

Money

Banks are ubiquitous in San Francisco. Avoid ATMs that are not in banks or credit unions; they charge outrageous fees.

49-MILE SCENIC DRIVE

Laid out for the 1939–40 Treasure Island Exposition, the 49-Mile Drive covers almost all the city's highlights, from Coit Tower to the Golden Gate Bridge. Although the route is well marked with instantly recognizable seagull signs, it's a good idea to have a map and an alert navigator. Pick up the route map from the San Francisco Visitors Information Center.

Travelex (Map pp96-7; ☎ 362-3453; 75 Geary St, Union Square; ⊗ 9am-5pm Mon-Fri, 10am-4pm Sat) Offers currency exchange; there's another branch at San Francisco International Airport in the International Terminal.

Post
Civic Center Post Office (Map pp96-7; ☎ 563-7284, 800-725-2161; 101 Hyde St) To receive mail here, address it this way: your name, c/o General Delivery, Civic Center Post Office, 101 Hyde St, San Francisco, CA 94142, USA.
Post office (Map pp96-7; downstairs, Macy's department store, Union Square; ⊗ 10am-5:30pm Mon-Sat, 11am-5pm Sun)

Tourist Offices
San Francisco Visitors Information Center (Map pp96-7; ☎ 391-2000; www.sfvisitor.org; lower level, Hallidie Plaza, cnr Market & Powell Sts; ⊗ 8:30am-5pm Mon-Fri, 9am-3pm Sat & Sun) Near Union Square, at the terminus of the primary cable-car lines. Carries maps, guidebooks, brochures, phonecards and the driving map to the 49-Mile Drive (see above). Operates a 24-hour automated phone line, with recorded information (☎ 391-2001).

DANGERS & ANNOYANCES
San Francisco is pretty safe, with few trouble spots to avoid. Drive-by shootings are the province of Oakland and Los Angeles, not San Francisco.

Unless you know where you're going, stay out of the Tenderloin, the area of downtown bordered by Polk St to the west, Powell St to the east, Market St to the south and O'Farrell St to the north. Also avoid 6th St between Market and Folsom Sts. Market St between 5th St and Van Ness Ave can be sketchy in spots, but it's not terrible. In the Mission District, drug-dealers and junkies hang around Mission St between 15th and 17th.

The biggest nuisance comes from aggressive panhandlers loitering by the cable-car turnaround on Market St and on Powell St near Union Square. Kids and bicycle thieves linger at the east end of Haight St by the park. Don't be cowed. Ambivalence and fear are the psychological inroads by which scoundrels exploit tourists. In a polite tone, simply say 'No, thanks,' and confidently continue on your way.

SIGHTS & ACTIVITIES
There's plenty to do in San Francisco. The following sights and activities focus on waterfront areas. If you stay for a while, pick up Lonely Planet's guide to San Francisco.

Angel Island   Map p84
A great day trip is the 750-acre **Angel Island State Park** (☎ 435-1915, ranger's office ☎ 435-5390, ferry service ☎ 705-5444, reservations ☎ 800-444-7275; www.angelisland.com). Visitors bike and hike over 12 miles of trails, have picnics and tour old military buildings. Call about **bicycle rentals**, **snack-bar** hours and **tram tours** (☎ 897-0715). Bring food and layered clothing. Ferries depart from Pier 41 ($12 return); for other departure points contact the park.

Alcatraz Island   Map pp92-3
America's most notorious prison from 1933 to 1963, 12-acre Alcatraz Island sits isolated by chilly waters and strong currents. You can tour 'The Rock' by booking a ferry and self-guided audio tour through **Blue and Gold Fleet** (information ☎ 773-1188, reservations ☎ 705-5555; ferry & audio tour $13), which sails daily from 9:30am to 2:30pm (to 4:15pm summer). Reservations are essential. Ask about the docent-led 'Alcatraz After Dark' tours.

Treasure Island   Map pp92-3
For a lesser-known perspective on San Francisco, cross the first span of the eastbound Bay Bridge. In the middle of the bridge, exit at the 10mph hairpin Treasure Island exit ramp, on the left side of the road. Continue to the overlook, where you can view the skyline by day or night. On the way back, you'll have beautiful views from the upper deck of the bridge. (Tour not recommended in rush hour.)

The Embarcadero   Map pp96-7
Stroll the eastern waterfront, from South of Market to Fisherman's Wharf, along wide sidewalks and take in views of Treasure Island and the Bay Bridge. Once the center

INLAND SAN FRANCISCO

North Beach

San Francisco's vibrant Italian district brims with locals and tourists alike. Stroll Columbus Ave and stop for cappuccino and cannoli, watch a game of bocce ball in Washington Square Park, poke your head into shops on Grant Ave, and eat plates and plates of pasta. This is the one San Francisco neighborhood that has successfully kept out corporate chain stores. Looming above, **Coit Tower** (Map pp98-9; ☎ 362-0808; admission $3.75; ☯ 10am-6pm) stands atop Telegraph Hill. Visitors can ride the elevator to the top of the 210ft-tall tower. The neighborhood extends north from Broadway along Columbus Ave and Grant Ave.

Chinatown

The largest Chinatown outside China stretches along Grant Ave and Stockton St, south of Broadway. Tourists flock to Grant Ave to see the pagoda-style **Chinatown Gate** (Map p96-7; cnr Bush St) and the many nearby souvenir shops and restaurants. But the real action is on Stockton St, where local matrons shop for bok choy and still-swimming fish; come during market hours – unless you're squeamish, in which case, stick to Grant Ave.

The Castro

Ride vintage street cars up Market St to the Castro, the social and political epicenter of the gay and lesbian communities. On weekends, the streets teem with people. Stroll beneath towering palms on Market St, catch a classic film at the beautiful 1920s **Castro Theatre** (Map p106; ☎ 621-6120; 429 Castro St), window-shop or wander the side streets and see the area's many Victorian houses.

Haight Street

The Haight rose to fame during the 1967 Summer of Love, when tripped-out hippy mystics danced in the streets. The psychedelic love-fest ended, almost overnight, when the Black Panthers started dealing speed and the yogis got strung out on China white. Now there's a Gap store at the corner of Ashbury St, and the Haight seems a parody of its former self, but it's fun to shop the many shoe stores and used-clothing boutiques. If street urchins annoy you, stay away. The 'hood begins at Masonic Ave and extends to Golden Gate Park.

Nob Hill

People who still wear fur in San Francisco do so on Nob Hill. Though luxury hotels stand at the crest of the hill, the neighborhood remains a residential area for the skirt-and-sweater elite. **Grace Cathedral** (Map pp96-7; ☎ 749-6300; 1100 California St) lords over very-civilized Huntington Park. All cable-car lines cross at California and Powell Sts. The only Nob Hill mansion that didn't burn after the 1906 earthquake stands at California and Mason Sts.

Russian Hill

Northwest of Nob Hill, crooked **Lombard St** twists and turns downhill for one block, east of Hyde St. Most take the Powell-Hyde cable-car line to the top, then walk down. But if you ascend the hill from Leavenworth St (a short walk from the Wharf), you can reward yourself at the top with a delicious homemade scoop of **Swensen's Ice Cream** (Map pp98-9; ☎ 775-6818; cnr Union & Hyde Sts). There are some terrific neighborhood restaurants along Hyde St between Washington and Union Sts.

of the city's bustling port and later a symbol of urban decay, the Embarcadero has been redeveloped into a delightful bayside promenade.

At the southern end of the Embarcadero, the San Francisco Giants play baseball at Pac Bell Park. Further north, at the foot of Market St, the **Ferry Building** has stood elegantly since 1898; the building houses a bustling **farmers market** (☎ 353-5650; www.ferry plazafarmersmarket.com) and the **Sausalito ferries** (Golden Gate Ferry; ☎ 923-2000) dock outside.

You can ride vintage street cars along the Embarcadero; they run from Fisherman's Wharf to the Ferry Building, then up Market St to the Castro district.

DOWNTOWN SAN FRANCISCO

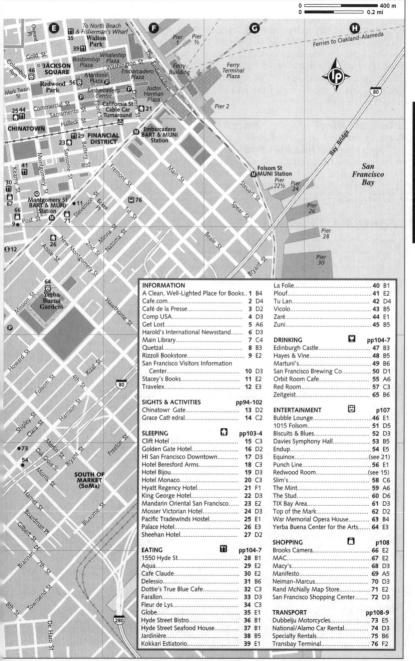

Four skyscrapers mark the huge **Embarcadero Center**, which continues four blocks west, starting on the Embarcadero at Justin Herman Plaza. At the base lie shops, restaurants, great movie theaters and a post office. Pop into the **Hyatt Regency Hotel** and ride the glass elevators to the '70s-modern atrium-lobby; in the evening have a drink in its revolving rooftop lounge.

Fisherman's Wharf Map pp98-9

North of the Embarcadero, **Pier 39** marks the beginning of **Fisherman's Wharf**, the epicenter of tourism and the home of the city's fishing fleet. Not much of a working wharf anymore, it better resembles a waterfront shopping mall with rows of theme stores selling tchotchkes masquerading as collectibles. But two cable-car lines end here, there are attractions for kids, you can eat-to-go crab from fish stands, and there's a sea-lion colony off Pier 39.

Splurge on a 30-minute seaplane flight with **San Francisco Seaplane Tours** (☎ 332-4843; www.seaplane.com; Pier 39; adult/child $139/99) for a bird's-eye bay view.

For a bay tour, **Blue and Gold Fleet** (☎ 773-1188; www.blueandgoldfleet.com; Pier 41; adult/child $20/11) operates hour-long cruises; book on-line for discounts. Alternatively, stroll the wharf and talk to fishermen; many give boat rides for less.

At Pier 45 you can see the **Musée Mécanique** (☎ 346-2000; www.museemecanique.com; Pier 45, Shed A;

SAN FRANCISCO & THE BAY AREA

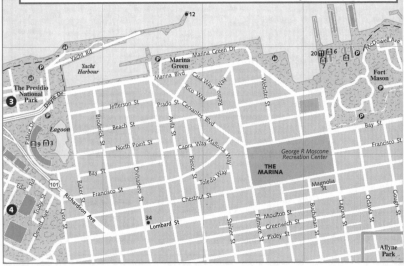

FISHERMAN'S WHARF

SIGHTS & ACTIVITIES pp94-102		Hotel San Remo........................ 15 G3		Tommaso's................................ 26 H4
African-American Historical & Cultural Society.. 1 D3		Washington Square Inn............. 16 H4		Trattoria Contadina................. 27 G4
Coit Tower................................. 2 H3				
Exploratorium............................ 3 A3		EATING ▥ pp104-7		DRINKING ▯ pp104-7
Ghirardelli Square...................... 4 E3		Buena Vista Café....................... 17 F3		Caffe Trieste............................. 28 H4
Maritime Museum....................... 5 E3		Cafe Jacqueline......................... 18 H4		
Museo Italo-Americano.............. 6 D3		Frascati.................................... 19 F4		ENTERTAINMENT ▣ p107
Museum of Craft & Folk Art....... 7 D3		Frjtz Fries...............................(see 4)		Beach Blanket Babylon............. 29 G4
Musée Mécanique...................... 8 F2		Ghirardelli Chocolate Shop		Lou's Pier 47..............................30 F2
Palace of Fine Arts.................... 9 A3		& Cafe...............................(see 4)		The Saloon.............................(see 25)
SF Museum of Modern Art Artists' Gallery........(see 7)		Greens..................................... 20 D3		
SS Jeremiah O'Brien................. 10 F2		L'Osteria del Forno................... 21 G4		TRANSPORT
USS Pampanito.......................... 11 F2		Mandarin Restaurant..............(see 4)		Blazing Saddles Bicycle Rentals... 31 G2
Wave Organ............................. 12 B2		McCormick & Kuleto's.............(see 4)		Blazing Saddles Bicycle Rentals... 32 F3
		Mo's Grill................................. 22 H4		Blazing Saddles Bicycle Rentals... 33 G2
SLEEPING ▣ pp103-4		Molinari's................................. 23 H4		
Dockside Boat & Bed................. 13 H2		Swensen's Ice Cream................ 24 F4		OTHER
Hotel Bohème.......................... 14 H4		The House............................... 25 H4		Walgreen's Pharmacy............... 34 B4

admission free; 10am-8pm) and its working collection of 19th-century carnival games.

Two historic vessels are moored at Pier 45: the **USS Pampanito** (☎ 775-1943; adult/senior & child $7/4; 9am-8pm Thu-Tue, 9am-6pm Wed), a WWII US Navy submarine; and the **SS Jeremiah O'Brien** (☎ 544-0100; Pier 45; adult/child $7/4; 9am-5pm), the sole-surviving, still-navigable WWII Liberty ship.

At the foot of Hyde St, **San Francisco Maritime National Historic Park** (☎ 561-7100; www.nps.gov/safr; adult/child $5/free) honors the waterfront's heritage with a **Maritime Museum** (300 Beach St; admission free; 10am-5pm) and preserves five classic ships at the **Hyde St Pier** (2905 Hyde St; 9:30am-5:30pm), including an 1886 iron-hull square-rigger.

Rent a bicycle from **Blazing Saddles** (☎ 202-8888; www.blazingsaddles.com; Pier 41, Pier 43½ & 2715 Hyde St; hourly/daily $7/28; from 8am), ride over the Golden Gate Bridge and take the ferry back from Sausalito.

You can walk out to the fishing pier at **Aquatic Park**, which has restrooms and a sandy beach safe for swimming – if you dare, brave the icy water.

Fort Mason & the Marina   Map pp98-9

West of Aquatic Park, **Fort Mason Center** (☎ 441-3400; www.fortmason.org) began as a Spanish fort before being taken over by the US military. During WWII, the navy built ships here and soldiers sailed off to war from the still-standing piers.

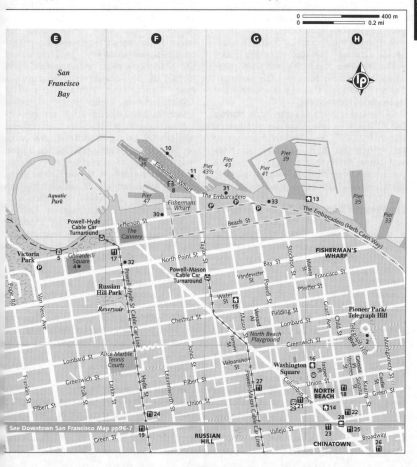

Part of the GGNRA, Fort Mason serves as a cultural complex housing nonprofits, theaters, galleries and museums, including the **Museum of Craft & Folk Art** (☎ 775-0991), the **San Francisco Museum of Modern Art Artists Gallery** (☎ 441-4777), the **Museo Italo-American** (☎ 673-2200) and the **African-American Historical & Cultural Society** (☎ 441-0640). For current theater listings, contact the center.

A footpath climbs up and down a wooded hill toward the Marina, neighborhood of multimillion-dollar homes standing on seismically unstable ground. Stroll past the yacht harbor onto **Marina Green**, a six-block-long esplanade great for kite-flying, picnicking, skating and watching windsurfers. At the tip of the breakwater, past the Golden Gate Yacht Club, the curious **Wave Organ** produces subtle sounds when incoming waves pound against its open tubes.

Bordering the Presidio, Bernard Maybeck's artificial classical ruin, the **Palace of Fine Arts** (Baker St at Bay St), was so popular when it was built for the 1915 Panama–Pacific Exposition that it was spared from its intended demolition.

Behind the ruin, see the **Exploratorium** (☎ 561-0360; www.exploratorium.edu; 3601 Lyon St; adult/child $12/8; ☻ closed Mon), a museum of art, science and human perception. Kids and adults all love the Tactile Dome, a pitch-black dome through which you crawl, climb and slide (make reservations!).

The Presidio & Fort Point   Map pp92-3

For years the US Army occupied the northwest corner of the San Francisco Peninsula. The area remains largely undeveloped and much remains green, despite Hwys 1 and 101 merging here en route to the Golden Gate Bridge.

Established in 1776 and overseen by the Spanish, then Mexican, and finally the American military, the Presidio occupies 1480 acres currently under authority of the GGNRA and the NPS. Debates rage over how best to use the valuable land and how to make the park financially self-sufficient by 2013, as mandated by Congress.

The **Presidio Visitors Center** (☎ 561-4323; www.nps.gov/prsf; cnr Montgomery St & Lincoln Blvd; ☻ 9am-5pm) has books, exhibits and information.

Along the bay, former military airstrip **Crissy Field** has been restored to a tidal marsh, with hiking and biking trails, and

picnic areas with BBQs. The **Crissy Field Center** (☎ 561-7690; www.crissyfield.org; cnr Old Mason & Halleck Sts; ☻ 9am-5pm Wed-Sun) has information, a café and bookstore.

Directly under the southern span of the Golden Gate Bridge, the **Fort Point National Historic Site** (☎ 556-1693; www.nps.gov/goga; ☻ 10am-5pm Fri-Sun) was built at the start of the 1861–65 Civil War, but it never saw battle and was abandoned in 1900. The triple-tiered brick fortress stands off Marine Dr.

Along the ocean side of the peninsula, **Baker Beach** has craggy rock formations abutting the cliffs. Currents and cold water make swimming unappealing, but it's popular with sunbathers – with or without swimsuits.

Golden Gate Bridge   Map p84

The jewel in the crown of the GGNRA, the 1937 Golden Gate Bridge (☎ 921-5858; www.goldengatebridge.org; pedestrian walkway ☻ 6am-6pm Nov-Apr, 5am-9pm May-Oct; bicycles 24hr) remains San Francisco's most enduring symbol. A marvel of 20th-century engineering, it's nearly 2 miles long, with a main span of 4200ft. The name comes from the straits it crosses, not its color, which is actually 'international orange.' (Despite conventional wisdom, the bridge is *not* constantly being repainted; it constantly gets *touched-up* and hasn't received a full coat since 1993.)

Start your tour from the parking lot at the bridge's south end (via Lincoln Blvd through the Presidio; or via Hwy 101 northbound to the 10mph-hairpin exit marked 'Last SF Exit,' just before the toll plaza). There's a lookout here, along with a gift shop and a must-see cutaway of the 3ft-thick suspension cable. Follow the path to the bridge sidewalk. (If you're on a bicycle, follow signs to the appropriate sidewalk.) Bring a jacket, even if it's sunny inland. MUNI buses No 28 and 29 run to the toll plaza.

If you drive across, stop at the first exit north of the bridge marked **Vista Point**. The views are superb, but you'll pay a $5 toll to return (there's no outbound toll). Before heading back, see Marin Headlands (p89).

Lincoln Park, Point Lobos, Ocean Beach & Fort Funston   Map pp92-3

From the north-facing cliffs of **Lincoln Park**, west of the Golden Gate, the **California Palace of the Legion of Honor** (☎ 863-3330; adult/child $8/5, free Tue; ☻ 9:30am-5pm Tue-Sun), one of San

Francisco's best art museums, shows medieval to 20th-century European art, including Rodin's sculpture *The Thinker,* located in the courtyard where Isadora Duncan once danced. Have lunch in the café. The museum is surrounded by an 18-hole **golf course** (☎ 750-4653, 221-9911).

At **Point Lobos**, the city's westernmost tip, the latest incarnation of the **Cliff House** (☎ 386-3330; www.cliffhouse.com) overlooks the Pacific Ocean. There's a lounge, gift shop and fairly good restaurant inside, but views are the highlight. At press time, the building was getting a much-needed renovation, scheduled to open mid-2004. On the other side of the road, up the hill, there's **Sutro Heights Park**.

Behind the restaurant, definitely see the mesmerizing 1946 **Camera Obscura** (☎ 750-0415; admission $2; ☽ 11am-sunset), Leonardo da Vinci's invention that projects the view from outside the building onto a giant parabolic screen inside.

The ruins in the cove just north of the Cliff House are all that remain of the **Sutro Baths**, the magnificent six-pool, 3-acre indoor swimming-pool palace Adolph Sutro built in 1896. Hike the trail from the parking lot above.

South of Point Lobos, wide-open **Ocean Beach** stretches 4 miles along the ocean. It's *not* safe for swimming, but you can have beach fires; call the NPS **park police** (☎ 561-5505) for regulations. Find wood at grocery stores.

The Great Hwy runs along Ocean Beach. Turn left on Sloat Blvd for the **San Francisco**

Zoo (☎ 753-7080; www.sfzoo.org; Sloat Blvd & 45th Ave; adult/child $10/4; ☽ 10am-5pm), a conservation-friendly menagerie.

One mile south, watch hang gliders float above **Fort Funston**, and hike atop windswept cliffs to the beach below.

Golden Gate Park   Map pp92-3

One of the world's finest urban parks, Golden Gate Park stretches nearly half way across the peninsula. Pick up information at **McLaren Lodge** (☎ 831-2700; park's western entrance, cnr Fell & Stanyan Sts; ☽ 8am-5pm Mon-Fri).

The very elegant **Conservatory of Flowers** (☎ 666-7001; www.conservatoryofflowers.org; admission $5; ☽ 9am-4:30pm Tue-Sun), the oldest building in the park, houses rare species of plants – some more than 120 years old – from 50 countries around the world. It's a must-see for any gardener.

At the **California Academy of Sciences** (☎ 750-7145; www.calacademy.org; adult/student $8.50/5.50, free 1st Wed of month), see the large natural-history museum and Morrison Planetarium. Also inside is Steinhart Aquarium, with its 100,000-gallon tank. Show a current MUNI transfer for discounted admission. The academy plans to renovate in 2004; call for details.

The popular **Japanese Tea Garden** (☎ 831-2700; adult/child $2/1; ☽ 9am-6:30pm summer, 8:30am-6pm winter) has many features, including a pagoda, gates, bridges, statues and a lovely teahouse which serves green tea and fortune cookies for $2.

The **Strybing Arboretum & Botanical Gardens** (☎ 661-1316) encompasses several gardens

---

HITCHCOCK'S SAN FRANCISCO *by Ryan Ver Berkmoes*

In San Francisco, you can revisit the dark and dramatic scenes from Alfred Hitchcock's *Vertigo*. Major sites easily recognizable today include:

- ▪ Scottie Ferguson's (Jimmy Stewart) apartment is at 900 Lombard St.
- ▪ Mission Dolores and its cemetery (there is no headstone for Carlotta Valdes) lie at 16th and Dolores Sts.
- ▪ Fort Point stands at the southern base of the Golden Gate Bridge; you can walk close to the spot where Madeline Elster (Kim Novak) took her plunge.
- ▪ Judy Barton (Kim Novak, again but with gaudier make-up) holed up at the Hotel Empire, now called the York Hotel (940 Sutter St).
- ▪ Judy/Madeline takes her first, then second and final plunge from Mission San Juan Bautista (p114), 91 miles south of San Francisco off Hwy 1. The mission remains unchanged since the film was shot in 1958, but the tower never existed.

within 70 acres, including the Garden of Fragrance, the California Collection of Native Plants and the Japanese Moon-Viewing Garden. True garden enthusiasts might like to stop by the bookstore at the entrance for details on daily tours.

The park is packed with sporting facilities, including 7½ miles of bicycle trails, countless miles of jogging trails, 12 miles of equestrian trails, an archery range, baseball and softball diamonds, fly-casting pools, a nine-hole golf course, lawn bowling greens, four soccer fields and 21 tennis courts. Rent rowboats and pedal boats from the **Stow Lake boathouse** (☎ 752-0347; $13-17 per hour; ☺ 10am-4pm).

On Sunday, John F Kennedy Dr closes to traffic, and hordes of in-line skaters,

bicyclists and street hockey players fill the roadway. Rent a bicycle from **Golden Gate Cyclery** (☎ 379-3870; 672 Stanyan St; $30 per day). Rent skates from **Skates on Haight** (Map pp92-3; ☎ 752-8375; 1818 Haight St; $6/24 per hour/overnight; ☺ closed Mon).

TOURS

The visitors information center has a complete list of tour operators. Try **City Guides** (☎ 557-4266; www.sfcityguides.org), sponsored by the San Francisco Public Library; savvy local historians lead a fantastic variety of free walking tours.

The **Victorian Home Walk** (☎ 252-9485; www.victorianwalk.com) leads architectural walking tours that cost $20 per person and last about 2½ hours.

THE HIDDEN COAST by Luci Yamamoto

Don't overlook the *east* side of the bay. Running from Richmond in the north to Hayward in the south is the low-key East Bay; you won't see many tourists here, but you'll find open fields where dogs romp off-leash, parks with ample parking and spectacular views of San Francisco. For information on East Bay parks, see www.ebparks.org.

Hidden among neatly manicured townhouses lies the **Rosie the Riveter Memorial** (www.rosietheriveter.org) in Richmond, an outdoor World War II memorial honoring the American women on the WWII home front. The memorial is simple and spare – a modern sculpture displaying photographs and quotations against the backdrop of a quiet marina. To get here, take I-80 to I-580 west, exit Marina Bay Parkway and proceed to Regatta Way.

A local favorite, 2000-acre **Tilden Park** (☺ 8am-10pm) in North Berkeley has something for everyone: hiking trails, miles of cycling, a golf course, giant carousel, botanical garden and plenty of picnic tables with BBQ grills. Access is from streets off Grizzly Peak Blvd and Wildcat Canyon Rd.

Stop and smell the roses at the **Berkeley Rose Garden** in North Berkeley, where there are 1700 rose bushes (showcasing 250 varieties). Peak bloom season is late spring to early summer. Before visiting, drink hard-core java from the original gourmet-coffee pioneer, **Peet's coffee** (Vine St). To get here, take Euclid Ave (at Glen Ave).

At one end of University Ave sits UC Berkeley, at the other, the **Cesar Chavez Park** and **Berkeley Marina**, with panoramic bay views. Weekend afternoons bring kite-flyers and dog-walkers. Neighboring the marina is North Waterfront Park, where windsurfing and sea kayaking lessons and rentals are on offer.

Smack in the middle of downtown Oakland, **Lake Merritt** is ideal for an urban jog or walk in nature. You'll spot hundreds of Canada geese (not to mention gobs of mossy goose poop) along a 3.5-mile perimeter path. Kids love the Children's Fairyland. Rent a boat and float beside Oakland's revitalized downtown.

For organic produce, artisan-baked breads, fresh flowers and free tastings, check out the Sunday farmers market at **Jack London Square** (www.jacklondonsquare.com). At night, head to **Yoshi's** (☎ 510-238-9200; www.yoshis.com; 510 Embarcadero West), an iconic Oakland jazz club and Japanese restaurant. From I-880, exit at Broadway/Alameda.

Alongside the San Mateo Bridge, the minimalist **Hayward Shoreline Interpretive Center** (☺ 10am-5pm Tue-Sun) is geared toward the elementary-school set. But 817 acres of shoreline provide a surprising perspective on the bay's tides, birds and marshland. Expect high winds. Bring sunglasses. Take I-880 to Hwy 92 west, exit Clawiter Rd/Eden Landing Rd and turn right on Breakwater Ave.

SLEEPING

San Francisco lodging is expensive. Always ask about packages and discounts, and check the Internet. Rates given here are *published* high-season rates; you can usually do better. The **Visitors Information Center** (☎ 888-782-9673; www.sfvisitor.org) runs a reservation line, good in a pinch or if you want a comprehensive list of lodgings.

Union Square

Union Square has lots of hotel rooms near department stores, cable-car lines and theaters, but it's bordered on the west by a sketchy neighborhood, the Tenderloin (see Dangers & Annoyances, p94).

HI San Francisco Downtown (Map pp96-7; ☎ 788-5604; 312 Mason St; dm members/nonmembers $22/25) This large, well-equipped hostel, a stone's throw from Union Square, has over 280 beds, a few dozen private rooms (from $60 per night) and 24-hour access.

Golden Gate Hotel (Map pp96-7; ☎ 392-3702, 800-835-1118; www.goldengatehotel.com; 775 Bush St; r without/with bath $85/115; P ⧉) Attentive owners take good care of the Golden Gate, which has comfortable rooms in a 1913 Edwardian hotel safely up the hill from the Tenderloin.

King George Hotel (Map pp96-7; ☎ 781-5050, 800-288-6005; www.kinggeorge.com; 334 Mason St; r $80-129; P ⧉) One of downtown's good hotel bargains, the nine-story King George, opened in 1912, has comfortable – if small – rooms. It serves breakfast, has a wine bar and offers weekend English tea service.

Sheehan Hotel (Map pp96-7; ☎ 775-6500, 800-848-1529; www.sheehanhotel.com; 620 Sutter St; r $79-165; P ⧉ ⧉) The only downtown non-luxury property with an indoor pool, the Sheehan has 64 clean, tourist-class guest rooms up the hill in a safe neighborhood.

Hotel Beresford Arms (Map pp96-7; ☎ 673-2600, 800-533-6533; www.beresford.com; 701 Post St; r $99-129; P ⧉) Because it was built as an apartment house, guests get bigger-than-average hotel rooms here for reasonable prices; some have kitchenettes, making it good for families.

Orchard Hotel (☎ 362-8878, 888-717-2881; www.theorchardhotel.com; 665 Bush St; r $129-189; P ⧉) Expect modern, spacious, comfortable rooms with luxury-hotel amenities at tourist-hotel prices. Central location. Breakfast included.

Also a bargain, the charming, well-kept 1905 **Andrews Hotel** (☎ 563-6877, 800-926-3739; www.andrewshotel.com; 624 Post St; r $105-145; P) has small but comfy accommodations; request a quiet room if it matters.

Hotel Monaco (Map pp96-7; ☎ 292-0100, 800-214-4220; www.monaco-sf.com; 501 Geary St; r $230-399; P ⧉) One of Union Square's best luxury-boutique hotels, the Monaco's smartly decorated, plush rooms have lovely fabrics and eclectic furnishings. There's a fireplace in the lobby beside a marble staircase, as well as a terrific restaurant and bar. It's also pet-friendly.

The Clift (Map pp96-7; ☎ 775-4700, 800-652-5438; www.clifthotel.com; 495 Geary St; r $325-455; P ⧉) Philippe Starck redesigned San Francisco's most fashionable luxury hotel, and every detail from furniture to flowers has been impeccably styled for maximum chic. For cocktails, stop by the famous Redwood Room, carved entirely from a single tree.

North Beach & Fisherman's Wharf

Stay in the old Italian neighborhood made famous by Jack Kerouac and Lawrence Ferlinghetti, and people-watch at sidewalk cafés. On the downside, parking is next to impossible.

Hotel San Remo (Map pp98-9; ☎ 776-8688, 800-352-7366; www.sanremohotel.com; 2237 Mason St; r $55-95; P) One of the city's most charming budget hotels, San Remo has rooms with shared baths. Its location between North Beach and the wharf makes it perfect for sightseers.

Washington Square Inn (Map pp98-9; ☎ 981-4220, 800-338-0220; www.wsisf.com; 1660 Stockton St; r $145-245; P ⧉) Right on Washington Square, this discrete, well-maintained inn has 15 very comfortable rooms furnished with antiques. Rates include in-room breakfast and evening wine and hors d'oeuvres.

Dockside Boat & Bed (Map pp98-9; ☎ 392-5526; www.boatandbed.com; office: C Dock, Pier 39; boats nightly per couple $125-375; P) Spend the night aboard a sailboat or yacht, and awaken to the sound of water lapping against the hull. Continental breakfast included.

Also consider the **Hotel Bohème** (Map pp98-9; ☎ 433-9111; www.hotelboheme.com; 444 Columbus Ave; r $164-184) in the middle of North Beach.

Downtown & Financial District

Staying near the foot of Market St puts you near the Embarcadero, the bay and all public

SAN FRANCISCO
& THE BAY AREA

transportation lines. It's a neighborhood of high-rise offices, not Victorian houses.

Pacific Tradewinds Hostel (Map pp96-7; ☎ 433-7970, 800-486-7970; http://san-francisco-hostel.com; 680 Sacramento St; dm $24) This clean and well-maintained, 4th-floor hostel has free high-speed Internet, a fully equipped kitchen and no curfew or chore requirements.

Hotel Bijou (Map pp96-7; ☎ 771-1200, 800-738-7477; www.hotelbijou.com; 111 Mason St; r $105-149; P 🖳) The Bijou is an oasis of hip civility at the edge of the Tenderloin. (Ignore the junkies down the street.) If the very comfortable rooms were further up the hill, they'd cost another $75. In the plush lobby there's a small theater which screens nightly movies, filmed in San Francisco.

Mandarin Oriental San Francisco (Map pp96-7; ☎ 276-9888, 800-622-0404; www.mandarinoriental.com; 222 Sansome St; r from $475) All rooms have spectacular views at downtown San Francisco's finest luxury hotel, on the top 10 floors of the city's third-tallest tower. Beds have exquisite 260-thread-count Egyptian cotton sheets and in certain guestrooms you can sit in a bubble bath and look out at the skyline through one-way glass. Service is of course superb. Don't rule out staying here before you check rates on-line, especially on weekends.

Palace Hotel (Map pp96-7; ☎ 512-1111, 888-627-7196; www.sfpalace.com; 2 New Montgomery; r $210-260; P 🖳 🏊) Also good for a splurge, the Palace has luxurious accommodations in an 1875 building; even if you're not staying here, see the opulent and beautiful Garden Court, where you can sip tea.

The Castro

The city's gayest neighborhood gets some of San Francisco's best weather (ie least foggy). Its many shops, restaurants and cafés stay busy into the evening.

Beck's Motor Lodge (Map p106; ☎ 621-8212, 800-227-4360; 2222 Market St; r in summer $99-125; P) In expensive San Francisco, this two-story, standard-issue motel is good value and has a great location, convenient to all the Castro sights.

The Parker Guest House (Map p106; ☎ 621-3222, 888-520-7275; www.parkerguesthouse.com; 520 Church St; r $119-199; P 🖳) The Castro's best inn, a 1909 Edwardian mansion, has deliciously comfortable beds in the rooms and two very comfortable parlors downstairs. Continental breakfast is included.

Also consider the **Inn on Castro** (Map p106 ☎ 861-0321; www.innoncastro2.com; 321 Castro St r $100-185).

Ocean Beach

Seal Rock Inn (Map pp92-3; ☎ 752-8000, 800-732-5762 www.sealrockinn.com; 545 Point Lobos Ave; r $115-135) I you're a purist and must stay on the ocean you'll do all right at this standard-issue motel, across from the Cliff House, and far from downtown.

EATING & DRINKING
Waterfront

The Ramp (Map p92-3; ☎ 621-2378; 855 China Basin St; dishes $7-12; 🕒 lunch/brunch only) Locals drink Bloody Marys on the patio and eat sandwiches in an industrial shipyard. There's live music on weekends. The Ramp is a the foot of Mariposa St, off 3rd St.

Greens (Map pp98-9; ☎ 771-6222; Fort Mason, Bldg A; lunch $8-13, dinner $14-19; 🕒 lunch Tue-Sun, dinner Mon-Sat) The city's best haute-vegetarian also has sweeping views of the Golden Gate There's great takeout too.

Beach Chalet (Map pp92-3; ☎ 386-8439; 1000 Great Hwy; dishes $8-24; 🕒 breakfast, lunch, dinner) This is the only restaurant on Ocean Beach that makes its own beer and it has pretty good food to accompany it. Make reservations There's occasional live music and a full bar

Waterfront Restaurant & Cafe (Map pp92-3 ☎ 391-2696; Pier 7, The Embarcadero; dishes $14-28 Book a table upstairs for Euro-Cal cooking and gorgeous bay views, or visit the less expensive café downstairs for simpler fare

For views of the touristy wharf, try the **Mandarin** (Map pp98-9; ☎ 673-8812) for upscale Chinese, or **McCormick & Kuleto's** (Map pp98-9 ☎ 929-1730) for pricey but OK seafood They're both in Ghirardelli Square.

Downtown & Union Square

Dottie's True Blue Cafe (Map pp96-7; ☎ 885-2767; 52 Jones St; breakfast under $10; 🕒 closed dinner) There no better place for breakfast than Dottie's.

Tu Lan (Map pp98-9; ☎ 626-0927; 8 6th St; dishe under $10) The place is a dump, but the food fantastic at Tu Lan. Beware the lousy neighborhood (approach from Market St).

Cafe Claude (Map pp98-9; ☎ 392-3505; 7 Claud Lane; lunch $7-11, dinner $12-14; 🕒 closed Mon dinner Sun) Francophiles lust for this très sexy cafe and its authentic French-café scene. It has outdoor seating and weekend jazz.

Vineyard, **Sonoma Wine Country** (p79)

LEE FOSTER

Jedediah Smith Redwoods State Park (p45)

MARK NEWMAN

Bowling Ball Beach (p74), Anchor Bay

WES WALKER

Lone hiker on the **Lost Coast** (p61)

COREY RICH

JOHN E

Point Reyes National Seashore (p85)

MARY JANSON

A cable car on the move, **San Francisco** (p91)

Landmark Transamerica Pyramid,
San Francisco (p91)

CURTIS MA

RICHARD CUMMINS

City Hall's impressive dome,
San Francisco (p91)

Plouf (Map pp96-7; ☎ 986-6491; 40 Belden Place; dishes $14-24; ☯ closed Sat lunch & Sun) Plouf means 'splash' in French, and splashy it is. One of the city's best for seafood (try the mussels), it's bustling and loud, hip without being overbearing. Sexy waiters. Full bar. Great wines. Outdoor seating.

Globe (Map pp96-7; ☎ 391-4132; 290 Pacific Ave; dishes $14-24; ☯ 'til 1am Mon-Sat, closed lunch Sat & Sun) When chefs get off work, they head to Globe for dinner. Enjoy excellent European-Californian cooking and a stark but stylish room. Book a table.

Slanted Door (☎ 861-8032; Ferry Bldg; lunch $9-17, dinner $9-26) For superb Californian-Vietnamese and a great wine list, book a table at this minimalist-chic restaurant.

Atop Russian Hill lie several neighborhood restaurants. For seafood, try **Hyde Street Seafood House** (Map pp96-7; ☎ 931-3474; 1509 Hyde St; dishes $14-17; ☯ dinner). You'll need a reservation for the authentic Gallic bistro fare at tiny **Hyde Street Bistro** (Map pp96-7; ☎ 292-4415; 1521 Hyde St; dishes $12-15, 3-course prix-fixe $25; ☯ dinner Mon-Sat). **1550 Hyde St** (Map pp96-7; ☎ 775-1550; 1550 Hyde St; dishes $16-19; ☯ dinner Tue-Sun) has a wine bar and great Euro-Cal cooking. For down-to-earth Mediterranean, Russian Hill meets the Italian countryside at **Frascati** (Map pp98-9; ☎ 928-1406; 1906 Hyde St; dishes $17-22; ☯ dinner).

Kokkari Estiatorio (Map pp96-7; ☎ 981-0983; 200 Jackson St; lunch $15-23, dinner $19-28; ☯ lunch Mon-Fri, dinner Mon-Sat) Retsina best accompanies the big Greek and eastern Mediterranean flavors at Kokkari; reserve a table or sit at the bar with the Bacchanalian revelers.

Zaré (Map pp96-7; ☎ 291-9145; 568 Sacramento St; lunch $15-19, dinner $20-25; ☯ closed Sat lunch & Sun) Charming Zaré serves downtown's best central Mediterranean cooking.

Make reservations and dress for downtown's top restaurants:

Aqua (Map pp96-7; ☎ 956-9662; 252 California St; lunch $16-22, dinner $27-40; ☯ lunch Mon-Fri, dinner nightly) To find better than Aqua's exquisite haute-contemporary French-California preparations of seafood (and foie gras), you'd have to go to Paris or New York.

Fleur de Lys (Map pp96-7; ☎ 673-7779; 777 Sutter St; tasting menus $65-80; ☯ dinner Mon-Sat) Gracious and refined Fleur de Lys crafts sumptuous New French cuisine, including a superb vegetarian tasting menu. Gents: remember to wear a jacket.

La Folie (Map pp96-7; ☎ 776-5577; 2316 Polk St; tasting menu $75; ☯ dinner Mon-Sat) Intimate and casually elegant La Folie transforms food into art – and the art is magical; try the Discovery Menu.

Farallon (Map pp96-7; ☎ 956-6969; 450 Post St; lunch $14-16, dinner $27-32; ☯ lunch Tue-Sat, dinner nightly) For hubbub and splash, try the coastal cuisine at Farallon.

The trendy **Red Room** (Map pp96-7; ☎ 346-7666; 827 Sutter St) mixes drinks in a sexy, all-red lounge; while dart players drink glasses of stout at **Edinburgh Castle** (pp96-7; ☎ 885-4074; 950 Geary St).

North Beach & Fisherman's Wharf

North Beach is famous for its mom-and-pop Italian restaurants.

Trattoria Contadina (Map pp98-9; ☎ 982-5728; 1800 Mason St; dishes $10-20; ☯ dinner only) You can enjoy great pastas and friendly service here – if you reserve a table.

L'Osteria del Forno (Map pp98-9; ☎ 982-1124; 519 Columbus; dishes $8-14; ☯ closed Tue) Off-the-boat waiters serve authentic Italian trattoria-style dishes at this tiny restaurant.

Tommaso's (Map pp98-9; ☎ 398-9696; 1042 Kearny St; dishes $11-17; ☯ dinner Tue-Sun) Tommaso's bakes pizzas and roast meats in the oldest brick oven on the coast.

Cafe Jacqueline (Map pp98-9; ☎ 981-5656; 1454 Grant Ave; dishes $25-50; ☯ Wed-Sun dinner) Romantic, cozy Cafe Jacqueline only serves soufflés.

The House (Map pp98-9; ☎ 986-8612; 1230 Grant Ave; lunch $8-17, dinner $11-22; ☯ closed Sun lunch) The House is loud, and serves up some dynamite Asian-fusion dishes.

Pick up Italian deli food at **Molinari's** (Map pp98-9; ☎ 421-2337; 373 Columbus Ave); great burgers at **Mo's Grill** (Map pp98-9; ☎ 788-3779; 1322 Grant Ave; dishes under $10); pub food at the city's oldest microbrewery, **San Francisco Brewing Co** (Map pp96-7; ☎ 434-3344; 155 Columbus Ave; dishes under $10); and organic raw food at **Juicey Lucy's** (☎ 786-1285; 703 Columbus Ave; dishes under $10; ☯ 11am-6pm).

At the wharf, you can eat crepes and hand-cut french fries at **Frjtz Fries** (Map pp98-9; ☎ 928-1475; 900 North Point St; dishes under $10) and drink Irish coffee at **Buena Vista Café** (Map pp98-9; ☎ 474-5044; 2765 Hyde St).

To meet a single frat boy or party girl, head down to the Marina to the many bars around Fillmore St, between Union and Lombard Sts.

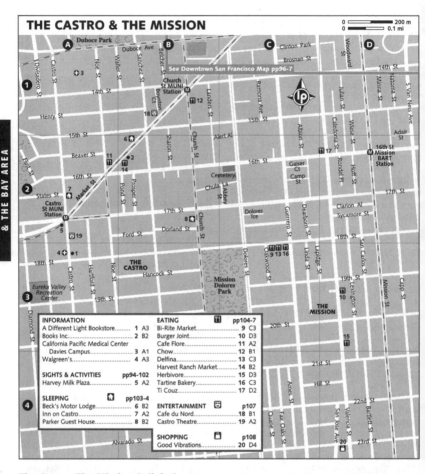

THE CASTRO & THE MISSION

0 — 200 m
0 — 0.1 mi

See Downtown San Francisco Map pp96-7

THE CASTRO

THE MISSION

Mission Dolores Park

INFORMATION		
A Different Light Bookstore	1	A3
Books Inc	2	B2
California Pacific Medical Center		
Davies Campus	3	A1
Walgreen's	4	A3

SIGHTS & ACTIVITIES	**pp94-102**	
Harvey Milk Plaza	5	A2

SLEEPING	**pp103-4**	
Beck's Motor Lodge	6	B2
Inn on Castro	7	A2
Parker Guest House	8	B2

EATING	**pp104-7**	
Bi-Rite Market	9	C3
Burger Joint	10	D3
Cafe Flore	11	A2
Chow	12	B1
Delfina	13	C3
Harvest Ranch Market	14	B2
Herbivore	15	D3
Tartine Bakery	16	C3
Ti Couz	17	D2

ENTERTAINMENT	**p107**	
Cafe du Nord	18	B1
Castro Theatre	19	A2

SHOPPING	**p108**	
Good Vibrations	20	D4

The Castro, The Mission & Civic Center

The Mission lies east of the Castro and has better restaurants.

For quick meals, try the salad bar at **Harvest Ranch Market** (Map p106; ☎ 626-0805; 2285 Market St; lunch $4-8); excellent prepared foods at **Bi-Rite Market** (Map p106; ☎ 241-9760; 3639 18th St); or delicious **Delessio** (Map pp96-7; ☎ 552-5559; 1695 Market St), where you can also eat in.

Burger Joint (Map p106; ☎ 824-3494; 807 Valencia St; dishes $7) makes the best burgers; vegans dig **Herbivore** (Map p106; ☎ 826-5657; 983 Valencia; dishes $6-12); **Tartine Bakery** (Map p106; ☎ 487-2600; 600 Guerrero St; dishes $6; ☻ no dinner; closed Mon) has fabulous pastries and real sourdough; and **Ti Couz** (Map p106; ☎ 252-7373; 3108 16th St; dishes $7-13) serves buckwheat crepes and hard cider.

Chow (Map p106; ☎ 552-2469; 215 Church St; dishes $5-12) Chow satisfies diverse tastes with everything from pizzas to pork chops.

Delfina (Map p106; ☎ 552-4055; 3621 18th St; dishes $10-19; ☻ closed lunch) Down-to-earth urban sophisticates and savvy food-lovers flock to Delfina for deliciously simple contemporary Italian cuisine; make reservations.

Thep Phanom (Map pp92-3; ☎ 431-2526; 400 Waller St; dishes $8-12; ☻ closed lunch) San Francisco's best Thai restaurant has a charming staff, but it's busy so make reservations.

Vicolo (Map pp96-7; ☎ 863-2382; 201 Ivy St; slices $4) At Civic Center, Vicolo serves great salads and deep-dish cornmeal-crust pizzas.

Wine aficionados rush to **Hayes & Vine** (Map pp96-7; ☎ 626-5301; 377 Hayes St), and piano-bar lovers lounge at mostly gay **Martuni's** (Map pp96-7; ☎ 241-0205; cnr Market & Valencia Sts).

Zuni (Map pp96-7; ☎ 552-2522; 1658 Market St; lunch $8-18, dinner $12-28; ⌚ closed Mon) Hobnob with San Francisco's *bon vivants* and sup on casually sophisticated, flavor-packed Cal-Med specialties prepared in a wood-fired brick oven. Try the roasted chicken. Make reservations.

Jardinière (Map pp96-7; ☎ 861-5555; 300 Grove St; dishes $24-33; ⌚ closed lunch) For supper-club style and Champagne toasts, you can't beat sophisticated Jardinière, one of the city's best for Cal-French cuisine. Dress to impress and make reservations.

Cafe Flore (Map p106; ☎ 621-8579; 2298 Market St) Nicknamed the Cafe Floorshow, this café in the Castro serves coffee, beer and food.

You can drink beer with hip bikers at **Zeitgeist** (Map pp96-7; ☎ 255-7505; 199 Valencia St) or sip '50s-style cocktails with the Vespa crowd at the **Orbit Room Cafe** (Map pp96-7; ☎ 252-9525; 1900 Market St).

ENTERTAINMENT
The *Sunday Chronicle's* 'Datebook' section lists almost everything happening around town. Also pick up the *San Francisco Bay Guardian* and the *SF Weekly*, free at boxes located all over the city.

TIX Bay Area (Map pp96-7; ☎ 433-7827; www.theatre bayarea.org; Union Square; ⌚ closed Mon) This free-standing kiosk on Powell St sells half-price, day-of-performance tickets and full-price advance tickets. It also carries MUNI passes. Cash only for same-day seats.

Clubs & Live Music
DOWNTOWN & FISHERMAN'S WHARF
Twirl in a cocktail dress at **Top of the Mark** (Map pp96-7; ☎ 616-6916; 999 California St), atop the Mark Hopkins Hotel; drink Champagne at the **Bubble Lounge** (Map pp96-7; ☎ 434-4204; 714 Montgomery St); or head to **Biscuits & Blues** (Map pp96-7; ☎ 292-2583; 401 Mason St) for nightly music and down-home Southern cookin'.

In North Beach, **Caffe Trieste** (Map pp96-7; ☎ 392-6739; 601 Vallejo St) harks back to the Beat days (opera singers perform Sundays), while **The Saloon** (Map pp98-9; ☎ 989-7666; 1232 Grant Ave), the city's oldest bar, hosts local blues stalwarts.

At the wharf, **Lou's Pier 47** (Map pp98-9; ☎ 771-5687; 300 Jefferson St) hosts live music every night.

SOUTH OF MARKET
The highest concentration of bars and clubs is around 11th St near Folsom St.

Slim's (Map pp96-7; ☎ 621-3330; 333 11th St) This place books an impressive string of rock, blues, country and R&B artists.

1015 Folsom (Map pp96-7; ☎ 431-1200; 1015 Folsom St) The city's foremost dance club, 1015 hosts popular straight and gay club nights. Unlike most places in the city, it stays open after 2am.

Endup (Map pp96-7; ☎ 357-0827; 995 Harrison St) Dance in the morning at the Endup, which hosts mixed late-night and morning parties.

The Stud (Map pp96-7; ☎ 863-6623; cnr 9th & Harrison Sts) The Stud hosts Trannyshack, the city's best drag show, at midnight Tuesdays; other nights it's a gay dance bar with a pool table.

THE CASTRO & THE MISSION
After hitting the Castro's many bars, sing karaoke at **The Mint** (Map pp96-7; ☎ 626-4726; 1942 Market St) or hear indie bands at **Cafe du Nord** (Map p106; ☎ 861-5016; 2170 Market St).

Live Theater
Beach Blanket Babylon (Map pp98-9; ☎ 421-4222; www.beachblanketbabylon.com; Club Fugazi, 678 Green St) If you see only one show, make it the hilarious Beach Blanket Babylon.

Teatro Zinzanni (Map pp92-3; ☎ 438-2668; http://zinzanni.org; Pier 27) For dinner and a show, Zinzanni puts on a 19th-century, European-style circus with a five-course meal.

The San Francisco Symphony performs in **Davies Symphony Hall** (Map pp96-7; ☎ 864-6000; www.sfsymphony.org; cnr Grove St & Van Ness Ave).

The beautiful **War Memorial Opera House** (Map pp96-7; ☎ 864-3330; 301 Van Ness Ave) hosts the San Francisco Opera and the **San Francisco Ballet** (☎ 865-2000; www.sfballet.org), which also performs at **Yerba Buena Center for the Arts** (Map pp96-7; ☎ 978-2787; cnr Howard & 3rd Sts).

For comedy, head to the **Punch Line** (Map pp96-7; ☎ 397-4337; 444 Battery St).

Sport
San Francisco 49ers (☎ 656-4900; www.sf49ers.com) The 49ers play football at Candlestick Park (known as 3-Com Park), south of the city.

San Francisco Giants (☎ 972-2000; www.sfgiants .com) The Giants play baseball for the crowds at the Pac Bell Park at the southern end of the Embarcadero.

SHOPPING

If you've forgotten underwear or need a toaster or a fur coat, head directly to Union Square. **Macy's** (Map pp96-7; ☎ 397-3333) and the nearby **Neiman-Marcus** (Map pp96-7; ☎ 362-3900) lie on the Geary St side. East along Post and Geary Sts lies San Francisco's highest concentration of brand-name stores and high-fashion boutiques. **MAC** (Map pp96-7; ☎ 837-0615; 5 Claude Lane) carries men's designer and retro gear. MAC's **North Beach branch** (☎ 837-1604; 1543 Grant Ave) stocks women's apparel.

Nordstrom (☎ 243-8500) sits atop upscale **San Francisco Shopping Centre** (Map pp96-7; cnr Market & 5th Sts). For souvenirs, go to Fisherman's Wharf and Pier 39. For more civilized tourist shopping, go to **Ghirardelli Square** (Map pp98-9), at the wharf's west end; buy the famous chocolate at **Ghirardelli Chocolate Shop & Caffe** (☎ 474-1414).

Don't get ripped off on electronics or cameras in Chinatown; instead look for bargain-priced cookware and herb-and-tea shops. If you need a camera, reputable **Brooks Camera** (Map pp96-7; ☎ 362-4708; 125 Kearny St) sells, rents and repairs them.

The cashmere-clad tend to shop in small boutiques in Pacific Heights, along Fillmore St between Bush and Sacramento Sts. Small designer stores and high-end gift shops line Union St between Franklin and Fillmore Sts, in Cow Hollow; look for places tucked in hidden courtyards.

For au courant underground shopping, head to Hayes Valley, on Hayes St between Franklin and Laguna Sts, near Civic Center. Check out Manifesto (Map pp96-7; ☎ 431-4778; 514 Octavia St), run by local designers.

Shop for vintage clothing and music on busy Haight Street, from Masonic Ave to Stanyan St. **Amoeba Records** (Map pp92-3; ☎ 831-1200; 1855 Haight St), near Stanyan St, carries the best indie selection of music in town.

In the Mission District, hit Valencia St, between 16th and 24th Sts, for vintage shops, locally designed clothing and Mexican folk art. Women owned and operated, **Good Vibrations** (Map p106; ☎ 974-8980; 1210 Valencia St) is the street's most famous store and carries sex-positive adult toys.

GETTING THERE & AROUND
Air

The Bay Area has three airports: **San Francisco International Airport** (Map p84; SFO; ☎ 650-876-7809; www.flysfo.com), 15 miles south of the city via Hwy 101 or I-280; **Oakland International Airport** (OAK; ☎ 510-577-4000; www.flyoakland.com), 12 miles away, via the Bay Bridge and I-880; and **San Jose International Airport** (SJC; ☎ 408-277-4759; www.sjc.org), 45 miles south. Most international flights arrive at SFO. It's often cheapest to fly into Oakland.

To/From the Airport

Take **BART** (Bay Area Rapid Transit; ☎ 989-2278; www.bart.gov) trains ($5) directly from SFO or OAK right into downtown San Francisco.

Taxis charge about $35 for a trip into the city; follow signs from the arrival areas at any airport. Add 15% gratuity to the metered fare.

SFO Airporter (☎ 650-246-2768) operates buses ($13) to downtown hotels.

Door-to-door shuttle vans cost less than taxis. Vans leave the departures level outside terminals. Try **Lorrie's** (☎ 334-9000) and **Super Shuttle** (☎ 558-8500). Fares are about $17. Call for city pick-ups.

For service from OAK, reserve with **Bayporter Express** (☎ 467-1800; $26 for 1st passenger, $12 for each additional).

Bus

Intercity buses operate from the **Transbay Terminal** (Map pp96-7; 425 Mission St at 1st St). Take **AC Transit** (☎ 510-839-2882) to the East Bay, **Golden Gate Transit** (☎ 932-2000) to Marin and Sonoma counties, and **SamTrans** (☎ 800-660-4287) buses to points south.

Greyhound (☎ 495-1575, 800-231-2222; www.greyhound.com) operates nationwide buses.

Train

CalTrain (☎ 800-660-4287; www.caltrain.com; cnr 4th & Townsend Sts) operates commuter lines down the peninsula. MUNI's N-Judah streetcar line serves the station.

Amtrak (☎ 800-872-7245; www.amtrak.com) stops in Emeryville and Oakland, with connecting bus services to San Francisco.

Car & Motorcycle

Avoid driving, if only because of limited parking. When parallel parking on hills, curb your wheels or face fines.

Be aware that parking restrictions are strictly enforced. Read the signs. For towed vehicles, you need to call **City Tow** (☎ 621-8605; 850 Bryant St, Room 145).

It's a good idea to rent a car for excursions out of the city. For good service, reserve with the downtown office of **National/ Alamo** (Map pp96-7; ☎ 292-5300; www.nationalcar.com, www.alamo.com; 320 O'Farrell St).

For the best 4x4s and convertibles, call at **Specialty Rentals** (Map pp96-7; ☎ 701-1900; www .specialtyrentals.com; 1600 Mission St).

If you'd like to rent a motorcycle, contact **Dubbelju** (Map pp96-7; ☎ 495-2774; www.dubbelju.com; 271 Clara St).

Public Transportation

MUNI (☎ 673-6864; www.sfmuni.com) runs buses, streetcars and cable cars. Get the *Street & Transit Map* ($2) at newspaper stands around Union Square. Buses cost $1, cable cars $2. Transfers are good for two more trips within 90 minutes, except on cable cars. Buy multi-day passes at the Visitors Information Center or the TIX kiosk on Union Square.

BART (☎ 989-2278; www.bart.gov) runs trains beneath Market and Mission Sts, linking San Francisco and the East Bay via the Transbay Tube. From downtown, it's a 10-minute ride to the Mission district. Intra-city fares cost $1.10; intercity trips cost $2 to $5.

Taxi

Taxi fares start at $2.85 for the first mile and cost 45¢ per fifth of a mile thereafter. Be warned that taxis are almost impossible to find during Friday-evening rush. Call **Luxor Cab** (☎ 282-4141), **Veteran's Cab** (☎ 552-1300), **De Soto Cab** (☎ 970-1300) or **Yellow Cab** (☎ 626-2345).

SOUTH OF THE BAY

The urban landscape disappears along the rugged and largely undeveloped coast. In the 68 miles between San Francisco and Santa Cruz, winding Hwy 1 passes beach after beach, many hidden from view. But across the peninsula by the bay, it's a world of freeways – notably Hwy 101, which roughly parallels Hwy 1 – connecting a 50-mile stretch of suburbia; to see notable bayside towns and cities, get off the freeway in San Bruno, San Mateo, Redwood City, Palo Alto or San Jose and head for the downtown districts.

PACIFICA TO HALF MOON BAY
☎ 650

Fifteen miles from downtown San Francisco, Pacifica marks the end of coastside suburbs. It's a nothing-special town, but has two sandy beaches: **Rockaway Beach** to the north, popular for fishing, and **Pacifica State Beach**, popular with surfers (beware rip currents). The latter has outdoor showers and restrooms.

Just south of town, Hwy 1 emerges from eucalyptus forests at an unstable cliff area called Devil's Slide. Drive carefully. The road often washes out during winter rains. On the upside, it's a beautiful stretch of coastline.

A half mile south of Devil's Slide, **Gray Whale Cove State Beach**, one of the coast's most popular clothing-optional beaches, has steep steps to the sand. Park on the east side of Hwy 1; be careful crossing the road!

Montara State Beach lies a mile further south and encompasses **McNee Ranch State Park**, a northern section of the Santa Cruz Mountains. To ascend the pristine hills, hike the trails leading from the Martini Creek parking lot on the inland side of Hwy 1.

Point Montara Lighthouse HI Hostel (☎ 728-7177; cnr Hwy 1 & 16th St; dm/r $18/48) stands next to a 1928 lighthouse; make reservations.

The **Fitzgerald Marine Reserve** (☎ 728-3584), at Moss Beach, protects extensive tidepools. Be careful on the slippery rocks, and obey posted regulations. From Hwy 1 in Moss Beach, turn west onto California Ave.

Stop for a bite at the **Moss Beach Distillery** (☎ 728-5595; cnr Beach Way & Ocean Blvd; dishes over $15), overlooking the ocean; follow directional signs from Hwy 1.

Just south, Princeton-by-the-Sea stretches around Pillar Point Harbor. Eat fried fish and coleslaw at **Barbara's Fishtrap** (☎ 728-7049; 281 Capistrano Rd; dishes $8-18). If you want to fish, call **Huck Finn Sportfishing Center** (☎ 726-7133), which offers day-long salmon-fishing trips for about $60 per person.

At the west end of Pillar Point, **Maverick's** attracts the world's top surfers to its huge, steep and very dangerous waves. The annual Quiksilver/Maverick's surf contest happens between December and March, depending on conditions.

Near Pillar Point Harbor, **Harbor View Inn** (☎ 726-2329; 51 Alhambra Ave; r $120-140) has clean ocean-view rooms and standard-issue furnishings.

SAN FRANCISCO & THE BAY AREA

HALF MOON BAY
☎ 650 / pop 11,300

Half Moon Bay attracts visitors with its wide-open beaches, but agriculture remains the major industry, particularly the cultivation of humid-climate crops such as strawberries, broccoli and pumpkins, which you can sample at the many roadside fruit-and-vegetable stands. Since it's the main town between San Francisco (28 miles north) and Santa Cruz (40 miles south), it's a good place to stop for lunch or to spend a couple of days exploring nearby parks and preserves.

Orientation & Information

Hwy 92 connects Half Moon Bay to inland freeways, providing access to the South Bay; avoid Hwy 92 during commute hours, unless traveling against traffic. Locally, Hwy 1 is called Cabrillo Hwy.

Shops, cafés and restaurants line five-block-long Main St, just east of Hwy 1. The **Half Moon Bay Coastside Chamber of Commerce** (☎ 726-8380; www.halfmoonbaychamber.org; 520 Kelly Ave; ☷ 9am-4pm Mon-Fri) provides visitor information.

Sights & Activities

Play on 4 miles of open sandy beach at **Half Moon Bay State Beach** (☎ 726-8819; day-use fee $4); access via Kelly Ave or further north at Venice Blvd.

Rent a horse at **Seahorse Ranch** (☎ 650-726-2362, 650-726-9903; www.horserentals.com). Two-hour rides cost $50; between 8am and 10am, it's only $30. Kids under five ride ponies.

Celebrate the harvest at the annual **Art & Pumpkin Festival** (☎ 726-9652). The October event kicks off with the World Championship Pumpkin Weigh-Off; the winning pumpkin sometimes exceeds 1000lb.

Sleeping & Eating

San Benito House (☎ 726-3425; www.sanbenitohouse.com; 356 Main St; r $80-176) Rent Americana-style rooms upstairs; stop downstairs at the deli for the town's best sandwiches (lunch under $10). The **restaurant** (dishes $16-19, dinner Thu-Sun) serves very good Euro-Cal cooking; on Thursday, dinner entrees cost under $10. There's a full bar nightly.

Old Thyme Inn (☎ 726-1616, 800-720-4277; www.oldthymeinn.com; 779 Main St; r $135-300) This charming 1898 inn has cheerful rooms and lovely herb gardens.

Mill Rose Inn (☎ 726-8750, 800-900-7673; www.millroseinn.com; 615 Mill St; r $150-310) The Mill Rose provides luxurious amenities, such as a outdoor Jacuzzi and landscaped gardens.

Half Moon Bay Lodge (☎ 726-9000, 800-368-2468; www.woodsidehotels.com; 2400 S Cabrillo Hwy; r $190-220; ☳) Stay at this lodge for well-appointed hotel rooms, some with fireplaces and a with garden-view terraces.

Ritz-Carlton Half Moon Bay (☎ 712-7000, 800-241-3333; www.ritzcarlton.com; Miramontes Pt Rd; r $275-625; ☐ ☳) There's no more luxurious place t stay between San Francisco and Monterey than this sprawling seaside resort. Dine on fine chinaware with silver cutlery, the bed down on 300-thread-count Egyptian cotton sheets. There's also a 36-hole gol course and spa.

Cameron's Restaurant & Inn (☎ 726-5705; 1410 Cabrillo Hwy; r $90-110; dishes from $8) Eat pub food drink beer and play darts at Cameron's, century-old English-style pub. If you don mind noise, rent a room upstairs.

Getting There & Away

SamTrans (☎ 800-660-4287) runs regular dail buses to Half Moon Bay. Take bus No 11 from BART Daly City station, or bus No 11 from Colma station. Travel to Linda Mar i Pacifica, then connect with bus No 294 t Half Moon Bay. Each bus costs $1.25.

DETOUR TO PESCADERO

Fifteen miles south of Half Moon Bay, turn east from Hwy 1 onto Pescadero Creek Rd and see the little town of Pescadero. Though visually attractive, with its white-washed, steepled church, the best reason to visit is to eat at dressed-down **Duarte's Tavern** (☎ 879-0464; cnr Stage & Pescadero Rds; dishes $11-14; ☷ 7am-9pm). It's most famous for the artichoke soup and olallieberry pie, but staff also make homemade goat-cheese ravioli with cheese from a nearby farm, and great fish dishes such as sand dabs and Petrale sole; in season, try the delicious crab cioppino ($20). Kids are always welcome. After lunch, burn off the extra calories at 2200-acre **Butano State Park**, where you can hike to grassy hilltops on trails lined with second-growth redwoods (no dogs on trails); there's also a campground. Take Cloverdale Rd 4½ miles south from Pescadero.

HALF MOON BAY TO SANTA CRUZ

San Gregorio State Beach ($4 day-use fee) lies 10 miles south of Half Moon Bay. It has a clothing-optional stretch to the north, but it's often windy and cold. **Pomponio** and **Pescadero** state beaches extend further down the coast. All have picnic tables; Pescadero does *not* have restrooms.

Twenty miles south of Half Moon Bay, the 1872 **Pigeon Point Lighthouse** (☎ 650-879-2120) stands 115ft tall. Because of decaying ironwork, the lighthouse remains closed indefinitely, but the point is a dramatic spot to watch migrating gray whales from January to March. Volunteer docents lead tours of the grounds from 10am to 4pm Friday to Sunday. The old lightkeeper's quarters have been converted into a very popular **hostel** (☎ 650-879-0633; 210 Pigeon Point Rd; dm/r $18/51).

Año Nuevo State Reserve
☎ 650
This reserve lies 27 miles south of Half Moon Bay. Elephant seals breed here in greater numbers than anywhere else in the world. It's wonderful to behold, but to see them, you must plan well ahead (see below for guided walks).

Between 1800 and 1850, the elephant seal was driven to the edge of extinction by trappers. Only a handful survived around the Guadalupe Islands off the Mexican state of Baja California. With the development of substitutes for seal oil and the advent of ecological conservation, the elephant seal has made a comeback, reappearing on the Southern California coast around 1920. In 1955, seals returned to Año Nuevo beach.

The peak mating-and-birthing season falls between mid-December and the end of March; seal pups leave by April. During these months visitors are only allowed on the reserve for guided walks; book at least eight weeks ahead. The **park office** (☎ 879-0227) can give advice, but to make reservations, call ☎ 800-444-4445 or 916-638-5883. Tours cost $4, plus $4 for parking. From the ranger station it's a 3- to 5-mile round-trip hike to the beach; the visit takes two to three hours. If you haven't booked, bad weather tends to bring last-minute cancellations. The rest of the year, advance reservations aren't necessary, but you'll need a visitor permit from the entrance station; arrive before 3pm.

Big Basin Redwood State Park
☎ 831
Big Basin (☎ 338-8860; day-use fee $4) became California's first state park in 1902, following heated battles between conservationists and loggers. Many trees here have stood more than 1500 years. The park encompasses 25 sq miles in the Santa Cruz Mountains. Hike along creeks and streams through old-growth redwood forests, with stands of fir, cedar, bay, madrone and oak.

You can access some trails from Hwy 1, but the main entrance lies off Hwy 236, which connects with Hwy 9 about 15 miles north of Santa Cruz. The park has 146 family **campsites** (☎ 800-444-7275 reservations; sites $14). There are also 36 **tent cabins** (☎ 800-874-8368; cabins $49) with two double-bed platforms and wood-burning stoves.

SANTA CRUZ
☎ 831 / pop 56,000
In the beachside city of Santa Cruz, the specter of 1960s counterculture lives in aging hippies and granola-fed university students. In recent years, though, Silicon Valley commuters have moved in and driven up real estate prices. Now there are as many Range Rovers as VW vans, but the University of California's (UCSC) 13,000 idealistic, left-leaning students keep the traditional spirit of the city alive and well.

Fun-seeking crowds pack the beaches and boardwalk on summer weekends. Unfortunately it's not all peace and love with some of the street punks downtown. Hang loose but remain aware of your surroundings. Unlike the North Coast, the weather in summer can be quite warm and sunny – still, carry a sweater; this isn't San Diego.

Orientation
Santa Cruz faces south on giant Monterey Bay. The city can be confusing, with roads winding uphill and downhill, disappearing, then reappearing across the San Lorenzo River. The city bleeds into neighboring Capitola. Pacific Ave is the main street of downtown Santa Cruz, with Front St one block east.

Information
Santa Cruz County Conference & Visitors Council (☎ 425-1234, 800-833-3494; www.santacruz.org; 1211 Ocean St; 🕑 9am-5pm Mon-Sat, 10am-4pm Sun) has

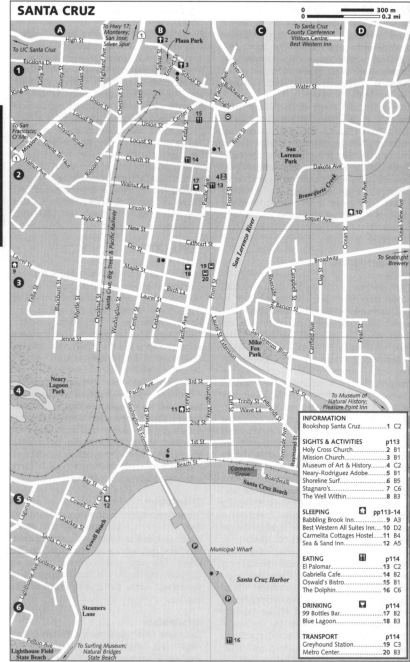

SANTA CRUZ

0   300 m
0   0.2 mi

SAN FRANCISCO & THE BAY AREA

plenty of useful brochures, maps and lodging information.

Metro Santa Cruz (www.metroactive.com/cruz), the town's free weekly newspaper, has event, film and restaurant listings.

Pick up books at **Bookshop Santa Cruz** (☎ 460-3254; 1520 Pacific Ave).

Sights
WATERFRONT
The West Coast's oldest beachfront amusement park, the **boardwalk** (☎ 423-5590; www .beachboardwalk.com; rides $2-4, all-day passes $24; ☉ daily Jun-Aug, Sat & Sun Sep-May) opened in 1906. There's a 1924 wooden roller coaster and a 1911 carousel – both National Historic Landmarks.

Drive right onto the **wharf**, lined with seafood restaurants and souvenir shops. If you want to fish, you can rent poles and tackle. Noisy pods of sea lions laze beneath the wharf.

MISSION SANTA CRUZ
The **Holy Cross Church** is all that remains of the 1791 Mission Santa Cruz, the town's namesake mission. **Santa Cruz Mission State Historic Park** (☎ 425-5849; 144 School St; ☉ 10am-4pm Thu-Sun), one block off Mission Plaza, includes one original structure, the 1791 **Neary-Rodríguez Adobe**. The 1931 **mission church** (cnr High & Emmet Sts) stands as a half-size replica; inside there's a **gift shop** (☎ 426-5686).

MUSEUMS
The small **Museum of Art & History** (☎ 429-1964; 705 Front St; adult/student $4/2; ☉ 11am-5pm Tue-Sun, to 7pm Thu) has historical exhibits and contemporary art.

The **Santa Cruz City Museum of Natural History** (☎ 420-6115; 1305 E Cliff Dr; donation welcome; ☉ 10am-5pm Tue-Sun) includes an ancient seacow fossil and a touch-friendly tidepool.

The tiny **Surfing Museum** (☎ 420-6289; admission free; ☉ noon-4pm Thu-Mon), at Lighthouse Point on W Cliff Dr, overlooks the most popular surfing break in Santa Cruz.

UNIVERSITY OF CALIFORNIA, SANTA CRUZ
Sights on the 1965 **UCSC** (☎ 459-0111; www.ucsc .edu) campus include galleries, a renowned arboretum and structures from the 1860s Cowell Ranch, around which the campus was built. West of town, see an 87ft whale skeleton and marine exhibits at UCSC's

Seymour Marine Discovery Center (☎ 459-3800; near Delaware Ave & Swift St; adult/student $5/3; ☉ 10am-5pm Tue-Sat, noon-5pm Sun).

NATURAL BRIDGES STATE BEACH
West of town at the end of W Cliff Dr, **Natural Bridges** (☎ 423-4609; day-use fee $4) has tidepools, rock formations and wintertime whale-watching. It's also the state's only Monarch butterfly preserve. Between November and March, thousands of them roost in the trees. Call for tour information.

Activities
SPAS
If you want to soak in a hot tub, check out **The Well Within** (☎ 458-9355; 417 Cedar St; $22-27 per couple) and **Kiva Retreat House** (☎ 429-1142; 702 Water St; private/communal tub $20/16).

WATERSPORTS
The north side of Monterey Bay is warmer than the south, which is cooled in summer by water from underwater Monterey Canyon.

Surfing is popular in Santa Cruz, especially at Steamer Lane; Pleasure Point Beach, on E Cliff Dr toward Capitola; and Manresa State Beach, beyond Capitola. Rent equipment at **Shoreline Surf** (☎ 458-1380; 125 Beach St; $30 per day).

Learn to surf with **Club Ed** (☎ 459-9283; www.club-ed.com) or **Richard Schmidt Surf School** (☎ 423-0928; www.richardschmidt.com). Both charge $80 for a two-hour group lesson or a one-hour private lesson, including equipment.

WHALE-WATCHING & HARBOR CRUISES
Whale-watching trips, fishing expeditions and harbor cruises depart year-round from the municipal wharf. Try **Stagnaro's** (☎ 427-2334), a long-standing operator, which offers whale-watching trips (adult/child $30/16), fishing trips (adult $55 to $60, child $45 to $50) and one-hour sightseeing tours (adult/child $8/5).

Sleeping
Rooms in Santa Cruz are overpriced in summer, particularly on weekends (expect rates to be lower at other times). Rates shown below reflect high-season tariffs.

Carmelita Cottages Hostel (☎ 423-8304; 321 Main St; dm $20, d $46-80) Make advance reservations for Santa Cruz's best lodging bargain.

Best Western All Suites Inn (☎ 458-9898, 800-428-2627; www.bestwestern.com; 500 Ocean St at Soquel Ave; r $95-275; 🖭) Every room is a suite at this comfortable property near downtown. Near the highway, consider its sister property, **Best Western Inn** (☎ 425-4717, 800-428-2627; 126 Plymouth St; r $85-235).

Sea & Sand Inn (☎ 427-3400; 201 W Cliff Dr; r $159-359) It's just a motel, but the Sea & Sand has ocean-view rooms on a cliff away from the noisy boardwalk.

Pleasure Point Inn (☎ 469-6161, 877-557-2567; www.pleasurepointinn.com; 3665 E Cliff Dr; r $165-265) In a quiet residential area right on the water, this inn has four spartan, but luxurious and modern rooms. Highlights include a rooftop hot tub and deck overlooking the sea, and full breakfast is included.

Babbling Brook Inn (☎ 427-2437; www.babbling brookinn.com; 1025 Laurel St; r $180-250) The inland Babbling Brook Inn has well-appointed rooms with featherbeds; some have Jacuzzi tubs and gas fireplaces. Outside there's a pleasant garden with a running stream. Full breakfast is included.

Eating

First stop for self-caterers should be the year-round **farmers market** (cnr Lincoln & Center Sts; 🕑 2:30-6:30pm Wed). Pacific Ave and Front St downtown are lined with cheap eats.

Silver Spur (☎ 475-2725; 2650 Soquel Dr; dishes under $10) For hearty breakfasts, head to Silver Spur, north of Hwy 1 on the east side of town.

Seabright Brewery (☎ 426-2739; 519 Seabright Ave; dishes from $8) After the beach, bring the kids here for burgers, salads, sandwiches or steaks.

The Dolphin (☎ 426-5830; dishes from $14) For fish on the wharf, you'll get the most bang for your buck at this little diner at the end of the pier.

O'Mei (☎ 425-8458; 2316 Mission St; dishes $8-12) In town, O'Mei serves the city's best Chinese; make reservations.

Gabriella Cafe (☎ 457-1677; 910 Cedar St; dishes from $14) Dine on rustic Italian-inspired dishes at Gabriella, in a cozy candlelit room.

El Palomar (☎ 425-7575; 1336 Pacific Ave; dishes $10-22) This hugely popular place serves great Mexican staples (try the *ceviches*). Great tequilas too.

Oswald's (☎ 423-7427; 1547 Pacific Ave; dishes $18-23; 🕑 dinner Tue-Sun) For superb Euro-Ca cooking, reserve a table at tiny Oswald's Santa Cruz's best.

Drinking

Choose from 40 beers on tap at **99 Bottles Bar** (☎ 459-9999; 110 Walnut Ave).

Dance with students and the local gay crowd at the **Blue Lagoon** (☎ 423-7117; 923 Pacific Ave).

Getting There & Away

Next door to the **Greyhound station** (☎ 423-1800; 425 Front St), **Santa Cruz Metropolitan Transit** (☎ 425-8600) operates local bus services from the **Metro Center** (920 Pacific Ave).

CAPITOLA

☎ 831

Five miles east of Santa Cruz, the little seaside town of Capitola is quieter than Santa Cruz, with affluent crowds less inclined to hold drum circles on the beach. Downtown you'll find shops, galleries, restaurants and pretty houses. Streets can get crowded and parking tight; leave the car in the lot behind City Hall, off Capitola Ave at Riverview Dr.

The **Capitola Chamber of Commerce** (☎ 475-6522; www.capitolachamber.com) has local tips and

---

DETOUR TO SAN JUAN BAUTISTA

Made famous in Alfred Hitchcock's *Vertigo*, sleepy San Juan Bautista preserves the state's only remaining original Spanish plaza. On one side, stands **Mission San Juan Bautista** (☎ 623-4528; $2 donation; 🕑 9:30am-4:45pm). Founded in 1797 it's the largest of California's mission churches. The ridge along the north side of the church marks the San Andreas Fault. North of the **cemetery**, look for old El Camino Real, the state's first road, built to link the missions; much of Hwy 101 follows the original route. The buildings around the plaza make up the **state historic park** (🕑 831-623-4526; admission $2; 🕑 10am-4:30pm). Tour the 1814 **Plaza Hotel** and the adjacent **Castro-Breen Adobe**. The **blacksmith shop** and **Plaza Stable** hint at San Juan Bautista in its heyday, when it was central California's largest town and 11 stagecoaches a day passed through. Take Hwy 156, 3 miles east of Hwy 101 to get here.

SAN FRANCISCO & THE BAY AREA

information about the **Capitola Art and Wine Festival**; it's held in mid-September. Also visit www.capitola.com. The **Begonia Festival** (☎ 476-3566), on Labor Day weekend, features a flotilla of flowered floats on Soquel Creek.

The **Capitola Historical Museum** (☎ 464-0322; 410 Capitola Ave; ☽ noon-4pm Fri-Sun) hosts two-hour summer-weekend walking tours; make reservations.

Stop for coffee and a book at **Capitola Book Cafe** (☎ 462-4415; 1475 41st Ave).

Dine by the beach at contemporary, eclectic **Paradise Beach Grill** (☎ 476-4900; 215 Esplanade; dishes $8-21); make reservations.

Ride the tram to **Shadowbrook** (☎ 475-1511; 1750 Wharf Rd; lunch $7-14, dinner $14-24; ☽ closed Sat lunch), a huge old wooden house turned restaurant; open since 1947, it's surrounded by vast gardens and is beside Soquel Creek.

ELKHORN SLOUGH
☎ 831

Nearly 75% of California's coastal wetlands have wound up beneath roads, houses and shopping malls. They are crucial habitats for some migratory birds and certain fish and mammals, and also support human settlements by stabilizing the shorelines and filtering water. You can hike 5 miles of trails, spot eagles and pelicans and see how Monterey Bay naturally meets the land at 1400-acre **Elkhorn Slough National Estuarine Research Reserve** (☎ 728-2822; www.elkhornslough.org; 1700 Elkhorn Rd, off Hwy 1, Watsonville; adult/child $2.50/free; ☽ 9am-5pm Wed-Sun), just south of the Monterey County line. Call for docent-led tour times. Lest you forget how drastically humankind has altered the landscape, the giant smokestacks of the adjacent power plant stand as a reminder.

Central Coast

CENTRAL COAST

Hugging the Pacific from Monterey to Ventura, California's Central Coast offers a stunning variety of destinations, both of nature's making and of human design. Its natural delights include extraordinary marine life and brilliant wildflowers, coastal bluffs and steep mountain canyons, elusive, wave-battered coves and sparkling, easily reached sandy beaches. The Channel Islands, sitting offshore, provide glimpses of plant and animal species not visible on the mainland.

People have also shaped the Central Coast, from Native Americans such as the Ohlone, Esselen, Salinan and Chumash, going back thousands of years; to Spanish explorers, missionaries, Mexican and US settlers; and modern-era cultural figures, corporations and environmentalists. Museums, historic buildings, universities and parks abound.

In the region's north, Monterey is home to a world-class aquarium and the wharves once populated by the characters who inspired John Steinbeck. Big Sur, 90 moody beautiful miles of coastline, offers peaceful getaways and is the quintessential stretch of Hwy 1. Just south, Hearst Castle perches on the hills, beckoning art lovers and wannabe millionaires. San Luis Obispo, slightly inland, is a funky town which has sprung up around its beautiful mission, while larger, wealthier Santa Barbara has fine beaches and strikingly consistent Spanish-style architecture. Ventura, a laid-back beach town, is also the gateway to the Channel Islands.

The Central Coast has endless opportunities for hikers, kayakers, divers, surfers and cyclists. And anyone who wishes to end a day spent in the outdoors with a delicious repast and comfortable quarters will be well rewarded.

CENTRAL COAST

HIGHLIGHTS

- Sipping cocktails at sunset in Montecito's **Biltmore Hotel** (p142) in Santa Barbara
- Eating out in Mediterranean-style cafés in **Carmel** (p126)
- Hiking **Bishop's Peak** (p135) in San Luis Obispo
- Beach-combing on **Pfeiffer Beach** (p128)
- Watching whales and dolphins en route to the **Channel Islands** (p144)
- Discovering the many delights of **Big Sur** (p127)
- Gasping at the opulence of **Hearst Castle** (p131)
- Catching the distinctive 'Pink Moment' sunset in **Ojai** (p143)
- Driving or bicycling down the stunning **17-Mile Drive** (p124)
- Sun-worshiping on the beaches of **Santa Barbara** (p141)

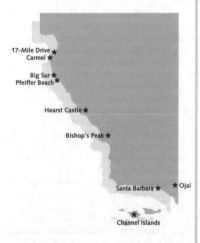

Climate

In the Monterey area the weather is mild
with average temperatures of 57°F. Rain
comes November through April; spring
and fall bring warm days and cool nights.
Morning and evening coastal fog is common
in summer. Big Sur is foggy in the summer,
warmer and clearer in fall, and rainy in the
winter, with temperatures dipping low but
never to freezing. Spring is windy. Inland,
San Luis Obispo experiences mostly sun-
shine, with rain only from January to April.
In winter, temperatures can drop to almost
freezing, but highs on the same day can be
in the 60s. Summer offers near-100°F highs.
Santa Barbara delivers 60s and 70s year-
round, with some rain November through
April. Throughout the region, inland temperatures are more extreme.

National & State Parks

California's Central Coast is home to the
Channel Islands National Park (p144), a
chain of islands in the Santa Barbara Channel. Inhabited for thousands of years by
the Chumash Indians, the islands are now
known for their biological diversity: 10% of
plants and 30% of animals on the islands
are endemic.

Numerous **state parks and beaches** (camping reservations ☎ 800-444-7275, international callers
☎ 916-638-5883, TDD ☎ 800-274-7275; www.parks.ca
.gov) grace California's Central Coast. A quick
introduction to them is *California Escapes*
(www.caescapes.com), the official guide to
California State Parks. Monterey State Beach
and Monterey Bay (p122) are great for water
sports while Monterey State Historic Park
(p122) features restored buildings revealing
the area's Spanish and Mexican heritage.
Point Lobos State Reserve (p126) offers wildlife viewing and hiking, while Garrapata State
Park (p128) is a hidden gem for hikers.

Pfeiffer Big Sur is a good entry point
into magical Big Sur. Montaña de Oro
(p133) comes alive with wildflowers and
Refugio State Beach (p142) has a palm tree–
bedecked campground, while El Presidio
de Santa Barbara's (p140) restored historic
buildings take visitors back in time.

State beaches and parks, including Gaviota (p142), Refugio (p142) and Carpinteria
(p142), will make available beach wheelchairs that dip into the ocean. Call the **local
authority** (☎ 805-968-1033) to make a booking.

Getting There & Around

From the north, the Central Coast is
reached by the coastal Hwy 1, also called
the Pacific Coast Hwy, or the inland Hwy
101–El Camino Real, which originally connected California's missions. In the south
of this region, in Ventura, Hwy 1 and Hwy
101 are the same road. Regional airports include the Monterey Peninsula Airport and
the Santa Barbara Airport, although flying
into San Francisco, San Jose or Los Angeles
and then busing, training or driving to the
Central Coast may be cheaper. Amtrak
serves Salinas, San Luis Obispo and Santa
Barbara and has connector buses to some
other cities. Greyhound buses from either
San Francisco or Los Angeles serve Salinas,
Monterey, San Luis Obispo and Santa Barbara (see p216 for more information).

MONTEREY

☎ 831 / pop city 29,700, peninsula 138,460

Monterey is a lively, friendly town rich in
natural beauty and history – and not the
least bit shy about benefiting from its main
industry, tourism. Monterey Bay is one of the
world's most varied marine environments,
and offshore the Monterey Canyon plum-
mets to a depth of over 10,000ft. In summer
the upwelling currents carry cold water from
this deep submarine canyon, sending a rich
supply of nutrients toward the surface level
to feed the bay's diverse marine life. These
frigid currents also account for the bay's
generally low water temperatures and the fog
that blankets the peninsula in summer.

History

The Ohlone tribes, who were on the peninsula from about 500 BC, may have spotted
Spanish explorer Juan Rodríguez Cabrillo,
who sailed by in 1542. He was followed in
1602 by Sebastián Vizcaíno, who landed
near the site of today's downtown Monterey
and named it after his patron, the Duke of
Monte Rey. The Spanish returned in 1770
to establish Monterey as their first presidio
in Alta California. Monterey became the
capital of Alta California after Mexico broke
from Spain in 1821, and then became a bustling international trading port. The American takeover during the Mexican American
War (1846–48) signaled an abrupt change
in the town's fortunes, and San Jose soon
replaced Monterey as the state capital.

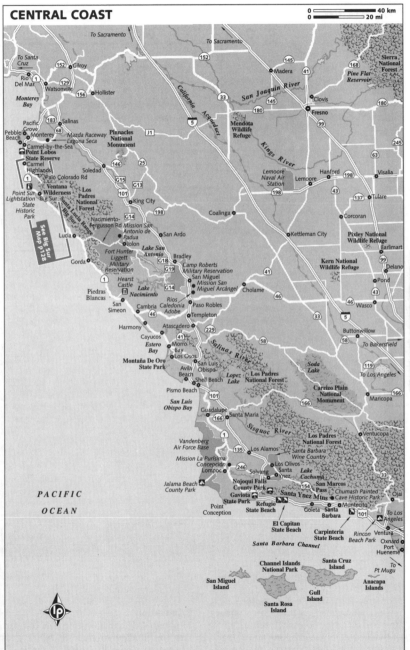

CENTRAL COAST

0 ——————— 40 km
0 ——————— 20 mi

See Big Sur Map P.128

To Sacramento

To Sacramento

Gilroy

To Santa Cruz

Rio Del Mar

Watsonville

Hollister

Monterey Bay

Pacific Grove

Pebble Beach

Monterey

Salinas

Mazda Raceway Laguna Seca

Carmel-by-the-Sea

Point Lobos State Reserve

Carmel Highlands

Pinnacles National Monument

Palo Colorado Rd

Point Sur Lightstation State Historic Park

Ventana Wilderness

Big Sur

Soledad

Los Padres National Forest

King City

Santa Lucia Range

Big Sur

Nacimiento-Fergusson Rd

Lucia

Fort Hunter Liggett Military Reservation

Gorda

Mission San Antonio de Padua

Jolon

Lake San Antonio

San Ardo

Bradley

Camp Roberts Military Reservation

San Miguel

Mission San Miguel Arcángel

Cholame

Piedras Blancas

Hearst Castle

Lake Nacimiento

San Simeon

Cambria

Rios Caledonia Adobe

Paso Robles

Templeton

Harmony

Atascadero

Cayucos

Estero Bay

Morro Bay

Los Osos

Montaña De Oro State Park

San Luis Obispo

Avila Beach

Shell Beach

Lopez Lake

Pismo Beach

San Luis Obispo Bay

Guadalupe

Santa Maria

Los Padres National Forest

Salinas River

Soda Lake

Carrizo Plain National Monument

Maricopa

Vandenberg Air Force Base

Mission La Purísima Concepción

Lompoc

Los Alamos

Los Olivos

Santa Ynez

Los Padres National Forest

Santa Barbara Wine Country

Lake Cachuma

Nojoqui Falls County Park

Solvang

San Marcos Pass

Chumash Painted Cave Historic Park

Ojai

Jalama Beach County Park

Gaviota State Park

Refugio State Beach

Point Conception

Santa Ynez Mtns

Montecito

Goleta

Santa Barbara

El Capitan State Beach

Carpinteria State Beach

Rincon Beach Park

Ventura

Oxnard

Port Hueneme

To Los Angeles

To Pt Mugu

Santa Barbara Channel

PACIFIC OCEAN

Channel Islands National Park

San Miguel Island

Santa Rosa Island

Santa Cruz Island

Gull Island

Anacapa Islands

Sierra National Forest

Pine Flat Reservoir

San Joaquin River

Madera

Fresno

Clovis

Kings River

Mendota Wildlife Refuge

California Aqueduct

Lemoore Naval Air Station

Lemoore

Hanford

Visalia

Coalinga

Kettleman City

Pixley National Wildlife Refuge

Earlimart

Kern National Wildlife Refuge

Delano

Pond

Wasco

Buttonwillow

To Bakersfield

To Los Angeles

Corcoran

Tulare

Sisquoc River

To Los Angeles

LP

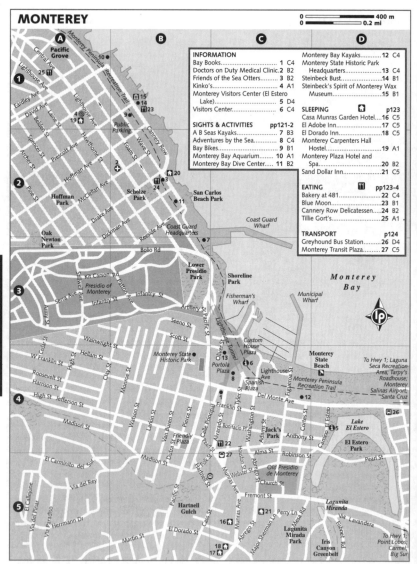

MONTEREY

| 0 | 400 m |
| 0 | 0.2 mi |

In the late 19th century, people began to capitalize on the teeming marine life in Monterey Bay, and the first sardine canneries soon opened. By the 1930s, Cannery Row had made the port the 'Sardine Capital of the World,' but overfishing and climatic changes caused the industry's sudden collapse in the 1950s. Fortunately, tourism has come to the rescue and modern Monterey attracts large numbers of visitors.

Orientation

Monterey's historic downtown is a compact area surrounding Alvarado St, which ends in Custom House Plaza, near Fisherman's Wharf. This area is known as Old Monterey, as distinct from Cannery Row, about a mile northwest. Cannery Row segues straight into Pacific Grove ('PG'), a less touristy town.

Information

BOOKSTORES

Bay Books (Map opposite; ☎ 375-1855; 316 Alvarado St) Has a superb range of books, especially regarding the history, culture and environment of Monterey and the Central Coast. It is a good place to pick up specialized hiking and other activity maps and guides to the area – and coffee.

INTERNET ACCESS

Internet access is free at a couple of places in town:

Friends of the Sea Otter (Map opposite; ☎ 642-9037;381 Cannery Row, Suite Q; ☺ 10am-6pm, 10am-7pm summer)

Kinko's (Map opposite; Lighthouse Ave & Irving; ☺ 24hr).

MEDICAL SERVICES

Community Hospital of Monterey Peninsula (Map p125; ☎ 624-5311; 23625 Holman Hwy)

Doctors on Duty Medical Clinics (Map opposite; ☎ 649-0770; 501 Lighthouse Ave; ☺ 8am-8pm)

TOURIST OFFICES

When you've arrived, also pick up copies of *Go!* and the *Coast Weekly*, with events, activities and entertainment listings.

Monterey County Convention & Visitors Bureau (☎ 888-221-1010, calls answered 9am-5pm Mon-Fri; 24hr recording 831-649-1770; www.montereyinfo.org)

Monterey Visitors Center (Map opposite; ☎ 888-221-1010; fax 648-5373; cnr Camino El Estero & Franklin St; ☺ 9am-6pm Mon-Sat & 9am-5pm Sun Apr-Oct, 9am-5pm Mon-Sat & 10am-4pm Sun Nov-Mar) On the shore of El Estero Lake, east of Old Monterey.

Visitors Center (Map opposite; ☎ 649-7109; www.mbay.net/~events; 20 Custom House Plaza; ☺ 10am-5pm) Centrally located in the Stanton Center near Fisherman's Wharf.

Sights

MONTEREY BAY AQUARIUM

Monterey's most mesmerizing experience is a visit to the **aquarium** (Map opposite; ☎ 648-4888, toll-free in California ☎ 800-756-3737; www.mbayaq.org; 886 Cannery Row; adult/student/child age 3-12 $18/16/9; ☺ 9:30am-late May–early Sep & holidays, 10am-6pm rest of year), built on the site of what was once the city's largest sardine cannery. You'll encounter countless aquatic denizens, from slow-moving starfish and slimy sea slugs to animated sea lions and sea otters.

CRITTERS YOU 'OTTER' NOT MISS

Sea otters are one of the Monterey Bay Aquarium's major attractions, but these charming creatures can be found all around Monterey Bay.

Not long ago, the sea otter was on the brink of extinction, ruthlessly hunted down by fur traders because of its exceptionally dense fur (sea otters can have more than a million hairs per square inch, the thickest fur of any mammal). In 1977, the US Fish and Wildlife Service placed sea otters on the endangered species list. These days, otters enjoy special protection along the entire length of Big Sur in what is called the California Sea Otter Game Refuge.

Sea otters have a playful nature and laid-back appearance, and are one of the few animals to use tools. They may be seen floating on their backs using a rock to break open shellfish. Besides the Monterey Bay Aquarium, good places to see otters are Fisherman's Wharf (p122) in Monterey, the rocky points along 17-Mile Drive (p124) and Point Lobos State Reserve (p126). For more information about these animals, contact the nonprofit **Friends of the Sea Otter** (Map opposite; ☎ 642-9037; 381 Cannery Row, Suite Q; ☺ 10am-6pm, 10am-7pm summer).

The top prize goes to the **Jellies: Living Art** exhibit, which presents these pulsing creatures in all their ethereal beauty and amazing variety. Standing in the infinity mirror room surrounded by what seems like millions of moon jellies is otherworldly.

Vanishing Wildlife: Saving Tunas, Turtles & Sharks exposes a previously unseen million-gallon gallery that is home to huge tuna, green sea turtles and hammerhead sharks. The exhibit explains the human impact on these magnificent creatures – and modern-day efforts at conservation.

Meanwhile, the gigantic **kelp forest** teems with hundreds of animals – from sharks to sardines – which are fed at 11:30am and 4pm. Also fun are the **sea otter feeding sessions** at 10:30am, 1:30pm and 3:30pm.

Small children love **Splash Zone**, an interactive area that is home to the penguins. The touch pools, where you can get close to sea cucumbers, bat rays and other animals, are also a winner.

To avoid long lines in summer, on weekends and on holidays, book ahead by phone or on the Internet; the booking fee is $3.

MONTEREY STATE HISTORIC PARK

Old Monterey is home to an extraordinary assemblage of 19th-century brick and adobe buildings, administered as the **Monterey State Historic Park** (admission free). Pick up a brochure describing the 2-mile-long self-guided walking tour called the *Path of History* at the **Visitors Center** (Map p120; ☎ 649-7109; www.mbay.net /~events; 20 Custom House Plaza; ☻ 10am-5pm), inside the Stanton Center. You can also pick it up from the **State Historic Park Headquarters** (Map p120; ☎ 649-7118; docent-led tours available) across the street in the historic Pacific House, which also houses a **museum of state history** (☻ 10am-5pm).

FISHERMAN'S WHARF

Like its larger namesake in San Francisco, the wharf is a tourist trap at heart, but good fun nonetheless. Noisy seals make regular visits to the wharf, and it's also the base for a variety of boat trips.

CANNERY ROW

In his novel, *Cannery Row*, John Steinbeck depicted the dreams and schemes of an amazing cast of characters and immortalized the sardine-canning business that Monterey lived on for the first half of the 20th century. Alas, the sardines' days were numbered. Predictions that overfishing could destroy the business were ignored when the catch reached a peak of 250,000 tons in 1945. Just five years later, figures plummeted to 33,000 tons, and by 1951 most of the sardine canneries had closed, many of them mysteriously catching fire.

Nowadays, Cannery Row packs in tourists rather than sardines. Many shoot photos of the bronze bust of the writer at the bottom of Prescott Ave, right next to the restored warehouse containing the **Steinbeck's Spirit of Monterey Wax Museum** (Map p120; ☎ 375-1010; adult/child 7-12 $4.95/2.95; ☻ 9am-9pm). If you like wax figures, stop here.

Activities
DIVING

The waters of **Monterey Bay** and nearby **Carmel Bay** are excellent for diving and snorkeling. The kelp is healthy and marine life abounds. **Monterey Bay Dive Center** (Map p120; ☎ 656-0454; www.mbdc.to; 225 Cannery Row; snorkeling/scuba kit $39/69, private one-tank/group two-tank tour $59/75) is a great place to rent gear or to sign up for a private guided tour. Call or visit the website to book ahead.

KAYAKING

To get up close to Monterey Bay's kelp forests, sea otters, birds and harbor seals, take a guided kayak tour with **A B Seas Kayaks** (Map p120; ☎ 866-0824-2337; www.montereykayak.com; 32 Cannery Row #5; ☻ 9am-5pm) daily at 10:30am or 1:30pm for $50, or paddle solo. Also offering tours and rentals for comparable prices is **Monterey Bay Kayaks** (Map p120; ☎ 800-649-5357; www.montereybaykayaks.com; 639 Del Monte Ave; ☻ 9am-6pm Sun-Thu, 9am-8pm Fri-Sat).

BICYCLING

The paved **Monterey Peninsula Recreational Trail** travels for 18 car-free miles along the waterfront from Lovers Point in Pacific Grove to Seaside, passing by Fisherman's Wharf and Cannery Row in Monterey. Also well worth pedaling – and best done in spring or fall with fewer tourists around – is the famous 17-Mile Drive (see p124).

For bike rentals, try **Adventures by the Sea** (Map p120; ☎ 372-1807; www.adventuresbythesea.com; 201 Alvarado Mall; ☻ 9am-8pm depending on fog). Rentals cost $6/18 for one/four hours or $24 per day. There is also Cannery Row's **Bay Bikes** (Map p120; ☎ 646-9090; www.montereybaybikes.com; 640 Wave St; ☻ 9am-5pm, open later depending on weather), where bikes go for $15/20 per half/full day and tandems cost $30/40. Small/large surreys are fun for families and rent for $15/25 per hour.

Tours

Several dive and kayak outfitters offer guided tours (see Diving this page). For whale-watching, possible year-round, try **Monterey Bay Whale Watch** (Map p120; ☎ 375-4658; www.gowhales.com; Sam's Fishing Fleet, Fisherman's Wharf). In winter and spring, gray whales migrate through Monterey Bay, one of the best places to see them. Three-hour trips cost $27/18 per adult/child under 12 (children under three are free). In summer and fall see humpback and blue whales during four- to six-hour trips for $43/$35 adult/child. Dolphins and, much rarer, killer whales, are also seen in the area.

Festivals & Events

The popular **Monterey Wine Festival** (☎ 800-656-4282; www.montereywine.com) happens April, and the internationally famed **Monterey Jazz Festival** (☎ 373-3366; www.montereyjazzfestival.org) in September; reserve tickets well in advance for both.

Sleeping

Rates are highest May to mid-September. Call for specials year-round.

BUDGET

Monterey Carpenters Hall Hostel (Map p120; ☎ 649-0375; www.montereyhostel.org; 778 Hawthorne St; dm member/nonmember $18/22, r $54-84) This HI-affiliated hostel is the best deal in town. Dorms are light and airy and the hostel has a large living room with high ceilings, comfortable couches, a large dining table and games. Pancake batter is available for frying at breakfast daily in the spacious kitchen.

Laguna Seca Recreation Area (☎ 755-4899, reservations 888-588-2267; Monterey-Salinas Hwy 68; tent/RV sites $18/22) Since budget is hard to find in Monterey, enjoy camping amid the oaks about 9 miles east of town on Hwy 68. This campground is nicely maintained, with 175 spaces (102 with hookups), hot showers, flush toilets, picnic tables and firepits.

MID-RANGE

Asilomar Conference Grounds (Map p125; ☎ 642-4242; www.asilomarcenter.com; 800 Asilomar Blvd; r from $117; ☒) In PG, this lovely compound began in 1913 as a YWCA retreat. Designed by architect Julia Morgan, it is nestled in the trees – and near the beach. A number of buildings, some on the National Register of Historic Places, have guest rooms with private bathrooms and common areas with fireplaces. Breakfast is included.

Affordable rooms can be found along Monterey's motel row, about 2.5 miles northeast of Old Monterey on N Fremont St, east of Hwy 1 (take the Fremont St exit).

El Dorado Inn (Map p120; ☎ 373-2921, 800-722-1836; fax 831-758-4509; 900 Munras Ave; r $45-195) Close to central Monterey, this small motel is within walking distance of Old Monterey. Rates include a small in-room breakfast.

El Adobe Inn (Map p120; ☎ 372-5409, 800-433-4732; 936 Munras Ave; r $49-1990) Next door to El Dorado is a similar inn, but with a bit more charm. Rates include continental breakfast,

free local calls and use of a hot tub. There's also **Sand Dollar Inn** (Map p120; ☎ 372-7551, 800-982-1986; www.sanddollarinn.com; 755 Abrego St; r $69-149; ☒) with a Jacuzzi and breakfast.

TOP END

Monterey Plaza Hotel and Spa (Map p120; ☎ 646-1077, 800-368-2468; 400 Cannery Row; r $185-505; ☒) Worth the splurge, this hotel has tastefully decorated common areas with bay views, pool, spa, restaurant and bistro. The rooms are just-so neat and tidy, and everything seems sparkling new. The aquarium package for two includes a room and two adult tickets for $210.

Casa Munras Garden Hotel (Map p120; ☎ 375-2411, CA only 800-222-2446, US only 800-222-2588; www.casamunras-hotel.com; 700 Munras Ave; r $139-209; ☒) This hacienda-style hotel is made up of 11 buildings, and has spacious rooms decorated in bright colors (some with fireplaces). Dip in the kidney-shaped pool.

Eating & Drinking

Cannery Row Delicatessen (Map p120; ☎ 645-9549; 101 Drake Ave; breakfast $2-6, lunch & dinner $4-7; ☻ 7:30am-5pm Mon-Tue, 7:30am-9pm Wed-Sun) Although they give a 10% discount to locals, the staff of this charming deli treat travelers right too. A patio overlooks the bike path. Try the hot salami or vegie deli melt.

Tillie Gort's (Map p120; ☎ 373-0335; 111 Central Ave, Pacific Grove; dishes $7-10) While waiting for your inspired healthy cuisine, leaf through *The Hippie Dictionary: A Cultural Encyclopedia of the 1960s and 1970s* to learn what 'sweets' are or brush up on your anti-war movement history. No-meat loaf is served, along with vegie lasagna, stir fries and a few carnivorous dishes. Locals meet here for lunch and the staff are super friendly. It's right across the border in PG.

Bakery at 481 (Map p120; ☎ 648-1481; 481 Alvarado St; dishes $6-8; ☻ breakfast & lunch) Francophiles must run this bakery. Seated indoors, catch a glimpse of the alchemy happening behind the counter. Or relax in the open-air entry way, sipping coffee and sampling brioche French toast, or soups and savory treats (pine nut gorgonzola focaccia!).

Blue Moon (Map p120; ☎ 375-4155; 654 Cannery Row; dishes $7-26; ☻ to late) The decor here is calming, somewhat reminiscent of the aquarium's Jellies exhibit. Glide along the pebble path to your table with an excellent view of the bay. Yellow lights glow, complementing all the blue. The cuisine, dubbed 'East West,' has something for everyone, from seafood to steak to good vegie options.

For snacks and inexpensive eats, visit the **Monterey Bay Certified Farmers Market** (☎ 655-2607; Alvarado St; ⏱ 4-8pm Tue summer, 4-7pm Tue winter) between Pearl St and Del Monte Ave.

Getting There & Around

The **Monterey Peninsula Airport** (☎ 648-7000; www.montereyairport.com) is on Olmstead Rd, off Hwy 68, 4 miles from town. American, America West and United Express fly here. **Monterey-Salinas Transit** (MST; ☎ 899-2555; www.mst.org) bus No 21 travels from the airport to the **Monterey Transit Plaza** (Map p120; Alvarado St). Other nearby airports are San Francisco and San Jose. The **Monterey-Salinas Airbus** (reservations ☎ 373-7777) shuttles passengers from these two airports to the Monterey Transit Plaza several times a day (one way/round trip $30/55).

Amtrak (☎ 800-872-7245) runs the *Coast Starlight*, which stops in Salinas. Bus service to Monterey is considered a 'through ticket,' and should be included in the ticket price; ask when making a reservation. Greyhound makes the trip four times daily from San Francisco ($19), and three times daily from Santa Cruz ($12.50) and Santa Barbara ($37.50), as well as from other cities. (For more information on car rentals, Amtrak and Greyhound, see p216).

Monterey-Salinas Transit (MST; ☎ 899-2555; www.mst.org) operates bus services throughout the peninsula, inland to Salinas and south to Point Lobos (p126) and Big Sur (p127) as far as Nepenthe. Tickets cost from $1.75 to $3.50 and all-day passes are available. Routes converge at the Monterey Transit Plaza. From here, bus No 1 makes the trip out to Cannery Row and Pacific Grove. Other useful routes include bus Nos 4 and 5 to Carmel; No 22 to Big Sur via Carmel (May through September only) and Nos 20 and 21 to Salinas (No 21 goes via Laguna Seca and the airport). All buses are wheelchair and bicycle accessible.

From late May to early September take the free **WAVE** (Waterfront Area Visitors Express; ☎ 899-2555), a shuttle that loops around Old Monterey, Fisherman's Wharf and Cannery Row from 9am to 6:30pm.

17-MILE DRIVE

To get to Carmel from Pacific Grove take the stunningly beautiful **17-Mile Drive** through the Pebble Beach Resort and residential area, open sunrise to sunset. Entry is via guarded gates, and costs $8.50 per car. Bicycles enter free, but on weekends and holidays cyclists can only use the Pacific Grove gate. Use caution when bicycling, as drivers tend to be *very* distracted by the views. Cyclists, on the other hand, may be distracted by the wind.

From the north, enter via the Pacific Grove gate off Sunset Dr. You'll get a map explaining various sights along the route (both natural and commercial). **Spanish Bay**, where Spanish explorer Juan Portola and crew camped in 1769 while searching for Monterey Bay, is rugged and magnificent. Look seaward to **Point Joe** and the **Restless Sea**, with offshore turbulence caused by Joe's underwater formations. Further on, stop at Seal Rock picnic area, and view **Bird Rock**, home to harbor seals and sea lions as well as our feathered friends.

Perhaps the most famous spot on the drive is the **Lone Cypress**. The fact that the striking silhouette of this 250-year-old arboreal wonder is a trademark of Pebble Beach doesn't detract one bit from its solitary beauty. Another Monterey Cypress, the **Ghost Tree**, deserves a look: its trunk is white, bleached from the harsh coastal elements.

If you want to be at the epicenter of the time-on-their-hands golf set, visit **Pebble Beach Lodge**, open to the public for dining and shopping. When you've seen enough of the 17-Mile Drive, you can exit at Pacific Grove, Hwy 1 or Carmel.

CARMEL-BY-THE-SEA

☎ 831 / pop 4080

In 1914 literary figures Robinson and Una Jeffers arrived in Carmel and decided they had found their 'inevitable place.' The natural beauty of this town, established in the 1880s as a planned seaside resort, attracted many other artistic types as well. The literary 'colony' included Mary Austin, Sinclair Lewis and Jack London. But over time the unavoidable happened; too many people wanted a piece of Carmel, and despite its charter emphasizing its residential rather than commercial character, residences and businesses proliferated. In 1986, residents

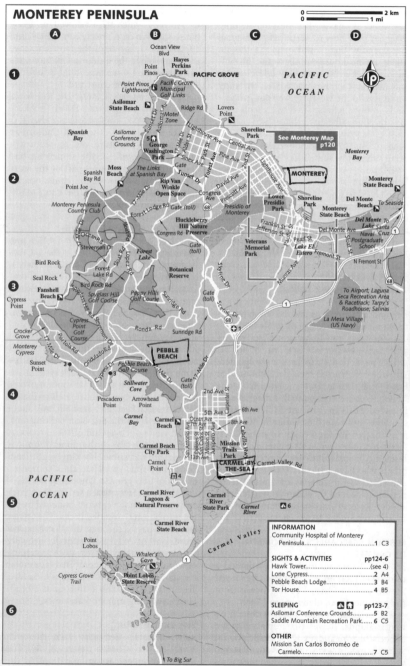

MONTEREY PENINSULA

0 — 2 km
0 — 1 mi

A **B** **C** **D**

1

Ocean View Blvd
Point Pinos
Hayes Perkins Park
PACIFIC GROVE
Point Pinos Lighthouse
Pacific Grove Municipal Golf Links
Asilomar State Beach
Ridge Rd
Lovers Point

PACIFIC OCEAN

2

Spanish Bay
Asilomar Conference Grounds
George Washington Park 5
Motel Zone
Shoreline Park
Central Ave
Pine Ave
See Monterey Map p120
Monterey Bay

Spanish Bay Rd
Moss Beach
The Links at Spanish Bay
Sunset Dr
Gate
Sinex Ave
Forest Ave
David Ave
Lighthouse Ave
MONTEREY
Monterey State Beach

Point Joe
Rip Van Winkle Open Space
Congress Ave
Prescott Ave
Presidio of Monterey
Lower Presidio Park
Shoreline Park
Monterey State Beach
Del Monte Beach
To Seaside

Monterey Peninsula Country Club
Forest Lodge Rd
Gate (toll)
Huckleberry Hill Nature Preserve
Congress Rd
Franklin St
Jefferson St
Pacific St
Del Monte Ave
Fremont St
Del Monte To Lake Santa
Lake El Estero
Naval Postgraduate School
N Fremont St

3

Bird Rock
Seal Rock
Fanshell Beach
Cypress Point
Crocker Grove
Monterey Cypress
Sunset Point
Stevenson Dr
Ocean Rd
Forest Lake Rd
Forest Lake
Bird Rock Rd
Spyglass Hill Golf Course
Botanical Reserve
Poppy Hills Golf Course
Gate (toll)
Sunridge Rd
Skyline Dr
Veterans Memorial Park
Murras Ave
Gate (toll)
Scenic Dr
1
To Airport; Laguna Seca Recreation Area & Racetrack; Tarpy's Roadhouse; Salinas
La Mesa Village (US Navy)

Ronda Rd
Sunridge Rd
68 1

CENTRAL COAST

4

Crocker Grove
Tor Iola Dr
Ondulado Rd
Cypress Dr
PEBBLE BEACH
Pebble Beach Golf Course 3
17 Mile Dr
Gate (toll)
2nd Ave
Carpenter St

Stillwater Cove
Pescadero Point
Arrowhead Point
5th Ave
6th Ave
8th Ave
Ocean Ave
7th Ave
Dolores St
San Carlos St
Mission St
Junipero Ave
Caballo Hwy

Carmel Bay
Carmel Beach
Carmel Beach City Park
Carmel Point
Mission Trails Park
13th Ave
CARMEL-BY-THE-SEA
Carmel Valley Rd

5

PACIFIC OCEAN

Carmel River Lagoon & Natural Preserve
Carmel River State Park
Carmel River
6

Carmel River State Beach
Carmel Valley

Point Lobos
1

6

Cypress Grove Trail
Whaler's Cove
Point Lobos State Reserve

To Big Sur

INFORMATION
Community Hospital of Monterey
Peninsula...................................**1** C3

SIGHTS & ACTIVITIES pp124-6
Hawk Tower.............................(see 4)
Lone Cypress................................**2** A4
Pebble Beach Lodge....................**3** B4
Tor House...................................**4** B5

SLEEPING pp123-7
Asilomar Conference Grounds....**5** B2
Saddle Mountain Recreation Park....**6** C5

OTHER
Mission San Carlos Borroméo de
Carmelo....................................**7** C5

elected business-friendly movie star Clint Eastwood as mayor. But despite ongoing struggles over how to keep this town small and friendly, there's still magic in the air. There are no house numbers and no billboards, trees grow in the middle of roads and the sand at the beach is an uncanny white, due to the wearing away of the headlands' granite. Jeffers said it was a landscape of 'superfluous beauty,' that it was 'crying out for tragedy.' The tragedy, perhaps, has been in the form of bulldozers, but the beauty somehow remains.

Orientation

It isn't hard to find the center of town – just follow the traffic to Ocean Ave, Carmel's main strip of shops, galleries, restaurants and hotels. Parallel 5th, 6th and 7th Aves and perpendicular Dolores, San Carlos and Mission Sts hold many attractions, too.

Sights & Activities

TOR HOUSE & HAWK TOWER

From the nearby beach, poet Robinson Jeffers and stonemasons carried the boulders to build **Tor House** (Map p125; ☎ 624-1813; 26304 Ocean View Ave; tours adult/student $7/4; ☯ hourly guided tours 10am-3pm Fri & Sat), which he, his wife Una and their twin sons inhabited. Later he constructed the adjacent 40ft-high **Hawk Tower**, inspired by ancient Irish stone towers. Famous visitors to this magical spot included Edna St Vincent Millay, Charlie Chaplin and Martha Graham. Inspired and affected by the beauty of nature, Jeffers came to believe in its supremacy – and humanity's insignificance. Unfortunately, others who have settled in Carmel have not chosen to live in Jeffers' low-impact manner, as evidenced by elaborate neighboring abodes. Reservations are recommended and no children under 12 are allowed.

MISSION SAN CARLOS BORROMÉO DE CARMELO

In 1770, Padre Junípero Serra founded a mission at Monterey. A year later, he moved the mission to Carmel to distance it from the presidio. Serra died here in 1784.

The original wooden mission church no longer stands. It was first replaced by an adobe structure and, in 1793, by the present stone church. It was secularized in 1834 and virtually abandoned in 1836 when the padres moved to Monterey. The ruin was roofed over in 1884, which at least slowed the decay, but restoration didn't really commence until 1931. Today it is one of the most attractive and complete of the California missions. It's worth spending some time in the beautifully landscaped outdoor courtyard.

Carmel's **mission** (☎ 624-1271; 3080 Rio Rd; museum & church adult/child age 5-17 $4/1; ☯ 9:30am-4:30pm Mon-Sat, 10:30am-4:30pm Sun), off Hwy 1, is just south of town. As with all Californian missions, the literature and museum displays are the work of the somewhat bias church faithful, and omit part of the story of the interaction between the missionaries and the Native Americans they came to live among – and convert.

POINT LOBOS STATE RESERVE

This **land reserve** (Map p125; ☎ 624-4909; www .ptlobos.org; admission $5 per vehicle; ☯ 9am-7pm, 9am-5pm winter), 4 miles south of Carmel on Hwy 1, is a must-see. With almost 600 acres of dramatic, tree-covered headlands, ancient coves and grassy meadows, plus 750 submerged acres, Point Lobos has served as pasture for livestock and housed a whaling station and abalone cannery. Luckily, around 1898, AM Allan began to buy up the land and seek public support to preserve it. In 1933 it became part of the new state park system.

As well as being a popular spot for divers, there are a number of short trails in the reserve. **Sea Lion Point** and **Sand Hill Trail**, about a half mile from the Sea Lion parking area, afford views of coves and offshore rocks. A portion of the trail – the upper loop – is wheelchair accessible. Looking north from Sea Lion Point, you'll see cliffs composed of Santa Lucia granite. Underfoot is the so-called **Carmelo Formation**, a sedimentary rock around 39 million years old, softened by the sea into bumpy, rounded rocks. The **Cypress Grove Trail** passes through the **Allan Memorial Grove**, one of only two naturally growing stands of Monterey cypress trees remaining on earth. These trees, contorted from their constant struggle with the forces of nature, are breathtaking. This trail rounds a headland, providing many ocean views.

Sleeping & Eating

Saddle Mountain Recreation Park (Map p125; ☎ 624-1617; fax 624-4470; sites $25-35; ☯) The only true budget accommodations in the

Carmel area is camping. Try one of the 25 tent sites or 25 full hookups for RVs. From Hwy 1 in Carmel take Carmel Valley Road about 5 miles and turn right on Schulte Rd. The park is in an oak grove by the Carmel River (it's a trickle) at the end of the road.

Pine Inn (☎ 624-3851, 800-228-3851; www.pine-inn .com; Ocean Ave btwn Monte Verde St & Lincoln St; r $125-250) Originally named Hotelo Carmelo, this 114-year-old structure (now with more recent additions) was rolled on pine logs four blocks down the road to its current location and renamed Pine Inn. It is now a luxury inn with formal, dark-wood walls and Victorian furniture. Ask the friendly, knowledgeable reception staff for stories about the 'old days' in Carmel.

Cypress Inn (☎ 624-3871, 800-443-7443; cnr Lincoln St & 7th Ave; r $125-295) This Spanish-style building wraps around a beautiful courtyard. Individual rooms are unique, and some have balconies and cozy seating areas. The hotel has its own cocktail lounge and nice staff and welcomes pets.

Candle Light Inn (☎ 624-6732, 800-433-4732; www.innsbythesea.com; San Carlos St, btwn 4th & 5th Ave; r $129-275) Though not as architecturally interesting as other accommodations in the area, many rooms at the Candle Light Inn do have kitchens and fireplaces.

Casanova (☎ 625-0501; 5th Ave btwn San Carlos & Mission Sts; lunch $11-15, 3-course dinner $26-43) In a house once inhabited by 'Aunt Fairy Bird,' cook to Charlie Chaplin, Casanova has been wining and dining Carmelites since 1977 and is a real treat. In the intimate, low-lit rooms of the house, or on the festive heated patio, you'll feel like you've stepped into a Mediterranean country estate. The salads, seafood dishes, pastas and meats are all first rate.

For cheaper eats, head to **Lenny's Deli** (☎ 624-5265; dishes $3-12; ☻ from 11am) in Carmel Plaza (enter off Mission St south of Ocean Ave). It offers soups, sandwiches, salads and Jewish specialties, with counter and open-air seating.

Galleries & Shopping
Carmel is known for its galleries and shops. Art ranges from derivative to daring; merchandise from tacky to tasteful.

For a look at work by some of the biggest names in photography, such as Ansel Adams, Edward Weston, Imogen Cunningham and Alfred Stieglitz, as well as some working photographers, visit the **Weston Gallery** (☎ 624-4453; www.westongallery.com; 6th Ave btwn Dolores & Lincoln Sts; ☻ 10:30am-5:30pm Tue-Sun).

Getting There & Around
Carmel is 5 miles south of Monterey by Hwy 1. **Monterey-Salinas Transit** (MST; ☎ 899-2555; www.mst.org) buses No 4 and 5 go north to Monterey and south to the Mission.

BIG SUR
☎ 831

'El país grande del sur,' the big country of the south, was how Carmel mission residents referred to the unknown terrain to the south, bestowing upon it a kind of reverence, but no precise meaning. Big Sur continues to defy definition, though poetic descriptions of the land stretching from Carmel to San Simeon are numerous. In 1542, Juan Cabrillo, sailing in view of the region's north–south Santa Lucia Mountains, the steepest coastal range in the contiguous US, wrote: 'There are mountains which seem to reach the heavens, and the sea beats on them; sailing along close to the land, it appears as though they would fall on ships.'

It's impossible to know what the Esselen tribe, native to Big Sur at least 3000 years ago, thought of their dramatic home where acorns, rabbits, deer and bears sustained them; tragically the tribe was wiped out by diseases imported by the Spanish.

In more recent times, Pico Iyer wrote that 'much of the power of Big Sur arises from the feeling that you are entering somewhere ancient, pre-human almost.' Despite the tourists who flock here, the electricity that arrived in the 1950s, the TV reception that some residents chose in the 1980s, and the expensive inns, it's the trees, tides, fog and prevailing winds that rule.

Orientation & Information
The mountains rise to greater heights to the east. A few words of advice: cell phones won't work; resist the urge to seek Internet access; bring cash; fill the gas tank elsewhere; and be careful, as the closest hospital is in Monterey (p121).

Plan ahead by contacting the **Big Sur Chamber of Commerce** (☎ 667-2100; www.bigsur california.org). In Big Sur, visit the **Ranger Station** (☎ 667-2315; ☻ 8am-6pm). *El Sur Grande*, widely available, is a free guide to the area.

Sights & Activities

Park at Soberanes Point to access trails through redwoods or stands of cacti and coastline at **Garrapata State Park** (☎ 624-4909).

Point Sur Lightstation (☎ 625-4419; Hwy 1; adult $5, child $2-3; guided tours 10am & 2pm Sat, 10am Sun) is the only intact lightstation on the Central Coast open to the public. Docents lead tours of this 19th-century beacon perched 361ft above dangerous surf.

At **Andrew Molera State Park** (☎ 372-8016, ranger 372-4076), a half-mile trail leads from the campground to a beach past sycamore trees and the Cooper Cabin, one of the oldest structures in Big Sur. Trails head south along the bluffs. The first-come, first-served walk-in **campground** (sites $1), about a third of a mile from the parking lot, has firepits, vault toilets and drinking water. **Molera Horseback Tours** (☎ 625-5486, 800-942-5486; www.molerahorsebacktours.com; rides $25-59; ⊗ Apr-Jan) runs guided trail rides. Also here is the **Big Sur Cultural & Natural History Center** (☎ 455-9514), maintained by the Ventana Wilderness Society.

Pfeiffer Big Sur State Park (☎ 667-2315), named after Big Sur's first European settlers, has rustic administration buildings and the 1930s, CCC-built Big Sur Lodge (p130). A **campground** (☎ 800-444-7275; sites $12, hiker-biker sites $2) is in a valley shaded by redwoods; facilities include showers and laundry but no hookups. Hiking trails loop through the park and head into the adjacent Ventana Wilderness (see the Detour on p129). The nature trail in Day Use Area One is wheelchair accessible. **Pfeiffer Falls**, a 1.4-mile round-trip, heads through a primeval redwood grove to 60ft falls. Highly recommended is the **Valley View Trail**, which continues from the falls another half mile, uphill, to expansive views of Point Sur and Big Sur Valley. In spring the path will be lined with wild irises, fairy lanterns and Indian paintbrush; the soundtrack will be birdsong.

Sycamore Canyon Rd (unmarked except for a sign prohibiting large trucks) winds 2 miles down to remarkable **Pfeiffer Beach**. Standing on the purplish-pink sand you can see from one end of the slightly curved beach to the other, with the steep cliffs at your back. It's beautiful and slightly overwhelming. The Pacific is relentless against the shore; waves foam and recede through carved arches of rock, evidence of the ocean's persistence; a steady roar proof of its power.

Henry Miller Library (☎ 667-2574; www.henry miller.org; admission by donation $1; ☼ 11am-6pm Wed-Mon), set back from the road amid greenery, is a bookstore/hangout/arts venue/shrine, and a fine place to stop and ponder life and literature. Here are all of Miller's written works, many of his paintings, translations of his books and a collection of Big Sur and Beat generation material.

The **Coast Gallery** (☎ 667-2301; admission free; ☼ 9am-5pm), housed in redwood water tanks, exhibits crafts by local and national artisans and watercolors, limited edition prints, books and historic memorabilia of Henry Miller.

A steep dirt fire road (take the hairpin turn 2 miles north of Julia Pfeiffer Burns State Park) descends half a mile along a creek to **Partington Cove**, once used for loading tanbark, a cross between an oak and a chestnut whose bark was used in tanning leather. During Prohibition this was allegedly a bootleggers' landing. Great tidepools!

Julia Pfeiffer Burns State Park (☎ 667-2315), named for a Big Sur pioneer woman, features redwood, tan oak, madrona and chaparral. The **Ewoldsen Trail** offers good views of the ocean and the Santa Lucia Range. There's also California's only coastal waterfall, the 80ft **McWay Falls**, which drops straight into the sea (onto the sand at low tide). To get here, take the trail heading west from the park entrance and cross beneath Hwy 1. Nearby, two walk-in **campgrounds** (☎ reservations 800-444-7275; sites $12) sit on a semi-protected bluff. Register at Pfeiffer Big Sur campground (see opposite).

Marked only by a lighted sign reading 'Esalen Institute, By Reservation Only,' the **Esalen Institute** (☎ 667-3005; www.esalen.org; Hwy 1) is world-renowned for its seminars and natural **hot springs**. Workshops deal with anything that 'promotes human values and potentials.' When space is available, you may stay without...evolving. Rooms sleep up to three people (per person $130 to $150) or in four- to six-bed dorms ($90 to $95); three meals are included.

Limekiln State Park (☎ 667-2403; day-use $3) gets its name from the four remaining lime-kilns built here in the 1880s to smelt lime to powder. A half-mile trail through a redwood grove leads to the site. The **campground** (☎ 800-444-7275; sites $12) sits by the entrance tucked under a bridge next to the ocean; it has flush toilets and free hot showers.

DETOUR TO VENTANA WILDERNESS

The 167,000-acre Ventana Wilderness is the backcountry of the Big Sur coast. It lies within the northern part of Los Padres National Forest, which straddles the Santa Lucia Range and runs parallel to the coast for its entire length. Most of the wilderness is covered with oak and chaparral, though canyons cut by the Big Sur and Little Sur rivers support virgin stands of coastal redwoods. Scattered pockets of the endemic Santa Lucia fir grow in rocky outcroppings at elevations above 5000ft.

The Ventana is popular with hikers and backpackers. There are 237 miles of trails with access to 55 designated backcountry trail camps. One favorite destination is **Sykes Hot Springs**, natural hot mineral pools (ranging from 98°F to 110°F) framed by redwoods, about 10 miles from the wilderness boundary via the Pine Ridge Trail. The trailhead is at the Big Sur Ranger Station and has parking, fresh water and restrooms. Backcountry and fire permits are available here. Note that Ventana has the country's largest concentration of mountain lions (one cat per 10 sq miles).

Sleeping
CAMPING & CABINS

See Sights & Activities (p128) for information on state park campgrounds. In addition, camping is offered at the following resorts, some of which also rent out cabins.

Ventana Campground (☎ 667-2712; www.ventana inn.com; sites Sun-Thu $25, Fri-Sat $35; ☼ Apr-Oct) Just south of Pfeiffer Big Sur State Park and set in a 40-acre redwood grove, Ventana has beautiful secluded campsites and a general store.

Big Sur Campground & Cabins (☎ 667-2322; sites $26, tent cabins $50, cabins with bath & kitchen $90-180) Nice sites and small cabins are shaded by mature redwoods along the Big Sur River. A store stocks the basics, and there are laundry facilities, hot showers, volleyball and basketball courts, and a playground.

There's also **Riverside Campground & Cabins** (☎ 667-2414; sites $28, cabins $60-115), where the cheaper cabins don't have private bathrooms.

INNS & RESORTS

Most places do not have telephones or TVs. Enjoy the silence.

Deetjen's Big Sur Inn (☎ 667-2377; www.deetjens .com; r $75-195, breakfast $4.50-11, dinner $15-29) Built by a Norwegian immigrant in the early 1930s, magical Deetjen's has a handful of funky, uniquely furnished cabins with names such as 'Van Gogh' and 'Chateau Fiasco.' If you stay, walk back into the property, along Castro Creek, to see the albino redwood tree. The restaurant is excellent.

Big Sur Lodge (☎ 667-3100, 800-424-4787; www .bigsurlodge.com; cottages $99-229; ☒) This well-designed resort boasts pretty cottages within steps of great hikes. The pricier ones also have kitchens and/or fireplaces, and sleep up to six people. Rates include admission to the state parks, and there's a **restaurant** (dishes $12.50-23) and store.

Glen Oaks Motel (☎ 667-2105; www.glenoaksbigsur .com; r $69-104, cottages $130-145) Clean, airy rooms and cottages are set amid trees and flowers.

Ripplewood Resort (☎ 667-2242; www.ripplewood resort.com; cabins $75-125) All cabins have kitchens and private bathrooms; some with fireplaces. Riverside units are quieter than ones on the Hwy 1 side. Grab a basic breakfast at the café and groceries at the market.

Big Sur River Inn (☎ 667-2700, 800-548-3610; www.bigsurriverinn.com; r $85-140; ☒) There are cozy country-style lodgings and an all-day restaurant here. Call for updated rates.

Post Ranch Inn (☎ 667-2200; www.postranchinn .com; r $485-935; ☒) If you want to splurge, this is the place. The most famous – and luxurious – inn and spa along the California coast perfectly pampers its guests in discreet style, while carefully preserving the coastal bluffs on which it stands. Arrive before dark for stunning views from the superb French-Californian restaurant, **Sierra Mar** (breakfast $12-20, dinner $25-39).

Ventana Inn & Spa (☎ 667-2331, 800-628-6500; www.ventanainn.com; r $300-975; ☒) The perfect couples' retreat, serene and romantic Ventana is known for its Japanese bathhouse and beautiful grounds. The restaurant, **Cielo** (lunch $11-17, dinner $25-35), looks like a Zen ski lodge, has great daytime views and serves good modern-American dishes.

Eating
Good food is neither hard to find nor cheap in Big Sur.

Big Sur Road House (☎ 667-2264; dishes $14-20; ☒ dinner, closed Tue) In addition to inns and resorts that offer food, there's this road-house with outdoor seating and inventive dishes such as mushroom empanadas or grilled salmon with green cabbage and mango salad.

Nepenthe (☎ 667-2345; dishes $11-30) Known for its vivid gardens and breathtaking cliff-top location, Nepenthe has arresting views from both the large outdoor terrace and through the panoramic windows in the dining room. The downstairs, self-service **Cafe Kevah** (dishes $8-12; ☒ 9am-4pm Mar-Dec) is cheaper and has similar views. There's a wonderful gift shop here, too.

Getting There & Around
Monterey–Salinas Transit (MST; ☎ 899-2555; www .mst.org) bus No 22 runs here from Monterey from May through September.

SAN SIMEON
☎ 805 / pop 360
San Simeon began life in the 1850s as a whaling station. In 1865, George Hearst bought 45,000 acres of land and established a beachside settlement on the western side of Hwy 1, across from today's entrance to Hearst Castle. The Hearst Corporation still owns much of the land here.

Adjacent to the houses, **Hearst Memorial State Beach** (day-use fee $2) has a pleasant sandy stretch with intermittent rock outcrops and a rickety wooden pier (fishing permitted).

Three miles south of the original San Simeon (just off the Hearst Corporation's property), the town of San Simeon is a mile-long strip of unexciting motels and equally unimpressive restaurants.

About 7 miles north of San Simeon, stop at the **Piedras Blancas elephant seal rookery** to watch these lovable creatures basking on the beach in huge blubbery piles. In springtime, the hills around here are covered with wild lupins, a blanket of purplish-blue.

San Simeon State Park embraces the **San Simeon Natural Preserve**, a popular wintering spot for monarch butterflies; and the **Pânu Cultural Preserve**, the site of archaeological finds dating back 6000 years. A 3-mile trail meanders through the park, which is fringed by a long sandy beach. Camping at the two campgrounds here is pleasant. **San Simeon Creek** (☎ 927-2035, reservations 800-444-7275; www.cal-parks.ca.gov; reservation fee $7.50, sites $17-19) has 133 sites for tents or RVs, water, flush toilets and coin-operated showers. **Washburn**

(☎ 927 2035; sites $10-12), up on the bluff above it, is less developed.

The nicest hotel in San Simeon is the **Best Western Cavalier** (☎ 927-4688; www.cavalier resort.com; 9415 Hearst Dr; r $119-259; ☒). Rooms are set on a manicured lawn overlooking the ocean. The on-site **restaurant** (breakfast $5-11, lunch $5-14, dinner $7-20) has friendly staff, good wine and delicious food with good options for vegetarians, such as the elaborate spinach salad.

The **Silver Surf Motel** (☎ 927-4661, 800-621-3999; fax 927-3225; 9390 Castillo Dr; r $49-104; ☒) is nothing special but it's decent value for money and has a small indoor pool and spa. Other lodging is close by in Cambria (see below).

HEARST CASTLE
☎ 805

Perched high on a hill – dubbed 'the Enchanted Hill' by the man who conceived it, William Randolph Hearst – and overlooking vast pastureland and the Pacific Ocean in the distance, **Hearst Castle** (☎ 927-2020; www.hearst-castle.org) is a monument to wealth and ambition. The estate sprawls over 127 acres of lushly landscaped gardens, accentuated by shimmering pools and fountains and statues from ancient Greece and Moorish Spain. Designed by architect Julia Morgan, it has 165 rooms in four houses, all of them furnished with Italian and Spanish antiques.

The four organized tours available (see p132 for more information) start at the visitors center at the bottom of the hill. A free exhibit covers the history of Hearst, and you don't need tour tickets to see it. The five-story large-screen **National Geographic Theater** (☎ 927-6811) shows a 40-minute propaganda piece on Hearst and the construction of the castle. Admission to the theater is included in Tour 1. If you're on another tour but still want to see the movie, you can get discounted tickets for $6/4 per adult/child; otherwise admission is $7.50/5.50.

CAMBRIA
☎ 805 / pop 6500

About half a mile inland, Cambria is a pleasant though touristy village with streets lined with knick-knack stores. Residents refer to the 'West Village' and 'East Village,' both centered along Main St. Drop in at the **Chamber of Commerce** (☎ 927-3624;

www.cambriachamber.org; 767 Main St; ☺ 9am-5pm Mon-Fri, 10am-2pm Sat & Sun) for more information. **Cambria Village Transit** (☎ 927-0468; www.cambriatransit.org) runs the free **Otter Bus** (9am-6pm Thu-Mon July 1-Sep 15; Fri-Mon Sep 16-Jun 30) from San Simeon Pines Seaside Resort (see below) into town.

Dramatically beautiful and good for a dip and a walk is **Moonstone Beach**, named for the opalescent stones once abundant here. It has low bluffs and a sand beach. At the northern end, **Leffingwell Landing** offers a picnic area shaded by Monterey cypress trees.

Quirky **Nitt Witt Ridge** (☎ 927-2690; 881 Hillcrest Dr; tours adult/child $10/5) is a whimsical 50-year-in-the-making work of the now-deceased Arthur Harold Beal. The three-level house is built entirely out of recycled materials – from abalone shells to beer cans, and tiles to toilet seats. Call ahead to arrange tours.

For a contrast, climb the short, steep road at the east end of Main St to the **Old Santa Rosa Chapel & Cemetery**, an 1870 classic New England–style chapel with faded wooden grave markers in the yard.

South of Cambria, off Hwy 1, **Harmony** (population less than 20) consists of just a handful of buildings. One houses **Harmony Pottery** (☎ 927-4293), a studio and gallery. Call for tasting room hours at **Harmony Cellars** (☎ 927-1625, 800-432-9239; www.harmonycellars.net).

Sleeping & Eating

Cambria Shores Inn (☎ 927-8644, 800-433-9197; www.cambriashores.com; 6276 Moonstone Beach Dr; r $95-180) The resident innkeepers at Cambria Shores will make you feel at home, with sparkling rooms and a breakfast basket delivered in the morning, hung on an iron hook outside the door. Adirondack chairs on the lawn are a perfect spot for staring at the ocean while enjoying the complimentary cheese and crackers or homemade cookies. Dogs are pampered. Another option is **San Simeon Pines Seaside Resort** (☎ 927-4648; www.sspines.com; 7200 Moonstone Beach Dr; r $95-120; ☒).

Robin's (☎ 927-5007; 4095 Burton Dr; dishes $11-17) Serving creative, fresh dishes such as roasted vegetable cannelloni, catering to vegetarians and the unreformed alike, Robin's is the best in town. Make reservations.

Linn's (☎ 927-0371; 2277 Main St; dishes $5.50-14) is famous for potpies and outlandish desserts. **Sow's Ear Cafe** (☎ 927-4865; 2248 Main St; dishes $13-23; ☺ dinner) is a more formal place.

HEARST CASTLE *by Ryan Ver Berkmoes*

William Randolph Hearst was not very much like Charles Foster Kane in *Citizen Kane*. Not that he wasn't bombastic, conniving and larger than life – indeed he was – but from the 1920s through to the 1940s he also had a ball, ever-enlarging his castle, constantly entertaining and running a media empire. The moody recluse of *Kane* he was definitely not.

As it did with Hearst's construction budget, the castle will devour as much of your time as you allow. It's grand, sumptuous, historic (beloved guest Winston Churchill penned anti-Nazi essays here in the 1930s) and will make you wish you had a spare billion or two so you could move in. Fortunately the entire complex is a state park which minimizes crass commercialism. To see any part of the vast hilltop estate, you'll need to take a tour. Don't even think of coming without a reservation. In peak summer months book, well in advance.

There are four tours, each departing from the large and accommodating visitors center. Regardless of the number of tours you book, you'll still have to make the 10-minute bus ride up and down the hill each time, but the views are great and the surrounding terrain largely unspoiled: it gives a sense of California before the Europeans arrived. Start with the Experience Tour (formerly Tour 1); it gives an overview of the estate and a chance to see a film about Hearst's life. It answers all the basic questions and preps you for deeper discovery. Unless you only have a passing interest in the castle, you'll likely want to take more tours. Each includes the Neptune Pool, which tempts many on hot days, but diving in will get you quickly thrown out. The castle's interiors astound, but also check out the gardens. Hearst compulsively shopped for Europe's artistic glories, vacuuming up artifacts, complete rooms and even entire monasteries, all of which his architect, Julia Morgan, integrated artfully into the whole.

Tours 2, 3 and 4 are much less crowded than Tour 1, and allow more time to speak with the professional guides, who appreciate thoughtful, unusual questions. While it's possible to take all four tours in one day – each lasts about two hours – this could leave you feeling exhausted and spent. Spreading your visit over two days allows time to see the good (and free) museum in the visitors center, as well as the town of Cambria to the south and the elephant-seal colony to the north. Facilities at the visitors center (there's no eating or drinking up the hill) are geared for industrial-sized mobs; we don't recommend them. Rather, get a picnic lunch in Cambria and sit on the sand at San Simeon beach, across from the entrance.

Tours start at 8:20am; the last leaves at 3:20pm. The Experience Tour costs $18/9 per adult/child; the others cost $12/7. There are no discounts if you book more than one. Parking is free. For reservations and information, telephone ☎ 800-444-4445 (☎ 916-414-8400 from overseas) or log onto www.hearstcastle.com. The website provides details on all the tours, including special nighttime and garden visits. Note that weather can vary between the castle's hilltop location and the visitors center. The gloomy fog at the base can open up to blazing sunny skies, so wear layers. Hearst Castle stands about 230 miles from both San Francisco and Los Angeles. If you're driving the 93 miles south from Monterey, take your time on beautiful, winding Hwy 1.

CAYUCOS

☎ 805 / pop 3400

At Estero Bay's northern end, small and slow-paced Cayucos (ki-*you*-kiss) is less commercial and sleepier than Morro Bay. Ocean Ave, which parallels Hwy 1, is the main thoroughfare, with historic storefronts and most of the hotels and restaurants. At the town's northern end is the long pier, built in 1875, from which you can fish without a license.

Cayucos' gentle waves are good for beginner surfers. **Cayucos Surf Company** (☎ 995-1000; 95 Cayucos Dr), just a few steps north of the pier, rents out surfboards for $10/20 per half/full day. Just half a block from the beach, **Tidewater Inn** (☎ 995-3670, 800-965-2699; 20 S Ocean Ave; r $55-85) is a small motel with spiffy, newly renovated rooms sporting flowery decor.

Sea Shanty (☎ 995-3272; 296 S Ocean Ave; dishes $4-18) has good desserts.

MORRO BAY

☎ 805 / pop 9700

Home to a large commercial fishing fleet, the biggest claim to fame of Morro Bay is its namesake **Morro Rock**, a 578ft peak that rises dramatically from the ocean floor just offshore. It's part of a chain of nine such volcanic rocks stretching between here and San Luis Obispo, which formed some 21 million years ago. Unfortunately, panoramic views of the bay and rock are compromised by the trio of cigarette-shaped smokestacks of a coal power plant that squats at the bay's northern end.

The bay itself is a giant estuary inhabited by two dozen threatened and endangered species, including the brown pelican, sea otter and steelhead trout. Morro Rock is home to peregrine falcons, and in winter, about 120 migratory bird species move in.

Leading south from Morro Rock is the **Embarcadero**, a fairly scruffy waterfront lined by touristy shops and restaurants.

Three blocks inland from the Embarcadero is the more pleasant **Main St** with interesting shopping and the local **Chamber of Commerce** (☎ 772-4467; www.morrobay.com; 880 Main St; ☺ 8am-5pm Mon-Fri, 10am-3pm Sat).

Sights & Activities

The 1965-acre **Morro Bay State Park** incorporates an 18-hole golf course, a marina with kayak rentals and a campground. Also here is the **Museum of Natural History** (☎ 772-2694; Morro Bay State Park Rd; adult/child $5/1; ☺ 10am-5pm). Exhibits examine the impact of oceanic, atmospheric, geologic and human forces on the environment and shed light on how living things adapt to changes.

Just north of the museum is a eucalyptus grove that harbors the **Heron Rookery State Reserve**, one of the last remaining great blue heron rookeries in California; from late February to May you can spot them feeding their young.

The paddle wheeler **Tiger's Folly II** (☎ 772-2257; 1205 Embarcadero; adult/child $10/5) makes trips around the harbor daily from May to September and on weekends in winter; check-in at the Harbor Hut (see this page).

For views of kelp forests and schools of fish, take a spin on **Seaview** (☎ 772-9463; 699 Embarcadero No 8; adult/child $12.50/5.50), a semi-sub which plies the waters daily; it departs from the Embarcadero at the bottom of Pacific St.

If you'd rather explore the area under your own steam, rent a canoe or kayak from **Canoe 2 U** (☎ 772-3349; 699 Embarcadero No 9; half-hour/half-day $4/19.50) next door.

Sleeping & Eating

Morro Strand State Beach Campground (☎ 772-8812, reservations ☎ 800-444-7275; sites $12) North of town, this campground has 81 sites behind the sand dunes. There are flush toilets and cold showers but no hookups.

Morro Bay State Park Campground (☎ 772-7434, reservations ☎ 800-444-7275; tent/RV sites $12/18) About 2 miles south of town, Morro Bay State Park has beautiful sites fringed by eucalyptus and cypress trees. It has hot water, and trails leading to the beach.

Motels cluster along Main and Harbor Sts. Rates drop in the off-season; make reservations for summer stays.

El Morro Masterpiece Motel (☎ 772-5633, 800-527-6782; www.masterpiecemotels.com; 1206 Main St; r $69-325) Sporting the look of a Mediterranean castle, El Morro is decorated with framed art throughout. The staff are friendly and rooms are a good size with a relaxed European-style ambience.

Embarcadero Inn (☎ 772-2700, 800-292-7625; www.embarcaderoinn.com; 456 Embarcadero; r $95-225) A friendly Morro Bay base. Most of the large rooms have balconies with views of 'the Rock' and all feature upscale bathrooms, VCRs and refrigerators. Some also have gas fireplaces. Rates include continental breakfast and daily newspaper.

Dorn's (☎ 772-4415; 801 Market Ave; dishes $4.50-25; ☺ breakfast, lunch & dinner) Going strong since 1942, Dorn's is famous for its clam chowder, fresh fish and extensive wine list.

Harbor Hut (☎ 772-2255; 1205 Embarcadero; lunch $8-17, dinner $15-34) With tropical tiki looks and a casual ambience, Harbor Hut has a menu heavy on steaks and seafood.

Creperie Sophie (☎ 772-4727; 355 Morro Bay Blvd; dishes $5-8) The French-Canadian owners of Creperie Sophie serve up vichyssoise, savory and sweet crepes, and good beer.

MONTAÑA DE ORO STATE PARK
☎ 805

About 6 miles southwest of Morro Bay, Montaña de Oro State Park covers about 13,000 acres of undeveloped mountain and seaside terrain. Its coastal bluffs are a favorite spot for hiking, mountain biking and horseback riding. The northern half of the park includes a row of sand dunes (85ft high) and the 4-mile sand spit that separates Morro Bay from the Pacific. The park's southern section consists of finger-like bluffs and an ancient marine terrace, which after seismic uplifting is now a series of 1000ft peaks. In spring the hills are blanketed by bright poppies, wild mustard and other wildflowers that give the park its name, meaning 'mountain of gold' in Spanish.

The state park's **visitors center** (☎ 528-0513; ☽ 11am-3pm daily Apr-Aug, 11am-3pm Thu-Sun Sep-Mar), about 3 miles south of the park boundary, does triple duty as a ranger station and natural history museum. Several hiking trails start near here, including the **Bluff Trail**, which skirts the cliffs and has beach access points.

A short walk east of the visitors center is a great **campground** (☎ 528-0513, reservations 800-444-7275; sites $7) with 50 sites, each near the creek or against the hillside, with picnic tables, firepits, pit toilets and drinking water, but no showers.

The park is about 7 miles from Hwy 1. Exit at South Bay Blvd and follow the signs.

SAN LUIS OBISPO

☎ 805 / pop 44,200

San Luis Obispo (SLO; san loo-*iss* obispo), about 8 miles inland, is one of the most charming towns of the Central Coast, perhaps because it seems to maintain a sort of balance. It's relaxed, yet not sleepy; attractive, yet not manicured or artificial; a worthy tourist destination, yet a true community in itself.

Like so many Californian cities, it grew up around a mission, this one founded in 1772 by Padre Serra. SLO is also home to the California Polytechnic State University (Cal Poly), which has 17,000 students.

Visit on Thursday evening, when the famous farmers market turns the main drag of Higuera St into a giant street party from 6pm to 9pm. Bike the back roads – yearround – or hike in the volcanic peaks that surround the town.

Orientation

SLO's downtown is bisected by the main commercial arteries of Higuera St, which travels one way going southwest, and Marsh St, running one way northeast. San Luis Obispo Creek flows through downtown parallel to Higuera St. The best exits from Hwy 101 are Marsh St and Monterey St. Parking is free for the first hour in several downtown parking garages.

Information

If you're out of cash, you'll find banks along Higuera and Marsh Sts.

Chamber of Commerce (☎ 543-1255, 800-676-1772; www.visitslo.com; 1039 Chorro St) Has plenty of free printed matter, including the *Points of Interest* brochure and a useful city map ($2.95).

Main post office (cnr Marsh & Morro Sts)

Novel Experience (☎ 544-0150; 787 Higuera St) Stocks an extensive array of books, guides and maps to the area.

San Luis Obispo County General Hospital (☎ 781-4800; 2180 Johnson Ave) Half a mile southeast of Monterey St.

Sights & Activities

Mission San Luis Obispo de Tolosa (☎ 543-6850; church admission free, museum donation $2; ☽ 9am-5pm Apr-Oct, 9am-4pm Nov-Mar), on Monterey St between Chorro and Broad Sts, sits on Mission Plaza. With its public bathrooms, beautiful floss silk trees providing shade, and many places to sit down and relax, SLO's mission area feels more like a town square – for enjoyment by all and sundry – than some of California's other missions. Often called the 'Prince of the Missions,' its church has an unusual L-shape with a flat open-beam ceiling and whitewashed walls; there's also a garden courtyard. The museum displays several artifacts from the Chumash, including arrowheads, bowls, whistles and flutes – but with very little interpretation. Items from the mission period are interpreted from the church's perspective.

Follow the two walking tours in the chamber of commerce's brochure *Points of Interest* to see sites of architectural note, including several adobes.

Support the visual arts and visit the **San Luis Obispo Art Center** (☎ 543-8562; www.sloartcenter.org, 1010 Broad St, cnr Monterey; admission free; ☽ 11am-5pm Wed-Mon, 11am-5pm daily summer). Open since 1967, the four-wing gallery exhibits fine art and crafts. The **San Luis Artists' Gallery** (☎ 547-9396; www.sanluisartistsgallery.com; cnr Higuera & Nipomo Sts; admission free; ☽ 11am-5pm) is an artists cooperative showing work by more than a dozen local working artists. On the first Friday of every month galleries stay open until 9pm and the artistically minded come out for Art After Dark.

Great hikes are numerous here, especially in the **Nine Sisters**, volcanic peaks offering panoramic views (not all are open to the public). Highly recommended i

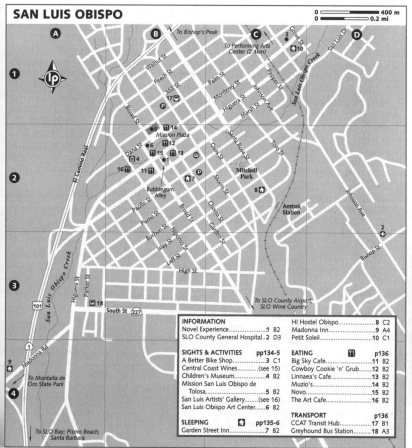

SAN LUIS OBISPO

the tallest, **Bishop's Peak** (1559ft). The trail (about 2.5 miles) starts in a lovely grove of live oaks and then heads steeply along rocky, exposed switchbacks, home to many lizards. Scramble up boulders at the top for the view. To get to the hike, head west on Foothill Rd, turn right on Patricia and left on Highland; the road dead-ends in the trailhead.

Road and mountain biking are popular in the region. Rent bikes at the appropriately named **A Better Bike Shop** (☎ 543-1148; www.abetterbikeshop.com; 1422 Monterey St; ☑ 10am-6pm Mon-Sat, noon-5pm Sun).

Franciscans planted the region's first grapes some 200 years ago, and wine has been produced here ever since. But in the last 10 years, vineyards in the Edna and Arroyo Grande Valleys have flourished. For tasting in town and advice on visiting nearby vineyards, stop in at **Central Coast Wines** (☎ 784-9463; www.ccwines.com; 712 Higuera St; ☑ 11am-6pm Sun-Wed, 11am-9pm Thu, 11am-8pm Fri & Sat).

Sleeping
HI Hostel Obispo (☎ 544-4678; fax 544-3142; www.hostelobispo.com; 1617 Santa Rosa St; dm $17.50-20, r $40-60; check-in 7:30-10am & 4:30-10pm, hostel closed 10am-4:30pm; ☐) In a Victorian house on a residential street, this hostel is clean and welcoming. It's just one minute from the Amtrak station and a 10-minute walk from downtown. Amenities include a laundry, nicely equipped kitchen and living room.

Petit Soleil (☎ 549-0321; www.petitsoleilslo.com; 1473 Monterey St; r $99-200) This B&B has taken decoration, comfort and hospitality to a wonderful level. The bright yellow building sits along a plant-filled stone courtyard. Each tastefully decorated room has a different French country theme. Breakfast is served on the sunny patio.

Garden Street Inn (☎ 545-9802; 1212 Garden St; r with breakfast $90-160) Stay in this restored 1887 Victorian for the high ceilings, friendly staff and the colorful stained-glass windows. The rooms are super clean.

Madonna Inn (☎ 543-3000, 800-543-9666; www .madonnainn.com; 100 Madonna Rd; r $137-330) This place is worth a look – it's the pinnacle of kitsch. There are 109 unique rooms, including the popular caveman room (carved from solid rock).

There's also camping in Montaña de Oro State Park (see p134).

Eating

Muzio's Grocery (☎ 543-0800; 870 Monterey St; ☽ 9am-6pm Mon-Sat) From a high-ceilinged 1912 building, Muzio's sells delectable Italian treats and makes excellent sandwiches (fresh mozzarella and basil $6.95). There are a few tables but it's even nicer to take your sandwich over to Mission Plaza.

Art Cafe (☎ 788-0330; 570 Higuera St, #105; dishes $3-10; ☽ breakfast & lunch) The baker here whips up amazing loaves like spice white pepperjack and honey whole wheat. Omelettes, salads, soups and sandwiches are fresh and tasty. There are many vegetarian options. Local art graces the walls.

Big Sky Cafe (☎ 545-5401; 1121 Broad St; dishes $6-16) Have dinner here to people-watch or space out – there's plenty of room. Tuck into such global fare as the Big Sky noodle bowl.

Novo (☎ 543-3986; 726 Higuera St; tapas $6-15, mains $10-24) Another good dinner spot, with dahl, meat and salads…you name it.

Linnaea's Cafe (☎ 541-5888; 1110 Garden St) For good coffee and hanging out with locals, while away a morning at Linnaea's or come in the evening for acoustic entertainment.

Cowboy Cookie 'n' Grub (☎ 788-0212; 1035 Chorro St; dishes $2-5; ☽ 10am-5pm Mon-Fri, 11am-4pm Sat) Look for the saddle and steer horns at this tiny, charming restaurant where soups, salads and cookies are on offer at reasonable prices.

Getting There & Around

The **SLO County Airport** (☎ 541-1038), 3 miles south of downtown between Hwy 1/101 and Broad St, is served by America West, American Airlines and United Airlines. **Greyhound** (☎ 543-2121; 150 South St) passes through town. SLO is the northern terminus of Amtrak's *Pacific Surfliner*. The *Coast Starlight* also stops at SLO daily. The station is at the southern end of Santa Rosa St.

Regional buses operated by **Central Coast Area Transit** (CCAT; ☎ 541-2228) travel north to Morro Bay, Cambria and San Simeon and south to Pismo Beach. Lines converge at the **transit hub** (cnr Palm & Osos Sts).

The free **SLO Trolley** (☽ noon-5pm, noon-9pm Thu) loops around Marsh, Higuera, Nipomo, Monterey and Palm Sts.

SLO Transit (☎ 541-2277) operates local buses (fares $0.75). The nonprofit **Ride-On Transportation** (☎ 541-8747) offers 'Safe Rides' within SLO for just $2 between 9pm and 3am Thursday, Friday and Saturday night.

AVILA BEACH

☎ 805 / pop 1250

Avila Beach is a survivor. In the late 1990s, this lovely beach town was all but wiped off the map by a massive oil spill courtesy of the nearby Unocal refinery. A costly clean-up, which required replacing the contaminated soil, tearing down structures and moving much of the population, was completed in 2001. The 'New Avila' comes with a redesigned waterfront and a once-again clean and white sandy beach. Avila's south-facing location keeps it mostly fog-free. Nearby is the ominous, heavily guarded access road to the Diablo Canyon nuclear power plant.

The **Sea Barn** (Front St) rents out boogie boards ($7 per day) surfboards ($6 per hour) and other beach stuff like umbrellas and chairs. It even has a free ocean-dipping wheelchair.

Stay at the **Inn at Avila Beach** (☎ 595-2300; fax 595-9560; 256 Front St; r $79-199). Sip the wonderful caffeinated creations of the **Espresso Diva cart** (Front St).

PISMO BEACH

☎ 805 / pop 8600

In the words of a local: 'Pismo, it's about the clam chowder, the beach; it's kick back.' Pismo Beach, the largest of the bay towns, is a conglomeration of tourist shops and

JUDY BELLAH

Extravagant Neptune Pool,
Hearst Castle (p131)

STEPHANIE DIANI

Surfers at sunset, **Leadbetter Beach** (p141),
Santa Barbara

JOHN BORTHWICK

Roller coaster, **Santa Cruz** (p113)

Monterey's touristy but fun **Fisherman's Wharf** (p122)

RICHARD CUMMINS

RICHARD CUM

Getty Center (p149) architecture, Los Angeles

DALLAS STRIBLEY

Muscle-men on Ocean Front Walk,
Venice Beach (p166)

Old Town State Historic Park (p182),
San Diego

RICHARD CUM

RICK GERHARTER

Lattes in **Little Italy** (p185), San Diego

restaurants around Pismo Pier, along a wide sandy beach. The town is called the 'Clam Capital of the World' because the tasty mollusks were once found here. These days, the beach is pretty much clammed out.

Butterflies are Pismo's most prevalent animal attraction these days. Tens of thousands of the migrating monarchs descend upon the town between late November and March, making their winter home in the secluded **Monarch Butterfly Grove**. Forming dense clusters in the tops of eucalyptus and pine trees, these beautiful, dark orange creatures perfectly blend into the environment and are easily mistaken for leaves. Free access to the grove is via the North Beach Campground, south of town off Hwy 1.

For area information visit the **Pismo Beach Chamber of Commerce** (☎ 773-4382, 800-443-7778; www.pismochamber.com; 581 Dolliver St; ☾ 9am-5pm Mon-Sat, 10am-4pm Sun). Buses run here from San Luis Obispo (see Getting There & Around on p136).

Sleeping & Eating

North Beach Campground (☎ 489-2684, reservations 800-444-7275; sites $12) About 1 mile south of the Pismo Pier, off Hwy 1, North Beach has 103 grassy sites in the shade of eucalyptus trees. It offers easy beach access, flush toilets and hot showers but no hookups.

Pismo Beach has dozens of motels; prices rise between May and September.

Ocean Breeze Inn (☎ 773-2070, 800-472-7873; www.surfinn.net; 250 Main St; r $89-159, ste with kitchen $89-199; 🏊) A block from the beach, this inn offers rooms with a small breakfast and use of the heated pool.

North of town, toward rocky Shell Beach (technically part of Pismo Beach), several upscale resorts squat atop scenic bluffs. A good option is **Spyglass Inn** (☎ 773-4855, 800-824-2612; www.spyglassinn.com; 2705 Spyglass Dr; r $79-199), with some ocean-view rooms.

You'll find several casual cafés and restaurants along Pomeroy Ave, directly up from the pier.

Splash Cafe (☎ 773-4653; 197 Pomeroy Ave; dishes $1.75-7.75) This buzzing hole-in-the-wall café makes award-winning clam chowder and great grilled ahi tuna sandwiches ($4.50).

Giuseppe's (☎ 773-2870; 891 Price St; lunch $8-12, dinner $16-24) A few blocks inland, Giuseppe's is a top-ranked Italian restaurant serving fine pizza and pasta.

SOUTH OF PISMO
☎ 805

Southbound from Pismo there are the two tiny towns of Los Alamos and Los Olivos, and one over-the-top tourist spot of Solvang. The back roads here – and even Hwy 101 – are incredibly scenic.

In Los Alamos stop for a meal at **Cafe Quackenbush** (☎ 344-5181; www.generalstoreca.com; 485 Bell St; dishes $7-15; ☾ 7am-5pm Tue-Sun).

TWO HIDDEN BEACHES
by Ryan Ver Berkmoes

South of Pismo Beach and west of the town of Lompoc lie two excellent beaches well worth visiting.

Ocean Beach and **Surf Beach** are really one beach on the grounds of the huge Vandenberg Air Force Base. During the 9-mile drive west of Lompoc on Ocean Ave you'll pass mysterious-looking structures used to support launches of both spy and commercial satellites. At the coast you'll find parking for Ocean, then Surf Beach. The dunes are untrammeled, and there are good signs explaining the ecology of the nearby estuary. Surf Beach even boasts an Amtrak train station, but the schedules prohibit a day trip from LA since the *Coast Starlight* runs southbound in the morning and northbound at night. Be aware that the endangered snowy plover nests here. It's a tiny bird with a total population under 2000. The beaches usually close on weekdays from March to September to allow them some solitude. Because they are so skilled at camouflaging their nests in the sand, the average frisbee-throwing Joe can easily trample them.

Five miles south of Lompoc on Hwy 1, look for Jalama Rd. Its 14 miles of twisting tarmac traverse pastoral ranch and farm lands. But the real reward is at the end of the road at Jalama Beach County Park. Utterly isolated, it's home to a terrific beachfront **campground** (day-use $6 per vehicle, sites from $18 per night). There are no reservations, but look for the 'campground full' sign, back at Hwy 1, and save yourself the 14-mile drive. To secure one of the private beachside sites, arrive near dawn. For information, phone ☎ 736-3504. A tiny store sells very fine cheeseburgers ($4.50).

In Los Olivos walk through the sculpture garden at the **Judith Hale Gallery** (☎ 688-1222; www.judithhalegallery.com; 2890 & 2884 Grand Ave; admission free; ☷ 10am-5pm Mon-Sat, 11am-5pm Sun). Artist Phillip Glashoff's metal sculptures of animals and people, incorporating everyday objects, are joyful.

From Los Olivos, drive out on Figueroa Mountain Rd to visit area **wineries**. In April, head all the way to the road's end (45 minutes) to see amazing **wildflowers**.

Solvang is on Hwy 246, just east of Hwy 101. In 1911, three Danish farmers established the Atterdag College Folk School in the Santa Ynez Valley to pass on their Danish traditions to future generations. The small town that grew up around the school was Solvang. Stop in at the **visitors bureau** (☎ 688-6144, 800-468-6765; www.solvangusa.com; 1511 Mission Dr) for information.

Elverhøj Museum (☎ 686-1211; cnr 2nd St & Elverhøj Way; admission by donation; ☷ 1-4pm Wed-Sun), housed in a replica 18th-century Jutland farmhouse, is the town's local history museum; it's for Nordic enthusiasts only.

Better than the human-made environment in these parts are the rolling hills and other natural wonders. From Solvang take Alisal Rd south to **Nojoqui Falls County Park** (about 5 miles) and take the short walk to the falls.

Stay at the **Royal Copenhagen Inn** (☎ 688-5561; www.royalcopenhageninn.com; 1579 Mission Dr; r $70-105; ☒). For cultural culinary balance, eat tasty Italian food at **Cafe Angelica** (☎ 686-9970; 490 First St; lunch $7-10, dinner $13-22).

DETOUR TO CHUMASH PAINTED CAVE STATE HISTORIC PARK

Scenic Hwy 154 veers east of Hwy 101 just south of Los Alamos. It passes through the little town of Los Olivos, bisecting Santa Barbara Wine Country, the Santa Ynez Valley and part of the Los Padres National Forest, before rejoining Hwy 101 in Santa Barbara.

About 8 miles north of Santa Barbara, look for the turn-off to Painted Cave Rd and go to **Chumash Painted Cave State Historic Park** (☎ 968-3294; ☷ dawn-dusk) to see vivid pictographs painted by the Chumash about 200 years ago. The cave is protected by a metal screen, so a flashlight is helpful for getting a good view. The rough road to the park isn't suitable for RVs.

SANTA BARBARA

☎ 805 / pop 92,300

Santa Barbara calls itself the American Riviera, and indeed its weather, beauty, cleanliness and affluence make it seem like a playground for the rich. But underneath the glitter there is a real community here and many attractions for travelers – free or otherwise.

The town occupies a prime position between the Pacific Ocean and the Santa Ynez Mountains. Riding the waves or climbing the hills, everyone seems active here, encouraged by the year-round dry and mild climate. But in case there is a little nip in the air, a wisp of fog or a drop of rain, Santa Barbara offers museums, notable architecture, a zoo and a botanic garden.

Santa Barbara is an easy jaunt from San Francisco or Los Angeles, and a relaxing break from those urban centers.

Orientation

All you need to remember in Santa Barbara is that the beach is to the south, not the west, and the mountains are to the north The downtown area is a grid – its main artery is north to south State St, full of shops (too many of them chains), restaurants and bars. Locals identify as from the west side or the east side, State being the dividing line. Milpas St, east of State, is home to many Latino businesses. Cabrillo Blvd hugs the coastline and becomes Coast Village Rd as it enters the eastern suburb of Montecito; heading west it becomes Shoreline Dr. The 'APS,' short for Alameda Padre Serra, runs along the foothills of the mountains to the mission.

Santa Barbara is surrounded by small wealthy communities: Hope Ranch to the west, Montecito and Summerland to the east. The University of California Santa Barbara is just west of Hope Ranch in Isla Vista, and most of Santa Barbara's college crowd lives around the campus or in neighboring Goleta. A cautionary note, as sung by Camper van Beethoven: 'Baby don't you go, don't you go to Goleta.' There's nothing there.

Information

To find out what's happening in town, pick up the free Santa Barbara *Independent*, or check it out online at www.independent.com. Banks and ATMs are on State St.

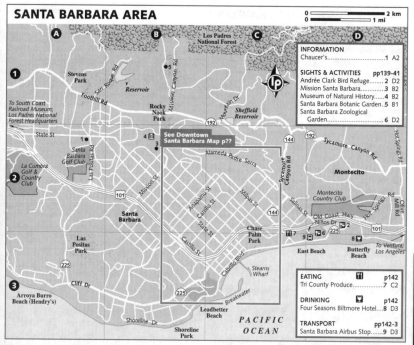

SANTA BARBARA AREA

INFORMATION
Chaucer's..................................1 A2

SIGHTS & ACTIVITIES   pp139-41
Andrée Clark Bird Refuge........2 D2
Mission Santa Barbara..............3 B2
Museum of Natural History......4 B2
Santa Barbara Botanic Garden.5 B1
Santa Barbara Zoological
Garden..6 D2

EATING   p142
Tri County Produce..................7 C2

DRINKING   p142
Four Seasons Biltmore Hotel...8 D3

TRANSPORT   pp142-3
Santa Barbara Airbus Stop.......9 D3

Beachfront Visitors Center (Map p140; ☎ 965-3021; www.santabarbaraca.com; 1 Garden St; ☉ 9am-5pm Mon-Sat, 10am-5pm Sun Sep-Jun; 9am-6pm Jul-Aug) Be sure to get a map of the self-guided 12-block *Red Tile Tour*, an excellent way to take in major downtown sights and historic landmarks.
Chaucer's (Map above; ☎ 682-6787; 3321 State St) The best bookstore in town, with plenty of books and maps on local history, culture and activities. Located in Loreto Plaza where State St meets Positas Rd.
Main Post Office (Map p140; 836 Anacapa St).
St Francis Medical Center (Map p140; ☎ 962-7661, emergency 568-5712; 601 East Micheltorena St) Centrally located.

Sights

Stepping into the 1929 **Santa Barbara County Courthouse** (Map p140; ☎ 962-6464; 1100 Anacapa St; admission free; ☉ 8am-5pm Mon-Fri, 10am-5pm Sat & Sun; tours 10:30am Mon, Tue & Fri, 2pm Mon-Sat) is like stepping into a tale from the *Arabian Nights*. Built in Spanish-Moorish revival style, it features hand-painted ceilings and tiles from Tunisia and Spain. The clock tower offers a panoramic view and the grassy courtyard is great for picnics.

The 'Queen of the Missions,' **Mission Santa Barbara** (Map above; ☎ 682-4713; 2201 Laguna St; adult/child $4/free; ☉ 9am-5pm), sits on a majestic perch half a mile north of downtown. Three adobe structures preceded the current stone version, built in 1820. The church features Chumash wall decorations and the oldest known photographs of the mission; one is from the 1850s. The side courtyard is home to a mature, lush **Moreton Bay fig tree** from Australia (c 1890).

The 65-acre **Santa Barbara Botanic Garden** (Map above; ☎ 682-4726; 1212 Mission Canyon Rd; adult/child ages 1-3/student $5/1/3; ☉ 9am-sunset) is extraordinary – a true must-see. The garden, devoted to California's native flora and divided into sections such as 'canyon,' 'island,' 'desert' and 'meadow,' offers 5.5 miles of trails that meander through cacti, redwoods, oaks and manzanita. Do not miss the 'ceanothus' section, across Mission Canyon Rd from the parking area. Its Porter Trail erupts with springtime wildflowers including the matilija poppy, whose blooms sit atop stems as tall as 8ft. That swooshing noise you hear is the lizards underfoot.

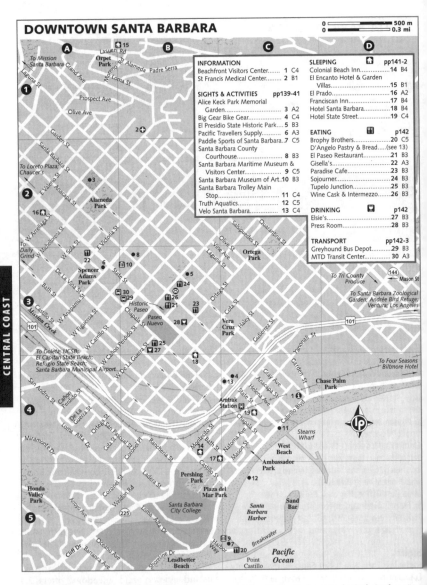

DOWNTOWN SANTA BARBARA

0 — 500 m
0 — 0.3 mi

INFORMATION
Beachfront Visitors Center...... 1 C4
St Francis Medical Center........ 2 B1

SIGHTS & ACTIVITIES   pp139-41
Alice Keck Park Memorial
Garden................................. 3 A2
Big Gear Bike Gear.................. 4 C4
El Presidio State Historic Park.... 5 B3
Pacific Travellers Supply.......... 6 A3
Paddle Sports of Santa Barbara..7 C5
Santa Barbara County
Courthouse.......................... 8 B3
Santa Barbara Maritime Museum &
Visitors Center..................... 9 C5
Santa Barbara Museum of Art.10 B3
Santa Barbara Trolley Main
Stop................................. 11 C4
Truth Aquatics...................... 12 C5
Velo Santa Barbara............... 13 C4

SLEEPING   pp141-2
Colonial Beach Inn.................14 B4
El Encanto Hotel & Garden
Villas.................................15 B1
El Prado.............................16 A2
Franciscan Inn......................17 B4
Hotel Santa Barbara...............18 B4
Hotel State Street.................19 C4

EATING   p142
Brophy Brothers....................20 C5
D'Angelo Pastry & Bread.....(see 13)
El Paseo Restaurant...............21 B3
Gisella's.............................22 A3
Paradise Cafe.......................23 B3
Sojourner............................24 B3
Tupelo Junction....................25 B3
Wine Cask & Intermezzo.........26 B3

DRINKING   p142
Elsie's...............................27 B3
Press Room.........................28 B3

TRANSPORT   pp142-3
Greyhound Bus Depot.............29 B3
MTD Transit Center...............30 A3

El Presidio de Santa Barbara State Historic Park (Map above; ☎ 966-9719; E Cañon Perdido St, btwn Anacapa & Santa Barbara St; admission by donation; ☺ 10:30am-4:30pm), a former 18th-century Spanish fort, harbors some of the city's oldest structures. The chapel's interior explodes in kaleidoscopic color and features some interesting trompe l'oeil effects.

The **Santa Barbara Zoological Garden** (Map p139; ☎ 962-5339; 500 Niños Dr; adult/child under 12 $8/6; ☺ 10am-5pm) is home to 700 animals from around the world, including a crooked-necked giraffe.

At the nearby **Andrée Clark Bird Refuge** (Map p139; 1400 E Cabrillo Blvd; admission free), observe nesting freshwater birds.

Santa Barbara Museum of Art (Map opposite; ☎ 963-4364; 1130 State St; adult/student $7/4, free Thu & 1st Sun of month; ☺ 11am-5pm Tue-Thu & Sat, 11am-9pm Fri, noon-5pm Sun) presents works by European and American masters. Free out front is the only intact mural in the US by world-renowned Mexican muralist David Alfaro Siqueiros, called *Portrait of Mexico Today, 1932*.

Alice Keck Park Memorial Garden (Map opposite; 1500 Santa Barbara St), often called 'Alice Keck Park,' has picture-perfect lily pads in a goldfish pond and a 'sensory path,' along which visually impaired people – or anyone – can listen to recorded messages with instructions to smell and touch certain plants.

Activities

BEACHES & SURFING

Santa Barbara (and environs) is a beach-lover's paradise. **East Beach** is the long sandy stretch between Stearns Wharf and Montecito; it's Santa Barbara's largest, most popular beach. At its eastern end, across from the Biltmore Hotel, Armani swimsuits and Gucci sunglasses abound at **Butterfly Beach**.

Between Stearns Wharf and the harbor, **West Beach** has calm water and is popular with families and tourists staying in nearby motels. On the other side of the harbor, **Leadbetter Beach** is a good spot for surfing and windsurfing, with access to a grassy picnic area atop the cliffs.

West of Santa Barbara, near the junction of Cliff Dr and Las Positas Rd, is popular **Arroyo Burro Beach** (also called Hendry's).

Santa Barbara county has many other spots that surfers frequent, including **Jalama Beach** and the **Rincon Beach Park** (www.sbparks.org; Hwy 101 at Bates Rd).

HIKING

The **Santa Ynez Mountains** are 20 minutes by car from downtown. The hills are full of trails, most of which cut through rugged chaparral and steep canyons offering incredible coastal views. Most also cut in and out of private property; this is allowed, but be respectful and/or prepared for unexpected restrictions. One excellent, moderately strenuous walk is **Hot Springs Loop**. To get there, take Hwy 101 south to the Hot Springs exit; turn left on Hot Springs Rd and drive 3.2 miles. Turn left on Mountain Dr and take it a quarter of a mile to the

trailhead. Don't hike without a map. Find them at **Pacific Travellers Supply** (Map opposite; ☎ 963-4438; 12 W Anapamu St). The Los Padres chapter of the Sierra Club published the excellent *Santa Barbara Trail Guide* (1995), which has access descriptions, maps and notes on geology, flora and fauna. Most of the trails it details still exist.

BICYCLING

Contact the **Santa Barbara Bicycle Coalition** (☎ 962-1479; www.sbbike.org) or pick up the *Santa Barbara County Bike Map* to plan a route into the hills or through Hope Ranch (part of the Pacific Coast Bike Route). You can also just ride along the beach on the Cabrillo Blvd bike path. Rent bikes at **Big Gear Bike Gear** (Map opposite; ☎ 962-5962; 324 State St; cruiser/mountain bike $15/20 per day). Racers or bike tourists can ship their own bikes to **Velo Santa Barbara** (Map opposite; ☎ 884-0917; 331 Motor Way) for assembly ($30).

KAYAKING

Paddle Sports of Santa Barbara (Map opposite; ☎ 899-4921, 888-254-2094; 117B Harbor Way; ☺ 10am-6pm summer; noon-6pm Tue-Fri, 10am-5pm Sat-Sun winter) rents out single/tandem/touring kayaks for $20/30/40 per two hours and $40/50/60 per day. It also leads trips such as a moonlight tour of the harbor ($60).

Tours

Santa Barbara Trolley (Map opposite; ☎ 965-0353; adult/child $12/7) makes a 90-minute loop with narration past Stearns Wharf, the courthouse, the art museum and the mission. Tickets are valid all day, allowing you to get off and on as you please. The first trolley leaves from Stearns Wharf at 10am, and the last one at 4pm (5:30pm June to September).

Sleeping

BUDGET

Mid-May to mid-September budget accommodations are practically nonexistent in Santa Barbara. Even a cheap motel room that may cost just $50 in November can soar to as much as $150.

Hotel State Street (Map opposite; ☎ 966-6586; fax 962-8459; 121 State St; r in summer $40-70) This is one of the best deals in town for those willing to share a bathroom. The building is basic but it's only two blocks from the beach.

A number of nearby state parks have campgrounds. Call ☎ 968-1033 for information on all the following. Right on the beach off Hwy 101 are **Refugio State Beach** (sites $12) and **El Capitan State Beach** (sites Oct-Feb $13, Mar-Sep $16), 17 miles west of town. Refugio is a popular surf spot and student hangout, while El Capitan, perched on low bluffs, is more popular with families. Amenities include flush toilets, hot showers, picnic tables and BBQs. **Gaviota State Park** (sites winter $11, spring & summer $14), 30 miles north of town on Hwy 101 has first-come, first-served sites.

Carpinteria State Beach Campground (☎ 684-2811, reservations 800-444-7275; sites $16-26, hiker/biker $2) Off Hwy 101 (Casitas Pass Rd exit), Carpinteria State Beach has hookups, showers and restrooms

MID-RANGE & TOP END

El Prado (Map p140; ☎ 966-0807, 800-669-8979; 1601 State St; r $90/140 low/high season; ☜) Staff are chatty and nice. The small but clean and pleasant rooms are newly renovated; many overlook the pool. Snacks are available in the lobby.

Franciscan Inn (Map p140; ☎ 963-8845; fax 564-3295; 109 Bath St; r in summer $105-220, winter $85-175; ☜) Staying at the Franciscan Inn feels like having your own home in a quiet Santa Barbara neighborhood. It also has a nice pool, a spa and guest laundry, and its rates include breakfast and afternoon drinks.

Colonial Beach Inn (Map p140; ☎ 966-2219, 800-468-1988; www.sbhotels.com; 223 Castillo St; r $126-188) The clean Colonial Beach has southern decor, and some units have kitchenettes.

Hotel Santa Barbara (Map p140; ☎ 957-9300, 888-259-7700; www.hotelsantabarbara.com; 533 State St; r $129-229) This classy place in the heart of town has a spacious lobby that gives way to quiet rooms with flowery curtains.

El Encanto Hotel & Garden Villas (Map p140; ☎ 687-5000, 800-346-7039; www.elencantohotel.com; 1900 Lasuen Rd; cottages $229-800) Sitting on a hill above the mission, El Encanto has a great view of downtown and the ocean. Its secluded cottages are nestled among 10 acres of lush gardens.

Eating

Sojourner (Map p140; ☎ 965-7922; 134 E Cañon Perdido St; dishes $4-12) The food is delicious, with excellent vegetarian options, and the people working here are down-to-earth.

Tupelo Junction (Map p140; ☎ 899-3100; 739 Chapala St; breakfast & lunch $4-15, dinner $12-21; ☺ Wed-Sat) Wait staff in overalls serve gourmet quality dishes such as red beans and rice with shallots, tomatoes and greens or blackened molasses salmon.

Gisella's (Map p140; ☎ 963-8219; 1311 State St; dishes $10-23) This charming place is just far enough south on State St to walk to and from Santa Barbara's attractions, and just far enough north to cater to more locals than tourists. Extremely friendly staff serve great Italian pizzas and homemade pasta.

Paradise Cafe (Map p140; ☎ 962-4416; 702 Anacapa St; dishes $5-20) This quintessential California café has mouth-watering inventive salads, light pastas, seafood and steak. Eat on the outdoor patio (no smoking) or at the lunch counter. Note the man and woman depicted in the mural...in paradise.

Brophy Brothers (Map p140; ☎ 966-4418; Breakwater; dishes $7-18) Beloved for its clam chowder and seafood, its bubbly atmosphere and its salty setting right in the marina.

Two great breakfast and lunch spots are **D'Angelo Pastry & Bread** (Map p140; ☎ 962-5466; 25 W Gutierrez St; dishes $2-7), with Parisian white coffee cups and good jam on toast; and the **Daily Grind** (☎ 687-4966; 2001 De La Vina St; dishes $2-7; ☺ 5:30am-11pm), with 10-plus types of coffee, including 'industrial,' (strength) and great sandwiches. Taquerias line Milpas St.

Tri County Produce (Map p139; ☎ 965-4558; 335 South Milpas) is a good grocery store.

Drinking

Bars are not hard to find, especially on lower State St, but most are cavernous places with no distinct identity. Exceptions include the **Press Room** (Map p140; ☎ 963-8121; 15 E Ortega St), with posters of punk-rock idols, a juke box and no nonsense barstaff pulling pints; and **Elsie's** (Map p140; 117 W De la Guerra St), a few rooms with couches and a small back patio with twinkling lights.

The most magical place to clutch your cocktail, however, is the **Four Seasons Biltmore Hotel** (Map p139; ☎ 969-2261; 1260 Channel Dr, Montecito). The view of the ocean will make you feel like a movie star.

Getting There & Around

The **Santa Barbara Municipal Airport** (☎ 683-4011; 500 Fowler Rd, Goleta) serves the city.

Santa Barbara Airbus (Map p139; ☎ 964-7759, 800-423-1618) shuttles between LA International Airport (LAX) and Santa Barbara (one way/round-trip $37/69, 14 times a day).

Greyhound (Map p140; ☎ 965-7551; 34 W Carrillo St) has up to nine daily buses to Los Angeles ($12) and up to seven to San Francisco ($32). **Amtrak** (Map p140; lower State St) has direct train and coach services to Los Angeles ($20) and San Luis Obispo ($22).

Santa Barbara is bisected by Hwy 101. For downtown, take the Garden St or Cabrillo Blvd exits. Parking on the street and in any of the 10 municipal lots is free for the first 90 minutes (all day Sunday).

The downtown–waterfront shuttle bus runs every 10 to 15 minutes from 10:15am to 6pm along State St to Stearns Wharf. A second route travels from the zoo to the yacht harbor at 30-minute intervals. The fare is 25¢ per ride; transfers between routes are free.

Buses run by **Santa Barbara Metropolitan Transit District** (MTD; ☎ 683-3702) cost $1 per ride and travel all over town and adjacent communities, including Goleta and Montecito. The **MTD transit center** (Map p140; 1020 Chapala St) has details on route schedules.

SOUTH OF SANTA BARBARA
Ojai
☎ 805 / pop 8000

About 35 miles southeast of Santa Barbara and 14 miles inland from Ventura off Hwy 33, Ojai (pronounced *oh*-hi, meaning 'Moon' to the Chumash) is a town that has long drawn artists and new agers. Several spiritual institutes, including the Krishnamurti Foundation and the Krotona Institute of Theosophy are here. Ojai is famous for the rosy glow that emanates both from its mountains at sunset – the **Pink Moment** – and from the faces emerging from spa treatments. In fact, the scenery here is so stunning that Frank Capra chose it to represent the mythical Shangri-La in his 1937 movie *Lost Horizon*.

For information, go to the **Ojai Chamber of Commerce** (☎ 646-8126; www.the-ojai.org; 150 W Ojai Ave; 🕑 9:30am-4:30pm Mon-Fri, 10am-4pm Sat & Sun).

Ojai is famous for its annual **Ojai Music Festival** (☎ 646-2053; www.ojaifestival.org), a long-standing classical music fest.

Arcade Plaza, a maze of mission revival-style buildings on Ojai Ave (the main thoroughfare), contains cutesy shops and art galleries.

The **Table of Contents Book Store** has a varied range and a café. **Firehouse Pottery & Gallery** (☎ 646-9453; www.firehouse-pottery.com; 109 S Montgomery St) is a spacious place with ceramics and interesting hand-blown glassware.

The 9-mile **Ojai Valley Trail**, converted from old railway tracks, is popular with walkers, joggers, cyclists and equestrians. It links with Ventura's Foster Park.

Ojai Valley Inn & Spa (☎ 646-5511, 800-422-6524; r & ste $279-450; 🏊), at the western end of town, is a luxurious golf and spa resort with amazing gardens and architecture. A funkier place with little red cottages is the **Rose Garden Inn** (☎ 800-799-1881; www.rosegardeninnofojai.com; 615 West Ojai Ave; r low/high season $71/137, cottages $125/219; 🏊).

Mingle with locals at the **farmers market** (301 E Matilija St; 🕑 9am-1pm Sun). Across the street is friendly Java & Joe, with good coffee.

Get 'grrrowllers' (glass jugs) of takeout Big Bad John Brown or Red Potato Caboose Ale at the small **Ojai Brew Pub** (☎ 805-646-8837; 423 E Ojai Ave No 101; dishes $4-10) or dine in.

The only direct bus service is from the city of Ventura. Take the Greyhound bus or Amtrak train to Ventura, then board **SCAT** (☎ 487-4222) bus No 16 ($1, 45 minutes, hourly) at Main & Figueroa Sts, which goes straight to downtown Ojai.

Ventura
☎ 805 / pop 104,500

Ventura has a charming historic downtown along its Main St, but otherwise is first and foremost a setting off point for travelers en route to the Channel Islands. The **visitors center** (☎ 648-2075, 800-333-2989; 89 S California St, Suite C; 🕑 8:30am-5pm Mon-Fri, 9am-5pm Sat & 10am-4pm Sun) is well stocked.

Ventura Harbor, southwest of Hwy 101 via Harbor Blvd, is where boats depart for the Channel Islands (p144). Even if you don't embark on an island adventure, **Channel Islands National Park Visitors Center** (☎ 658-5730; 1901 Spinnaker Dr; 🕑 8:30am-5pm) has an interesting natural history display and a three-story lookout, from which you can see the islands on a clear day.

Since boats depart early, you may want to stay in Ventura. **Bella Maggiore Inn** (☎ 652-0277; 67 S California St; r $75-175) is a 'haunted' B&B with a courtyard restaurant. The **Vagabond Inn** (☎ 648-5371; 756 East Thompson Blvd; r $90-150; 🏊) is right near a beach-access walkway.

There's also camping and RV-ing nearby at **Ventura Beach RV Resort** (☎ 643-9137; 800 Main St; RV sites $44). Heading south on Hwy 101 take the Main St exit and turn right; heading north, exit at California St, turn right on California and left on Main; travel a mile to the resort entrance. Also north of town on Hwy 101, take the 'State Beaches' exit for **Faria County Campground** (☎ 654-3951; tent/RV sites $22/35); it's on the left 3 miles after exiting.

Caffeinate at locally owned **Kelly's Coffee & Fudge Factory** (☎ 641-9951; 533 E Main St) or buy thin-crust pizzas and yummy pasta at **Capriccio Restaurant** (☎ 643-7115; 298 Main St; dishes $8-15) serves thin-crust pizzas and yummy pasta.

Greyhound (☎ 653-0164; 291 E Thompson Blvd) runs up to five buses daily from Los Angeles ($12) en route to Santa Barbara ($8.25).

CHANNEL ISLANDS NATIONAL PARK

☎ 805

The Channel Islands are an eight-island chain lying off the coast from Santa Barbara almost as far south as San Diego. Five of the islands – San Miguel, Santa Rosa, Santa Cruz, Anacapa and tiny Santa Barbara – comprise the Channel Islands National Park. The islands have unique flora and fauna and extensive tidepools and kelp forests. More than 100 plant and animal species found here are not found anywhere else in the world, which is why the park is sometimes nicknamed 'California's Galapagos.' Note that many of these species are plants – do not expect to disembark and immediately see a parade of unknown wildlife. The feeling is a bit subtler than the National Park Service brochure illustration leads one to believe.

Originally inhabited by the Chumash and Gabrielino Indians (who were taken to the mainland missions in the early 1800s), the islands were subsequently taken over by sheep ranchers and the US Navy until the mid-1970s, when conservation efforts began. San Miguel, Santa Rosa, Anacapa and Santa Barbara Islands are now owned by the **National Park Service** (NPS; www.nps.gov/chis), which also owns about 20% of Santa Cruz. The NPS has its work cut out for it. Human use in the modern era has left a far-reaching legacy. In ranching days, livestock overgrazed, causing erosion, and rabbits fed on native plants. The US military even practiced bombing techniques on San Miguel. Still an environmental threat today, remaining feral pigs dig deep trenches looking for bulbs (you may encounter these pigs – or signs of their hooved handiwork), while invasive plant species like mustard, ice plant and range grasses squeeze out native plants.

Anacapa, which is actually three separate islets, offers a memorable introduction to the islands' ecology. This is the home of thousands of brown pelicans who nest and raise chicks here. It's a conservation success story: in 1970 only one chick survived, on West Anacapa. Scientists figured out that DDT (a pesticide) flowing from the sewage system into the ocean, made its way into the kelp that fish ate. When pelicans feasted on contaminated fish, the DDT caused the shells of their eggs to become so fragile the eggs broke under the parent bird's weight. This discovery led to a 1972 ban on DDT.

Santa Cruz, the largest island, has two mountain ranges with peaks as high as 2450ft (Mt Diablo). Here you can swim, snorkel, scuba dive and kayak. There are excellent hikes, too. One is the **Scorpion Canyon–Island Jay hike**. Starting in the upper campground, scramble across the old stream bed and then head steeply uphill to the old oil well and fantastic views. Connect with Smugglers Rd atop the hill and loop back to Scorpion Anchorage.

The Chumash called **Santa Rosa** 'Wima' or 'driftwood' because of the logs that often came ashore here. They built plank canoes called *tomols* from the logs. This island has rare Torrey pines, sandy beaches and nearly 200 bird species. In 1959 an archaeologist hiking in **Arlington Canyon** discovered a human femur 30ft below the surface of the ground – exposed by stream bank erosion. 'Arlington Woman' dates from the end of the last Ice Age, about 13,000 years ago.

San Miguel, the most remote of the four northern islands, offers solitude and a wilderness experience, but it's often shrouded in fog and is very windy. Some sections are off-limits to prevent disruption of the fragile ecosystem.

Santa Barbara is home to the humongous northern elephant seal and Xantus' murrelets, a bird that nests in cliff crevices.

The islands receive most of their visitors from June to September; however, the nicest times to visit are during the spring wildflower season (April and May) and in September and October, when the weather conditions are the calmest.

Sleeping

All the islands have primitive **campgrounds** (☎ reservations 800-365-2267; www.nps.gov; sites $10), which are open year-round. Each one has pit toilets and picnic tables, but you must take everything in (and out, including trash). Water is only available on Santa Rosa and Santa Cruz Islands. Due to fire danger, campfires are not allowed, but enclosed camp stoves are OK. Be prepared to carry your stuff up to 1.5 miles to the campground from the landing areas.

The campground on Santa Barbara is large, grassy and surrounded by hiking trails, while the one on Anacapa is high, rocky and isolated. Camping on San Miguel, with its unceasing wind, fog and volatile weather, is only for the hardy. Santa Rosa's campground is sheltered by a canyon with wonderful views of Santa Cruz, whose own site is within a eucalyptus grove in a canyon (it can be very windy). Del Norte, a backcountry campground on Santa Cruz Island, is in a shaded oak grove a 3.5-mile hike away from the landing.

Getting There & Away

To get to the Channel Islands National Park Visitors Center and boat docks when going north on Hwy 101, exit at Victoria Ave, turn left on Victoria and right on Olivas Park Dr to Harbor Blvd; Olivas Park Dr runs straight into Spinnaker Dr. Going south, exit Seaward onto Harbor Blvd, then turn right on Spinnaker Dr.

Island Packers (☎ 642-1393, recorded information ☎ 642-7688; www.islandpackers.com; 1867 Spinnaker Dr), near the visitors center, offers day trips and packages to all the islands. Rates range from $20 to $60; call for details. Overnight campers pay more. The company's whale-watching tours cost $24/16 per adult/child for the 3½-hour gray whale trip (January to March) and $58/47 for the all-day blue and humpback whale-watching trip (July to September). Island Packer staff are knowledgeable. En route to the islands they will point out – and slow down for – marine life such as dolphins and whales. They also talk about the history and ecology of the islands, and lead hikes when park rangers are busy.

Truth Aquatics (☎ 962-1127; www.truthaquatics .com; 301 W Cabrillo Blvd), the park's Santa Barbara-based operator, offers similar excursions to Island Packers.

Most trips require a minimum number of participants and may be canceled anytime due to surf and weather conditions. This means if you camp overnight and the seas are rough the next day, you could get stuck on the island. In any case, landing is never guaranteed. Reservations are recommended for weekend, holiday and summer trips, and credit card or advance payment is required.

Boating to the islands can be rough; those prone to seasickness should take preventive drugs, and might even want to consider taking a 25-minute flight to Santa Rosa Island with **Channel Islands Aviation** (☎ 987-1301; 305 Durley Ave, Camarillo; trips $125-175).

Los Angeles Area

CONTENTS

Los Angeles (city population 3.7 million, county population 9.8 million) is an urban area of baffling proportions, with no real center. It's a patchwork of communities, separate worlds, linked by an astounding maze of highways, choked with traffic. You need to pull off, pull over and explore one neighborhood at a time. There's something for everyone, from world-class art museums to working artists, canyon hikes to carousels, dark bars to sunny beaches.

Inhabited first by Chumash and Gabrielino Indians, in 1781 people from the two Mission communities of the area founded an agricultural community, El Pueblo de Nuestro Señora la Reina de los Angeles del Río Porciúncula (The Town of Our Lady the Queen of the Angels of the Porciuncula River) that grew into a thriving farming community. Statehood and city incorporation came in 1850, and railroads arrived in 1876 and 1885. Then came the fruit industry, the harbor, the discovery of oil, the aircraft industry and...drumroll please...the film 'Industry'. Through it all LA has survived earthquakes, race riots and, so far, an unquenchable thirst for water.

Get out the dark glasses; it's sunny here. The average temperature is 70°F, with summer highs usually in the mid-80s to low 90s and winter lows in the mid-50s to low 60s. Offshore breezes keep beach communities 10° to 15°F cooler. Evenings tend to be cool, even in summer. Rain falls almost exclusively between November and April, with storms raging in January and February.

HIGHLIGHTS

- Taking the Mt Hollywood Hiking Trail in **Griffith Park** (p159)
- Sipping on a happy-hour margarita at **Toppers** (p166), high above Santa Monica
- Strolling down Chinatown's **Chung King Rd** (p153), full of old herbalists and young artists
- Wandering along the canals of **Venice** (p166)
- Marvelling at the architecture and tile handiwork at Malibu's **Adamson House** (p164)
- Enjoying the **Getty Center** (p149) art collection, from Michelangelo to Van Gogh to Manuel Alvarez Bravo
- Eating at **Grand Central Market** (p156), where anything goes but chain stores
- Visiting the sublime **Greene & Greene Gamble House** (p160) in Pasadena
- Dancing on the deck of the **Queen Mary** (p170) in Long Beach
- Picnicking on the **Laguna Beach** (p173) waterfront

LOS ANGELES AREA

INLAND LOS ANGELES

Downtown is a collection of neighborhoods: There's Chinatown, Little Tokyo and El Pueblo de Los Angeles. Nearby is one of the most handsome train stations in the country and then there's Grand Central Market, where you can find every edible item imaginable. The Arts District buzzes with the collective creativity of students at the Southern California Institute of Architecture. And don't miss the LA 'River,' a concrete trench great for inline skating, if not fishing.

West of Downtown, Hollywood doesn't exude the glamour associated with its name, but no one has stolen the stars from the sidewalk yet, so it's worth a visit for celebrity lovers. Nearby neighborhoods include trendy Silver Lake and friendly Los Feliz ('Fe-liss') with good restaurants and bars. West Hollywood, LA's gay and lesbian epicenter, has the Sunset Strip. Most TV and movie studios are north of Hollywood in the San Fernando Valley.

ORIENTATION

Los Angeles is bordered to the north by the San Gabriel Mountains and to the west by the Pacific. Downtown is 12 miles east of the ocean. Hollywood is a vast area bordering Griffith Park, Los Feliz and Silver Lake, Melrose Ave and West Hollywood. Everything south of Hollywood, spread west from Downtown to Beverly Hills, can be called 'Mid-City.' East LA and South Central border Downtown.

INLAND LA FOR THE WEEKEND

Have breakfast at the **Farmers Market** and then head for the **Getty Center**. When you've exhausted yourself on art, have a lazy lunch at Groundwork in the **Arts District** and walk through **El Pueblo**, **Little Tokyo** and **Chinatown**. Hit **Hank's Bar** in the Stillwell Hotel and then dance the night away at the **Mayan**. After a glamorous stay at the **Millenium Biltmore Hotel**, head to Pasadena to see the **Gamble House** and the **Huntington Museum** and botanic garden. Return to the city and dine in **Los Feliz** at Simply Thai. If you can still stand...swing dance at the **Derby**.

LA's coastal communities are detailed in the Coastal Los Angeles section (p162).

Maps

Lonely Planet makes a laminated Los Angeles map available in bookstores or at www .lonelyplanet.com. Detailed street maps are available at gas stations and bookstores. The Automobile Association of Southern California maps are useful.

INFORMATION
Bookstores

Book Soup (☎ 310-659-3110; 8818 Sunset Blvd) For general interest, head to this hip bookstore in West Hollywood, which has a sizable gay and lesbian section.
Form Zero Books (Map p154; ☎ 213-620-1920; 811 Traction Ave) Architecture specialist in the Arts district.

Internet Access

Central Library (Map p154; ☎ 213-228-7000; 630 W Fifth St; 😊 10am-8pm Mon-Thu, 10am-6pm Fri-Sat; 1pm-5pm Sun) You can check email here for free.

Media

Major newspapers include the *Los Angeles Times*, the San Fernando Valley–based *Daily News* and Spanish Language *La Opinión*. The *LA Weekly* (http://laweekly.com) is a thick freebie that appears every Thursday and is good for events listings. For showbiz news, pick up *Variety* and the *Hollywood Reporter*.

Medical Services

Hollywood Presbyterian Hospital (Map p157; ☎ 323-660-5350; 1300 N Vermont Ave)
UCLA Medical Center (Map pp150-1; ☎ 310-825-9111; 10833 LeConte Ave)

Post

Call ☎ 800-275-8777 to locate the nearest post office.

Telephone

All telephone numbers in the Inland LA section are accompanied by the appropriate area code (LA has five).

Tourist Offices

Downtown LA Visitors Center (Map p154; ☎ 213-689-8822; www.lacvb.com; 685 S Figueroa St; 😊 8am-5:30pm Mon-Fri) Offers maps, brochures, lodging information and tickets to theme parks and other attractions.
Little Tokyo Visitors Center (Map p154; ☎ 213-613-1911; 307 E 1st St; 😊 10am-5:30pm Mon-Sat)

DANGERS & ANNOYANCES

Walking around in the daytime is generally safe anywhere, although extra caution should be exercised in East Los Angeles, South Central, some sections of Hollywood and the MacArthur Park neighborhood west of Downtown, which are plagued by interracial gang activity, drugs and prostitution. Stay away from these areas after dark. Ditto for Venice (p166). Also exercise a bit of extra caution in Silver Lake and West Hollywood. Westside communities such as Westwood and Beverly Hills, as well as the beach towns (except Venice) and Pasadena, are generally the safer areas.

LA is infamous for smog. On bad air quality days (usually on hot summer days), even a healthy person can suffer from an irritated throat. It's best to avoid strenuous outdoor activities on days like this.

SIGHTS & ACTIVITIES
Art Museums
GETTY CENTER

The **Getty Center** (Map pp150-1; ☎ 310-440-7300; www.getty.edu/museum; 1200 Getty Center Dr; admission free; ☒ 10am-6pm Tue-Thu & Sun, 10am-9pm Fri & Sat) is on a 110-acre Richard Meier–designed 'campus.' Four two-story pavilions house the permanent collection, while a fifth presents changing exhibitions. Enjoy paintings, sculptures, illuminated manuscripts, drawings and furniture, and the compound's architecture, landscaping and superb views.

Some recent acquisitions include a pre-Impressionist painting by Edgar Degas, *The Convalescent*; and *Head with Horns*, a rediscovered wooden sculpture made by Paul Gauguin in Tahiti.

Admission is free, but parking reservations ($5) are mandatory – except after 4pm weekdays, all day weekends and on any day for college students. Alternatively, park in the lot on Sepulveda Blvd at Constitution Ave (just north of Wilshire Blvd) and take the free shuttle. MTA bus No 761 works too.

The **Getty Villa**, a recreation of a 1st-century Roman country house and the site of the original museum, is being renovated. Check the website for updates.

LOS ANGELES COUNTY MUSEUM OF ART

The **LACMA** (☎ 323-857-6000; www.lacma .org; 5905 Wilshire Blvd; adult/student/child $7/5/1; ☒ noon-8pm Mon, Tue & Thu, noon-9pm Fri, 11am-8pm Sat & Sun)

HOLLYWOOD CITY PASS

The **Hollywood City Pass** (www.citypass.net; adult/child age 3-11 $69/39) is a ticket booklet with coupons good for one-time admission within a 30-day period to Universal Studios Hollywood, American Cinematheque at the Egyptian Theatre, the Autry Museum of Western Heritage, the Museum of Television & Radio, the Hollywood Entertainment Museum and the Petersen Automotive Museum. A city tour with Starline Tours is included. Purchase at participating sites, the Downtown LA Visitors Center or online.

houses European art, including Italian baroque paintings and works by Rembrandt, Degas and Gauguin; and Ancient art from Egypt, Greece, Rome, Turkey and Iran is also on display.

MUSEUM OF CONTEMPORARY ART

The acclaimed **Museum of Contemporary Art** (Map p154; MOCA; ☎ 213-626-6222; www.moca-la.org; 250 S Grand Ave; admission $8, free after 5pm Thu; ☒ 11am-5pm Tue-Sun, 11am-8pm Thu) is housed in a stunning building by Japanese architect Isozaki Arata. Its collection of paintings, sculptures and photographs from the 1940s to the present includes works by Mark Rothko, Jackson Pollock and Willem de Kooning.

WATTS TOWERS

South Central's main attraction is the intriguing **Watts Towers** (☎ 213-847-4646; 1765 E 107th St; adult/concession/child under 17 $2/1/free; tours half-hourly 11am-2:30pm Tue-Fri, 10:30am-2:30pm Sat, 12:30pm-3pm Sun). On the National Register of Historic Places, this curious and unique folk-art monument is the life's work of Italian immigrant Simon Rodia. In 1921 Rodia set out to 'make something big' – and then spent the next 33 years at it. Supporting his towers are slender columns containing steel reinforcement, which he wrapped with wire mesh and covered with cement by hand. Incorporated into the facade are glass, mirrors, sea shells, rocks, ceramic tile and pottery.

The adjacent **Watts Towers Art Center** (☎ 213-847-4646; admission free) has changing art exhibits by local and national artists.

LOS ANGELES AREA

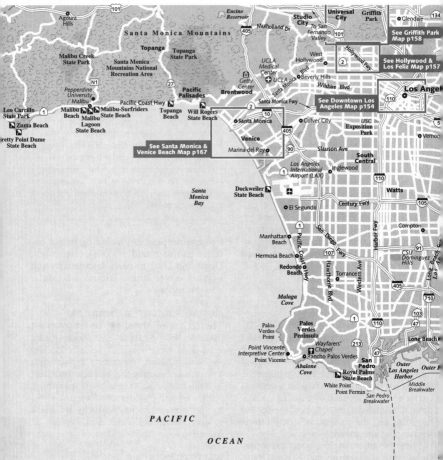

PACIFIC

OCEAN

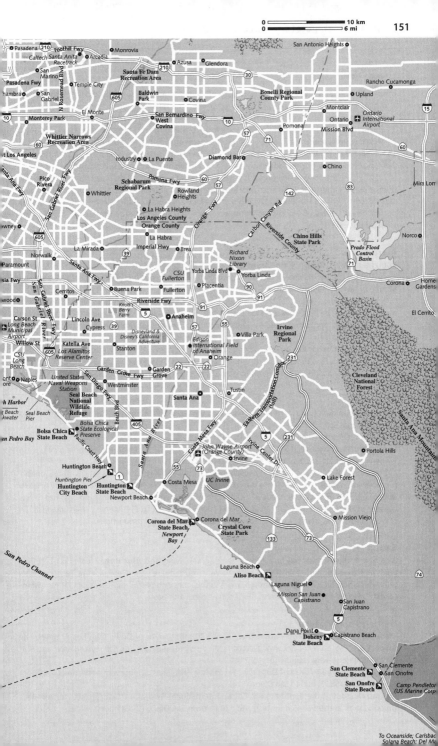

DISNEYLAND

Innovative animator and enigmatic figure Walt Disney tapped into something deep in the American psyche when, in 1955, he decided to open a theme park. The world-famous theme park is based in Anaheim, 30 miles south of Downtown, and is still going strong.

Disneyland (☎ 714-781-4565, 213-626-8605; www.disneyland.com; ✆ 8am-midnight summer, 10am-8pm off-season) is 'imagineered' to be the happiest place on earth, from the impeccable, pastel sidewalks to the personal hygiene of the roughly 21,000 park employees, called 'cast members.' In February 2001, a second park opened adjacent to the original: **Disney's California Adventure**.

You'll need at least one day for each park, and more if you want to go on all the rides. One-day admission to either park is $45, or $35 for children aged three to nine. 'Multi-Day Park Hopper Tickets' cost $114/90 for three days and $141/111 for four days of admission within a two-week period. These tickets give access to both parks, but you can only visit one park per day. Parking is an additional $8.

Attractions

You enter Disneyland on **Main Street USA**, which is a cheery re-creation of small-town America circa 1900, with myriad shops and the **Candy Palace**. Have your picture taken with Mickey and Minnie or any of the other jumbo Disney characters.

Main Street ends in the Central Plaza. On your right is **Tomorrowland**, home to many of the high-tech rides. The best ones are **Star Tours**, where you find yourself clamped into a StarSpeeder vehicle for a wild and bumpy ride through deep space. **Space Mountain** will have you screaming long and loud as you hurtle into complete darkness at a frightening speed.

Disney's California Adventure, paying homage to California, is divided into three themed sections on 55 acres. Don't miss the astonishing **Soarin' Over California**, a virtual hang-gliding flight over the state's most beautiful landscapes and sights, including the Golden Gate Bridge.

Sleeping

Many Anaheim motels and hotels offer packages that combine lodging with tickets to Disneyland and other area attractions.

About 5 miles north of Disneyland is **HI Fullerton** (☎ 714-738-3721; fax 714-738-0925; 1700 N Harbor Blvd; dm members/nonmembers $16.50/18.50; closed 11am-4pm; ⓟ ▣), a clean and friendly facility with 20 beds in three dorms, a nice porch, Internet access and kitchen facilities.

The area around Disneyland – especially Harbor Blvd and Katella Ave – teems with reasonably priced accommodations. Try **Alamo Inn** (☎ 714-635-8070, 800-378-9696; fax 714-778-3307; 1140 W Katella Ave; r $49-99; ⓟ ⚄), a generic but pleasant option with a small pool and free movies. Top-End is the rule at **Disney's Grand Californian Hotel** (☎ 714-635-2300; fax 714-300-7300; 1600 S Disneyland Dr; r $275-350; ⓟ), a Craftsman-style place with a lobby of cathedral proportions.

Eating

A captive audience must pay any price. In the original Disneyland, **Blue Bayou** (dishes $23-29) offers Louisiana-style cuisine. At Disney's California Adventure, there's the **Golden Vine Terrace** (dishes $10), which has outdoor seating and gourmet sandwiches and pastas. In Downtown Disney, **Rainforest Cafe** (☎ 714-772-0413; dishes $10-25) serves pizza and pasta.

Getting There & Away

Disneyland is just off I-5 on Harbor Blvd, about 30 miles south of Downtown Los Angeles. The **Airport Bus** (☎ 800-772-5299; www.airportbus.com) runs between LAX and Disneyland area hotels at least hourly (one-way/round-trip $16/25).

Greyhound (☎ 714-999-1256; 100 W Winston Rd) has frequent departures to/from Downtown LA ($8.25) and to San Diego ($14).

Amtrak stops at the depot next to Edison International Field of Anaheim. Tickets to/from LA's Union Station are $9.50 (45 minutes), and $20 to/from San Diego (three hours).

LOS ANGELES AREA

Downtown
FINANCIAL DISTRICT
Decide for yourself if the **Bunker Hill Steps** (Map p154), saving Angelinos from walking straight up a hill (hear the San Franciscans laughing), are really 'more pleasing' than the Spanish Steps in Rome, as the plaque says.

CHINATOWN
LA's Chinese community dates back to the mid-19th century, with many Chinese arriving several years later to work on the railroad. In the 1930s, the original Chinatown was demolished to make way for Union Station. These days, the 16-square-block Chinatown is north of El Pueblo along Broadway and Hill St. Though fewer than 5% of LA's 170,000 Chinese make their home here, this district is still a social and cultural center and is continually evolving, most recently beckoning artists.

Browse the **Chinatown Farmers Market** (Map p154; 727 North Hill; 3pm-7pm Thu) at the public parking lot between Alpine and Ord to be immersed in the community. **Kong Chow Temple** (Map p154; 931 N Broadway; donation box) is on the 2nd floor of the Kong Chow Benevolent Association. Enter, ascend the stairs and ring the bell. If someone is there you'll be let in...but don't expect a lot of interpretation of the site.

North of here, off Hill Street, is a T-shaped pedestrian-only area called **Chung King Rd** (Map p154), home to Chinese businesses and artists' live-work-show spaces. Visit the **Black Dragon Society** (213-620-0030; www.black-dragon-society.com; 961 Chung King Rd) and **Diannepreuss Gallery** (213-687-8226; 945 Chung King Rd).

EL PUEBLO DE LOS ANGELES
This 44-acre State Historic Park commemorates the founding site of LA and preserves some of the city's earliest buildings. The park's main attraction is **Olvera St**, a narrow passageway which has been an open-air Mexican marketplace since 1930. Volunteers lead free one-hour walking tours of El Pueblo on Tuesday to Saturday mornings from the **visitors center** (213-628-3562; 622 N Main St; 10am-3pm Mon-Sat) in the Sepulveda House (1887).

To be transported to a more glamorous era than the present, loiter in LA's 1939 **Union Station** (Map p154; Alameda St).

LA FOR CHILDREN

It's easy to keep kids entertained in LA and surrounds. There's plenty to explore on the beach, in the mountains and even in the urban core. Here is a short list of suggestions:

- Aquarium of the Pacific, Long Beach (p170)
- Autry Museum of Western Heritage, Griffith Park (p159)
- Cabrillo Marine Aquarium, San Pedro (p169)
- Santa Monica Pier (p165)
- Los Angeles Zoo, Griffith Park (p159)
- *Queen Mary*, Long Beach (p170)

Generations of Angelenos have grown up with **Bob Baker Marionette Theater** (Map p154; 213-250-9995; 1345 W 1st St, Echo Park). Since 1963, it has enthralled kids with its singing and dancing marionettes and stuffed animals.

In Santa Monica, the **Puppet and Magic Center** (Map 166; 310-656-0483; 1255 2nd St) is a 40-seat theater with regularly scheduled performances as well as puppet workshops and a puppet museum.

The Calendar supplement of the Thursday *Los Angeles Times* as well as the Sunday Calendar section have special listings of youth-appropriate activities.

LITTLE TOKYO
Established by Japanese immigrants in the 1880s, **Little Tokyo** was effectively decimated during WWII by the internment of US-born Japanese into camps. The community took decades to recover but today, Little Tokyo is the social, economic and cultural center for nearly 250,000 Japanese Americans.

On view at the **Japanese American National Museum** (Map p154; JANM; 213-625-0414; 369 E 1st St; adult/senior/student $6/5/3, free after 5pm Thu & every 3rd Thu of month; 10am-5pm Tue-Wed & Fri-Sun, 10am-8pm Thu) are objects of work and worship, photographs and art relating to the history of Japanese immigration to, and life in, the USA.

Most charming is the **Japanese Village Plaza** (Map p154), an outdoor, pedestrian-only shopping area, with sushi bars, and shops.

0 |===========| 600 m
0 |===========| 0.4 mi

SIGHTS & ACTIVITIES	pp149-55
Brewery Art Complex.................	6 F1
Chinatown Farmers Market.........	7 A1
Japanese American National Museum..8 A3	
Kong Chow Temple.....................	9 A1
Museum of Contemporary Art	
(MOCA)...................................	10 C2
Sepulveda House........................	(see 3)
Southern California Institute of	
Architecture............................	11 E3

SLEEPING	🛏	pp155-6
Best Western Dragon Gate Inn.....		12 A1
Figueroa Hotel...........................		13 B3
Millennium Biltmore....................		14 C3
Stillwell Hotel...........................		15 C3

EATING	🍴	pp156-60
Chow Fun.................................		16 A2
Clifton's Brookdale Cafeteria.......		17 C3
Frying Fish Sushi........................		18 A3
Grand Central Market..................		19 D3
Groundwork..............................		20 E3
Joy-Mart..................................		21 A3
Ocean Seafood..........................		22 A1
Shabu Shabu House....................		(see 21)
Via Cafe...................................		(see 27)

DRINKING	pp156-60
Hank's Bar................................	(see 15)

ENTERTAINMENT	🎭	pp160-1
Bob Baker Marionette Theater......		23 C1
Dorothy Chandler Pavilion...........		(see 24)
Mark Taper Forum......................		24 D2
The Mayan................................		25 C4

SHOPPING	🛍	p161
No Reply..................................		26 A3
Old Chinatown Plaza..................		27 A1
Shop Chuey..............................		(see 27)
Wing Wa Hing Gifts & Arts..........		28 A1

TRANSPORT	pp161-2

INFORMATION	
Central Library............................	1 C3
Downtown LA Visitors Center........	2 C3
El Pueblo Visitors Center..............	3 A2
Form Zero Books........................	4 E3
Little Tokyo Visitors Center...........	5 A3

Echo Park

Chinatown

El Pueblo de Los Angeles

Civic Center

Civic Center/Tom Bradley

Little Tokyo

Arts District

Financial District

Pershing Square

7th St/Metro Center

Jewelry District

Fashion District

South Park

Los Angeles Convention Center

Bunker Hill Steps

LA County Museum of Art

Metro Red Line

Metro Blue Line

Union Station/Patsaouras Transit Plaza

Terminal Annex Post Office

Gateway Transit Center

Japanese Village Plaza

James Irvine Garden

Flower Market

Metrolink Station

See Enlargement

To Los Angeles; Watts Towers

To Santa Monica

ARTS DISTRICT

In the somewhat deserted industrial section south and east of Little Tokyo is a creative zone. The **Southern California Institute of Architecture** (Map opposite; Sci-Arc; ☎ 213-613-2200; 960 E 3rd St) is here in a low structure housing a gallery and many minds hard at work contemplating the built environment. **Form Zero Books** (see Bookstores on p148) holds readings and displays Sci-Arc work.

Northeast, across LA's trickling 'river' is the **Brewery Art Complex** (Map opposite; 2100 N Main St), a self-contained artists' colony.

Hollywood

This may be your only chance to step on the stars, more than 2000 of them, embedded in the sidewalk along the **Hollywood Walk of Fame** (Map p157), stretching east on Hollywood Blvd from La Brea Ave to Gower St and south along Vine St between Yucca St and W Sunset Blvd. Call the **Hollywood Chamber of Commerce** (☎ 323-489-8311) for a schedule of induction ceremonies.

In 1927, movie mogul Sid Grauman conceived what would become the most famous of Hollywood movie palaces, **Mann's Chinese Theater** (Map p157; ☎ 323-464-8111; 6925 Hollywood Blvd). To get inside, see one of the first-run films shown here. Or just enjoy the famous forecourt, where more than 150 legends of the silver screen have left handprints.

Bicycling

Visit **LA Bike Tours & Cyclery** (Map p157; ☎ 888-775-2453; 6731 Hollywood Blvd; ⏰ 10am-8pm Mon-Sat, 10am-6pm Sun, closed 2-3pm) to rent a bike ($20/10/60 per day/additional day/week) and get route advice. The staff heads into the Hollywood hills for an hour's ride daily from 2pm; perhaps you may join them. Call to ask about other specialty LA bike tours.

TOURS

Universal Studios (Map p158; ☎ 818-508-9600; 100 Universal City Plaza; adult/child $43/35; ask about special packages; ⏰ vary seasonally) is the world's largest movie and TV studio, and sprawls across 413 acres. Head for the 45-minute **Backlot Tour**, part educational trip, part thrill-ride. A tram whisks you and about 250 other visitors past the studio's maze of 35 sound stages with voice and video narration by Ron Howard. You'll see where scenes from *Jurassic Park* and *Apollo 13* were filmed,

and rumble past outdoor sets such as Courthouse Square, best known from *Back to the Future*; and the Bates Hotel featured in Hitchcock's *Psycho*.

For a rare behind-the-scenes glimpse of one of Hollywood's oldest movie and TV production facilities, take the two-hour **Warner Bros Studios Tour** (Map p158; ☎ 818-972-8687; 4000 Warner Blvd, Burbank; tours $32, half-hourly 9am-3pm). Reservations are required; children must be over eight years of age.

FESTIVALS & EVENTS

Biggies in LA are the January 1 **Tournament of Roses Parade & Rose Bowl** in Pasadena, a celebration of football; the **Venice Art Walk**, an artists' open studios event in May; and the **Gay & Lesbian Pride Celebration** in June. See p209 for a comprehensive listing of festivals statewide.

SLEEPING
Downtown

Stillwell Hotel (Map p154; ☎ 213-627-1151, 800-553-4774; 838 S Grand Ave; s/d from $49/59) A touch of 1920s glamour survives here for budget prices. This historic property features 250 basic but nicely appointed rooms with TV. The adjacent bar, Hank's, with its plaid carpet and booths, is a fine place to shun the LA sun.

Best Western Dragon Gate Inn (Map p154; ☎ 213-617-3077, reservations 800-282-9999; www.dragongateinn.com; 818 N Hill St; r $70-139, ste $139-179; Ⓟ) This family-run hotel in the heart of Chinatown exudes Asian flair in its decor and friendly attentiveness in its service. Rooms are sparkling and the pedestrian-only entrance courtyard has a café, post office and even an herbalist. Stay here for easy access to transport (at the time of research, the Chinatown Metro Rail station was about to open).

Figueroa Hotel (Map p154; ☎ 213-627-8971, 800-421-9092; www.figueroahotel.com; 939 S Figueroa St, South Park; s $94-124, d $104-136, ste $165-195) A 1927 gem, this hotel has a lofty lobby with touches of Morocco and Spanish hacienda – the theme continues in the rooms. The outdoor pool has big umbrellas for relaxing under, and there's also an open-air bar.

Millennium Biltmore (Map p154; ☎ 213-624-1011, 800-245-8673; www.regalbiltmore.com; 506 S Grand Ave; r $129-275; Ⓟ) This over-the-top establishment, with a decadent tiled indoor pool room, has a pedigree going back to 1923.

Hollywood & West Hollywood

Student Inn International Hostel (Map opposite; ☎ 323-469-6781, 800-557-7038 in LA only, www.student inn.com; 7038½ Hollywood Blvd; dm/r $15/43) Undergoing some upgrading but not yet sparkling, this hostel is right in the thick of Hollywood. The vibe is 20-something, and alcohol and smoking are permitted.

Highland Gardens Hotel (Map opposite; ☎ 323-850-0535, 800-404-5472, www.highlandgardenshotel.com; 7047 Franklin Ave; r $75, ste $85-175; P ⚲) This is très LA, wrapped around a leafy courtyard and pool. Spacious, clean rooms come with breakfast. 'Industry' types in town on business kip here long-term. And it was at the Highland Gardens, in room 105, that Janis Joplin overdosed on October 3, 1970.

Magic Castle Hotel (Map opposite; ☎ 323-851-0800, 800-741-4915; www.magiccastlehotel.com; 7025 Franklin Ave; r & ste $69-169; P ⚲) One of Hollywood's most popular hotels. Doubles and suites have kitchens, the decor is modern and there's a large heated pool.

Hollywood Roosevelt Hotel (Map opposite; ☎ 323-466-7000, 800-950-7667; www.hollywoodroosevelt.com; 7000 Hollywood Blvd; r $199-399; P 🖳 ⚲) This glamorous 1927 Spanish Colonial has been completely redone in luxurious style. Extras include high-speed Internet access, free stays for children under 18 with parents, and poolside cabanas for privacy. Ask about special deals.

Chateau Marmont (☎ 323-656-1010, 800-242-8328; fax 323-655-5311; 8221 W Sunset Blvd; r $250, ste $325-1950; P) This French-style castle looks out of place looming over West Hollywood, but that never bothered famous guests such as Greta Garbo. On a tragic note, comedian John Belushi overdosed in Bungalow 2 (or 3, depending on your source) in 1982.

EATING & DRINKING
Downtown
FINANCIAL DISTRICT

Grand Central Market (Map p154; 317 Broadway) 'Feeding Los Angeles since 1917' is the motto here, with plenty of self-serve eateries with dishes for under $5. **China Cafe** has huge, steamy, delicious bowls of noodle soup.

Clifton's Brookdale Cafeteria (Map p154; ☎ 213-627-1673; 648 S Broadway; dishes $3-7) This ultracamp LA institution has been in business since 1932. After filling your tray, you'll sit down in an 'enchanted forest' with faux trees, squirrels and deer.

Drinks in the dark can be had at **Hank's Bar** (Map p154; ☎ 213-627-1151, 800-553-4774; 838 S Grand Ave) in the Stillwell Hotel. If you like red decor, head west of Downtown to Koreatown where **The Prince** (Map p154; ☎ 213-389-2007; 3198 W 7th St) pours stiff drinks.

CHINATOWN & EL PUEBLO DE LOS ANGELES

Chow Fun (Map p154; ☎ 213-626-1238; 686 N Spring St, Suite 126; dishes $4-8) This recent addition to Chinatown has big windows and decor modeled after Chinese 'peasant style.' The food ranges from traditional dishes like pickled cabbage & shredded pork noodle soup to noodles with spaghetti sauce. Vegetarians will do fine here.

Ocean Seafood (Map p154; ☎ 213-687-3088; 757 N Hill St) A budget dim sum takeout ($2 to $12) is on offer, but there's also a spacious Hong Kong-style dining room complete with choose-your-own-crustacean tanks ($8 to $28).

Via Cafe (Map p154; ☎ 213-617-1481; 451 Gin Ling Way; ☽ 8am-7pm) Via serves up a variety of teas and coffee drinks along with noodle soups ($4 to $5).

Las Anitas (☎ 213-623-1153; W-26 Olvera St; dishes $7-10; ☽ 10am-8pm, closed Tue) Soak up the festive atmosphere of El Pueblo here.

In Union Station, **Traxx** (dishes $8-27) offers seafood and salad in an unbeatable atmosphere.

LITTLE TOKYO & ARTS DISTRICT

Joy-Mart (Map p154; ☎ 213-680-9868; 137 Japanese Village Plaza; dishes $6-12) In Little Tokyo, you will feel joy at this cozy restaurant and sake bar when you sample the intoxicant for $5/14 per hit/3-kind sampler, and $30 to $80 per bottle. Food ranges from Bento boxes and curry to *donburi* and sushi. The staff are gracious. Bring cash, as no credit cards are accepted.

Shabu Shabu House (Map p154; ☎ 213-680-3890; 127 Japanese Village Plaza; dishes $8-13.60 dinner) This aptly named restaurant is one of the best places for the culinary ritual of *shabu shabu*, the Japanese version of fondue.

Groundwork (Map p154; ☎ 213-626-8650; 811 Traction Ave; ☽ 7am-8pm) This Arts District eatery sells strong coffee and sandwiches prepared with an artist's slow contemplation and creativity.

Frying Fish Sushi (Map p154; ☎ 213-680-0567; 120 Japanese Village Plaza; sushi $1.50-4.50) has some of the best prices.

INFORMATION	
Hollywood Presbyterian Hospital	1 F2

SIGHTS & ACTIVITIES	pp149-55
LA Bike Tours & Cyclery	2 A2
Mann's Chinese Theater	3 A2

SLEEPING	pp155-6
Highland Gardens Hotel	4 A2
Hollywood Roosevelt Hotel	5 A2
Magic Castle Hotel	6 A2
Student Inn International Hostel	7 A2

EATING	pp156-60
Electric Lotus	8 F2
Mexico City	9 F1
Miceli's	10 A2
Mustard Seed Cafe	11 F1
Pig 'n' Whistle	12 A2
Simply Thai	13 F1

DRINKING	pp156-60
Tiki Ti	14 F2

ENTERTAINMENT	p160-1
Dresden Room	15 F2
The Derby	16 F1
The Hollywood Palace	17 B2

SHOPPING	p161
Larry Edmunds Bookshop	18 B2
Skylight Bookshop	19 F2
Squaresville	20 F2

TRANSPORT	pp161-2
Greyhound Bus Station	21 B2

West Hollywood & Hollywood

Farmers Market (☎ 323-933-9211; 6333 W 3rd St) Open since 1934, the market is the place to assemble a picnic from the cheese, sausage and bread vendors, or eat takeout on the central patio.

The market's New Orleans-style **Gumbo Pot** (☎ 323-933-0358; dishes $5-9) serves a tasty jambalaya (a spicy rice dish with chicken and sausage). At the hip Art-Deco **Kokomo** (☎ 323-933-0773; 6333 W 3rd St; lunch $5-8, dinner $8-15), you can belly up to the counter alongside 'industry' types for big breakfasts. There's also a bar with micro-brewed beer. Catch jazz from 7pm to 9pm on Thursdays on the west patio. Hot? Try **Bennet's Ice Cream**, near gate 15.

Miceli's (Map p157; ☎ 323-466-3438; 1646 N Las Palmas Ave; dishes $7-17; ⏲ lunch Mon-Fri, dinner nightly) Step into this dark restaurant with its carved booths and hundreds of empty Chianti bottles dangling from the ceiling.

Pig 'n' Whistle (Map p157; ☎ 323-463-0000; 6714 Hollywood Blvd; dishes $4-10) Opened in 1927, this pub claims to have regularly hosted the likes of Shirley Temple, Cary Grant, Clark Gable and others before closing in the 1950s. It has been lovingly restored; note the carved ceiling and comfortable half-circle booths. There is something delicious for everyone, including kids.

Los Feliz

Simply Thai (Map p157; ☎ 323-665-6958; 1850 Hillhurst Ave; dishes $5-15) The deep wall colors, lush plants and brilliant fabrics will soothe you after a day on LA's freeways. The food here tastes just-picked fresh and is not weighted down by heavy sauces. The service is great and the beer is cold.

Mustard Seed Cafe (Map p157; ☎ 323-660-0670; 1948 Hillhurst Ave; dishes $2-10; ⏲ breakfast & lunch) Any day but Monday you can get Huevos

---

GRIFFITH PARK   Map p158

One of the best spots in LA, in the rugged Santa Monica Mountains, Griffith Park is five times the size of New York's Central Park and blanketed by California oak, wild sage and manzanita. The land was bequeathed to the city in 1896 by Griffith J Griffith.

Hiking

For recent arrivals, this is the perfect place to come and get the lay of the land. Starting from the base of the observatory, take the **Mt Hollywood Hiking Trail** up to 1625ft for panoramic views, including that of Hollywood's most recognizable landmark, the Hollywood sign. Built atop Mt Lee in 1923, it was an advertising gimmick for a real estate development called Hollywoodland. Each metal letter is 50ft tall. Hiking to the sign is illegal.

Griffith Observatory & Planetarium

Clinging to the southern slopes of Mt Hollywood, the **Griffith Observatory & Planetarium** (☎ 323-664-1191; www.griffithobs.org; 2800 E Observatory Rd) has been a local landmark since 1935. The complex remains closed until 2005 for renovation.

Los Angeles Zoo

The **LA Zoo** (☎ 323-644-6000; www.lazoo.org; 5333 Zoo Dr; adult/senior/child $8.25/5.25/3.25; ⏲ 10am-5pm) is home to some 1200 animals representing 350 mammal, bird, amphibian and reptile species. They live in a dozen habitats laid out according to the animals' continental origins. A highlight is the chimpanzees of the Mahale Mountains (located in Tanzania); the Ahmanson Koala House is also a crowd favorite.

Autry Museum of Western Heritage

Anyone interested in the history of the American West will hit the mother lode at this delightful **museum** (☎ 323-667-2000; www.autry-museum.org; 4700 Western Heritage Way; adult/student/child age 2-12 $7.50/5/3, free 2nd Tue of month; ⏲ 10am-5pm Tue-Wed & Fri-Sun, 10am-8pm Thu). Its 10 galleries combine scholarship and showmanship to reveal how the West was 'discovered' again and again, by everyone from prehistoric tribes to missionaries.

Rancheros with no-nonsense service. Salads have special touches like pumpkin seeds.

Electric Lotus (Map p157; ☎ 323-953-0040; Vermont Ave; lunch $6-10, dinner $8-16) Visit here for good Indian food and, when you're done, dance to DJ spins (call for dance schedule).

Mexico City (Map p157; ☎ 323-661-7227; 2121 Hillhurst Ave; ⊗ lunch Wed-Sun, dinner nightly) Has good burritos ($8) and plenty of seating.

Tiki Ti (Map p157; ☎ 323-669-9381; 4427 Sunset Blvd) This garage-sized tropical tavern is where showbiz folks, blue-collar types and Silver Lake trendoids jostle up to the bar, which is engulfed in nautical kitsch. Smoking is okay here.

ENTERTAINMENT

Find the scoop on entertainment in the *Los Angeles Times* Calendar section and the free *LA Weekly*.

DETOUR TO PASADENA

Nine miles northeast of Downtown LA, Pasadena is well worth a visit, especially for advocates of the Arts & Crafts movement. The 1908 **Greene & Greene Gamble House** (☎ 626-793-3334; 4 Westmoreland Pl; adult/student/child $8/5/free) is one of the finest examples of the style, boasting sublime design, as well as sleeping porches, leaded art glass, fine furniture and Tiffany lamps. The surrounding streets (Arroyo Terr and Grand Ave) hold additional architectural delights.

Also in Pasadena is the **Huntington Library, Art Collection & Botanical Garden** (☎ 626-405-2100; 1151 Oxford Rd; adult/senior/student/child 5-11 yrs $10/8.50/7/4, free 1st Thu of month; ⊗ closed Mon). The sprawling garden has 14,000 species of trees, shrubs, flowering and nonflowering plants. The library houses rare English-language books, maps and manuscripts, including a 1455 Gutenberg Bible.

Pop in to the **Convention & Visitors Bureau** (☎ 626-795-9311; http://pasadenacal .com; 171 S Los Robles Ave) for information.

Stay overnight at the **Artists' Inn & Cottage** (☎ 626-799-5668, 888-799-5668, www .artistsinns.com; 1038 Magnolia St; r $115-205; **P**), in a lovely Victorian farmhouse. Thin crust pizza is delicious at **Avanto Cafe** (cnr Lake & Union Sts).

Tickets for most events are available by phone or direct from each venue's box office. Many venues also allow reservations via the Internet. **Ticketmaster** (☎ 213-480-3232; www.ticketmaster.com) collects exorbitant handling fees and service charges.

Downtown

The Mayan (Map p154; ☎ 213-746-4287; 1038 S Hill St; ⊗ Fri & Sat) Head to this pre-Columbian-style ex-movie palace for salsa and merengue on the main floor, and hip hop, disco and Spanish rock in the other rooms. No jeans or sneakers allowed.

Mark Taper Forum (Map p154; ☎ 213-628-2772; Music Center, 135 N Grand Ave) This downtown venue is considered the leading theater in SoCal.

Los Angeles' **Philharmonic Orchestra** (☎ 213-850-2000) and **Opera** (☎ 213-972-8001), the latter directed by Placido Domingo, perform downtown in the **Dorothy Chandler Pavilion** (Map p154 ☎ 213-972-7211; Music Center of LA County, 135 N Grand Ave).

Hollywood & West Hollywood

The Hollywood Palace (Map p157; ☎ 323-467-4572; 1735 N Vine St) A huge, glam Art Deco landmark, the Palace is a nightclub and concert venue with a state-of-the-art sound system.

West Hollywood is the heart of the gay and lesbian scene. **The Palms** (☎ 310-652-1595; 8572 Santa Monica Blvd) is the oldest lesbian bar, with everything from karaoke to salsa; and **Rage** (☎ 310-652-7055; 8911 Santa Monica Blvd) is a two-story gay bar and dance club.

Viper Room (☎ 310-358-1880; 8852 Sunset Blvd) Owned by Johnny Depp, the infamous Viper Room is a small hangout for celebs and their hangers-on. Lines wrap around the block.

Cat Club (☎ 310-657-0888; 8911 Sunset Blvd) But why wait in line? Head to this unpretentious club owned by Slim Jim Phantom of Stray Cats fame and presenting rock and roll.

Comedy clubs abound in West Hollywood, including the **Groundlings Theater** (☎ 323-934-9700; 7307 Melrose Ave), whose graduates include Lisa Kudrow and Pee-Wee Herman.

Los Feliz

Dresden Room (Map p157; ☎ 323-665-4294; 1760 N Vermont Ave) Enjoy the loud, campy singing duo barside or slide into a half-circle booth with your sweetie.

The Derby (Map p157; ☎ 323-663-8979; 4500 Los Feliz Blvd) LA's 'Swing Central' since 1993, The Derby was featured in the movie *Swingers*. Some of the best dancers in town jump 'n' jive around the pint-sized dance floor. Ask about free lessons.

Other Areas
Spaceland (☎ 323-833-2843; 1717 Silver Lake Blvd) In Silver Lake, Spaceland has a sign that offers 'dreams, food & spirits.' This is a no-attitude place to catch local bands as well as some bigger names. Smokers can see the show from a glassed-in smoking lounge.

SHOPPING
LA is all about image – how you look, what you wear, what you collect, so it's not surprising there are stores everywhere.

Downtown
Bargain clothing shoppers flock to the Fashion District, a frantic 56-block warren of fashion that is the epicenter of the city's clothing industry. Note that most stores only accept cash and that refunds or exchanges are uncommon.

In Chinatown, all things red and gold can be found at **Wing Wa Hing Gifts & Arts** (Map p154; N Broadway), along with exquisite orchids and 'lucky bamboo.' **Old Chinatown Plaza** (Map p154) is a plaza of gift shops and restaurants on the northern end of Broadway. The traditional – and somewhat rundown – mingles with the tongue-in-cheek trendy here: look for **Shop Chuey** (Map p154; ☎ 213-625-3787; 437 Gin Ling Way), 'exclusive home of the made-in-Chinatown, LA T-shirt,' a gift shop and art gallery.

Olvera St (Map p154) in El Pueblo de Los Angeles is a good place to find Mexican handcrafted leather and hand-woven clothing as well as children's toys and piñatas.

At **Japanese Village Plaza** (Map p154) you can stock up on kimonos and books, and toys and crafts, from origami art to fine spun pottery. Near here is **No Reply** (Map p154; ☎ 213-687-8903; 343 E 2nd St), a neat and tidy vintage clothing store with great finds.

Hollywood
Larry Edmunds Bookshop (Map p157; ☎ 323-463-3273; 6644 Hollywood Blvd) While in celebrity land, stop in at this long-time purveyor of film, theater and TV scripts etc.

Los Feliz
Squaresville (Map p157; ☎ 323-669-8464; 1800 N Vermont Ave) lets you assemble that funky Left Coast look at reduced prices.

Wander into **Skylight Bookshop** (Map p157; ☎ 323-660-1175; 1818 N Vermont Ave) for 'zines.

GETTING THERE & AROUND
See Transport (p216) for more detailed information.

Air
Los Angeles International Airport (Map pp150-1; LAX; ☎ 310-646-5252; www.lawa.org) is 17 miles southwest of Downtown LA. Touch-screen computer monitors in airport terminals give information on ground transport options. The Shuttle C bus, stopping at each terminal, goes to the LAX transit center for connection to city buses. Shuttle G bus goes to the Metro Rail green line.

Bus
The 24-hour **Greyhound Main Bus Station** (Map p154; ☎ 213-629-8401; 1716 E 7th St at Alameda St) is in a somewhat rough area. There's also a **Greyhound Bus Station** (Map p157; ☎ 323-466-6381; 1715 N Cahuenga Blvd) in Hollywood. Greyhound serves San Diego at least hourly ($14) and has up to 10 buses to/from Santa Barbara ($13). Services to/from San Francisco run almost hourly ($42).

Train
Amtrak (☎ 800-872-7245; www.amtrak.com; 800 N Alameda St) at **Union Station** (Map p154) runs the *Coast Starlight* to Seattle ($100), the *Southwest Chief* to Chicago ($150) and the *Pacific Surfliner* to San Diego ($27), Santa Barbara ($20) and San Luis Obispo ($31).

Car & Motorcycle
From San Francisco the fastest route to LA (six hours) is via I-5. Hwy 101 is slower (eight hours) but a bit more picturesque. The most scenic route is via Hwy 1 (10 hours). From San Diego and other points south, take I-5.

Public Transport
LA's **Metropolitan Transit Authority** (MTA; ☎ 800-266-6883; www.mta.net; phone answered ☷ 6am-8:30pm Mon-Fri, 8am-6pm Sat-Sun) has its headquarters (closed weekends) in Union Station (Map p154) and runs the buses ($1.35 one way, $1.85 to $3.85 freeway express, $11 weekly

pass). Check the website, call or stop by the station for a map of routes. Many routes are equipped with bicycle racks.

See Getting There & Around (p167) for details on Santa Monica's Big Blue Bus.

The MTA's **Metro Rail**, LA's 'subway,' may be maligned by immigrants from New York, but lines (fares $1.35) do connect Downtown, Hollywood, Long Beach, Redondo Beach and – soon – Pasadena. Bikes are allowed with an MTA permit, but not during rush hour (6am to 9am, 3pm to 7pm).

LA Department of Transportation (LADOT; ☎ 808-2273; www.ladottransit.com; fares $0.25) runs shorter-route buses in several communities, including Hollywood and Downtown.

Taxi

In LA, taxi fares are metered: $2 at flag fall plus $1.80 per mile. Call, rather than hail a cab here.

Checker ☎ 800-300-5007
Independent ☎ 800-521-8294

COASTAL LOS ANGELES

If you're in LA county, spend some time clinging to the edge of the continent. Most of LA's beaches are wide and sandy – and the water is tolerable by spring, peaking at about 70°F in August. On land, there's a beach community to almost anyone's liking. Malibu, exclusive and laid-back, has preserved a bit of its history, on display at the Adamson House. Santa Monica juxtaposes a developed pier for family fun with a city grid of fancy shops. Venice is home to artists and beach bums. San Pedro and Long Beach have the LA Port, a maritime museum and historic ocean cruiser. Laguna Beach, with a beautiful coastline park and arts festival, merits a longer visit.

SANTA MONICA MOUNTAINS NATIONAL RECREATION AREA

Not to be missed is the 150,050-acre Santa Monica Mountains National Recreation Area (SMMNRA), the world's largest urban park. Few visitors to LA realize that the metropolis actually borders wilderness in the park, which is a joint venture of national, state and local park agencies and private property owners, and is an easily accessible sample of California's rugged beauty.

The Santa Monica Mountains stretch from west of Griffith Park in Hollywood to the east of the Oxnard Plain in Ventura County. Their northern border is the Ventura Fwy, while in the south, they rise dramatically above the Pacific Ocean. Several canyon roads cut through the mountains, providing easy access to trails. Nearly 600 miles of trails crisscross the area, including the popular 65-mile Backbone Trail.

The park was founded in 1978 by the US Congress and boasts a number of ecological areas, such as oak woodlands, chaparral and coastal lagoons. More than 450 animal species, including deer, bobcats, mountain lions and coyotes, live here. Hawks, falcons and eagles circle above, while rattlesnakes reside beneath the brush. Many species are listed as rare, threatened or endangered under the Endangered Species Act.

The park also contains a number of archaeological sites related to the Chumash and Gabrielleno Indians who lived in these mountains. The Satwiwa Cultural Center preserves the culture of these tribes and that of the many other native cultures in Southern California.

As wild as the park is, it has not escaped the 'industry'. TV's *Dr Quinn, Medicine Woman* and other celluloid greats were filmed here.

Information

In the very western San Fernando Valley, the National Park Service (NPS) maintains a **visitors center** (☎ 805-370-2300; 401 W Hillcrest Dr, Thousand Oaks; ✆ 8am-5pm Mon-Fri, 9am-5pm Sat & Sun, closed major holidays). Take the Lynn Rd exit from Hwy 101 (Ventura Fwy), head north on Lynn Rd, east on Hillcrest Dr, left on McCloud Ave, and turn at the first driveway on your right. The center dispenses information and sells maps, hiking guides and books.

A State Park Ranger is on-site at **Trippet Ranch** (☎ 310-455-2465; 20825 Entrada Dr off Topanga Canyon Rd; ✆ 8am-sunset; maps $2, parking $5) in Topanga State Park.

Sights & Activities
HIKING

Visit in spring, when temperatures are moderate and wildflowers bloom. Summer can be hot and winter can bring mudslides. In general, most trails are rugged and require sturdy footwear. Look out for poison oak, which has waxy, glistening leaves that cause a rash. If you meet a mountain lion, hold your ground and try to appear large by raising your arms or grabbing a stick. If the lion gets aggressive, fight back, shout and throw objects at it.

You should always hike with a trail map. If you want more guidance, check out the excellent series of guides by John McKinney, including *Day Hiker's Guide to Southern California* ($15) and *Walking Los Angeles: Adventures on the Urban Edge* ($14).

In **Topanga State Park**, you can pick up a map from Trippet Ranch parking area and follow **Musch Trail** to the fire road to **Eagle Rock**, a difficult hike that rewards with views of Santa Ynez Canyon. Or take the **Santa Ynez Canyon Trail**, a moderate 6-mile round-trip that reaches a dead-end at a waterfall and pool – good for swimming in early summer.

MOUNTAIN BIKING

Most fire roads and some trails are open to mountain bikers. In general, if a path is wider than 4ft, it is open to bikes. On any road or trail, bicyclists must yield to hikers and horses and not exceed 15mph. The NPS visitors center has maps. For more on biking, including rentals, see p165.

SATWIWA NATIVE AMERICAN CULTURAL CENTER

This joint effort by the Friends of Satwiwa, UCLA and the NPS has exhibits on plants, mammal and insect specimens, as well as archaeological and cultural artifacts. Check the website (www.nps.gov/samo/fos) for basketry workshops, storytelling and performances. From Hwy 101 (Ventura Fwy) exit on Lynn Rd and head south 5.25 miles to Via Goleta where you'll see the entrance. Walk about a third of a mile on a gravel road to the center.

Camping

Malibu Creek State Park (☎ 818-880-0367, reservations 800-444-7275; sites $12) has 62 campsites. **Leo Carillo** (☎ 818-880-0350; reservations, 800-444-7275; sites $12; hiker-biker $1) has 138 sites. Sites at both parks are wheelchair accessible. **Topanga State Park** (☎ 310-455-2465; backcountry sites $1) has eight no-reservation sites. For camping at **Pt Mugu State Park**, at the western edge of the Santa Monica Mountains, contact the NPS visitors center (see opposite).

Getting There & Around

Hwy 101 (Ventura Fwy) borders the mountains on the north, and Hwy 1 and the Pacific Ocean form the southern boundary. Access to most park areas is available via many roads that cross the mountains between these two major highways.

Call **Thousand Oaks Transit** (☎ 800-438-1112) for bus information.

MALIBU
☎ 310 / pop 12,575

The name Malibu is derived from the Chumash name, which the Spanish spelled 'Umalibu,' probably their take on 'humal-iwu,' meaning 'it makes a loud noise all the time over there.' The Chumash were referring to the sound of the surf, music to the ears of many present-day residents and day-tripping surfers and beachcombers.

Malibu has been a celebrity enclave since the 1920s, when money troubles forced landowner May Rindge to lease out property. Clara Bow and Barbara Stanwyck were among the first to move to what became the 'Malibu Colony'. In addition to the pounding surf, another constant din is now audible in the homes of the biggest names in the entertainment industry. It's

---

HOW SAFE IS THE WATER?

It's LA...so, how clean is the water? **Heal the Bay** (☎ 310-453-0395, 800-432-5229 within CA only; www.healthebay.org) monitors the Santa Monica Bay and issues a monthly Beach Report Card with ratings A+ (excellent) to F. Swimming is usually prohibited for three days following a major storm, when sewer run-off pollutes the water.

Also dangerous are the strong currents, called riptides, which can drag swimmers away from shore. Look for white, frothy water and flat waves. To check on weather or tide conditions, there are several numbers to call:

- Northern Beaches (Zuma area)
  ☎ 310-457-9701

- Central Beaches (Santa Monica area)
  ☎ 310-578-0478

- Southern Beaches (Hermosa area)
  ☎ 310-379-8471

the clash of these wealthy property owners battling environmentalists over development. One ongoing struggle concerns the construction of seawalls protecting multimillion-dollar seaside homes from... well...the inevitable.

Information
Everything in Malibu is along – or just off – Hwy 1 (also called the Pacific Coast Hwy). The **Malibu Chamber of Commerce** (☎ 456-9025; www.malibu.org; 23805 Stuart Ranch Rd, Suite 100; ☽ 10am-4pm Mon-Fri) is just east of Hwy 1.

Sights & Activities
ADAMSON HOUSE & MALIBU LAGOON MUSEUM
A national historic site and a California landmark, the **Adamson House** (☎ 456-8432; www.adamsonhouse.org; 23200 Pacific Coast Hwy; tours $5) is a must-see for architecture buffs and tile enthusiasts. The 1929 Moorish–Spanish Colonial revival villa of Adamson House was designed by Stiles O Clements for Rhoda and Merritt Adamson, the daughter and son-in-law of the Rindges, the last owners of the Malibu Spanish land grant.

The house has lush grounds and perfect views of the Malibu lagoon and beach. The tiles (note the 'rug' in the downstairs hall) were made at the nearby Malibu tileworks, which carefully guarded its glaze recipes. A 1931 fire led to the tileworks' demise (though reproductions are available at the giftshop). Hour-long tours of Adamson House operate 11am to 2pm Wednesday to Saturday.

The adjacent **Malibu Lagoon Museum** (admission free; ☽ 11am-3pm Wed-Sat) has exhibits of local history.

TOPANGA CANYON
The most intriguing drive from Malibu into the mountains is via **Topanga Canyon**. An alternative-lifestyle community even before it was discovered by hippies in the '60s, Topanga still features a collection of homes that range from ramshackle to modern rustic.

The **Will Geer Theatricum Botanicum** (☎ 455-3723; 1419 N Topanga Canyon Rd) mounts a summer series of Shakespeare and other plays in a funky outdoor amphitheater (it's worthwhile having a walk around even if nothing is on). It was founded in 1953 by Will

Geer (best known as Grandpa Walton in the TV series), who was blacklisted during the McCarthy era.

See p163 for information on Topanga State Park.

J PAUL GETTY MUSEUM
Long before the Getty Center (p149) opened, there was the original **J Paul Getty Museum** (17985 Pacific Coast Hwy), housed in a replica of the Roman Villa dei Papiri. It's scheduled to be renovated but a reopening date had not been set at the time of research.

BEACHES
More than 20 beaches line Malibu's '27 miles of scenic beauty.' **Zuma** has volleyball nets and plenty of sand. **Pretty Point Dume Beach** is home to a state wildlife preserve. See surfers (or be one!) near the Adamson House at **Malibu-Surfriders State Beach**. 'Next door' is the famous – or infamous – 'gated' Malibu Beach of the uber-rich. Even plebeians may walk here – just stay below the high tide line.

Sleeping & Eating
Leo Carrillo State Beach Campground (☎ 805-488-5223, 800-444-7275 for reservations; 9000 Pacific Coast Hwy; sites $12) There's good camping at this kid-friendly campground, with 138 tent and RV sites, a general store, flush toilets and hot pay showers. Otherwise, stay in LA or Santa Monica.

Neptune's Net (☎ 457-3095; 42505 Pacific Coast Hwy; dishes $5-20) There's seaside dining in Malibu, too. Try Neptune's, near the Ventura County line, which serves superbly fresh seafood. Come at sunset, overlook the sea, peel a pile of shrimp and wash it all down with a cold beer.

For trendy shops and a myriad of eateries, turn off Hwy 1 on to Cross Creek Rd to the Malibu Country Mart, a compound of strip malls hugging parking lots. One surrounds a small park, with picnic tables, a playground and trees. Here you can purchase reasonably priced (for Malibu) food, such as burritos, sandwiches and falafels, and dine outside.

Getting There & Around
If you're on Hwy 1 between the Ventura County line and Santa Monica, you'll pass through Malibu.

SANTA MONICA

☎ 310 / pop 85,690

Since the early 1990s, Santa Monica has undergone a transformation from a quaint, slightly wacky seaside resort to a glitzy beach town. Developers are celebrating and travelers are increasingly drawn to this appealing destination. Santa Monica is safe, easily explored on foot, has good air quality, shopping, lodging, dining and miles of beach. But it must be said that in the transition something has been lost, too. Third St Promenade, a pedestrian-only area, is choked with chain stores. Rents have gone through the roof, ousting the independents. Visitors can seek out some of the charm of a bygone era on the less-than-polished pier, or pedal along the ocean-front bike path.

Information

BOOKSTORES

California Map & Travel (☎ 396-6277; 3312 Pico Blvd, Santa Monica) Good for travelers.

Hennessey & Ingalls (☎ 458-9074; 214 Wilshire Blvd) Visit here for art and architecture books.

The Midnight Special (☎ 310-393-292; 1450 Second St) Independent bookstore scheduled to reopen just after the time of research. The popular store, which hosts political gatherings and poetry readings, was ousted from its 10-year Third St Promenade location by skyrocketing rent.

TOURIST OFFICE

Santa Monica Visitors Center (☎ 393-7593; www .santamonica.com; 2nd flr, Santa Monica Place mall, cnr 2nd St & Colorado Blvd; 🕑 10am-4pm) Offers maps and general information.

Sights & Activities

THIRD STREET PROMENADE

The (consumer) heart of Santa Monica is this pedestrian mall between Broadway and Wilshire Blvd. Here you'll find street entertainment, restaurants, shops and movie theaters. The southern end of the promenade is anchored by Santa Monica Place, a shopping mall designed by Frank Gehry.

SANTA MONICA PIER

Two blocks west of the promenade, Ocean Ave parallels Palisades Park atop a bluff overlooking the ocean. Below is the famous **Santa Monica Pier** with restaurants and the 1920 **carousel** (🕑 11am-5pm Mon, Wed, Thu, 11am-7pm Fri-Sun) that starred alongside Paul Newman and Robert Redford in *The Sting*. Stroll

to the end to see photographs depicting the history of the pier (and the concurrent major events in US history). It must have been fun dancing in La Monica Ballroom overlooking the ocean – back in the good old days. Surfing life, going back as far as the 1920s, is also on display.

The pier's main draw is the **Pacific Park**, a small-scale amusement park with a roller coaster, a solar-powered ferris wheel, and a host of kiddy rides and arcade games. Ride tickets are $2 (the ferris wheel takes two tickets). Unlimited day use is $10.95 for kids (under 42in tall) and $19.95 for adults.

South of the pier a sign marks 'The Original location of **Muscle Beach**: Birthplace of the Physical Fitness Boom of the Twentieth Century.' The SoCal exercise craze began back in the 1930s; today brand-new equipment on the beach draws a new generation of bodybuilders...taking themselves very seriously.

WALKING & BICYCLING

The ocean-front walk and separate bike path are fine ways to take in the view. You can bike the 14-mile flat round-trip to Marina del Rey (p168), or 28-mile round-trip to Manhattan Beach (p168). Rent bikes on the pier at **Blazing Saddles** (☎ 393-9778; www.blazingsaddles.com; 🕑 9am-late; bikes $7-11 hourly, $28-48 daily; tandems $48 all day; kid's bike $15 all day). Cyclists can also head into the steep Santa Monica Mountains from here on the 18-mile 'moderate' Westwood–UCLA loop, take the 14-mile ride to Will Rogers Historical State Park or the 20-mile uphill to Sullivan Ridge.

BERGAMOT STATION

The 40 galleries berthed within this sprawling industrial complex called **Bergamot Station** (☎ 453-7535; 2525 Michigan Ave) have been a nexus of the LA arts scene since the complex opened in 1994. Also here is the **Santa Monica Museum of Art** (☎ 586-6488; suggested donation $2-3; 🕑 11am-6pm Tue-Sat, noon-5pm Sun), home of changing contemporary art exhibits.

Sleeping & Eating

HI Los Angeles-Santa Monica (☎ 393-9913, 800-909-4776; fax 393-1769; 1436 2nd St; dm $27-29, r $66-69) Right in the heart of things, this hostel has a kitchen, library, theater, laundry and travel store offering discounts on trips, such as the fabled tour of the stars' homes.

Cal Mar Hotel Suites (☎ 395-5555, 800-776-6007; www.calmarhotel.com; 220 California Ave; ste $99-159; P 🐾) Not much to look at from the exterior, Cal Mar is pleasant and airy, surrounding a courtyard with a pool. All suites have full kitchens.

Hotel California (☎ 393-2363, 800-537-8483, www.hotelca.com; 1670 Ocean Ave; r $169-279; P) Just steps from the beach, this hotel greets you with whimsical surf-inspired decor. The sunny rooms come with glossy hardwood floors and refrigerators, while suites have private patios and kitchenettes.

Sea Shore Motel (☎ 392-2787; fax 392-5167; 2637 Main St; r $75-130; P) Two blocks from the beach, the Sea Shore is clean, well run and popular with Europeans. Renovated rooms have lots of amenities.

Houston's (☎ 576-7558; 202 Wilshire Blvd; dishes $10-26; 🕑 lunch & dinner) Open, pleasing modern architecture is home to sleek wait staff serving sleeker guests delicious seafood, salads and burgers. Upstairs, enjoy a drink and the piano-cello duo.

Real Food Daily (☎ 451-7544; 514 Santa Monica Blvd; 🕑 lunch & dinner; dishes $7-14) Enjoy friendly service, organic vegan delights and puns ('Penne for Your Thoughts') here.

Try the **Border Grill** (☎ 451-1655; 1445 4th St; lunch $7.50-15, dinner $14-25) for boldly flavored south-of-the-border dishes. For a quick slice, pop into **Stefano's** (☎ 587-2429; 1310 3rd St) on the Promenade.

Cha Cha Chicken (Ocean Ave; dishes $7-12) On Ocean near Pico, look for the huge, brightly painted barrels sprouting lush plants that encircle the outdoor Cha Cha Chicken, where dishes such as spinach quesedilla or spicy black pepper shrimp caesar salad are available.

Toppers (☎ 393-8080; 1111 2nd St) For a margarita, happy hour snacks (4:30pm to 7:30pm daily; $2 munchies) and superb ocean sunsets, take the elevator to Toppers, atop the Radisson Huntley Hotel. On a clear day you can see forever.

Getting There & Around
From Downtown LA take Hwy 10 ('the' 10; also called the Santa Monica Fwy) west to Santa Monica. Hwy 1 connects to Malibu, north of here. Slightly inland heading south, it connects to Venice.

The Santa Monica–based **Big Blue Bus** (☎ 451-5444; www.bigbluebus.com) runs throughout the Westside, including Santa Monica, Venice, Westwood, Pacific Palisades and LAX. Bus No 14 goes to the Getty Center. The fare is 75¢; transfers to another Big Blue Bus are free and those to an MTA bus are 25¢. The express MTA bus No 10 is the fastest way to get to Downtown LA from Santa Monica ($1.75). Bus No 3 serves LAX.

VENICE BEACH
☎ 310 / pop 37,700
Venice Beach is famous for its Ocean Front Walk, its canals and a citizenry that blends hippies, artists, Industry types and students. Many people who came here for its low rents some 20 to 30 years ago, and recent arrivals alike, don't want to see their funky town become the next Malibu. People voice their opinions here – especially about development – at city council meetings.

But it was a developer who helped create Venice in the first place. Until about a century ago Venice was nothing but dreary swampland. Enter Abbot Kinney (1850–1920), a visionary, dreamer and developer, who drained the marshes, dug a 16-mile network of canals and built a promenade, pier and theater. Kinney even imported gondoliers from Italy to pole people through his beachfront paradise, which he dubbed 'Venice of America.'

In 1993 the surviving 3 miles of the historic canals were restored and are now lined with million-dollar-plus homes. The **Venice Canal Walk** is best accessed from either Venice or Washington Blvds near Dell Ave.

Sights & Activities
The chief attraction of modern Venice is its **Ocean Front Walk**, also known as the Venice Boardwalk. Bikini-clad bicyclists, henna tattoo artists, chainsaw-juggling entertainers, wannabe Schwarzeneggers and others come out to play. It's a roiling mass of humanity that must be seen to be believed. Strolling, biking or skating along this 1.5-mile stretch between Marine St and Venice Pier is public fun.

Venice is home to many artists, a presence reflected in the numerous galleries and abundant public art, including Jonathan Borofsky's 34ft Ballerina Clown at Rose Ave and Main St. Wander into **Robin's Sculpture Garden** (1632 Albert Kinney Blvd; www.robin.murez.com), an artist's studio 'en l'air', to see magical,

LOS ANGELES AREA

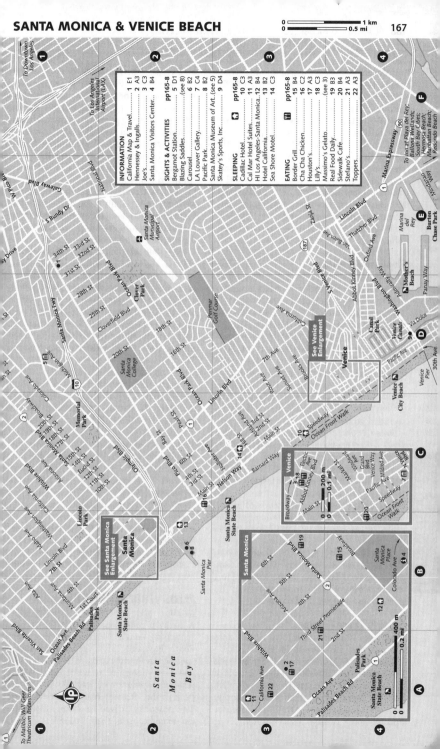

INFORMATION
California Map & Travel......... 1 E1
Hennessey & Ingalls............ 2 A3
Joe's.................................... 3 C3
Santa Monica Visitors Center.. 4 B4

SIGHTS & ACTIVITIES pp165-8
Bergamot Station.................. 5 D1
Blazing Saddles.................(see 8)
Carousel.............................. 6 B2
LA Louver Gallery................ 7 C4
Pacific Park......................... 8 B2
Santa Monica Museum of Art..(see 5)
Skatey's Sports, Inc.............. 9 D4

SLEEPING pp165-8
Cadillac Hotel...................... 10 C3
Cal Mar Hotel Suites............ 11 A3
HI Los Angeles–Santa Monica.12 B4
Hotel California.................... 13 B2
Sea Shore Motel.................. 14 C3

EATING pp165-8
Border Grill......................... 15 B4
Cha Cha Chicken................. 16 C2
Houston's............................ 17 A3
Lilly's.................................. 18 C3
Massimo's Gelato..............(see 3)
Real Food Daily................... 19 B3
Sidewalk Cafe..................... 20 B4
Stefano's............................. 21 A3
Toppers.............................. 22 A3

translucent glass sculptures and other works in resin and metal. **LA Louver Gallery** (☎ 822-4955; 45 N Venice Blvd; ⌚ 10am-6pm Tue-Sat) is internationally known.

In May, take the **Venice Art Walk** (☎ 392-8399) during which the many artists open their studios. It costs $50, but benefits the Venice Family Clinic and is a rare chance to see some of Southern California's artists up close and personal.

Skatey's Sports, Inc (☎ 823-7971; 102 Washington Blvd) can set you up with wheels for cruising the boardwalk. Mountain bikes or 10-speeds rent for $10/20/25 per hour/day/overnight; inline skates go for $5/10/15.

Sleeping & Eating

Venice is best visited by day for enjoying the beach and the galleries; it has a reputation for being unsafe after dark.

The Cadillac Hotel (☎ 399-8876; www.thecadillachotel.com; 8 Dudley Ave; dm $22, r $99, ste from $130; **P**) If you do want to stay over, try the rooms in this restored 1905 beachfront Art Deco building; all have ocean views, TV, phone and private bathroom. There's also a gym and sauna, rooftop sundeck and laundry.

Lilly's (☎ 314-0004; 1031 Abbot Kinney Blvd; dishes $10-19) This relaxed bistro has a flowery, secluded courtyard.

Joe's (☎ 399-5811; 1023 Abbot Kinney Blvd; dishes $20-22, 4-course prix-fixe menus $38 & $48) Next door to Lilly's is this classic neighborhood eatery serving Cal-French food.

On a hot day, try **Massimo's Gelato** nearby, where you can sit out the back in view of the Sculpture Gardens, a vendor of amazing plants. Breakfast and lunch (try the grilled vegetable panini for $7.50) are also on offer.

Sidewalk Cafe (☎ 399-5547; 1401 Ocean Front Walk; dishes $8-12) For 30 years the Sidewalk Cafe has served old-fashioned American fare to a steady stream of locals and tourists wanting a front-row seat on the boardwalk.

Getting There & Away

Take Hwy 10 from Downtown LA to Santa Monica, then head south on Hwy 1.

The Santa Monica–based **Big Blue Bus** (☎ 451-5444) runs throughout the Westside of LA, including Venice (see p167 for details). Bus No 2 runs from Venice and through Santa Monica (pick up multiple transfer options here). Bus No 3 serves LAX.

SOUTH OF VENICE BEACH
☎ 310

A number of beach towns stretch along the coast south of Venice Beach, ready to offer the traveler a room for the night and another beautiful slice of sea and sand.

The largest artificial small-craft harbor in the US, **Marina del Rey** is home to upscale salty types, living on boats or in apartment complexes. Just south of the marina area, the **Ballona Wetlands** are the last remaining wetlands in LA county. Developers and environmentalists battled over this land (sound familiar?). Eventually, an agreement allowed the marina, *with* the bird preserve.

The charming **Inn at Playa del Rey** (☎ 574-1920; 435 Culver Blvd; r $145-350) is perched alongside the bird sanctuary. Rooms are sparkling and wheelchair accessible, and rates include breakfast and evening wine and cheese. Nearby **Cafe Pinguini** (☎ 306-0117; 6935 Pacific Ave; dishes $11-20; ⌚ closed Mon) is recommended.

Just south, along the coast – within earshot of LAX – **Dockweiler State Beach** has an RV park (reservations ☎ 800-444-7275, 800-950-7275, 322-4951; sites $13-27) and is seaside RV heaven.

Beach and more beach is what you'll get from the well-to-do South Bay beach towns of **Manhattan**, **Hermosa** and **Redondo Beaches** (Map pp150-1), which typify the relaxed 'life's a beach' SoCal mentality. Surfers flock to Manhattan Beach's pier area, while volleyball enthusiasts hit both Manhattan's and Hermosa's wide stretch of sand. In Hermosa, call ahead to **Becker Surfboards** (☎ 372-6554; 301 Pier Ave) and ask about surf lessons. Redondo Beach is a bit narrower, and very family friendly. Pubs and restaurants abound in Manhattan and Hermosa. For something different, head to Redondo's **The Green Temple** (☎ 944-4525; 1700 S Catalina Ave #103; dishes $5-11), where tranquil wait staff serve inventive vegetarian fare.

PALOS VERDES PENINSULA
☎ 310

A rocky precipice rising from the sea and separating Santa Monica Bay from San Pedro Bay, the Palos Verdes Peninsula is spectacular – and exclusive. If you're lucky, you may encounter a few of Palos Verdes' resident population of peacocks, introduced back in the 1920s by real estate developers. The peacocks thrived to the point that the city exiled most of them in 1985.

The Palos Verdes coastline is unspoiled and comprises a series of coves. The only easily accessible sandy beach is **Malaga Cove**; **Abalone Cove** is an ecological reserve with large tidepools. Surfers ride the waves at **Royal Palms State Beach**, while scuba divers plow the waters at **White Point**.

Landlubbers can spot migrating Pacific gray whales from the observation area of **Point Vincente Interpretive Center** (☎ 377-5370, 31501 Palos Verdes Dr W; admission $2; ☺ 10am-5pm, later in summer). The whales travel by here en route from the Arctic Seas to Baja California and back between December and April. The facility, closed at the time of research, is scheduled to reopen in summer 2004; call ahead.

On a knoll above the cliffs of Portuguese Bend, the **Wayfarers' Chapel** (☎ 377-1650; 5755 Palos Verdes Dr S; ☺ 11am-4:30pm Mon-Fri, 10am-5pm Sat & Sun) was designed in 1949 by Lloyd Wright, Frank's son. When visitors step into the mostly-glass chapel, they are surrounded by a canopy of trees, and views of the sky.

SAN PEDRO
☎ 310 / pop 70,000

This slow-paced harbor community is far less affluent than its Palos Verdes Peninsula neighbor and sits on the fringe of 'Worldport LA' – the twin ports of LA and Long Beach. Together these form the third largest port in the world, after Singapore and Hong Kong. The ballet of leviathan tankers gliding slowly out to sea is impressive.

Before statehood, the Spanish allowed only two foreign ships a year to bring goods to the growing Los Angeles area, an act that fueled an active smuggling trade. In the 1870s, when Los Angeles was seeking a deepwater harbor after the arrival of the railroad, dredging work and construction of a breakwater began here. The town was incorporated in 1888 but was annexed to LA in 1909. Five years later, with the opening of the Panama Canal, San Pedro boomed.

The **San Pedro Chamber of Commerce** (☎ 832-7272; www.sanpedrochamber.com; 390 West 7th St) will steer you to local sights and restaurants. Pacific Ave is the main north–south drag, while 6th Ave heads east to the harbor.

Sights & Activities

The 75,000-sq-ft **Los Angeles Maritime Museum** (☎ 548-7618; www.lamaritimemuseum.org; Berth 84,

DETOUR TO SANTA CATALINA ISLAND

Head to Catalina Island where 88% of the land is protected by a conservancy and the other 12% is a luxury vacation destination fit for a king (that would be Arthur; the island's only town is called Avalon). It'll take about an hour to get to Avalon from San Pedro or Long Beach on the **Catalina Express** (☎ 519-1212, 800-618-5533; www.catalinaexpress.com; adult/senior/child $43/39/33), which runs eight times daily. This is the place for romance: dance in the beautiful ballroom of the 12-story-high round casino building, then take a moonlight stroll on the beach. For more information, check out the website of the **chamber of commerce** (www.catalina.com) and see Newport Beach (p172) for day-trip information.

bottom of 6th St; requested donation $1; ☺ 10am-5pm Tue-Sun), in a Streamline Moderne former car ferry terminal, contains more than 700 ship models, ship figureheads, navigational equipment and an operating amateur radio station. Just south of the Maritime Museum, Ports O' Call Village is a hopeless tourist trap. Skip it.

Definitely worth a visit is the **Cabrillo Marine Aquarium** (☎ 548-7562; www.cabrilloaq.org; 3720 Stephen White Dr; suggested donation adult/child $5/1, parking $6.50; ☺ noon-5pm Tue-Fri, 10am-5pm Sat & Sun). Among the 38 tanks displaying colorful fish and other marine life is one where visitors are encouraged to handle starfish, sea urchins, sea cucumbers and other critters. The museum is undergoing an expansion set to be completed in late 2004, but will remain open in the meantime. Not far away you'll find the recently restored 1932 **Cabrillo Beach Bathhouse** (☎ 548-7553; 3800 Stephen White Dr).

On the northern fringes of San Pedro's coast is the lovely little **White Point**, with a beach, playground and tidepooling ($2 to park Saturday and Sunday).

Point Fermin Park, the southernmost point in LA, is a grassy bluff for picnicking, complete with an 1874 Victorian lighthouse. Brave the winds atop neighboring Angels Gate Park to visit the **Korean Friendship Bell**, given to the US by South Korea and built on site by Korean craftspeople.

LOS ANGELES AREA

Sleeping & Eating

HI Youth Hostel (☎ 831-8109; 3601 S Gaffey St No 613; dm $19-23, semi-private r $21-24, private room $44-47; **P**) This hostel, in former WWII barracks, enjoys a million-dollar view.

Beach City Grill (☎ 833-6345; 376 W 6th St; ⏰ 11am-9pm Tue-Sat) If all the sightseeing has made you hungry, stop in at the Beach City Grill for unexpected Cajun and Caribbean treats like red beans and rice with vegie kebabs. The service is gruff but the food is worth it.

Whale & Ale (☎ 832-0363; 327 W 7th St) At the Whale & Ale, raise a pint to – or curse – Juan Cabrillo who claimed this land for Spain in 1542.

Getting There & Around

Hwy 110 heads here from Downtown LA.

A good way to get around the port and downtown San Pedro is by Electric Trolley, which runs Thursday to Monday at 15-minute intervals; rides cost only 25¢. The No 446 Metro Bus travels to Point Fermin.

LONG BEACH

☎ 562 / pop 461,520

Long Beach, the county's second-largest city, doesn't necessarily merit an overnight stay – unless you can splurge on a stateroom aboard the *Queen Mary* – but it's a worthwhile day trip from Downtown.

There's an **information kiosk** (⏰ 10am-6pm, Mar-Sep, 10am-4pm Fri-Sun Oct-Feb) next to the aquarium.

Sights & Activities

AQUARIUM OF THE PACIFIC

The $117-million **Aquarium of the Pacific** (☎ 590-3100; www.aquariumofpacific.org; 100 Aquarium Way; adult/senior/child $15/12/8, parking $6; ⏰ 10am-6pm) exhibits 17 large habitats and 30 smaller tanks covering three Pacific Rim regions: Southern California and Baja, the Northern Pacific, and the Tropical Pacific. More than 10,000 fish, and a few mammals and birds, call the aquarium home.

The most impressive gallery takes you to the tepid waters of the Tropical Pacific; in particular, it displays fish from the island archipelago of Palau in Micronesia (north of Australia), which is blessed with some of the world's most fecund and dazzling coral reefs.

RMS QUEEN MARY

The Titanic may have captured all the headlines, but the grand dame of ocean liners was the **RMS Queen Mary** (☎ 435-3511; www.queenmary.com; 1126 Queens Hwy; adult/senior & military/child $25/23/13, parking $8; ⏰ 10am-6pm, later in summer). The best deal is to board after 6pm and head for the Observation Bar for a cocktail. This way you don't pay admission but you can still wander the hallways and even dance on deck (to the music in your head). You will, however, still pay the $8 parking fee – unless you walk or bike here.

The 81,237-ton liner was launched in 1934 and made 1001 crossings of the Atlantic before being retired in 1964 and moored in Long Beach three years later. The lavish vessel transported Fred Astaire, Greta Garbo, Bob Hope and Marlene Dietrich. Winston Churchill signed the D-Day invasion papers in the 1st-class ladies' drawing room.

More than 1000ft long and 12 decks high, the *Queen Mary* accommodated its passengers in three classes. At $600, a 1st-class ticket cost three times as much as a 3rd-class ticket. The journey from Southampton to New York took 4½ days.

Much of the Queen Mary can be explored on a self-guided tour – or you can join the Royal Historic Guided Tour for an additional $8.

Part of the ship is now a pleasant **hotel** (☎ 435-3511, 800-437-2934; www.queenmary.com; cabins $99-129; staterooms $129-219; ste $350-650), with 365 rooms, elegant restaurants and lounges.

MUSEUMS

Long Beach is home to the exquisite **Museum of Latin American Art** (☎ 437-1689; 628 Alamitos Ave; adult/student & senior $5/3, free Fri; ⏰ 11:30am-7pm Tue-Fri, 11am-7pm Sat, 11am-6pm Sun), the only museum in the western USA to showcase contemporary Latin American art.

Sleeping & Eating

For a touch of luxury, book a stateroom aboard the Queen Mary (see above).

Restaurants cluster along Pine Row, providing some appealing options. **Madison** (☎ 628-8866; 192 Pine Ave; dishes $23-30; ⏰ lunch & dinner) is worth a peak for its dramatic restored 1916 building; while **King's Fish House** (☎ 432-7463; 100 W Broadway; dishes $14-30;

⊙ lunch & dinner) makes fish and seafood for the soul, all impeccably fresh.

Belmont Brewing Company (☎ 433-3891; 25 39th Place; lunch $6-12, dinner $9-25), away from the strip, is an oceanfront brew-pub with a deck perfect for watching sunsets.

Getting There & Around

Easily reached from Downtown LA by the Metro Rail Blue Line, it's a good day trip. Explore the center of town on foot or by local bus – called the Passport, there are four routes hitting places of interest (free within downtown, 90¢ otherwise). The AquaBus, a water taxi, travels hourly from 11am-6pm around Queensway Bay, with stops at the aquarium, the Queen Mary, Pine Ave and Shoreline Village ($2 per trip).

The Transit Information Center (223 E 1st St; ⊙ 7:30am-4:30pm weekdays), next to the Transit mall, has details. Also here is **Bikestation** (☎ 436-2453), renting out city, mountain and road bikes from $5 to $7 hourly, and $20 to $28 daily.

HUNTINGTON BEACH

☎ 714 / pop 196,290

Ever since the Hawaiian–Irish surfing star George Freeth gave surfing demonstrations here in 1914, Huntington Beach has been one of Southern California's most popular surf destinations. It even earned the title Surf City, USA, from rock and roll surf daddies, Jan and Dean.

Once the least polished and most low-key of Orange County's beach towns, gentrification has arrived in Huntington Beach. Along lower Main St, old-fashioned surf culture struggles to survive amid developer-driven cookie-cutter architecture. A new mega-development called 'Pacific City' is planned, hoping to break ground in 2004, though some residents oppose it. The surf museum might relocate to this area along Hwy 1 (called Pacific Coast Hwy here) between 1st and Huntington Sts, and there's talk of reopening the Golden Bear, a former music venue that once welcomed stars such as Janis Joplin, BB King and Bob Dylan.

For maps and information, drop in to the **visitors bureau** (☎ 969-3492, 800-729-6232; www .hbvisit.com; 301 Main St, Suite 208; ⊙ 9am-5pm Mon-Fri). Get the *Orange County Beach Access Map*, which is published by the California Coastal Commission ($2.50).

Sights & Activities

In September the Huntington Beach **Pro/ Am Surf Series Championship** – a landmark event in the sport – takes place just south of the Huntington Beach Pier. Also look for the **Surfing Walk of Fame** (cnr Pacific Coast Hwy & Main St), which immortalizes mostly local legends.

Huntington is home to the **International Surfing Museum** (☎ 960-3483; 411 Olive St; admission $2; ⊙ noon-5pm Wed-Sun), off Main St. Check out the display on 'women of surf.'

A bit of Huntington's old-school surf culture can be found at the **Java Jungle Coffee & Cigar House** (602 Pacific Coast Hwy), where it will cost you $20 to rent a board and wet suit for the day. The laid-back proprietor has some useful tips.

The 3-mile stretch of Pacific Coast Hwy north of Huntington Beach is flanked on one side by **Bolsa Chica State Beach**, which has dark sand facing a monstrous off-shore oil rig and **RV camping** (☎ 800-444-7275; sites $20 1-night stays only). Across the road is the **Bolsa Chica State Ecological Preserve**, which appears desolate (especially with the few small oil wells scattered about) but actually teems with terns, mergansers, pelicans, pintails and endangered Beldingís Savannah sparrows. A 1.5-mile loop trail starts from the parking lot.

Sleeping & Eating

Huntington City Beach (☎ 536-5280; sites $15) There's camping available for RV owners here, but reservations are only accepted during winter.

Colonial Inn Hostel (☎ 536-3315; www.hunting tonbeachhostel.com; 421 8th St; dm $18/100 day/week; 🖳) The Colonial Inn has dorms sleeping three to eight people and communal areas including a kitchen, living room and backyard. There's a laundry, Internet access, and free surfboard and bike rentals. Come here if you love surfing...not for cleanliness, decor or quiet.

Travellers won't go hungry with Lower Main St packed with casual eateries. Options include the **Sugar Shack** (☎ 536-0355; 213 Main St; dishes $5-10), a breakfast and lunch institution where local artifacts decorate the walls; and **Wahoo's Fish Taco** (120 Main St; dishes $2-7), where you can fill up cheaply on Mexican food or rice bowls with various toppings.

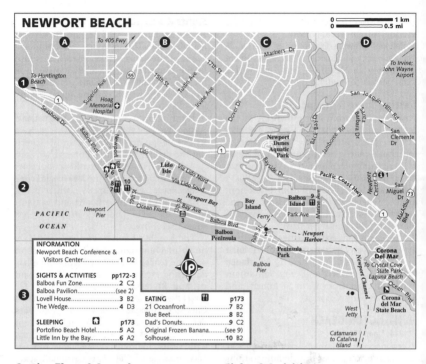

NEWPORT BEACH

0 — 1 km
0 — 0.5 mi

INFORMATION
Newport Beach Conference &
  Visitors Center....................1 D2

SIGHTS & ACTIVITIES   pp172-3
Balboa Fun Zone....................2 C2
Balboa Pavilion..........................(see 2)
Lovell House.............................3 B2
The Wedge.................................4 D3

SLEEPING   ☐   p173
Portofino Beach Hotel..............5 A2
Little Inn by the Bay................6 A2

EATING   🍴   p173
21 Oceanfront..........................7 B2
Blue Beet..................................8 B2
Dad's Donuts...........................9 C2
Original Frozen Banana.........(see 9)
Solhouse..................................10 B2

Getting There & Around

In the Orange County beach communities, Hwy 1 runs along the coast; Hwy 405 is parallel and inland, with exits for the coastal towns.

Call **Orange County Transportation Authority** (OCTA; ☎ 636-7433; single ride/day pass $1/2, express bus to LA $3) for bus schedules.

NEWPORT BEACH

☎ 949 / pop 75,630

Newport Beach is the largest of Orange County's beach towns, with one of the biggest pleasure craft harbors in the US. The main non-water-oriented pastime seems to be shopping.

The Pacific Coast Hwy (Hwy 1) passes through the part of Newport that centers around harbor activity. The Balboa Peninsula makes a natural 6-mile barrier between Newport Harbor and the ocean.

For more information about the sights, restaurants and accommodations, contact the **Newport Beach Conference & Visitors Bureau** (☎ 719-6100, 800-942-6278; www.newportbeach-cvb.com; 110 Newport Center Dr, Suite 120).

Sights & Activities

Balboa Peninsula, a strip of land a quarter-mile wide, has a white sand beach on its ocean side. Landward, look for the 1926 **Lovell House** (1242 W Ocean Front), designed by Rudolph Schindler, one of SoCal's influential modernist architects.

Hotels, restaurants and bars cluster around two piers – **Newport Pier**, near the peninsula's western end, and **Balboa Pier**, east of here. Near the latter is the **Balboa Fun Zone**, open since 1936. There's a ferris wheel, arcade games, touristy shops and restaurants and the 1905 **Balboa Pavilion**, beautifully illuminated at night. From the Fun Zone you can catch harbor cruises, fishing or whale-watching excursions, the **catamaran to Catalina Island** (departs daily at 9am, $37 round-trip) and the ferry to Balboa Island.

At the very tip of the peninsula, by the West Jetty, is the **Wedge**, a bodysurfing and knee-boarding spot famous for its perfectly hollow waves that can get up to 30ft high.

The Balboa Fun Zone is connected to **Balboa Island** via a tiny car and passenger ferry, which operates around the clock

($1.25 for car and driver, 50¢ per person). It lands at Agate Ave, about 11 blocks west of Marine Ave, the main drag. The free activity here is a stroll along its shoreline; it's about 1.5 miles around.

Nearby **Corona del Mar** is spread along Pacific Coast Hwy and hugs the eastern flank of the Newport Channel. The beach here lies at the foot of rocky cliffs. Children love the **tidepools** at Little Corona Beach. There are restrooms and volleyball courts. Parking costs $6; look for free spaces atop the cliffs behind the beach along Ocean Blvd.

Sleeping & Eating

The Little Inn by the Bay (☎ 673-8800, 800-438-4466; www.littleinnbythebay.com; 2627 Newport Blvd; r $89-229; **P**) At the Little Inn by the Bay, your day begins with a continental breakfast and newspaper delivered to your cheerfully decorated room. Bikes, boogie boards and beach chairs are also available for rent.

Portofino Beach Hotel (☎ 673-7030, 800-571-8749; www.portofinobeachhotel.com; 2306 W Ocean Front; r $130-300; **P**) This old-fashioned place right on the beach has a shared sitting area upstairs for watching the ocean on stormier days.

Solhouse (110 McFadden Pl; dishes $6-11) This may be one of the least pretentious or cheesy places left in such a touristy part of SoCal, with plants out front, a painted awning and art adorning the walls. Come for happy hour (5pm to 7pm).

Blue Beet (☎ 675-2338; 107 21st Place; lunch $4-8, dinner $7-19) Framed vintage posters and big armchairs, burgers, pasta and fish are on offer, but the place is best known for its nightly live jazz and blues concerts (with occasional cover charge).

21 Oceanfront (☎ 673-2100; 2100 W Ocean Front; dinner $20-60) Put on your fancier duds for 21 Oceanfront, which specialises in seafood dishes, including such rarities as beluga caviar and abalone.

Get your dessert on Balboa Island. Compare the frozen banana at **Dad's Donuts** (318 Marine), established 1960, with those at **The Original Frozen Banana** (a few doors down), established 1945.

Getting There & Around

See Huntington Beach Getting There & Around (see opposite).

LAGUNA BEACH

☎ 949 / pop 23,730

Stretching for about 7 miles along the Pacific coast, Laguna Beach has one of the most pleasant settings of any of SoCal's beach towns. And to Laguna's credit, much of the coastline has been developed into public space. Grassy parks for picnicking sit atop cliffs overlooking the ocean, and stairs plunge down to the seaside. Elsewhere, there are sandy beaches and volleyball courts.

Laguna Beach is exclusive – you can smell the money in the air – but the town also has a long tradition in the arts. It is the home of several famous festivals (see the Laguna Arts Festivals boxed text on p175) as well as the highly regarded **Laguna Playhouse** (☎ 497-2787; www.lagunaplayhouse.com; 606 Laguna Canyon Rd).

Laguna's earliest inhabitants, the Ute-Aztecas and Shoshone tribes, called the area Lagonas because of two freshwater lagoons in what is now Laguna Canyon. The name endured until 1904, when it was changed to Laguna. At roughly the same time, San Francisco artist Norman St Claire came to paint watercolors of the surf, cliffs and hills. His enthusiasm attracted others influenced by French impressionism, and they became known as the 'plein air' (outdoors) school.

Laguna swells with tourists on summer weekends, but away from the Village (town center) and Main Beach (where the Village meets the shore), there's plenty of room.

Information

Laguna Beach Visitors Bureau (☎ 497-9229, 800-877-1115; www.lagunabeachinfo.org; 252 Broadway; ☻ 9am-6pm Mon-Fri, 10am-3pm Sat, 11am-3pm Sun July & Aug only) Has the entire scoop on Laguna. Get the Public Art Brochure.

Sights & Activities

Laguna Beach has 30 public beaches and coves. Most are accessible by stairs off Pacific Coast Hwy; look for the beach-access signs, or pick up a copy of the *Orange County Beach Access Map* ($2.50) from the visitors bureau. **Main Beach** has volleyball and basketball courts and is best for swimming. Just north, the bluff-top **Heisler Park** gives access to several coves, including **Diver's Cove**, a deep protected inlet. **Crescent Bay**, north of town, has big hollow waves good for bodysurfing.

LOS ANGELES AREA

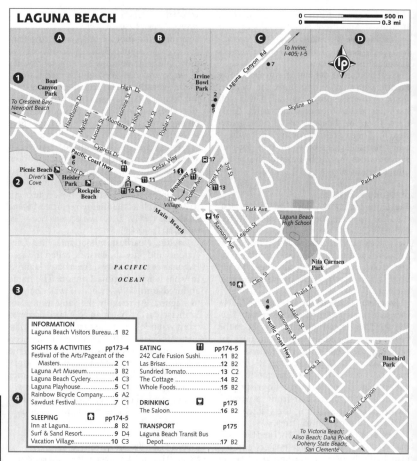

LAGUNA BEACH

0 —————— 500 m
0 —————— 0.3 mi

INFORMATION
Laguna Beach Visitors Bureau...**1** B2

SIGHTS & ACTIVITIES	pp173-4
Festival of the Arts/Pageant of the Masters.............................**2** C1	
Laguna Art Museum.............**3** B2	
Laguna Beach Cyclery...........**4** C3	
Laguna Playhouse.................**5** C1	
Rainbow Bicycle Company......**6** A2	
Sawdust Festival....................**7** C1	

SLEEPING	🏠 pp174-5
Inn at Laguna.......................**8** B2	
Surf & Sand Resort...............**9** D4	
Vacation Village...................**10** C3	

EATING	🍴 pp174-5
242 Cafe Fusion Sushi...........**11** B2	
Las Brisas............................**12** B2	
Sundried Tomato..................**13** C2	
The Cottage........................**14** B2	
Whole Foods.......................**15** B2	

DRINKING	🍺 p175
The Saloon..........................**16** B2	

TRANSPORT	p175
Laguna Beach Transit Bus Depot............................**17** B2	

About 1 mile south of the Village, **Victoria Beach** has volleyball courts and **La Tour**, a Rapunzel's tower-like structure from 1926. **Aliso Beach** has a fair amount of parking and is popular with surfers, as is **Salt Creek Beach** in nearby Laguna Niguel.

Bicycle rental places include **Laguna Beach Cyclery** (☎ 494-1522; 240 Thalia St) and **Rainbow Bicycle Co** (☎ 494-5806; 485 N Coast Hwy). The cost of a 24-hour rental is about $20 for cruisers and $25 to $35 for mountain bikes.

The breezy **Laguna Art Museum** (☎ 494-8971; 307 Cliff Dr; adult/concession/child under 12 $5/4/free, admission free Tue; ☑ 11am-5pm Tue-Sun) has changing exhibits usually featuring one or two California artists and a permanent collection heavy on California landscapes.

Sleeping & Eating

Budget-minded travelers should consider camping. Eight miles south of Laguna Beach is pleasant **Doheny State Beach** (☎ 496-6172; reservations ☎ 800-444-7275; sites $17-23) with 116 sites. There are no hook-ups but there's a dump station. There's a **blues festival** (☎ 262-2662), held near the campground in May.

San Clemente State Beach (☎ 492-3156; reservations ☎ 800-444-7275; tent sites $17-18, RV sites $23) has 88 tent sites and 72 with hook-ups.

Inn at Laguna (☎ 497-9722, 800-544-4479; fax 497-9972; 211 N Coast Hwy; r $99-499, in summer $149-529; 🅿 🐕) This is a treat, oceanside. The rooms have thick featherbeds, VCR, CD player, bathrobes and a continental breakfast – delivered.

LOS ANGELES AREA

Vacation Village (☎ 494-8566, 800-843-6895; www.vacationvillage.com; 647 S Coast Hwy; r & ste $83-251, in summer $92-339; P ☻) Southeast of the Village, this family-friendly place has 130 units, about half of them with kitchens, plus a pool and spa.

Surf & Sand Resort (☎ 497-4477, 800-524-8621; www.surfandsandresort.com; 1555 S Coast Hwy; r $225-375; ☻) Sporting a natural color scheme and luxurious rooms with all the trappings, this resort has some rooms with views of the private beach and ocean.

Las Brisas (☎ 497-5434; 361 Cliff Dr; dishes $11-20) This Laguna institution boasts great ocean views, serves Mexican seafood in the dining room and snacks ($7 to $12) on the patio.

The Cottage (☎ 494-3023; 208 N Coast Hwy; breakfast & lunch $5-10, dinner $11-17) Breakfast is served until 3pm (try the cranberry-orange pancakes) in this bungalow with a patio; otherwise, it's meaty American classics and pasta.

242 Cafe Fusion Sushi (☎ 494-2444; 242 N Coast Hwy; dinner $18) Helmed by a skilled sushi chef, 242 makes some of the best fishy morsels in town.

Sundried Tomato (☎ 494-3312; 361 Forest Ave; lunch & dinner $10-24) Sundried Tomato pairs a crisp Euro look with a casual patio for enjoying interesting salads, pastas and sandwiches.

For groceries, stop at **Whole Foods** (283 Broadway) in the Village.

Drinking
The Saloon (☎ 582-5909; 446 South Coast Hwy) is a standing room only, small friendly bar.

Getting There & Around
Hwy 1 runs along the coast; Hwy 5, inland, heads north to LA and south to San Diego. See Huntington Beach Getting There & Around (p172) for details on OCTA buses.

Laguna Beach Transit (☎ 497-0746) has its central bus depot on Broadway, just north of the visitors bureau in the heart of the village. It operates three routes at hourly intervals (no service between noon and 1pm and on Sunday). The Blue Line travels to the hotels and beaches along Pacific Coast Hwy.

SAN CLEMENTE
☎ 949 / pop 49,940

South from Laguna beach is San Clemente, where Richard Nixon ensconced himself after he famously lost the top job

---

LAGUNA ART FESTIVALS

The **Festival of the Arts** (☎ 497-6582, 800-487-3378; www.foapom.com; 650 Laguna Canyon Rd; adult/senior & student $5/3; ☺ from 10am daily Jul-Aug, closing hours vary), a seven-week juried exhibit, includes 160 artists whose work varies from paintings to handcrafted furniture to scrimshaw. Begun in 1932 by local artists who needed buyers, the festival attracts patrons and tourists from around the world. In addition to the art, there are free daily artists' workshops, a children's art gallery and live entertainment.

The most amazing aspect of the festival is the **Pageant of the Masters** (admission $15-65), where human models are blended seamlessly into re-creations of famous paintings. Order tickets weeks in advance, though you may be able to pick up last-minute cancellations at the gate. Nightly performances begin at 8:30pm.

In the 1960s, artists who did not get into the juried exhibition started their own festival to take advantage of the art seekers passing through town. They set up across from the festival, mocking its formal atmosphere by scattering sawdust on the ground. Thus, the so-called **Sawdust Festival** (☎ 494-3030; 935 Laguna Canyon Rd; www.sawdustartfestival.org; adult/child $6.50/2; ☺ 10am-10pm) was born.

---

in Washington. Nearby is the marine base, Camp Pendleton. Amtrak runs right along the ocean through San Clemente, which has a city beach with a playground, snack bar and the **Ole Hanson Beach Club** (☎ 361-8207), with a heated public pool.

Heading inland from the northern end of this beach, stop in at the decidedly non-touristy **Seaside Farms** (☎ 366-5849; 1624 N El Camino Real; dishes $3-7) for coffee, smoothies, soup, sandwiches, ice cream – and some cheap avocados (the owner has an avocado farm).

South of here is the **municipal pier** and the busier, more touristy part of town, with shops, restaurants and a few hotels. Farther along is **San Clemente State Beach** (☎ 492-3156), graced with sandstone bluffs topped with sage scrub. Surf, swim or use the sand wheelchair. Camp here and hear that lonesome whistle blow.

San Diego Area

CONTENTS

San Diego (city population 2.2 million, county population 2.8 million) has more than one flavor. Beach culture is big, with Ocean, Pacific and Mission Beaches pulsing with life – and crowds of tipsy suntanners. Yet San Diego has a refined side, one that pays homage to its history, its environment and the arts. There's also a vibrant gay and lesbian community, historic Old Town, Little Italy and La Jolla, a ritzy suburb offering excellent (non-alcoholic) ocean activities. The upside of this multiple personality is that San Diego has something for everyone.

The San Diego area was originally home to the Kumeyaay and the Luiseño/Juaneño peoples. Juan Rodríguez Cabrillo sailed into San Diego Bay in 1542, but it was Sebastian Vizcaíno who gave the city its name in 1602. In 1769, under Gaspar de Portolá and Padre Junípero Serra, 40 men founded the first of the California missions.

Following the bombing of Pearl Harbor in 1941, the headquarters of the US Pacific Fleet was moved from Hawaii to San Diego. The boom in wartime activity transformed the city: the harbor was dredged and landfill islands were built, vast tracts of instant housing appeared, and the population doubled in a couple of years. Postwar San Diego was a boom period, too.

The seafront location and climate – in the 70s with winter lows in the 'chilly' 60s year-round and only 10in of rain annually – make San Diego a major tourist destination. Though locals may mention the 'May Gray' and 'June Gloom,' caused by the marine layer right at the coast, most of the year, San Diegans enjoy sunny skies and some of the warmest weather in the country.

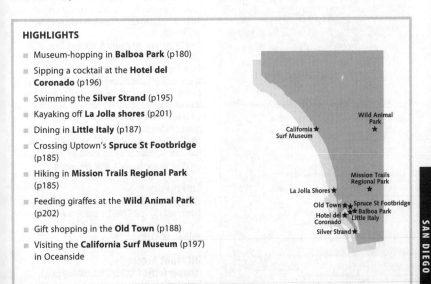

HIGHLIGHTS

- Museum-hopping in **Balboa Park** (p180)
- Sipping a cocktail at the **Hotel del Coronado** (p196)
- Swimming the **Silver Strand** (p195)
- Kayaking off **La Jolla shores** (p201)
- Dining in **Little Italy** (p187)
- Crossing Uptown's **Spruce St Footbridge** (p185)
- Hiking in **Mission Trails Regional Park** (p185)
- Feeding giraffes at the **Wild Animal Park** (p202)
- Gift shopping in the **Old Town** (p188)
- Visiting the **California Surf Museum** (p197) in Oceanside

Wild Animal Park ★

California ★
Surf Museum

Mission Trails
Regional Park ★

La Jolla Shores ★

Old Town ★★ Spruce St Footbridge
Hotel del ★★ Balboa Park
Coronado ★ Little Italy

Silver Strand ★

SAN DIEGO

INLAND SAN DIEGO

☎ 619

San Diego has its share of attractions for landlubbers, including excellent museums, a world-class zoo, noteworthy architecture, a range of live entertainment and good dining. Inland mountains beckon hikers.

ORIENTATION

San Diego is an easy place to navigate. The airport, train station and Greyhound terminal are all in or near the downtown area, a compact grid east of San Diego Bay. The main north–south freeway is I-5, which parallels the coast from the Camp Pendleton Marine Corps Base to the Mexican border. Interstate 8 runs east from Ocean Beach, up the valley of the San Diego River (called Mission Valley), past suburbs such as El Cajon and on to the Imperial Valley.

Waterfront attractions along the Embarcadero are west of the downtown grid. Balboa Park, with its many museums and famous zoo, is northeast of downtown, and Old Town is a couple of miles northwest of downtown. To the east of here is Hillcrest. Coronado is across San Diego Bay, accessible by bridge or ferry. Mission Bay, northwest of downtown, has lagoons, parks and facilities for recreation. The nearby coast is split into Ocean Beach, Mission Beach and Pacific Beach. La Jolla is to the north.

Maps

Tourist offices hand out a free map of downtown. Rand McNally's *San Diego City Map* and *San Diego County Regional Map* (both $3.95), and the American Automobile Association (AAA) maps *San Diego: Central & Southern Area* and *San Diego: North Area* ($3.95, free to members) are helpful.

Cyclists should acquire the free *San Diego Region Bike Map* from bike shops or **RideLink** (☎ 231-2453).

Cut back on pollution by using public transport, guided by *San Diego County's Regional Transit Map*. It's available at the Amtrak Station (Map p184), by calling ☎ 800-206-6883, or surfing to www.sdcommute.com.

INFORMATION
Bookstores

Bookhounds should peruse the old, new and rare offerings at bookstores on 5th Ave, between University and Robinson Aves, in Hillcrest.

The Bluestocking Books & Bindery (Map p181; ☎ 296-4214; 3817 5th Ave) A favorite in Hillcrest. The table displays are inspired, like placing an authentic old-fashioned *Boys Guide to Hunting and the Outdoors* next to Melissa Banks' novel *Girls Guide to Hunting and Fishing*.
Bountiful Books (Map p181; ☎ 491-0660; 3834 5th Ave)
Le Travel Store (Map p184; ☎ 544-0005; 745 4th Ave) Downtown bookstore with an excellent selection of maps.
Obelisk Bookstore (Map p181; ☎ 297-4171; 1029 University Ave) Hillcrest option that caters particularly to gay, lesbian, bisexual and transgender readers.

Emergency

24-hour Rape & Battering Hotline (☎ 233-3988)
Lifeguard (☎ 224-2708) For problems in the ocean or near the shore, contact the nearest lifeguard.
Police (☎ 911)

Internet Access

Internet Coffee (☎ 702-2233; 800 Broadway)
WebSurfCafe (Map p181; ☎ 858-296-6500; 416 University Ave, Hillcrest) Check your email here.

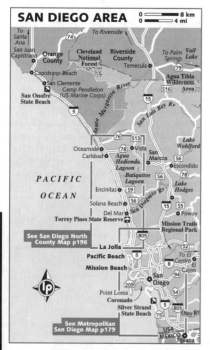

SAN DIEGO AREA   0 — 8 km / 0 — 4 mi

To Santa Ana
To Riverside
74
San Juan Capistrano
Orange County
Cleveland National Forest
Riverside County
To Palm Springs
Vail Lake
Temecula
79
Capistrano Beach
San Clemente
Camp Pendleton (US Marine Corps)
Agua Tibia Wilderness Area
516
San Onofre State Beach
15
Santa Margarita River
San Luis Rey Rv
76
513
Lake Wohlford
Oceanside
78
Vista
Carlsbad
Agua Hedionda Lagoon
San Marcos
56
Escondido
PACIFIC
Batiquitos Lagoon
56
78
OCEAN
Encinitas
59
Lake Hodges
Solana Beach
56
San Dieguito Rv
15
55
Del Mar
Poway
Torrey Pines State Reserve
Mission Trails Regional Park
See San Diego North County Map p196
805
La Jolla
52
Pacific Beach
5
To El Centro
8
El Cajon
Mission Beach
94
209
San Diego
54
Point Loma
Coronado
Silver Strand State Beach
5
805
75
Otay Rv
See Metropolitan San Diego Map p179
USA
MEXICO
Tijuana

SAN DIEGO

METROPOLITAN SAN DIEGO

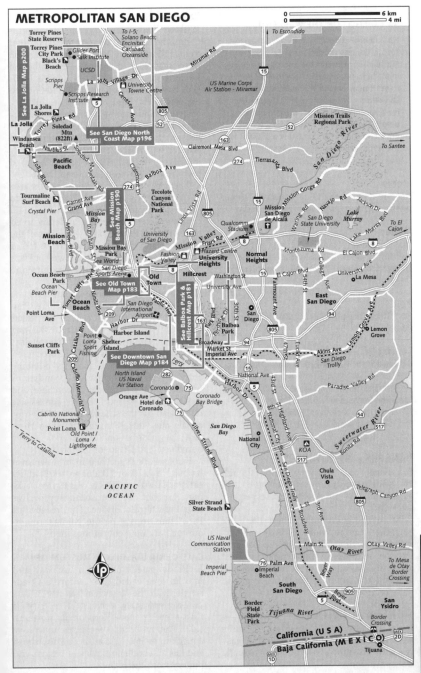

0 — 6 km
0 — 4 mi

Torrey Pines State Reserve
Torrey Pines City Park
Glider Port
Salk Institute
Black's Beach
UCSD
Scripps Pier
La Jolla Village Dr
University Towne Centre
Scripps Research Institute
See La Jolla Map p200
La Jolla Shores
Soledad Mtn (822ft)
See San Diego North Coast Map p196
La Jolla
Windansea Beach
Nautilus St
To I-5; Solano Beach; Encinitas; Carlsbad; Oceanside
Miramar Rd
To Escondido
US Marine Corps Air Station - Miramar
Mission Trails Regional Park
To Santee
San Diego River

Pacific Beach
Clairemont Mesa Blvd
Tierrasanta Blvd
Mission Gorge Rd
Navajo Rd
Jackson Dr

Tourmaline Surf Beach
Crystal Pier
Garnet Ave
Grand Ave
Balboa Ave
Tecolote Canyon National Park
Lake Murray
To El Cajon

Mission Bay
Mission Beach
University of San Diego
Mission Valley
Friars Rd
Qualcomm Stadium
Mission San Diego de Alcalá
San Diego State University
El Cajon Blvd
University Ave
La Mesa

Mission Bay Park
Sea World
San Diego Sports Arena
Fashion Valley
Hazard Centre
Normal Heights
Montezuma Rd
El Cajon Blvd

Ocean Beach Park
Ocean Beach Pier
See Old Town Map p183
Old Town
Hillcrest
Washington St
University Ave
Fairmount Ave
East San Diego
Lemon Grove
Akins Ave
San Diego Trolley

Point Loma Ave
Ocean Beach
San Diego International Airport
Harbor Dr
See Balboa Park & Hillcrest Map p181
San Diego
Balboa Park
Broadway
Market St
Imperial Ave
Paradise Valley Rd

Sunset Cliffs Park
Point Loma Sport Fishing
Harbor Island
Shelter Island
See Downtown San Diego Map p184
National Ave
National City

Cabrillo National Monument
Point Loma
Old Point Loma Lighthouse
Ferry to Catalina
North Island US Naval Air Station
Coronado
Orange Ave
Hotel del Coronado
Coronado Bay Bridge
San Diego Bay
KOA
Chula Vista
Telegraph Canyon Rd
Sweetwater River
Bonita Rd

PACIFIC OCEAN

Silver Strand State Beach
Silver Strand Blvd

US Naval Communication Station
Imperial Beach Pier
Palm Ave
Imperial Beach
South San Diego
Main St
Otay River
Otay Valley Rd
To Mesa de Otay Border Crossing

Border Field State Park
Tijuana River
San Ysidro
Border Crossing
California (USA)
Baja California (MEXICO)
Tijuana

SAN DIEGO

SAN DIEGO FOR THE WEEKEND

Hit **Balboa Park** bright and early to see the Timkin Gallery, the Botanical Building, the Museum of Man and the zoo. Have dinner in **Little Italy** at Mona Lisa and walk home to your pensione. In the morning, drive to **La Jolla** for breakfast at The Mission Coffee Cup Cafe. **Kayak** along La Jolla shores before heading back to town for a swim on the **Silver Strand** and to enjoy a cocktail at the **Hotel del Coronado**.

Media

Pick up the daily San Diego *Union-Tribune* or the free *San Diego Reader* (Thursday).

Money

You'll have no trouble accessing your holiday funds, with ATMs found everywhere. **Thomas Cook** (Map p184; ground level, Horton Plaza) Changes currency.

Post

Post Office (Map p184; 815 E St, Downtown; ☽ from 8:30am)

Tourist Offices

Old Town State Historic Park Visitors Center (Map p183; ☎ 220-5422; Robinson-Rose House, San Diego Ave; ☽ 10am-5pm) Offers information about state parks.
San Diego Convention & Visitors Bureau (Map p184; ☎ 236-1212; www.sandiego.org; Horton Plaza; ☽ 8:30am-5pm Mon-Sat year-round, 11am-5pm Sun Jun-Aug) Will mail you a complementary vacation planning guide.

DANGERS & ANNOYANCES

San Diego is a fairly safe city, though you should be cautious venturing east of about 6th Ave in downtown, especially after dark.

As in any community where there are bars, there can be trouble. Rowdy imbibers in beach neighborhoods and the Gaslamp Quarter may seem threatening (at least annoying) to lone women, or to gays and lesbians. It's safest to go out at night in pairs or groups.

SIGHTS & ACTIVITIES

Areas of interest to visitors are quite well-defined and mostly are within easy reach of downtown by foot or by public transportation.

Balboa Park
Map p181

With its museums, gardens and world-famous zoo, **Balboa Park** tops the list of what to see in San Diego. Maps dating from 1868 show that Alonzo Horton, 'the father of modern San Diego', had included a 1400-acre city park to his planned additions to the town. The land was still bare hilltops, chaparral and steep-sided arroyos (water-carved gullies) until 1892 when UC Berkeley botany graduate Kate Sessions started her nursery on the site, paying rent to the city in trees. By the early 1900s, Balboa Park had become a well-loved part of San Diego.

The park's main attractions are in the area bordered by Hwy 163 (Cabrillo Freeway) to the west and Park Blvd to the east. The main east–west thoroughfare is El Prado, anchored by the **Plaza de Panama**, and with most of the museums and theaters. More can be found around **Pan-American Plaza**, southwest of Plaza de Panama. The most stunning architecture is found around **Plaza de California**.

It would be impossible to cover all the attractions of this amazing park here. Plan ahead for your visit and start at the **Visitors Center** (☎ 239-0512; www.balboapark.org; 1549 El Prado; ☽ 9am-4pm), in the House of Hospitality. Available here are maps ($1), free brochures, the **Balboa Passport** ($30 good for one-time entry to each of the park's 13 museums within one week of the day of purchase) and the **Combo** ($50; passport plus zoo admission). Call ahead for the schedule of free days for certain museums. Many are closed on Monday. For information on the zoo, see the boxed text 'San Diego for Children' (p182).

Balboa Park is reached from downtown on bus No 7, 7A or 7B along Park Blvd. By car, Park Blvd provides access to free parking areas, but the most scenic approach is over the Cabrillo Bridge. The free Balboa Park Tram stops at various points throughout the park on a continuous loop.

CALIFORNIA BUILDING & MUSEUM OF MAN

El Prado passes under an archway and into an area called the California Quadrangle, with the **Museum of Man** (☎ 239-2001; www.museumofman.org; adult/child 6-17 $5/3, free 3rd Thu of month; ☽ 10am-4:30pm) on its northern side. The museum specializes in Native American artifacts from the US southwest and has an excellent display of baskets and pottery from the region.

BALBOA PARK & HILLCREST

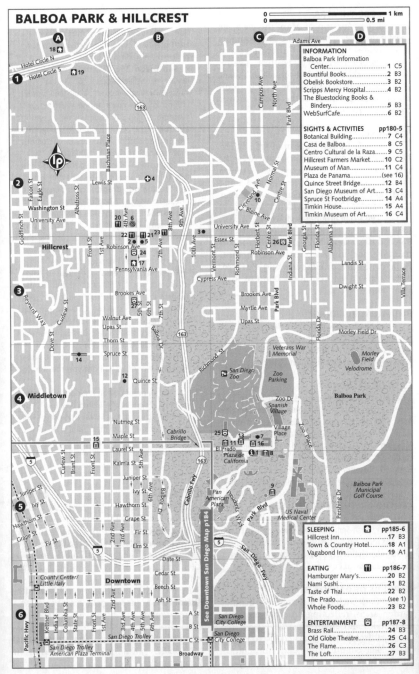

0 _____ 1 km
0 _____ 0.5 mi

INFORMATION
Balboa Park Information Center................................	**1** C5
Bountiful Books........................	**2** B3
Obelisk Bookstore....................	**3** B2
Scripps Mercy Hospital............	**4** B2
The Bluestocking Books & Bindery...................................	**5** B3
WebSurfCafe............................	**6** B2

SIGHTS & ACTIVITIES pp180-5
Botanical Building....................	**7** C4
Casa de Balboa.........................	**8** C5
Centro Cultural de la Raza........	**9** C5
Hillcrest Farmers Market..........	**10** C2
Museum of Man........................	**11** C4
Plaza de Panama.......................	(see 16)
Quince Street Bridge................	**12** B4
San Diego Museum of Art.........	**13** C4
Spruce St Footbridge...............	**14** A4
Timken House..........................	**15** A4
Timken Museum of Art............	**16** C4

SLEEPING 🏠 pp185-6
Hillcrest Inn.............................	**17** B3
Town & Country Hotel..............	**18** A1
Vagabond Inn..........................	**19** A1

EATING 🍴 pp186-7
Hamburger Mary's....................	**20** B2
Nami Sushi...............................	**21** B2
Taste of Thai............................	**22** B2
The Prado................................	(see 1)
Whole Foods............................	**23** B2

ENTERTAINMENT 🎭 pp187-8
Brass Rail.................................	**24** B3
Old Globe Theatre....................	**25** C4
The Flame................................	**26** C3
The Loft...................................	**27** B3

SAN DIEGO

OLD GLOBE THEATRE

Behind the Museum of Man, the **Old Globe Theatre** (also see Theater on p188) complex incorporates the Cassius Carter Stage and the outdoor Lowell Davies Festival Theatre. The namesake theater is a replica of Shakespeare's original Old Globe which stood on the southern bank of the Thames River from 1599 to 1642.

ART MUSEUMS

The 1924 **San Diego Museum of Art** (☎ 232-7931; www.sdmart.org; adult/senior & youth 18-24/child $8/6/3; ☒ 10am-6pm Tue-Wed & Fri-Sun, 10am-9pm Thu) houses European, American and some Asian art. The Sculpture Garden has pieces by Alexander Calder and Henry Moore.

The 1965 **Timkin Museum of Art** (☎ 239-5548; 1500 El Prado; admission free; ☒ closed Mon, Sun morning & Sep) houses a small but impressive group of paintings including works by Rembrandt, Rubens, El Greco, Cézanne and Pissarro. There's also a wonderful selection of Russian icons.

BOTANICAL BUILDING

This **building** (admission free; ☒ Fri-Wed) has a central dome and two wings covered with redwood lathes that let filtered sunlight shine on seasonally appropriate plant exhibits.

CASA DE BALBOA

The House of Commerce & Industry has three museums: the **Museum of Photographic Arts** (☎ 238-7559; adult/child $6/4, free 2nd Tue of month; ☒ to 5pm); the **San Diego Historical Society Museum** (☎ 232-6203; adult/child $6/2, free 2nd Tue of month; ☒ 10am-4:30pm Tue-Sun); and the **Model Railroad Museum** (☎ 696-0199; adult/student/child under 15 $5/3/free, free 1st Tue of month; ☒ closed Mon).

CENTRO CULTURAL DE LA RAZA

This **center** (☎ 235-6135; www.centroraza.com; donation; ☒ noon-5pm Thu-Sun) has exhibitions of Mexican and Native American art and is out on the fringe of the main museum area. Easiest access is from Park Blvd.

GARDENS OF BALBOA PARK

Balboa Park includes a number of distinct garden areas, reflecting different horticultural styles and environments. Take a free weekly **Offshoot Tour** (☎ 235-1114; meet at Botanical Bldg 10am) conducted by park horticulturists from mid-January to Thanksgiving.

SAN DIEGO FOR CHILDREN

San Diego is a great destination for families, with plenty of appealing activities to keep children's boredom at bay.

San Diego Zoo (Map p181; ☎ 234-3153, disabled-accessible facilities ☎ 231-1515, ext 4526; www.sandiegozoo.org; adult/child $20/12) is one of the city's biggest attractions, with more than 3000 animals representing about 800 species, exhibited in a beautiful landscaped setting, typically in enclosures that replicate their natural habitats.

Youngsters will love the **petting zoo** and the **animal nursery**. Also visit the koalas and the **Komodo dragon**. Just open at time of research was the **'Absolutely Apes'** exhibit, a re-creation of Indonesia's Asian rainforest ecosystem. The 8400 sq ft space allows orangutans and their smaller cousins, the siamangs, to cohabitate for the first time. Both species are endangered.

Tiger River, a realistic, re-created Asian rain forest, is a 'bioclimatic' exhibit. **Gorilla Tropics** is a replica African rainforest. Also take the kids to see the **Chinese pandas** and **African Rock Kopje** (outcrop), where klipspringers (small antelopes) demonstrate their rock-climbing abilities.

The zoo is in the northern part of Balboa Park. The No 7 bus will get you there from downtown.

Another great option for kids is the calm swimming waters of **Mission Bay** (p192) or the lovely sand of the **Silver Strand** (p195). There's also a good (flat) family bike ride on **Coronado Island** (p195). See p185 for bike rentals.

Old Town   Map p183

Under the Mexican government (which took power in 1821), this former pueblo was a square mile of land (roughly 10 times what is there today). It became the center of American San Diego – until the fire of 1872, after which the city's focus shifted to what is now downtown.

In 1968 the area became **Old Town State Historic Park**, archaeological work began, surviving original buildings were restored and other structures rebuilt. It's now a pleasant pedestrian district. The **visitors center** (☎ 220-5422; ☒ 10am-5pm, park tours 2pm) is in the Robinson-Rose House. Pick up a copy of the *Old Town San Diego State Historic Park Tour Guide & Brief History* ($2) or take a guided tour.

Across from the center is **Casa de Estudillo** (admission free), a restored adobe with original furnishings. The **Bazaar del Mundo**, just off the plaza's northwestern corner, is a colorful collection of shops and restaurants that is open late. Browse through collections of beautiful handicrafts from Mexico and other countries. Fabric aficionados should not miss the Guatemala Shop.

Two blocks from the Old Town perimeter sits **Whaley House** (☎ 298-2482; 2482 San Diego Ave; admission $5; ☺ 10am-4:30pm, closed Tue in winter), the city's oldest brick building.

The Old Town Transit Center, on the trolley line at Taylor St at the northwestern edge of Old Town, is a stop for the Coaster commuter train, the San Diego Trolley (orange and blue lines), and bus Nos 4 and 5 from downtown. Old Town Trolley tours stop southeast of the plaza on Twiggs St.

Downtown
Map p184
GASLAMP QUARTER
Fifth Ave was once San Diego's main street and home to such important industries as saloons, gambling joints and opium dens. It became known as the Stingaree, a notorious red-light district. By the 1960s it had declined to a skid row of flophouses and bars, but in the early 1980s, when developers started thinking about demolition and rebuilding, local protests and the Gaslamp Quarter Council saved the area.

Wrought-iron streetlamps, in the style of 19th-century gaslamps, were installed, along with trees and brick sidewalks. Restored buildings dating from the 1870s to the 1920s now house restaurants, bars, galleries and theaters. The 16-block area south of Broadway between 4th and 6th Aves is designated a National Historic District, and development is strictly controlled.

The **William Heath Davis House** (☎ 233-4692; 410 Island Ave), brought from Maine in 1850, contains a small museum with 19th-century furnishings. At 11am each Saturday, the Gaslamp Quarter Historical Foundation offers a two-hour guided walking tour from here ($5).

To get a feel for Gaslamp Quarter architecture and history, walk around during the day when you can fully appreciate the buildings.

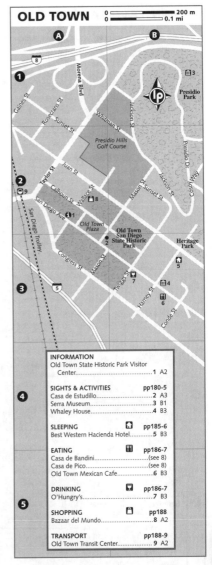

INFORMATION	
Old Town State Historic Park Visitor Center.............................1 A2	

SIGHTS & ACTIVITIES	pp180-5
Casa de Estudillo.............................2 A3	
Serra Museum.................................3 B1	
Whaley House..................................4 B3	

SLEEPING	pp185-6
Best Western Hacienda Hotel.............5 B3	

EATING	pp186-7
Casa de Bandini.............................(see 8)	
Casa de Pico.................................(see 8)	
Old Town Mexican Cafe...................6 B3	

DRINKING	pp186-7
O'Hungry's.....................................7 B3	

SHOPPING	pp188
Bazaar del Mundo............................8 A2	

TRANSPORT	pp188-9
Old Town Transit Center....................9 A2	

SAN DIEGO HARBOR/EMBARCADERO
Here's the place to take a pleasant stroll and view the **Maritime Museum** (☎ 234-9153; www.sdmaritime.org; N Harbor Dr & Ash St; adult/senior & military/child age 6-12 $7/5/4; ☺ 9am-8pm, to 9pm summer) on the impressive square-rigger *Star of India*. Docked nearby are several other beautiful ships with interesting histories.

DOWNTOWN SAN DIEGO

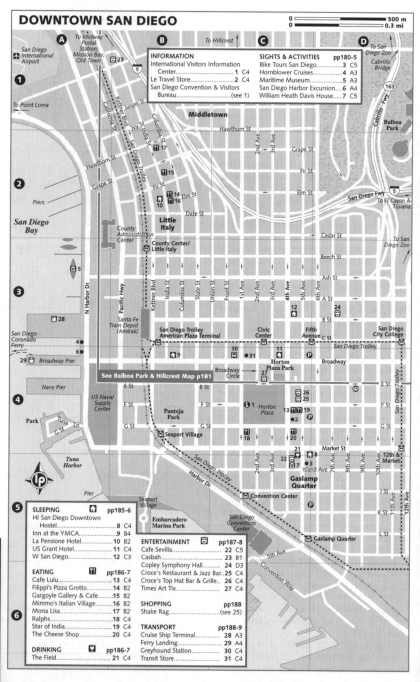

0 —————————— 500 m
0 —————————— 0.3 mi

Call or stop by **Hornblower Cruises** (☎ 725-8888; www.hornblower.com; ticket booth 1066 N Harbor Dr; 2hr cruise adult/child age 4-12 $20/10) for a variety of cruises. **San Diego Harbor Excursion** (☎ 234-4111, 800-442-7847; www.harborexcursion.com; 1050 N Harbor Dr) runs similar trips and there's also the **Coronado ferry** from the Broadway Pier ($1.50).

Little Italy   Map p184
Between Hawthorn and Ash Sts on the north and south, and Front St and the waterfront on the east and west, is San Diego's **Little Italy**. The area was settled in the mid-19th century by Italian immigrants, mostly fisherfolk and their families, who created a cohesive and thriving community.

When I-5 was completed in 1962, the heart (and, many say, soul) of the area was destroyed. Entire blocks were demolished. However, recent redevelopment has made Little Italy the hippest and most charming of downtown's neighborhoods.

Uptown & Hillcrest   Map p181
Uptown is a triangle north of downtown, east of Old Town and south of Mission Valley. Called Bankers Hill after some of the wealthy residents – or Pill Hill, because of the many doctors – these upscale heights had unobstructed views of the bay and Point Loma before I-5 was built.

A favorite pastime of residents old and new is crossing the 375ft **Spruce St Footbridge** that hangs over a deep canyon between Front and Brant Sts. The **Quince St Bridge**, between 4th and 3rd Aves, is a wood-trestle bridge built in 1905 and refurbished in 1988 after its proposed demolition was vigorously protested by community activists.

At the heart of Uptown is Hillcrest (bus Nos 1, 3 and 25 go to/from downtown along 4th and 5th Aves), the first suburban real-estate development in San Diego and now a lesbian and gay enclave. Hillcrest's **farmers market** (cnr Normal & Lincoln Sts; ☉ 9am-1pm Sun) is a fun place to people-watch.

Hiking
For a taste of what locals enjoy, visit **Mission Trails Regional Park** (Map p179; ☎ 668-3725; www.mtrp.org; One Father Junipero Serra Trail), a 10-minute drive away, which has several challenging trails. Two self-guided walks start at the visitors center; one identifies native

plants, while the other teaches about flora and fauna and the lifestyle of the Kumeyaay Indians who once lived here. There's also a **campground** (see Sleeping below).

Bicycling
Bike Tours San Diego (Map opposite; ☎ 238-2444; biketourssd@aol.com; 509 5th Ave; ☉ 8am-7pm Sat & Sun) rents out bikes (for all ages), recommends routes and offers tours.

TOURS
Old Town Trolley Tours (☎ 298-8687; adult/child $25/12, 10% on-line discount), in a green and orange bus done up to resemble an old-fashioned streetcar, does a loop around the main attractions near downtown and in Coronado. You can get on or off at any number of stops. Tours start at 9am and run every 30 minutes or so until 7pm. Trolley stops are marked with orange signs, usually next to a regular bus stop.

See the San Diego Harbor/Embarcadero (p183) section for tour boat information.

SLEEPING
Tourism is a major industry in San Diego. In summer (late May to early September), accommodation prices shoot up.

Budget
La Pensione Hotel (Map opposite; ☎ 236-8000, 800-232-4683; www.lapensionehotel.com; 1700 India St; s/d $65/75 year-round; Ⓟ) This is the best budget deal in San Diego. All the rooms are newly renovated and clean with plenty of natural light. In the heart of Little Italy, it's within walking distance of the harbor.

HI San Diego Downtown Hostel (Map opposite; ☎ 619-525-1531; 521 Market St; dm $16/19 members/nonmembers; ☉ 7am-midnight, pass code at night) This facility in the Gaslamp Quarter has lots of space for hanging out, an elevator and wheelchair-accessible rooms and bathrooms. It's a good deal but if you leave your windows open at night it can be noisy.

Hillcrest Inn (Map p181; ☎ 293-7078; 3754 5th Ave; r from $59) Friendly staff have their finger on the pulse of the gay community (but welcome straight guests, too). Ask for bar recommendations and you may get a free-drink coupon.

Inn at the YMCA (Map opposite; ☎ 234-5252; 500 W Broadway; r $55) This downtown budget option has rooms with shared bathroom, which are

SAN DIEGO

quite OK as a money-saving option. Some people stay here longer term, so weekly rates are available.

Kumeyaay Lake Campground (reservations ☎ 668-2748; sites $13) To get away from it all, head to Mission Trails Regional Park's campground, about a 20-minute drive from downtown. Three of the 47 sites are wheelchair accessible. There are bathrooms but no hookups. Take Hwy 8 east to Mission Gorge/Fairmont Ave. Turn north on Mission Gorge Rd and drive for 6 miles to the second Father Junipero Serra Trail entrance and turn left at the light. It's just a quarter of a mile further.

Mid-Range

Off either side of Hwy 8 in Mission Valley, Hotel Circle North and Hotel Circle South have a dozen or so mid-range chain motels.

The cheapest of these are **Vagabond Inn** (Map p181; ☎ 297-1691, 800-522-1555; 625 Hotel Circle S; r from $70; P) and **Comfort Inn Suites** (☎ 291-7700, 800-647-1903; 2485 Hotel Circle Place; r from $80; P), both with higher rates in summer.

Town & Country Hotel (Map p181; ☎ 291-7131, 800-772-8527; 500 Hotel Circle N; r from $125; P) Town & Country is a popular base for business gatherings as well as the leisure crowd. Price specials often keep rooms filled off-peak.

Best Western Hacienda Hotel (Map p183; ☎ 298-4707, 800-888-1991; 4041 Harney St; ste from $153; P) This lovingly looked after Spanish-style building is an excellent choice. Lounge in the comfortable lobby or relax poolside. Work out and then attend cocktail hour. Rates can go as low as $89, depending on availability.

Top End

W San Diego (Map p184; ☎ 231-8220; whotels.com; 421 W B St; r $249-500; P) Hopefully, you can stay more than one night here. If you don't, you'll never be able to use all the amenities, like Internet access and CD player in rooms or the gym and pool. If you get an in-room massage you might not have anything left to put in your in-room safe. But it's worth it all to sip cocktails at the rooftop Beach Bar, with sand underfoot. Check the website for specials.

US Grant Hotel (Map p184; ☎ 232-3121, fax 232-3626; 326 Broadway; s $150-180, d $165-200, ste from $295; P) This is the classiest hotel downtown and another place to go if money is no object. It's not very old (1910), but it was built by Ulysses S Grant Jr (son of the president). It has housed a host of famous guests, including Charles Lindbergh, Albert Einstein and Harry S Truman. Special packages can be substantially cheaper.

EATING & DRINKING

Supermarkets are ubiquitous. **Ralphs** (Map p184; ☎ 595-1581; 101 G St) is just south of Horton Plaza; and **Whole Foods** (Map p181; ☎ 294-2800; 711 University Ave, Hillcrest) sells organic produce and more.

Balboa Park   Map p181

Several of the park's museums have cafés.

The Prado (☎ 557-9441; lunch $9-19, dinner $16-26; lunch daily, dinner Tue-Sun) In the House of Hospitality, this four-star establishment has Mediterranean seafood, meat, pastas and a kid's menu.

Old Town   Map p183

Casa de Pico (☎ 296-3267; dishes from $6) Sip a margarita in the lively courtyard of this Mexican restaurant right in the Bazaar del Mundo. People queue up but it's worth it. The mariachi music will keep you entertained.

Another good Mexican option is **Casa de Bandini** (☎ 297-8211; 2660 Calhoun St; dishes under $11).

Old Town Mexican Cafe (☎ 297-4330; 2489 San Diego Ave; dishes $4-8; breakfast, lunch & dinner) This local favorite has a big bar, dining room and patio, and excellent food. The *carnitas* (roasted and shredded pork with onions and peppers) are famous, and served with lots of condiments – from cilantro to avocado – and warm tortillas which you can watch being made.

If you're thirsty, buy a round at Old Town's classic dive, **O'Hungry's** (☎ 298-0133; 2547 San Diego Ave).

Gaslamp Quarter   Map p184

The Gaslamp Quarter has numerous restaurants. Many are cavernous places featuring entertainment in the evening.

The Cheese Shop (☎ 232-2303; cnr 4th Ave & G St; snacks $4.50-7) Unpretentious and funky, it's no wonder that this day-time deli is much loved by locals for its great sandwiches and coffee.

SAN DIEGO

Cafe Lulu (☎ 238-0114; 419 F St; dishes $4-8; ✆ to 3am) This place breaks the mold. It's warm, inviting and small, with no glitz or bouncers scrutinizing long lines of people. Stop here for coffee and light meals.

Star of India (☎ 544-9891; 423 F St; buffet lunch $8, dishes $7-15) The North Indian food here is tasty (request your preferred spice level), though service may be slow (but smiling) on crowded nights.

The Field (☎ 232-9840; 546 5th Ave) The decor may be a bit over-the-top Irish but the Guinness goes down easy (if pricey, at $5 a pint). It's a bar in the early and late evening hours but at dinnertime many tables are reserved for those ordering fish 'n' chips.

Little Italy   Map p184

Gargoyle Gallery & Cafe (☎ 234-1344; 1845 India St; ✆ 8am-6pm) Cushioned benches sidle up to mosaic-covered tables at this great café, where the coffee and food are fresh and delicious. Try the hummus plate or Greek salad. Or wait...the fresh mozzarella and tomato sandwich with pesto. Breakfast is yummy too. This is the friendliest service you're likely to find in San Diego.

Filippi's Pizza Grotto (☎ 232-5094; 1747 India St; dishes $10) A heady mélange of garlic and onion, spices and tomato hangs in the air here. Pizza (feeds two to three) takes center stage.

Mimmo's Italian Village (☎ 239-3710; 1743 India St; snacks from $3) A few doors away from Filippi's, Mimmo's has hot and cold sandwiches and pasta salads.

North of Filippi's is **Mona Lisa** (☎ 234-4893; 2061 India St; dishes $6-11) for sit-down meals.

Uptown & Hillcrest   Map p181

Nami Sushi (☎ 297-7888; cnr University & 5th; dishes from $6) The vegetarian rolls here are divine; the beer cold. Come after dark for glowing views of the classic neon Hillcrest Sign.

Taste of Thai (☎ 291-7525; 527 University Ave; dishes $6-9) Another good choice, this Thai restaurant offers all levels of spiciness.

Hamburger Mary's (☎ 491-0400; 308 University Ave; dishes $7-14) A self-consciously gay eatery, but everybody is welcome to try their 'special tease,' a daily plate such as top sirloin steak with soup or salad and fries. Mary's has good margaritas and is famous for its Sunday champagne brunch buffet ($12.95).

ENTERTAINMENT

The free weekly *San Diego Reader* and San Diego *Union Tribune's* 'Night & Day' section hits the stands each Thursday with comprehensive listings and reviews. **San Diego Art + Sol** (www.sandiegoartandsol.com) is an excellent website with thorough information about the city's cultural landscape, including daily updated events listings.

Call **Ticketmaster** (☎ 220-8497) for event information and to book tickets. **Times Arts Tix** (Map p184; ☎ 497-5000), in the little Horton Plaza park on Broadway, sells half-price tickets for same-day evening or next-day matinee performances in theater, music and dance and full-price tickets to major events.

Clubs & Live Music

In Old Town, listen to mariachi bands in Bazaar el Mundo.

Ingrid Croce, widow of singer Jim Croce, is owner and executive chef at **Croce's Restaurant & Jazz Bar** (Map p184; ☎ 233-4355; 802 5th Ave; dishes $8-30) and Croce's **Top Hat Bar & Grill** (Map p184; ☎ 232-4338) next door. Both have live music and serve good but pretty pricey salads, pastas and contemporary American fare.

Cafe Sevilla (Map p184; ☎ 233-5979; 555 4th Ave; tapas $4-6, dishes $15-25) Live Latin American music and dancing is available most nights in Cafe Sevilla.

Casbah (Map p184; ☎ 232-4355; 2501 Kettner Blvd) Just when you thought there was no counterculture in San Diego...you saw a punk band at the Casbah, near Little Italy. Recommended are the dimly lit alcoves.

Gay & Lesbian

The Loft (Map p181; ☎ 296-6407; 3610 5th Ave) Grab a beer with locals at this friendly gay bar (all are welcome) and sing along to '80s tunes.

Brass Rail (Map p181; ☎ 298-2233; 3796 5th Ave) Perhaps the city's oldest gay bar, with a different music theme nightly, from Latino to African to Top 40. Competitive? Play pinball, pool or darts.

The Flame (Map p181; ☎ 295-4163; 3780 Park Blvd) A popular lesbian lounge, The Flame comes complete with pink padded walls, drapery and red lighting. It has a large dance floor and an indoor cigar bar.

Classical Music

The accomplished, nearly-100-year-old San Diego Symphony gives regular classical performances in the **Copley Symphony Hall** (Map p184; ☎ 235-0804; 750 B St). In summer, musicians move outdoors to the **Navy Pier** (Map p184; 960 N Harbor Dr) for a more light-hearted Summer Pops season.

Theater

Theater thrives in San Diego. Worth special mention is **Balboa Park's Old Globe Theatre Complex** (Map p181; ☎ 239-2255; www.theglobetheaters.org; tickets $17-55), where visitors to the 1935–36 Pacific-California Exposition enjoyed 40-minute renditions of Shakespeare's greatest hits. Saved from demolition in 1937, the theaters became home to a popular summer series of Shakespeare's plays, which were performed in full. In 1978 the whole complex was destroyed by an arson fire, but was rebuilt. It reopened in 1982, winning a Tony award in 1984 for its ongoing contribution to theater arts.

SHOPPING

Downtown shopping is concentrated in Horton Plaza, a mall with many chains. But just because you're in SoCal doesn't mean you must become a mall rat.

Shake Rag (Map p184; ☎ 237-4955; 440 F St) More inspired fashions can be found in the Gaslamp Quarter, at Shake Rag, in the basement of Croce's. Here, you can find 'an entire century's worth of fashion' presented on 6000 sq ft. It's not super-cheap (shirts from $12, jackets from $18), but the selection is unbeatable.

Hillcrest is also known for its hip fashions, vintage clothing and design stores, especially along University Ave.

Museums in Balboa Park have interesting shops selling books, toys and other items related to their exhibits.

Old Town is anchored by the Bazaar del Mundo, offering items from throughout Latin America. Fall in love with mirrors boldly framed with hundreds of bottle caps, or intricate beaded Huichol art from the Sierre Madre Mountains of Central Mexico.

GETTING THERE & AROUND
To/From Airport

Bus No 992 – The Flyer – operates at 10- to 15-minute intervals between the airport and downtown ($2). Buses make several stops along Broadway before heading north on Harbor Dr to the airport.

Several companies operate door-to-door shuttles from all three airport terminals. Per-person fares depend on the distance traveled; figure about $12 to Mission Valley's Hotel Circle, $8 to Old Town or downtown and $14 to La Jolla.

If you're going to the airport, call a day ahead to make arrangements for a pick-up time and location. **Cloud 9 Shuttle** (☎ 505-4950, 800-974-8885) is the most established service.

Air

Most flights into **San Diego International Airport–Lindbergh Field** (Map p178; ☎ 231-2100), about 3 miles west of downtown, are domestic. Coming in from overseas, you'll most likely change flights at one of the major US gateway airports, such as LA, San Francisco or New York City.

If you're flying to/from other US cities, it's almost as cheap to fly to/from San Diego as it is to LA. Airlines serving San Diego include Aeromexico, Delta, Northwest, Southwest and US Airways.

Boat

A regular **ferry** ($1.50) goes between Broadway Pier and Coronado.

Bus

Greyhound (☎ 800-231-2222, 239-3266; 120 W Broadway) serves San Diego from cities all over. The standard one-way/round-trip fare to and from LA is $16/28 (2¼ to 3¾ hours, several daily). Transfer in LA for San Francisco ($52/87, 11 hours). Greyhound offers direct services from San Diego to Tijuana, Mexico ($5/8, one hour, several daily).

Car

The big-name rental companies have desks conveniently located at the airport. For details see Transport (p216).

Public Transport
BUS

Metropolitan buses and the trolley lines are run by **Metropolitan Transit Service** (MTS; ☎ 233-3004, 800-266-6883, 685-4900 24hr recording; www.sdcommute.com; fares $1.75/2 regular/express). All sorts of local public transportation tickets, maps and information are available from the **Transit Store** (Map p184; ☎ 234-1060; 102 Broadway at 1st Ave; ☼ 8:30am-5:30pm Mon-Fri, noon-4pm Sat & Sun). Get the free *Regional Transit Map* here.

TRAIN

Regional Transit (☎ 233-3004, 800-266-6883 from North County; www.sdcommute.com; fares $3-3.75) runs a commuter rail service, the *Coaster*, from the Santa Fe train depot up the coast to North County, with stops in Solana Beach, Encinitas, Carlsbad and Oceanside. In the metropolitan area, it stops at the Sorrento Valley station (where there's a connecting shuttle to UCSD) and Old Town. Tickets are available from vending machines at stations and must be validated prior to boarding.

TROLLEY

Two trolley lines (fares vary with distance, up to $2.50) run to/from the downtown terminal near the Santa Fe train depot. The Blue Line goes south to the San Ysidro border and north to Old Town, then continues east through Mission Valley as far as the Mission San Diego de Alcalá. The Orange Line goes east, past the Convention Center to El Cajon and Santee. Trolleys run between 4:20am and 2:20am daily at 15-minute intervals during the day, and every 30 minutes in the evening. The Blue Line continues running all night on Saturday.

Taxi

Taxi fares are around $1.80 to start, and then about $1.90 per mile. There are several established companies:
American Cab (☎ 292-1111)
Orange Cab (☎ 291-3333)
San Diego Cab (☎ 226-7294)

Train

Amtrak (☎ 800-872-7245; www.amtrak.com) trains arrive and depart from the **Santa Fe train depot** (1050 Kettner Blvd) at the western end of C St. The *Pacific Surfliner* makes several daily runs to LA ($25, 2¾ hours), some continuing to Santa Barbara and San Luis Obispo. To get to San Francisco, transfer in Bakersfield.

COASTAL SAN DIEGO

San Diego has prime coastal real estate for surfing, sunning, swimming or just gazing at the horizon. Developed areas allow for merrymaking with the waves in sight, while quieter stretches of sand permit contemplation. The developed Mission Bay Park offers sheltered swimming for children, resorts,

boating and the animal extravaganza of SeaWorld. The San Diego Bay features a vibrant waterfront on the edge of downtown and the lovely Coronado Island just across the bay. La Jolla (p199) is covered in the San Diego North Coast section.

PACIFIC BEACH & MISSION BEACH
☎ 858

From Pacific Beach Point at the north end of Pacific Beach to the South Mission Jetty at the southern tip of Mission Beach are 3 miles of solid SoCal beach scene. Running the whole length, Ocean Front Walk, the beachfront boardwalk, can get crowded with joggers, in-line skaters and bicyclists and is one of the best people-watching venues in town. On warm weekends, parking becomes impossible and suntanned bodies blanket the beach. Families and fun-seekers flock to Belmont Park, and Mission Blvd gets so crowded that police often close it down.

Up in Pacific Beach, activity spreads inland, especially along Garnet Ave, which is well supplied with bars, restaurants and used clothing stores. The Crystal Pier is a popular place to fish or watch surfers. Down at the Mission Beach end, the hedonism is concentrated in a narrow strip between the ocean and Mission Bay.

Orientation & Information

Mission Blvd is the main drag, heading north-south through Pacific Beach (PB) and Mission Beach. In PB, Garnet Ave is a commercial strip running right down to the beach and Crystal Pier. Banks can be found along Garnet. For other information, including emergency services, see Information (p178) for Inland San Diego.

Sights & Activities
BELMONT PARK

This miniature Coney Island–style **amusement park** (Map p190; ☎ 228-9283; admission free, pay for attractions separately; ☀ 11am-10pm Sun-Thu, 11am-11pm Fri-Sat Jun-Sep; reduced hours off-season) has been a Mission Beach fixture since 1925. The star attraction here is the restored **Giant Dipper** (rides $3.50), a classic wooden roller coaster that was declared a National Historic Landmark in 1987. The creaky ride clocks in at just under two minutes and covers 2600ft; the highest drop is 70ft and the top speed about 50mph.

SAN DIEGO

MISSION BAY & THE BEACHES

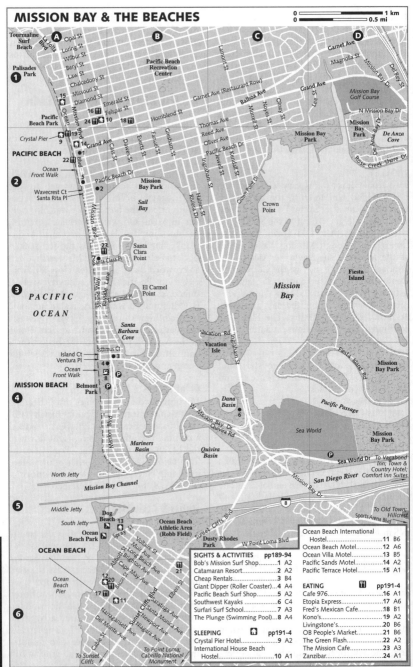

SIGHTS & ACTIVITIES	pp189–94
Bob's Mission Surf Shop	1 A2
Catamaran Resort	2 A2
Cheap Rentals	3 B4
Giant Dipper (Roller Coaster)	4 A4
Pacific Beach Surf Shop	5 A2
Southwest Kayaks	6 C4
Surfari Surf School	7 A3
The Plunge (Swimming Pool)	8 A4

SLEEPING	pp191–4
Crystal Pier Hotel	9 A2
International House Beach Hostel	10 A1
Ocean Beach International Hostel	11 B6
Ocean Beach Motel	12 A6
Ocean Villa Motel	13 B5
Pacific Sands Motel	14 A2
Pacific Terrace Hotel	15 A1

EATING	pp191–4
Cafe 976	16 A1
Etopia Express	17 A6
Fred's Mexican Cafe	18 B1
Kono's	19 A2
Livingston's	20 B6
OB People's Market	21 B6
The Green Flash	22 A2
The Mission Cafe	23 A3
Zanzibar	24 A1

Other big draws are **The Plunge**, an historic Olympic-sized indoor pool; the **Pirates Cove** children's play zone; and **Venturer II**, which features combination video game–virtual reality machines. Parking is $5.

SURFING

Surfing is the primary reason that a good number of San Diegans are here. The water can get crowded and several spots – **Sunset Cliffs** (Map opposite), in Ocean Beach, and **Windansea** (Map p200) in La Jolla – are somewhat 'owned' by locals, but in general San Diego is a great place for surfers of any skill level.

Fall offers the best chance to find strong swells and offshore Santa Ana winds. In summer, swells come from the south and southwest, and in winter, from the west and northwest. Spring brings more frequent onshore winds, but the surfing can still be good. For the latest beach, weather and surf reports, call **City Lifeguard** (☎ 619-221-8824).

Beginners planning to rent equipment should head to Mission Beach or Pacific Beach, where the waves are gentle. North of the Crystal Pier, **Tourmaline Surf Beach** (Map p190) is good to take your first strokes. Places such as **Bob's Mission Surf Shop** (Map opposite; ☎ 483-8837; www.missionsurf.com; 4320 Mission Blvd) and **Pacific Beach Surf Shop** (Map opposite; ☎ 488-9575; 747 Pacific Beach Dr) rent out boards ($5 to $8 per hour) and wet suits ($3).

For lessons, try **Surfari Surf School** (Map opposite; ☎ 337-3287; www.surfarisurf.com; 3780 Mission Blvd) in Mission Beach, started by a group of former lifeguards and a former school teacher. Reservations are required for 1½-hour lessons ($45/60 group/private) and the five-day surf camp ($250).

BICYCLING

Cheap Rentals (Map p190; ☎ 488-9070; www.cheap -rentals.com; 3685 Mission Blvd) has low prices and rents out everything from bikes and roller-blades to baby-joggers.

Sleeping

International House Beach Hostel (Map p190; ☎ 274-4325; 4502 Cass St; dm $18/20 student/non-student, r $40) This is not an HI-affiliated hostel so the atmosphere is a bit looser. With friendly staff and a decent facility, it attracts a young crowd.

Crystal Pier Hotel (Map opposite; ☎ 483-6983, 800-748-5894; 4500 Ocean Blvd; cottages $130-250 winter,

---

BEST SURF BREAKS

The best surf breaks, from south to north, are at **Imperial Beach** (especially in winter); **Point Loma** (reef breaks which are less accessible, but less crowded; best in winter); **Sunset Cliffs** in Ocean Beach; **Pacific Beach**; **Big Rock** (California's Pipeline); **Windansea** (hot reef break, best at medium to low tide, but crowded); **La Jolla Shores** (beach break best in winter); and **Blacks Beach** (a fast, powerful wave). Further up, in North County, there are breaks at **Cardiff State Beach**, **San Elijo State Beach**, **Swami's**, **Carlsbad State Beach** and **Oceanside**.

---

min 2-night stay; $170-280 summer, min 3-night stay) A series of bright white cottages actually on Crystal Pier, this is one of the most coastal places to stay. Dating from 1927, the distinctive arched entrance to the pier is a landmark at the end of Garnet Ave. Cottages sleep four to eight.

Cheaper is the well-positioned and well-worn **Pacific Sands Motel** (Map opposite; ☎ 483-7555; 4449 Ocean Blvd; r $55-60 winter; [P]); most rooms have a kitchen.

Pacific Terrace Hotel (Map opposite; ☎ 581-3500, 800-344-3370; www.pacificterrace.com; 610 Diamond St; ste $260-730; [P] [🛁]) Lap up the luxury at the Pacific Terrace in PB. These rooms are unbeatable: clean, classy and many with ocean views. If you're sick of the crowds on the Ocean Front Walk, lounge by the pool. Rates can drop significantly in the off-season.

Eating

Casual restaurants line Garnet Ave in PB; other dining and drinking spots are found near the pier, and along the Ocean Front Walk in both PB and Mission Beach.

Cafe 976 (Map opposite; ☎ 272-0976; 976 Felspar St; dishes $3-6) Believe it or not, there are a few folks in PB who believe there's more to life than the beach. They're here, sipping coffee or discussing literature. Breakfast, lunch and 'nighttime fare,' including sandwiches and soups, are cheap and good.

Zanzibar (Map opposite; ☎ 272-4762; 976 Garnet Ave; dishes $7-10) This place is open late – 365 days a year. Order at the counter from a long menu of soups, salads and sandwiches (try the focaccia pizzas). You may have to wait a while as this place gets busy, but the food is worth it. While you're waiting, people-watch in the large dining room.

Kono's (Map p190; ☎ 483-1669; 704 Garnet Ave) Also in PB is this long-time favorite across from the Crystal Pier. On a Saturday or Sunday morning, lines start wrapping around the block (well, almost) shortly after sunrise. The $5 breakfast burritos and blueberry pancakes are excellent, but anything served with the homemade potato dish is a winner.

Fred's Mexican Cafe (Map p190; ☎ 483-8226; 1165-B Garnet Ave; burritos $3) Avoid this place if you're on a diet: the burritos weigh more than a pound.

The Green Flash (Map p190; ☎ 270-7715; 701 Thomas Ave; dishes $12-22) On PB's section of the Ocean Front Walk, watch the suntanned and sweaty parade of humanity go by from the Green Flash. Hit happy hour from 3pm to 7pm Monday to Friday.

The Mission Cafe (Map p190; ☎ 488-9060; 3795 Mission Blvd; ⏱ 7am-3pm) In Mission Beach, this café offers 'conscientious cuisine' (their words) and has a fascinating mix of Chinese and Latino dishes. For breakfast, the egg dishes paired with rosemary-scented potatoes are popular; and lunches can bring concoctions like ginger-sesame chicken in tortillas.

Getting There & Around

For information on getting to San Diego, see Getting There & Around on p188. Bus routes serving Pacific Beach are Nos 30 and 34. The No 34 serves Mission Beach.

MISSION BAY

☎ 619

In the 18th century, the mouth of the San Diego River formed a shallow bay when the river flowed, and a marshy swamp when it didn't – the Spanish called it False Bay. After WWII, a combination of civic vision and coastal engineering turned the swamp into a 7-sq-mile playground, with 27 miles of shoreline and 90 acres of park. With financing from public bonds and expertise from the US Army Corps of Engineers, the river was channeled to the sea, the bay was dredged and millions of tons of sludge were used to build islands and peninsulas. A quarter of the new land has been leased to hotels and other businesses, repaying the bonds.

Sights & Activities

The attractions of Mission Bay include resort hotels, free outdoor activities and SeaWorld. Kite flying is popular in Mission Bay Park, and there's cycling and in-line skating on the miles of smooth paths (see below for rental information). Volleyball is big on Fiesta Island.

BOATING

Ocean kayaking is a good way to see marine life and explore cliffs and caves inaccessible from land. **Southwest Kayaks** (Map p190; ☎ 222-3616), near SeaWorld at the Dana Landing, has guided trips and classes, both starting at $35.

You can rent equipment at the Resort Waterspots, affiliated with **Catamaran Resort** (Map p190; ☎ 858-488-2582). Rentals range in price from $6 per hour for a boogie board to $80 per hour for a powerboat. Half-day and day rates are also available.

SEAWORLD

SeaWorld (Map p190; ☎ 226-3901; adult/child 3-11 $40/30, parking $8), opened in 1964, was the brainchild of four fraternity brothers from UCLA. What began with a few small shows and saltwater aquariums has evolved into a four-star attraction that appeals to people of all ages. Shamu, one of SeaWorld's killer whales, has become an unofficial symbol of the city.

The park is commercial, but nonetheless entertaining and slightly educational. Even if some of the animal shows are disturbingly reminiscent of old-fashioned circus acts, SeaWorld has a serious side, also working on animal conservation, rescue, rehabilitation, breeding and research. Beautiful landscaping – accomplished with more than 4500 plant species – throughout the park is a relaxing counterpoint to the sensory assault of the shows and attractions.

Ways to get the best value for your ticket include a re-entry stamp, which lets you go out for a break and return later the same day; and a two-day pass that gives you admission on two consecutive days ($44/34).

The shows starring trained animals distinguish SeaWorld from a regular zoo. **Shamu Adventure** is the most visually spectacular show, and the one you won't want to miss. Throughout the 30-minute program, the three star performers – Shamu, Baby Shamu and Namu – glide, leap, dive and flip through

SAN DIEGO

CROSSING THE US-MEXICAN BORDER

Every day an average of 226,000 people and 82,000 cars cross the US-Mexican border at San Ysidro, making it the world's busiest border crossing. Open 24 hours a day, the border is about 20 miles south of downtown San Diego and about a 10-minute walk from Tijuana. You can cross the San Ysidro border on foot, by car or by bus from either side. The alternative crossing at Mesa de Otay, 5 miles east of San Ysidro, is open 6am to 10pm. There is no public transport to Mesa de Otay.`

US citizens or permanent residents not intending to go past the border zone (in other words, beyond Ensenada), or to stay in the border zone for more than 72 hours, don't need a visa or even a passport to enter Tijuana. Do, however, bring some form of identification with your photo on it. Non-Americans can be subject to a full immigration interrogation upon returning to the US, so bring your passport and USA visa (if you need one).

San Diego Trolley

The San Diego Trolley Blue Line is the cheapest, easiest and most efficient way to travel to the border from central San Diego. Trollies leave on the 45-minute journey every 15 or 30 minutes from early morning to late at night and around the clock on Saturday. The fare is $2. If you're arriving at the airport and heading straight to the border, take bus No 992 and transfer to the trolley at America Plaza (request a transfer). The trolley terminus is on the US side of the border, from where you'll continue on foot.

Car & Motorcycle

Unless you're planning an extended stay or thorough exploration of Tijuana, taking a car across the border is probably more hassle than it's worth. If you do decide to take one, though, the most important thing you must do is get Mexican car insurance either beforehand or at the border crossing (available in numerous offices right at the Via de San Ysidro and Camino de la Plaza exits off I-5; about $8 per day). Expect to wait, as US security has tightened in recent years. The alternative crossing at Mesa de Otay is much less congested, but further from town.

You may also leave your car on the US side of the border and either walk or take a shuttle across. Several parking lots are located just off the Camino de la Plaza exit (the last US exit) off I-5. A popular lot is **Border Station Parking** (4570 Camino de la Plaza; $7 per day). Also here is a small tourist information kiosk with maps and pamphlets.

Walking

To cross the border on foot from San Ysidro, simply take the pedestrian bridge, then pass through the turnstiles and you're on Mexican soil. There's a tourist office about 150ft along the walkway and another by the yellow taxi stand. To reach Avenida Revolución, turn right just before the taxi stand, then continue west past souvenir hawkers and taco stands to a large outdoor mall called Plaza Viva Tijuana. From its far end, another pedestrian bridge leads across the Río Tijuana. From here continue west along Calle 1a (Calle Comercio), past countless more souvenir shops, to the foot of Avenida Revolución. The entire walk takes 10 to 15 minutes.

Walking from Tijuana to San Ysidro also involves a pedestrian bridge and turnstiles, and dealing with US Customs & Immigration.

the water while interacting with each other, the audience and their trainers.

Pirates 4-D is a 17-minute 3-D comedy movie that follows the adventures of a hapless pirate crew stranded on a Caribbean island. Written by Eric Idle of Monty Python fame, it also features actor Leslie Nielsen. The fourth dimension is provided by the audience, which is treated to a host of special effects (buzzing seats, water cannons, simulated bat attacks).

The shows are the park's flashy headliners, but to see animals close-up, visit the exhibits. In **Penguin Encounter**, king, macaroni and other penguin species share a habitat that faithfully simulates Antarctic living conditions. The temperature behind the glass-enclosed space is a constant 25°F, but light conditions change with the seasons just as nature dictates. So, if you're visiting in July (winter in Antarctica), you'll see them waddle and swim in near-darkness at all times.

The **Wild Arctic** takes you on a simulated-motion ride aboard a helicopter to Base Station Wild Arctic, a recreated research station with polar bears, beluga whales, walruses and seals. Kids love roaming through the polar bear dens (complete with growling sounds) and touching a 25ft ice wall, but watching the giant walrus in its crammed quarters is depressing.

Scary but true: you'll see dozens of sharks as you walk through a 57ft acrylic tube called **Shark Encounter**. Species include blacktip and whitetip, reef and sand tiger sharks, some of them impressively large.

Getting There & Around

For information on getting to San Diego from out of town or from the airport, see Getting There & Around (p188). From PB, take Ingraham St which runs south into Mission Bay to Vacation Isle and then to SeaWorld. From Mission Beach, take West Mission Bay Dr. I-5 runs along Mission Bay's east side. To get into Mission Bay or to SeaWorld from the highway, take SeaWorld Dr off I-5. By bus, take No 9 or No 27 from the Old Town Transit Center.

OCEAN BEACH
☎ 619

The community of Ocean Beach (OB) is a good place to get tattooed, shop for antiques or let it all hang out. Newport Ave, the main drag that runs perpendicular to the beach, is a compact zone of bars, surf shops, music stores, and used-clothing and antique stores. Bus No 23 connects OB to downtown.

The half-mile-long Ocean Beach Pier is good for fishing. North of the pier is the beach scene headquarters, with volleyball courts and sunset barbecues. North of here is Dog Beach, where dogs can run unleashed. A few blocks south of the pier is Sunset Cliffs Park, where watching surfers is mesmerizing and the sunset sublime.

Sights & Activities

If you're here on Wednesday afternoon, stop by the **OB farmers market** (☆ 4-7pm Wed, 4-8pm Jun-Sep) to see street performers and sample fresh food.

For more information on the area, also see Sights & Activities (opposite) for Point Loma.

Sleeping & Eating

This area has limited accommodations and it's a young scene.

Ocean Beach International Hostel (Map p190; ☎ 223-7873, 800-339-7263; 4961 Newport Ave; dm $16-20, d $35-40) If you're on a budget, try this hostel only a couple of blocks from the ocean. This friendly, fun place has helpful staff and is popular with European travelers.

Ocean Villa Motel (Map p190; ☎ 224-3481, 800-759-0012; 5142 W Point Loma Blvd; r from $120/75 summer/winter; P) This quiet, family-run motel is near Dog Beach (but no pets allowed).

Ocean Beach Motel (Map p190; ☎ 223-7191; 5080 Newport Ave; r $99-175; P) In the heart of OB's action and currently being renovated, the Ocean Beach Motel has rooms with ocean views. Upgrades include adding microwaves and refrigerators to some deluxe rooms.

OB People's Market (Map p190; ☎ 224-1387; cnr Voltaire St & Sunset Cliffs Blvd) For groceries and take-out meals, visit this organic co-operative with bulk foods, fresh soups and excellent pre-made sandwiches, salads and wraps, mostly under $5.

Etopia Express (Map p190; ☎ 224-3237; 5001-A Newport Ave; dishes $3-5; ☆ 10am-8pm) Don't miss Etopia Express, with smoothies, vegan pizza and wraps like the Cosmic Californian for $4.75. The incredibly friendly staff say they will stay open late if someone is hungry.

Livingstone's (Map p190; ☎ 224-8088; 5026 Newport Ave; dishes under $5) Saying 'lively' to describe Livingstone's is an understatement. Especially at sunset, the place brims with young folks downing beers by the pitcher and eating inexpensive Mexican food. Breakfast is served until 3pm.

Getting There & Away

To get to Ocean Beach, take Hwy 8 west from I-5. It ends in Sunset Cliffs Blvd, which intersects Newport Ave. Stay on Sunset Cliffs Blvd to reach the Sunset Cliffs Park. Bus No 35 connects Ocean Beach with downtown.

POINT LOMA
☎ 619

Point Loma is the peninsula that hangs down across the entrance to San Diego Bay, protecting it from the Pacific Ocean. Access to much of it is limited because of military installations, but there are still plenty of interesting sights to see in the area. San Diego's international airport, Lindbergh Field, forms the easternmost part of the peninsula.

San Diego's first fishing boats were based at Point Loma, and in the 19th century whalers dragged carcasses onto its shores to extract oil. Chinese fisherfolk settled on the harbor side of the point in the 1860s but were forced off in 1888 when the US Congress passed the Scott Act prohibiting anyone without citizenship papers from entering the area. Portuguese fishing families came 50 years later and established a permanent community. The Portuguese Hall is still a hub of activity and many people living on Point Loma are of Portuguese descent.

The tidal flats of Loma Portal, where Point Loma joins the mainland, were used as an airstrip in 1927 by Charles Lindbergh for flight-testing the *Spirit of St Louis*.

Sights & Activities
CABRILLO NATIONAL MONUMENT
On the southern tip of **Point Loma**, the peninsula that reaches south across the entrance to San Diego Bay, is **Cabrillo National Monument** (☎ 557-5450; www.nps.gov/cabr; admission $5/2 per car/bike or bus, good for 7 days; ☻ 9am-5:15pm Oct-Jul 3, 9am-6:15pm Jul 4-Sep). It commemorates and pays homage to Juan Rodríguez Cabrillo, the Portuguese-born explorer in the service of Spain who landed at San Diego Bay on September 28, 1542. He was the first European to land on what would later become the USA's West Coast. The visitors center has an excellent exhibition about the native inhabitants and the area's natural history.

At the time of writing, the grounds of the 1854 **Old Point Loma Lighthouse** were undergoing a facelift that includes a new interpretive exhibit shelter.

On the ocean side of the point, you can visit the **tidepools** to look for anemones, starfish, crabs, limpets and dead man's fingers (thin, tubular seaweed).

The **Bayside Trail** zigzags around the monument for about 2 miles, passing through native coastal sage shrub and nearby remnants of a WWII-era defense system, which includes gun batteries, fire-control stations and searchlight bunkers. A small **military exhibit** tells the story of the 19th Coast

Artillery at Fort Rosecrans, which defended San Diego, a prime military target, during WWII. The largest guns were at Battery Ashburn, northwest of the park entrance.

WHALE-WATCHING
The **Whale Overlook** in Cabrillo National Monument is the best place in San Diego to see the gray whale migration from land. Gray whales pass San Diego from mid-December to late February on their way south to Baja California, and again in mid-March on their way back up to Alaskan waters. Their 12,000-mile round-trip journey is the longest migration of any mammal.

Cabrillo National Monument has exhibits, whale-related ranger programs and a shelter from which to watch (bring binoculars).

Whale-watching cruises operate daily during the migration. The cost is around $15 to $20 for adults and $10 for children for a three-hour trip. Some outfits guarantee a sighting, and many have discount coupons in the *San Diego Reader*. Contact **Hornblower Cruises** (☎ 725-8888; www.hornblower.com) or **San Diego Harbor Excursion** (☎ 234-4111, 800-442-7847; www.harborexcursion.com).

BICYCLING
A great ride is from Sunset Cliffs Park out on the bike lane paralleling Hwy 209 – all the way to the Cabrillo monument. See Bicycling in Inland San Diego (p185) or in Mission Beach (p191) for rental information.

Getting There & Away
From Ocean Beach, head south on Santa Barbara St to connect with Catalina Blvd/ Hwy 209 that runs south along Point Loma. From the Old Town Transit Center, Bus No 26 heads all the way out to Point Loma and the Cabrillo National Monument.

CORONADO
☎ 619 / pop 28,500
Directly across the bay from downtown, Coronado is, administratively, a separate city and known for closely guarding its ambience and environmental quality. The spectacular 2.1-mile-long Coronado Bay Bridge (toll $1 with only a driver, and free with at least one passenger) joins Coronado to the mainland. The **Silver Strand** ($2 parking), a long, narrow sand spit, runs south to Imperial Beach.

It's windy but great for swimming in the Pacific. There are grills, outdoor showers and changing rooms. Exhaust yourself wave-diving, then visit the **Hotel del Coronado** (Map p179; ☎ 435-6611, 800-468-7337; 1500 Orange Ave; r $235-595; P ☺). The building is striking, with conical towers, cupolas, turrets, balconies and dormer windows. The cavernous public spaces reflect the background of James and Merritt Reed, who designed railroad depots. 'The Del' was where Edward (then the Prince of Wales) first met Mrs Simpson (then Mrs Spenser) in 1920; it achieved its widest exposure in the 1959 Marilyn Monroe movie, *Some Like It Hot*. Even if you can't afford to stay here, come for a cocktail or stroll on the pleasant beach nearby.

Bus Nos 901, 902 and 903 from downtown run the length of Orange Ave to the Hotel del Coronado.

SAN DIEGO NORTH COAST

The North Coast extends up the coast from the pretty seaside town of Del Mar to the Camp Pendleton Marine Base. This continuous string of beachside suburban communities resembles the San Diego of 30 years ago, though ongoing development (especially east of I-5) is turning North County into a giant bedroom community for San Diego and Orange County. Still, the beaches here are terrific, and the small seaside towns are good for a few days of relaxation. La Jolla is covered in this section.

The most coastal thoroughfare through this region is Old Hwy 101. Note that it changes it's name. You'll see SR21, North Coast Hwy, South Coast Hwy, Del Mar Blvd, among others. But it's pretty hard to get lost. Hwy 5 also runs north to south through the area.

Stop at the well-stocked **California Welcome Center** (☎ 760-721-1101, 800-350-7873; 928 North Coast Hwy) to chat with knowledgeable staff about the entire North Coast.

OCEANSIDE
☎ 760 / pop 161,000
Oceanside is home base for many of the employees who work on, or for, Camp Pendleton

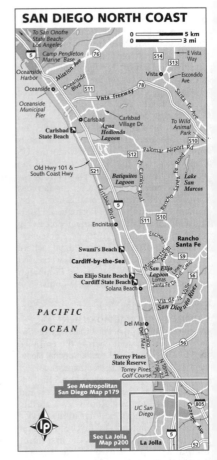

SAN DIEGO NORTH COAST

Marine Base on the town's northern border. Most attractions of interest to visitors are along the coast, although there are a few worthy restaurants on South Coast Hwy.

Sights & Activities
OCEANSIDE MUNICIPAL PIER
The main attraction in town is the wooden **Oceanside Municipal Pier**, extending more than 1900ft out to sea. There are snack bars, and bait and tackle shops, with poles to rent and lights for night fishing. Two major surf competitions – the West Coast Pro-Am and the National Scholastic Surf Association (NSSA) – take place near the pier in June.

At the northern end of the waterfront, the extensive Oceanside Harbor provides slips for hundreds of boats. **Helgren's** (☎ 722-2133; 315 Harbor Dr S) offers a variety of charter trips for sportfishing (half-/full day $29/55) and whale-watching (full day $18).

CALIFORNIA SURF MUSEUM

Recite the ancient Hawaiian surfing chant: '*Arise! Arise! Ye great surfs from Kahiki, The powerful curling waves! Arise with pohuehue, Well up, long raging surf*' at the **California Surf Museum** (☎ 721-6876; 223 N Coast Hwy; donations requested; ⏲ 10am-4pm Thu-Mon). It's amazing to see the old wooden boards that surfers used to ride. Many are on display, including Faye Baird Fraser's 8ft, 85lb redwood board. The museum also hangs a fine collection of old photos including one of Fraser surfing a 13ft tandem board at night, holding lighted flares. Makes one long for the old days. There is also memorabilia of Duke Kahanamoku (the Olympic gold medal swimmer and surfing pioneer who died in 1968).

SURFING

Visit **Action Beach Board Shop** (☎ 722-7101; www .actionbeach.com; 310 Mission Ave) to rent surfboards (two hours/full day $10/20), wet suits (two hours/full day $5/10) and other items.

There's also the year-round **Team Wahine Surfing School** (☎ 439-5679; www.teamwahine.com) offering lessons (hourly rate $55, lower rates on multiple lessons or groups, gear included) and camps for groms age 11 to 16.

Sleeping & Eating

San Onofre State Beach (☎ 949-492-4872; reservations 800-444-7275; sites $16; ⏲ Apr-Oct) This campground offers a chance to live dangerously: it is very close to the San Onofre Nuclear Generating Station, which provides 20% of the power to 15 million Southern Californians. The campground is on a 90ft-high bluff overlooking the ocean, with beach access via steep trails. There's a dump station, cold showers and toilets.

Guesthouse Inn & Suites (☎ 722-1904; 1103 N Coast Hwy; r from $65; P) Close to I-5 off the Coast Hwy exit, the Guesthouse Inn has a restaurant and harbor view.

Oceanside Days Inn (☎ 722-7661; 1501 Carmelo Dr; r from $60; P) With some views of the water, this inn has basic rooms.

Johnny Mañanas (☎ 721-9999; 308 Mission Ave; dishes $2-6.50) By the beach, this local chain restaurant is where you can eat 'guilt-free traditional healthy foods from Mexico' for as little as $2 for the guacamole taco to $6.50 for the shrimp enchiladas combo plate.

Hill Street Coffee House (☎ 966-0985; 524 S Coast Hwy; dishes $5-10) Out on the South Coast Hwy (Old Hwy 101; formerly Hill St) is this welcoming coffee house which breaks the town's crew-cut or surfer-tan mold. In this lovely Victorian house you'll be treated to a wide range of great meals made with organic produce (whenever possible). Sometimes there's random produce on a rack outside the door: fill the provided brown bags for just $2.

101 Cafe (☎ 722-5220; 613 S Coast Hwy; dishes $7-10) You can still hear them reciting the 1920s' town slogan, 'Oceanside, California's Pride,' at this café named for Hwy 101. Since 1928, in numerous incarnations, this place has been serving up all-American meals. Don't look for vegetarian here.

Getting There & Away

Amtrak, Greyhound, the *Coaster* and MTS buses all stop at the Oceanside **Transit Center** (235 S Tremont St).

CARLSBAD

☎ 760 / pop 78,200

Carlsbad is a good place to stay if you want to be within walking distance of shopping, restaurants and the beach. Rather than being stretched out along the highway like many North Coast towns, it has a solid downtown of four square blocks between I-5 and Carlsbad Blvd (which run north–south and are connected by Carlsbad Village Dr running east–west). The **Visitor Information Center** (☎ 434-6093; 400 Carlsbad Village Dr) is housed in the original 1887 Santa Fe train depot.

Like so many others, this town was made by the arrival of the railroad in the 1880s. John Frazier, an early homesteader, sank a well and found water with a high mineral content, supposedly the identical mineral content of spa water in Karlsbad (hence the town's name) in Bohemia (now the Czech Republic). Capitalizing on this aquatic similarity, he built a grand spa hotel, which prospered until the 1930s. The Queen Anne–style building is now **Neiman's Restaurant & Bar** (☎ 729-4131; 2978 Carlsbad Blvd), a place where the atmosphere is appreciably better than the overpriced food.

SAN DIEGO

Sights & Activities

BEACHES

The long, sandy beaches of Carlsbad are great for walking and seashell hunting. Good access is from Carlsbad Blvd, two blocks south of Carlsbad Village Dr, where there's a boardwalk, rest rooms and free parking.

The **Offshore Surf Shop** (☎ 729-4934; 3179 Carlsbad Blvd) rents out boards for $5/25 per hour/day and wet suits for $3/15. For lessons, call the **Carlsbad Surf School** (☎ 845-2272; 2hr group/private lessons $40/75).

FLOWER FIELDS

From March to May, the 50-acre flower fields of **Carlsbad Ranch** are ablaze in a sea of carmine, saffron and the snow-white blossom of ranunculus flowers. The fields are two blocks east of I-5; take the Palomar Airport Rd exit, go east, then left on Paseo del Norte Road – look for the windmill. Call ☎ 431-0352 for hours, prices or an events schedule.

BATIQUITOS LAGOON

South of Carlsbad is the **Batiquitos Lagoon**, one of the last remaining tidal wetlands in California. On a self-guided tour, you'll spot plenty of local plants, including the prickly pear cactus, coastal sage scrub and eucalyptus trees, as well as lagoon birds such as the great heron and the snowy egret. One of the artificial islands is a nesting site for the California least tern and the western snowy plover, both endangered species.

Sleeping & Eating

Surf Motel (☎ 729-7961, 800-523-9170; 3136 Carlsbad Blvd; r from $129/79 summer/winter; **P** **☻**) This friendly motel is close to the beach.

Carlsbad Inn (☎ 434-7020, 800-235-393; 3075 Carlsbad Blvd; r from $178; **P** **☻**) This top-end option is on the beachfront.

Vigilucci's Cucina Italiana (☎ 434-2500; 2943 State St; dishes from $12) Sit outdoors and choose from the extensive wine list at this Italian eatery.

The Armenian Cafe (☎ 720-2233; 3126 Carlsbad Blvd; dishes $6-12) Two blocks south of Carlsbad Village Dr, the Armenian is often chosen by locals for its excellent and authentic Armenian food.

Pizza Port (☎ 720-7007; 571 Carlsbad Village Dr; dishes $3-16) Serves up salads, pizza, locally brewed beer and surfing videos on TV.

LEGOLAND CALIFORNIA

Modeled loosely on the original Legoland in Denmark, **Legoland California** (☎ 918-5346; adult/child 3-16 $34/29, 2-day tickets $42/37; ☺ 9am-8pm mid-Jun–Sep, 10am-5pm Oct–mid-Jun) is an enchanting fantasy environment built entirely of those little colored plastic building blocks that many of us grew up with. There are bicycles to ride around the grounds, a boat tour of some exhibits, and many opportunities to build (and buy) your own Lego structures. It's all rather low-key compared with bigger, flashier parks such as Disneyland and therefore especially suited to younger children (10 and under). To get to Legoland, take the Legoland/Cannon Rd exit off I-5 and follow the signs. From downtown Carlsbad or downtown San Diego, take the *Coaster* to the Poinsettia Station, from where bus No 344 goes straight to the park.

Getting There & Away

Old Hwy 101 is Carlsbad Blvd through the center of town and heads north to Oceanside or south to La Jolla. Amtrak's *Coaster* stops here.

ENCINITAS

☎ 760 / pop 58,000

Yogi Paramahansa Yoganada founded his **Self-Realization Fellowship Retreat & Hermitage** here in 1937, and Encinitas has been a magnet for holistic healers and natural lifestyle seekers ever since. The gold lotus domes of the hermitage – easily spotted from Old Hwy 101 (S21) – mark the southern end of Encinitas and the turn-off for Swami's Beach, a powerful reef break surfed by territorial locals. There's a parking lot just south of the hermitage, on the western side of Old Hwy 101, which gives a good view of the surf. There is also a great vista from the hermitage's **Meditation Garden** (entrance 215 K St; ☺ 9am-5pm Tue-Sat, 11am-5pm Sun); the entrance is west of Old Hwy 101.

The heart of Encinitas is north of the hermitage between E and D Sts. Apart from outdoor cafés, bars and surf shops, the town's main attraction is **La Paloma Theater** (☎ 436-7469; 471 S Coast Hwy 101), built in 1928 and showing current movies nightly.

The inland hills are covered in commercial flower farms, most notably the **Paul Ecke**

Poinsettia Ranch (☎ 753-1134; www.ecke.com), established in 1928. In December there's an enormous poinsettia display at the ranch, and in spring the flowers grow in bands of brilliant color, which look spectacular from I-5.

The 30-acre **Quail Botanical Gardens** (☎ 436-3036; adult/child $5/2; ☉ 9am-5pm) has a large collection of Californian native plants, and sections planted with flora of various regions of the world, including Australia and Central America. From I-5, go east on Encinitas Blvd to Quail Gardens Dr.

SOLANA BEACH
☎ 858 / pop 13,000

Solana Beach has good **beaches** and the recently dubbed **Design District** (Cedros Ave), which has unique art and architecture studios, antiques stores and handcrafted clothing boutiques.

One of the first businesses here was **Belly Up Tavern** (☎ 481-2282, 481-8140; 143 S Cedros Ave), a converted warehouse which is still a popular music venue and regularly gets great bands. The cover charge is $5 to $10, or up to $20 for top attractions.

Wild Note Cafe (☎ 259-7310; dishes from $6) is affiliated with the Belly Up, and pleases guests for lunch or dinner.

DEL MAR
☎ 858 / pop 4400

Del Mar is the ritziest of North County's seaside towns. It has excellent restaurants, galleries, high-end boutiques and a horse-racing track, which is the site of the annual county fair. Downtown Del Mar (sometimes called the village) extends for about a mile along Camino del Mar. At its hub, where 15th St crosses Camino del Mar, is another of SoCal's monuments to consumerism, **Del Mar Plaza**. Overlooking the water, its terraces house expensive restaurants and boutiques, one of which sells clothing made solely from white fabric.

Sights & Activities
At the beach end of 15th St, **Seagrove Park** overlooks the ocean. This little chunk of well-groomed beachfront is a community hub frequented by locals.

The **Del Mar Racetrack & Fairgrounds** (☎ 755-1141; track admission $3), created in 1937 by a group including Bing Crosby and Jimmy Durante, has lush gardens and delightful, pink, Mediterranean-style architecture. The thoroughbred racing season runs from mid-July to mid-September.

Brightly colored hot-air balloons are a trademark of the skies above Del Mar. For pleasure flights, contact **Skysurfer Balloon Company** (☎ 481-6800; 1221 Camino del Mar).

The *Reader* lists other balloon companies and frequently contains hot-air excursion discount coupons. Flights are usually at sunrise or sunset and last about an hour ($130/150 on weekdays/weekends).

Sleeping & Eating
Del Mar Motel (☎ 755-1534, 800-223-8449; www.delmarmotelonthebeach.com; 1702 Coast Blvd; r from $120/90 summer/winter) The Del Mar Motel offers tidy rooms right on the beach.

L'Auberge Del Mar Resort & Spa (☎ 259-1515, 800-553-1336; 1540 Camino Del Mar; r from $225) If you're going to splurge, there are few places better to do it than this resort right across from Del Mar Plaza. Built on the grounds of the historic Hotel Del Mar – where Charlie Chaplin and Lucille Ball once frolicked (though not with each other) – its reincarnation continues to draw celebrities, including Bonnie Raitt and Mel Brooks.

Del Mar Pizza & Pasta (☎ 481-8088; 211 15th St; dishes $7-12) This Brooklyn-style pizzeria may be the least pretentious place in town. Eat with the plebs for $2.50 a cheese slice.

Cafe del Mar (☎ 481-1133; 1247 Camino del Mar; dishes $10-22) Enjoy brunch with the family or bring your love to the outside patio in the evening to sit under the twinkling white lights and shimmering tree leaves. The pasta or grilled salmon will delight.

Pacifica Del Mar (☎ 792-0476; dishes $18-25) At the top of the plaza, this restaurant has excellent fresh fish.

For self-catering, try the deli at **Good Nature Market** (☎ 481-1260), on the Plaza's lower level.

LA JOLLA
☎ 858 / pop 28,800

Immaculately landscaped parks, white-sand coves, upscale boutiques and a perfect site atop cliffs that meet deep, clear blue waters make it easy to understand why 'La Jolla' is often translated from Spanish as 'the jewel.' In fact, Indians who inhabited the area from 10,000 years ago to the mid-19th

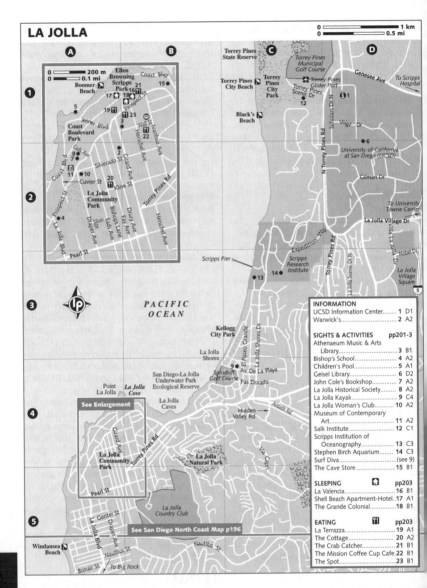

LA JOLLA

century called the place 'mut la Hoya, la Hoya' – the place of many caves. In any case, it's pronounced 'la *hoy-*ya' and is a great place to spend the day.

The area was subdivided in the 1880s and more intensively developed when Ellen Browning Scripps moved here in 1897. The newspaper heiress acquired much of the land along Prospect St, which she donated to various community uses. Not only did she support local institutions such as the **Bishop's School** (cnr Prospect St & La Jolla Blvd) and the **La Jolla Woman's Club** (715 Silverado St); she also had them designed by Irving Gill, who set the architectural tone of the community – an unadorned Mediterranean style characterized by arches, colonnades, lots of lush palm trees, red-tile roofs and pale stucco.

The surrounding area is home to the University of California San Diego, several renowned research institutes and a new-money residential area called the Golden Triangle, bounded by I-5, I-805 and Hwy 52. The space-age church in this area, which you see from I-5, is a Mormon Temple, completed in 1993.

Orientation

The compact town sits atop cliffs surrounded on three sides by the ocean. Distant views of Pacific blue are glimpsed through windows and from between buildings. The main thoroughfares, Prospect St and Girard Ave, are lined with restaurants, shops and galleries.

Information

Scripps Hospital (☎ 457-4123; 9888 Genesee Dr, La Jolla) Seek medical attention at the area's finest hospital.
Warwick's (☎ 454-0347; 2812 Girard Ave) Find the latest books here.

Sights & Activities

OLD TOWN

For a touch of old-style La Jolla, head northwest along Prospect St. **John Cole's Bookshop** (☎ 454-4766; 780 Prospect St) is in a cottage once owned by Ellen Browning Scripps and renovated to Irving Gill's design. Around the corner, the **La Jolla Historical Society** (☎ 459-5335; Eads Ave; ⊗ noon-4:30pm Tue-Thu) has vintage photos and beach memorabilia – think old bathing costumes, lifeguard buoys and the like.

The **Museum of Contemporary Art** (☎ 454-3541; 700 Prospect St; admission $4, free 1st Tue & 3rd Sun of month; ⊗ 11am-5pm winter, 11am-8pm Mon-Fri summer & Thu year-round, closed Wed) shows world-class exhibitions. Originally designed by Irving Gill in 1916 as the home of Ellen Browning Scripps, a redesign of the building was conceived by Philadelphia-born postmodern architect Robert Venturi. Also note the Andy Goldsworthy sculpture out front.

Walk east on Silverado St to Girard Ave. Here you'll find the latest from big names in fashion and the **Athenaeum Music & Arts Library** (☎ 454-5872; cnr Wall St & Girard Ave; ⊗ 10am-5.30pm Tue & Thu-Sat, 10am-8:30pm Wed), where you can see small art exhibits and read daily newspapers from around the globe.

THE COAST

Downhill from downtown, the La Jolla coastline is rugged and invigorating. Private properties going right down to the beach restrict access, and parking is limited at some points, but there is a wonderful walking path that skirts the shoreline for half a mile.

The path's western end begins at the **Children's Pool**, where a jetty protects the beach from big waves. Originally intended to give La Jolla's youth a safe place to frolic, the beach is now more popular with sea lions and is a great place to view them up close as they lounge on the shore.

Atop Point La Jolla, at the path's eastern end, **Ellen Browning Scripps Park** overlooks La Jolla Cove to the north. The cove's lovely little beach offers access to some of the best snorkeling around and is popular with rough-water swimmers.

The offshore area from Point La Jolla north to Scripps Pier, marked by white buoys, is the **San Diego–La Jolla Underwater Park Ecological Reserve**, with a variety of marine life, some kelp forests and interesting reefs and canyons. Waves have carved a series of caves into the sandstone cliffs east of La Jolla cove. The largest is called Sunny Jim Cave, which you can access ($2) from **The Cave Store** (☎ 459-0746; 1325 Cave St; ⊗ 9am-5pm).

The best place to surf and see surfers is 2 miles south of downtown (take La Jolla Blvd south and turn west on Nautilus St) at **Windansea Beach**. The surf's consistent peak (a powerful reef break, not for beginners) works best at medium to low tide. Immediately south, at the foot of Palomar St, **Big Rock** is California's version of Hawaii's Pipeline, with steep, hollow, gnarly tubes. The name comes from the large chunk of reef protruding from just offshore – a great spot for tidepooling at low tide.

LA JOLLA SHORES

Called 'the Shores,' this area northeast of La Jolla Cove is where La Jolla's cliffs meet the wide, sandy beaches that stretch north to Del Mar. Primarily residential, the Shores is home to **Kellogg City Park**, where the beachside playground is good for families. To reach the beach, take La Jolla Shores Dr north from Torrey Pines Rd and turn west onto Ave de la Playa. The waves are gentle enough for beginner surfers, and kayakers can launch from the shore without much problem.

Surf Diva (☎ 454-8273; www.surfdiva.com; 2160 Avenida de la Playa) offers weekend workshops for gals (only) of all ages. The cost is $98, or $115 from May to October.

Kayaking is fantastic here, as you can paddle amid the kelp forest or into the caves. You can also get close to the sea lions basking at Children's Pool. Rent kayaks (and wet suits if it's chilly) at **La Jolla Kayak** (☎ 459-1114; www.lajollakayak.com; 2199 Avenida de la Playa). Two hours ($40 for a two-seater, $5 wet suit) is a good amount of time. Ask about cave tours.

TORREY PINES STATE RESERVE & BEACH

Encompassing the land between N Torrey Pines Rd and the ocean from the Torrey Pines Glider Port to Del Mar, this **reserve** (☎ 755-2063; www.torreypine.org; 9am-sunset) preserves the last mainland stands of the Torrey pine (*Pinus torreyana*), a species adapted to sparse rainfall and sandy, stony soils. Steep sandstone gullies are eroded into wonderfully textured surfaces, and the views over the ocean and north to Oceanside are superb, especially at sunset.

The main access road, Torrey Pines Scenic Dr, off N Torrey Pines Rd (bus Nos 41 and 301) at the reserve's northern end, leads to a simple adobe which now acts as a **visitors center** (☎ 755-2063). Built as a lodge in 1922 for Ellen Browning Scripps, it now has exhibits on local flora and fauna. Rangers lead nature walks from here at 11am and 2pm weekends.

Entry and parking is $2 per car – if the ticket office is closed, get a permit from the yellow machine in the lower parking lot – or free if you walk in. Several walking trails wind through the reserve and down to the beach. If you want to hike, park near the driving range on N Torrey Pines Rd and take the paved path northwest until you reach a box of trail maps at the beginning of the Broken Arrow Trail.

Some of the best beaches in the county are north of the Shores in **Torrey Pines City Park**, which covers the coastline from the Salk Institute up to the Torrey Pines State Reserve. At extreme low tides (about twice a year), you can walk from the Shores north to Del Mar along the beach.

The Torrey Pines Glider Port (☎ 452-9858; 2800 Torrey Pines Scenic Dr; tandem flights $150 for 20min), at the end of Torrey Pines Scenic Dr, is the place for hang-gliders and paragliders to launch themselves into the sea breezes that rise over the cliffs. It's a beautiful sight. Down below is **Blacks Beach**, where bathing suits are technically required but practically absent. This is a popular hangout for gay men.

SALK INSTITUTE

The **Salk Institute** (☎ 453-4100, ext 1200; 10010 N Torrey Pines Rd) for biological and biomedical research was founded by Jonas Salk, the polio-prevention pioneer, in 1960. Designed by Louis Kahn and completed in 1965, it is regarded as a modern masterpiece, with its classically proportioned travertine marble plaza and cubist, mirror-glass laboratory blocks framing a perfect view of the Pacific. The facilities have been expanded, with new laboratories designed by Jack McAllister, a follower of Kahn's work. You can tour the Salk Institute with a volunteer guide at 11am and noon Monday to Friday.

UNIVERSITY OF CALIFORNIA, SAN DIEGO

A campus of the University of California, UCSD was established in 1960 and now has more than 18,000 students and an excellent academic reputation, particularly for its math and science programs. It lies on rolling coastal hills in a park-like setting, with many tall and fragrant eucalyptus trees. Its most distinctive structure is the **Geisel Library**, an upside-down pyramid of glass and concrete whose namesake, children's author Theodor Geisel, is better known as Dr Seuss, creator of *The Cat in the Hat*. He

DETOUR TO WILD ANIMAL PARK

Don't miss the **Wild Animal Park** (☎ 760-747-8702; www.wildanimalpark.org; adult/senior/child age 3-11 $27/24/20; 9am, closing hours vary by season) in the San Pasqual Valley, where you can see giraffes, elephants, lions, pandas and many other animals. Take the **Wagsa Bush Line Railway** 55-minute guided tour or book in advance for a **photo caravan** (☎ 619-718-3050) to bring home photo souvenirs and memories of feeding giraffes. To get here, take Hwy 15 and exit at Via Rancho Parkway. Follow signs to the park, 6 miles away. For public transport from San Diego, call ☎ 800-266-6883.

and his wife have contributed substantially to the library, and there is a collection of his drawings and books on the ground level.

The best access to the campus is off La Jolla Village Dr or N Torrey Pines Rd (bus Nos 41 and 301 from downtown); parking is free on weekends.

SCRIPPS INSTITUTION OF OCEANOGRAPHY
Marine scientists were working here as early as 1910 and, helped by donations from the ever-generous Scripps family, it has grown to be one of the world's largest marine research institutions. It is now part of UCSD, and its pier is a landmark on the La Jolla coast. The SIO is not to be confused with the Scripps Research Institute (10550 Torrey Pines Rd), a private, nonprofit biomedical research organization.

Affiliated with Scripps is the **Stephen Birch Aquarium** (☎ 534-3474; 2300 Exhibition Way, off N Torrey Pines Rd; adult/student/child $9.50/6.50/6; 9am-5pm daily), which is well worth a visit.

Sleeping
The Grande Colonial (☎ 454-2181; www.thegrandecolonial.com; 910 Prospect St; r from $230/170 summer/winter; P R) This place is the real deal. A National Trust for Historic Preservation member, the hotel occupies a hilltop corner and is adorned with blue and white awnings and flanked by tall palm trees. The rooms, some with ocean views, are plush.

La Valencia (☎ 454-0771; 1132 Prospect St; r $250-550 year-round; P) Yep, it's another ritzy place that exudes historic charm and unbridled California elegance. Great views, pink walls, palm trees and Mediterranean-style architecture (designed by William Templeton Johnson) have attracted movie stars and millionaires since it opened in the 1920s.

For a little less, try the **Shell Beach Apartment-Hotel** (☎ 459-4306, ☎ 800-248-2683; 981 Coast Blvd; r $139-219; P).

Eating
Dining is a pleasure in La Jolla, especially brunch.

The Mission Coffee Cup Cafe (☎ 454-2819; 1109 Wall St; dishes $6-9) Locals and tourists crowd this spot, spilling out onto sidewalk tables. Try the blackberry pancakes, or come for savory tamales or Asian-style wok dishes.

The Cottage (☎ 454-8409; 7702 Fay Ave; dishes from $6; 7:30am-3pm year-round, dinner Jun-Sep) This early 1900s cottage has been restored with a wonderful garden patio for outdoor dining. The 'Eat Your Vegetables' omelet is a good pick. Dinner features multiple salads and pastas.

La Terrazza (☎ 459-9750; 8008 Girard Ave; dishes $10-23) Service is friendly at this candlelit trattoria. Italian food is yummy here, from pizzas to pastas and seafood. Try the carciofini salad with warm baby artichokes, peppers, olives and tomatoes.

The Crab Catcher (☎ 454-9587; 1298 Prospect St; seafood dishes $15-30) In the Coast Walk complex, this is a good option for seafood and views. Drinks and appetizers during its nightly happy hour (3pm to 7pm) could make a nice meal for around $10.

The Spot (☎ 459-0800; 1005 Prospect St; dishes from $9) The Spot has meals until 1am. It's refreshingly un-glitzy for La Jolla, with a lively bar scene and a mixed crowd, from tourists to students to surfers.

Getting There & Around
From Pacific Beach in San Diego, head north on Mission and then follow La Jolla Blvd north. Alternately, hop on Hwy 5 if you're further inland, and exit on Ardath Rd. It'll loop around, first north then west, becoming Torrey Pines Blvd, which also takes you into town.

If you don't have wheels, bus No 34 connects La Jolla to downtown San Diego via the Old Town Transit Center.

Directory

CONTENTS

PRACTICALITIES

■ California lies within the Pacific Time Zone: Greenwich Mean Time minus eight hours.

■ The US uses the imperial system of weights and measures, but you'll sometimes see roadside mileage signs written in both kilometers and miles.

■ If your portable electrical appliances have adjustable current-selector switches, set them to 110V for US travel.

■ Video systems use the NTSC color TV standard, not compatible with PAL or Secam.

■ Six corporations own America's major media outlets. Listen instead for PRI (Public Radio International), Alternative Radio or more conservative NPR (National Public Radio) on the FM dial; for behind-the-corporate-veil news, see www.alternet.org or www.fair.com.

ACCOMMODATIONS

Accommodations in this book fall into one of three categories: budget ($40 to $80), mid-range ($80 to $175) and top end ($175+). Within each category, our top pick appears first on the list. However, just because something isn't at the top of our list doesn't mean it's not good. On the contrary. Each property we recommend meets a certain baseline standard for quality within its class.

Lodging in Coastal California is expensive. In some regions, like San Francisco, budget lodgings start at $75 a night. Prices listed reflect *published, high-season rates* for rooms. You can almost always do better, particularly mid-week or during the off-season, which along the coast means winter. Rates are generally highest in summer but they spike even higher around major holidays like Memorial Day, Independence Day and Labor Day, when you should expect two- and three-night minimum stays. Always ask about discounts, packages and promotional rates. If you have Internet access, check the web; some lodgings give better rates if you book over the Internet.

If you smoke, be sure to ask about the availability of smoking rooms. Many lodgings in California are exclusively non-smoking. In Southern California, nearly all lodgings have air-conditioning, but in Northern California, where it rarely gets hot, the opposite is true. If it matters, inquire when you book.

If you book a reservation on the phone with a motel or hotel, *always ask about the cancellation policy* before you give your credit-card number. If you plan to arrive late in the evening, call to confirm on the day of arrival. Hotels overbook, but if you've guaranteed the reservation with a credit card, they will accommodate you somewhere else and pick up the tab for the first night's stay as a way of apologizing. If they don't, squawk.

Where available, we have listed a property's toll-free information and reservation number in this book. If you're having trouble finding accommodations, consider using a hotel-reservation service such as the **Hotel Reservations Network** (☎ 800-964-6835; www.hoteldiscount.com) or the **Central Reservation Service** (☎ 800-873-4683; www.reservation-services.com). The service is free but its rates may not be the lowest.

Camping

Campgrounds abound in California, and most along the coast are open year-round. Facilities vary widely. Basic campsites usually have toilets, fire pits, picnic benches and drinking water and are most common in national forests and on Bureau of Land Management (BLM) land. The state- and national-park campgrounds tend to be the best equipped, featuring flush toilets, sometimes hot showers and RV hookups.

You can camp in national forests and on BLM land in any area where you can safely park your vehicle next to a road without blocking traffic. You are not allowed to park off undesignated roads (ie roads not shown on maps and that do not have signs that show the road number). Dispersed camping is not permitted in national parks, except for backpackers holding the appropriate permit. Check with a ranger station if you're unsure about where you can camp. Rangers also issue required fire permits (usually free).

Hostels

There are currently 23 hostels in California affiliated with **Hostelling International–American Youth Hostels** (HI-AYH; ☎ 800-909-4776; www.hiayh.org); check respective geographic chapters throughout this book. Reservations are advised during peak season.

Independent hostels have no curfew and more relaxed rules. Often these hostels are convivial places with regular guest parties and other events. Some include a light breakfast or other meals in their rates, arrange local tours and pick up guests at transportation hubs. Some hostels say they accept only international travelers, basically to keep out destitute locals – Americans who look like they will fit in with the other guests are usually admitted. A passport, HI-AYH card or international plane ticket should help establish your traveler credentials.

B&Bs

If you want a comfortable, atmospheric alternative to impersonal motel or hotel rooms, stay at a B&B. They're typically in restored old houses with floral wallpaper and antique furnishings; they charge over $120. Rates include breakfast, but rooms with TV and telephone are the exception, not the rule; some may share bathroom facilities. Most B&Bs require advance reservations, though some will accommodate the occasional drop-in guest. Smoking is prohibited.

Many places belong to the **California Association of Bed & Breakfast Inns** (☎ 831-462-9191; www.cabbi.com).

Motels & Hotels

Motels surround a parking lot and usually have some sort of a lobby. Hotels may provide extra services like laundry, but such amenities are expensive. If you walk in without reservations, always ask to see a room before paying for it, especially at motels.

Rooms are often priced by the size and number of beds in a room, rather than the number of occupants. A room with one double or queen-size bed usually costs the same for one or two people, while a room with a king-size bed or two beds costs more. There is often a surcharge for a third or fourth person. Many places advertise that kids stay free, but sometimes you'll have to pay extra for a crib or 'rollaway'.

Room location may also affect the price; recently renovated or larger rooms, or those with a view, are likely to cost a bit more. Hotels facing a noisy street may charge more for quieter rooms.

As a rule, motels offer the best lodging value for the money. Rooms won't often win design awards, but they're usually comfortably furnished and clean. Amenities vary, but expect telephone, TV, private bathroom, heating and air-conditioning, and an alarm clock. More and more places now offer a small refrigerator, coffeemaker and microwave. Many have swimming pools and spas, coin laundry and free local telephone calls.

Make reservations at chain hotels by calling their central reservation lines, but to learn about specific amenities and possible local promotions, call the property directly. Every listing in this book includes local direct numbers.

Luxury Hotels & Resorts

Luxury hotels provide every imaginable amenity. Expect very comfortable, attractive furnishings, a bathrobe, iron, ironing board, hair dryer, thick terry-cloth towels, firm mattress, high-thread-count sheets and both down and foam pillows on the bed. If there's something missing, pick up the phone and call the concierge or front desk (see Tipping, later in this chapter). Higher-end properties offer more services, such as in-room massage and evening turn-down. Some amenities cost extra. On the premises expect a restaurant of excellent caliber, serving three meals a day.

BUSINESS HOURS

In large cities, several supermarkets and restaurants are open 24 hours. Shops are open from 9am or 10am to 5pm or 6pm (often until 9pm in shopping malls), except Sunday when hours are noon to 5pm (often later in malls). Post offices are open 8am to 4pm or 5:30pm weekdays, and some are open 8am to 2pm on Saturday. Banks usually open from 9am or 10am to 5pm or 6pm weekdays; some also open until 1pm or 2pm on Saturday. Check with individual businesses for precise hours.

CHILDREN

Successful travel with young children requires planning and effort. Don't overbook your day. Cramming too many activities into a 12-hour day inevitably causes problems.

Ensure that the activities you choose include something for the kids as well – balance that morning at the art museum with a visit to the zoo or the beach. Include the kids in the trip planning; if they've helped figure out where you are going, they will be much more interested when they get there. For more information, advice and anecdotes, look at Lonely Planet's *Travel with Children*, by Cathy Lanigan.

Practicalities

Children's discounts are widely available for everything from museum admissions to bus fares and motel stays. The definition of a child varies – in some places anyone under 18 is eligible, while others only include children under six. Unless specified, prices quoted for children in this book refer to those aged three to 12.

Many hotels and motels allow children to share a room with their parents for free or for a modest fee, though B&Bs rarely do

and many don't allow children at all. Larger hotels often have a babysitting service, and other hotels may be able to help you make arrangements. Alternatively, look in the *Yellow Pages* for local agencies. Be sure to ask whether sitters are licensed and bonded, what they charge per hour, whether there's a minimum fee and whether they charge extra for meals and transportation. Always tip.

Most car-rental firms have children's safety seats for rent at a nominal cost, but be sure to book them in advance. The same goes for highchairs and cribs; they're common in many restaurants and hotels, but numbers are limited. The choice of baby food, infant formulas, soy and cow's milk, disposable diapers (nappies) and other necessities is great in supermarkets throughout California. Diaper-changing stations can be found in many public toilets in malls, department stores, some gas stations, major airports and even in some restaurants.

It's perfectly fine to bring your kids, even toddlers, along to casual restaurants (though not to upscale places at dinner-time). Children are generally welcome at daytime events.

Sights & Activities

Throughout this book you'll find family-friendly activities – Coastal California offers lots for kids to do. Aside from the many lighthouses along the shore, kids love Fisherman's Wharf (p98) in San Francisco, SeaWorld (p192) in San Diego and Disneyland (p152) and Universal Studios (p155) in Los Angeles, to just name a few. At national parks be sure to inquire at visitors centers for 'Junior Ranger' programs, in which kids complete specified activities and receive a badge or patch and certificate to take home. There's usually a nominal charge (less than $5) for the activity book. Many outdoor-activity tour operators have specially tailored gear for kids, depending on how little they are. Good activities along the coast include horseback riding, kayaking, bicycling and fishing. Check individual chapters for specific vendors.

CLIMATE CHARTS

Coastal California has a diversity of climates, with the cool, foggy North Coast (including San Francisco) and year-round temperate regions further south. For more climate information, see p9.

DIRECTORY

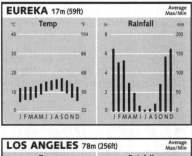

EUREKA 17m (59ft) — Average Max/Min — Temp / Rainfall

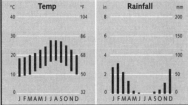

LOS ANGELES 78m (256ft) — Average Max/Min — Temp / Rainfall

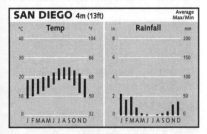

SAN DIEGO 4m (13ft) — Average Max/Min — Temp / Rainfall

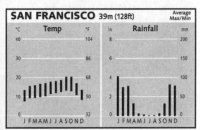

SAN FRANCISCO 39m (128ft) — Average Max/Min — Temp / Rainfall

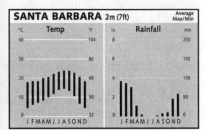

SANTA BARBARA 2m (7ft) — Average Max/Min — Temp / Rainfall

DANGERS & ANNOYANCES

By and large, California is not a dangerous place. The most publicized problem is violent crime, but this is confined to areas few visitors would go. Wildlife may pose some danger, and of course there is the dramatic, albeit unlikely, possibility of a natural disaster, such as an earthquake. Prepare for the worst, but expect the best.

Crime

Tourists will rarely get tricked, cheated or conned simply because they're tourists. Potential violence is a problem for all, but again it's mostly limited to off-the-beaten-path urban areas. Gang violence is a serious problem in parts of Oakland, as well as the Hunters Point and Bayview districts in San Francisco and some LA suburbs such as Compton, East LA and Watts. Avoid these places, especially after dark.

If you find yourself in a neighborhood where you'd rather not be, look confident. Don't stop every few minutes to look at your map, and hail a taxi if you can. If you're accosted by a mugger, there's no 100% recommended plan of action, but handing over whatever the mugger wants is better than getting attacked. Don't carry valuables or an excess of cash, and don't put it all in the same pocket or wallet. Keep some money separate, and hand it over fast. Muggers are not too happy to find their victims penniless.

While traveling, stash your money in several places, including a money belt worn underneath your clothing. At hotels, use their safe-deposit boxes or at least place valuables in a locked bag. Lock cars and put valuables out of sight or in the trunk. If your car is bumped from behind by another vehicle in a remote area, try to keep going to a well-lit area, gas station or even a police station.

That said, don't meditate on crime. The blood-thirsty American media tends to blow crime out of proportion, giving the impression that you're going to get shot if you set foot on the wrong street. Don't panic. Protect yourself as best you can, then focus your awareness on having a great trip. You'll save yourself a lot of unnecessary mental anguish.

Panhandlers & Homeless People

If you visit a city you're sure to encounter beggars. Many are homeless people suffering from medical or psychiatric problems, or the effects of alcohol and drug abuse; some are scam artists. Although a nuisance, most of them are harmless. Often they have witty signs like 'residentially challenged,' 'nonaggressive panhandler' and 'Let's be honest, I need a beer.'

It's an individual judgment call whether to offer them anything – you might just offer food if you have it. If you want to contribute toward a long-term solution, consider donating to a reputable charity that cares for the homeless.

Wildlife Dangers

Drivers should watch for stock or deer on highways. Hitting a large animal at 55mph will total your car, kill the animal and perhaps seriously injure you as well.

Bears are attracted to campgrounds, where they may find accessible food in bags, tents, cars or picnic baskets. Follow posted instructions at campgrounds. If a bear becomes habituated to human food, it will be shot by rangers. Use bear boxes when they're provided.

Mountain lions – also called 'cougars' or 'pumas' – are most common in the lower western Sierra, and the mountains and forests east of Los Angeles and San Diego, especially in areas with lots of deer, which includes some inland areas near the coast. Attacks on humans are rare.

Stay calm if you encounter one, pick up small children, stand your ground – unless you've cornered the animal, in which case give it an escape route – and appear as large (and confident) as possible by raising your arms or grabbing a stick. If the lion gets aggressive or attacks, fight back, shout and throw objects at it.

Snakes and spiders are found throughout California, and not just in wilderness areas, but they tend to prefer warmer inland areas. Attacks or fatalities are exceedingly rare; the following descriptions are necessarily general. If you get bitten, seek medical attention.

Watch your step when hiking, especially on hot summer afternoons in the inland hills and in the evenings, when rattlesnakes like to bask in the middle of the trail. They're often active at night. Most rattlesnakes have roughly diamond-shaped patterns along their backs and vary in length

from 2ft to 6ft. If you are bitten, you will experience rapid swelling, very severe pain and possible temporary paralysis, but victims rarely die. Antivenin is available in most hospitals. If the snake is dead, bring it in for identification, but don't attempt to catch it if there is even a remote possibility of being bitten again.

In Southern California, scorpions spend their days under rocks or woodpiles. The long stinger curving up and around the back is characteristic of these animals. The stings can be very painful but are almost never fatal; however, bear in mind that small children are at highest risk.

The most dangerous spider in the area is the black widow. The female has a small, round body marked with a red hourglass shape under its abdomen. She makes very messy webs, so avoid these, as the normally shy widow will bite only if harassed. The bite emits neurotoxins; they're painful but very rarely fatal.

The large (up to 6in in diameter) and hairy tarantula looks much worse than it is – it very rarely bites and then usually only when it is roughly handled. The bite is not very serious, although it is temporarily quite painful.

Earthquakes

Earthquakes happen frequently but most are so tiny they can only be detected by sensitive seismological instruments (see Environment on p29). If you're caught in a serious earthquake, get under a desk or table and follow it around the room. Alternatively head to an inside doorway. Protect your head and stay clear of windows, mirrors or anything that might fall. Don't head for elevators or go running into the street. If you're in a shopping mall or large public building, expect the alarm and/or sprinkler systems to come on.

If outdoors, get away from buildings, trees and power lines. If you are driving, pull over to the side of the road away from bridges, overpasses and power lines. Stay inside the car until the shaking stops. If you are on a sidewalk near buildings, duck into a doorway to protect yourself from falling bricks, glass and debris. Prepare for aftershocks. Use the telephone only if absolutely necessary. Turn on the radio and listen for bulletins.

DISABLED TRAVELERS

If you have a physical disability, there's no better place for travel within the US than California. The Americans with Disabilities Act (ADA) requires that all public buildings (including hotels, restaurants, theaters and museums) be wheelchair accessible. Buses and trains must have wheelchair lifts and telephone companies are required to provide relay operators (available via TTY numbers) for the hearing impaired. Many banks now provide ATM instructions in Braille, and you'll find curb-cuts at most intersections and sometimes audible crossing signals as well.

Larger private and chain hotels have suites for disabled guests. If you're worried about stairs, be sure to ask about the availability of an elevator. Major car-rental agencies offer hand-controlled vehicles and vans with wheelchair lifts at no extra charge, but you *must* reserve them well in advance.

All major airlines, Greyhound buses and Amtrak trains allow service animals (like guide dogs) to accompany passengers, but you must have documentation. Airlines must accept wheelchairs as checked baggage and have an onboard chair available, though you should always call in advance. Airlines will also provide assistance for connecting, boarding and disembarking flights; request assistance when making your reservation.

Most national and state parks and recreation areas have paved or boardwalk-style nature trails. For free admission to national parks, blind or permanently disabled US citizens and permanent residents can get a Golden Access Passport. Books worth checking out include *California Parks Access*, by Linda and Allen Mitchell, and *Easy Access to National Parks*, by Wendy Roth and Michael Tompane.

Organizations & Resources

A number of organizations and tour providers specialize in serving disabled travelers:
Access-Able Travel Source (☎ 303-232-2979; fax 303-239-8486; www.access-able.com) This excellent website has many good links.
Mobility International USA (☎ 541-343-1284; www.miusa.org) Advises disabled travelers on mobility issues and runs an educational exchange program.
Moss Rehabilitation Hospital's Travel Information Service (☎ 215-456-9600, TTY 456-9602;

www.mossresourcenet.org/travel.htm) Lists extensive useful contacts.
New Directions (☎ 805-967-2841, 888-967-2841; www.newdirectionstravel.com) Specializes in developmentally disabled travelers.
Twin Peaks Press (☎ 360-694-2462, 800-637-2256; http://home.pacifier.com/~twinpeak) Publishes a quarterly newsletter, as well as directories and access guides.

DISCOUNT CARDS

Many hostels in California are members of **Hostelling International–American Youth Hostel** (HI-AYH; ☎ 800-909-4776; www.hiayh.org), which is affiliated with the International Youth Hostel Federation (IYHF). You don't need an HI-AYH card in order to stay at these hostels, but having one saves you $3 a night. You can also buy one at the hostel when checking in.

If you're a student, bring along an International Student Identity Card (ISIC), a plastic ID with your photograph. These are usually available at your university or at student-oriented travel agencies and often entitle you to discounts on transportation and admission to sights and attractions. If you're a US student, carry your school or university ID card. Students can also buy the **Student Advantage Card** (☎ 877-256-4672; www.studentadvantage.com) for $22.50 for discounts on trains, buses, air fares and merchandise.

People over the age of 65 (sometimes 55, 60 or 62) often qualify for the same discounts as students; any identification showing your birth date should suffice as proof of age. Contact the **American Association of Retired Persons** (AARP; ☎ 800-424-3410; www.aarp.org), an advocacy group for Americans 50 years and older and a good resource for travel bargains, which offers membership cards for even greater discounts and extends its coverage to citizens over 50 years and those of other countries. A one-year membership is $8 for US residents and $10 for foreigners.

FESTIVALS & EVENTS

Local celebrations occur frequently in California. The following list is representative only. Check with local visitors bureaus or chambers of commerce, or contact the California Division of Tourism (see Tourist Information on p215) for more extensive listings.

JANUARY & FEBRUARY

Tournament of Roses Parade (☎ 626-449-4400; www.tournamentofroses.com) The famous New Year's Day parade of flower-coated floats, marching bands and equestrians held in the Los Angeles suburb of Pasadena.

Chinese New Year (San Francisco ☎ 415-391-9680, Los Angeles ☎ 213-617-0396) Held in late January/early February, Chinese New Year has free festivities, firecrackers, parades and lots of food, with the biggest celebrations held in San Francisco and Los Angeles.

Whalefest (☎ 831-649-1770, 888-221-1010) Held in Monterey each year in mid-January in celebration of the gray whales' annual migration, with music, exhibits and art.

MARCH & APRIL

San Diego Latino Film Festival (☎ 619-230-1938; www.sdlatinofilm.com) Screens films from throughout Latin America and the US in mid-March.

Toyota Grand Prix of Long Beach (☎ 888-827-7333; www.longbeachgp.com) A week-long auto racing spectacle through city streets, drawing world-class drivers.

San Francisco International Film Festival (☎ 995-275-9490; www.sfss.org) The country's oldest film festival, in late April to early May.

MAY

Bay to Breakers (☎ 415-359-2800; www.baytobreakers.com) The largest and craziest footrace in the world, it's a mob of costumed runners, world-class athletes and weekend warriors; held in San Francisco in mid-May.

Kinetic Sculpture Race (☎ 707-845-1717; www.kineticsculpturerace.org) On Memorial Day weekend, non-motorized contraptions of all sorts ride from Arcata to Ferndale in the North Coast's wackiest, most famous event.

JUNE

San Francisco Pride (☎ 415-864-3733; www.sfpride.org) Lesbian, gay, bisexual and transgender pride parade, in late June, attracts thousands of people to San Francisco.

JULY

Festival of the Arts & Pageant of the Masters (☎ 800-487-3378; www.foapom.com) Features exhibits by hundreds of artists and a pageant of art masterpieces 're-created' using real people; runs from early July to mid-August in Laguna Beach.

Annual US Open Sandcastle Competition (☎ 619-424-6663; www.usopensandcastle.com) Amazing sandcastle competition in mid-July; held at Imperial Beach, San Diego.

Carmel Bach Festival (☎ 831-624-2046; www.bachfestival.com) If you love baroque music, make it a point to be in Carmel in mid-July or early August for the many recitals, lectures, and performances.

AUGUST

Old Spanish Days Fiesta (☎ 805-962-8101; www.oldspanishdays-fiesta.org) Celebrates early rancho culture with parades, rodeo, crafts exhibits and shows; runs in Santa Barbara in early August.

Steinbeck Festival (☎ 831-796-3833; www.steinbeck.org) Celebrates California's Nobel laureate with films, theater and lectures on John Steinbeck in Salinas in mid-August.

Concours D'Elegance (☎ 831-659-0663; www.pebblebeachconcours.net) Presents vintage vehicles to modern concept cars in a world-class car parade in Pebble Beach in mid-August.

African Marketplace and Cultural Faire (☎ 323-734-1164; www.africanmarketplace.org) Celebrates African-American culture with traditional food, art and entertainment on three weekends in late August and early September in Los Angeles.

SEPTEMBER

Fringe Festival (☎ 415-931-1094; www.sffringe.org) This theater marathon in mid-September brings a variety of performers from around the world to the city of San Francisco.

Monterey Jazz Festival (☎ 831-373-3366; www.montereyjazzfestival.org) This is a long-running, big-name festival of traditional and modern styles of jazz, with workshops and exhibitions in mid-September.

Simon Rodia Watts Towers Jazz Festival (☎ 213-847-4646) Features jazz, gospel, R&B and other sounds in the shadow of the Watts Towers; runs on the last weekend of September in Los Angeles.

OCTOBER

World Championship Pumpkin Weigh-Off (☎ 650-726-4485; www.miramarevents.com) In Half Moon Bay, this is a competition of West Coast pumpkin growers, run in mid-October.

San Francisco Jazz Festival (☎ 415-788-7353, 800-850-7353; www.sfjazz.com) Features live music from top and new artists throughout the city from late October to early November.

NOVEMBER

Christmas Tree Lighting In late November many communities kick off the Christmas season by lighting up a large tree in a public place.

Hollywood Christmas Parade (☎ 323-469-2337) Features celebrities waving at fans lining Hollywood Blvd, classic cars, floats and marching bands.

DECEMBER

Truckers Christmas Convoy (☎ 707-442-5744) This memorable Eureka parade features 100 big rigs decked out with colorful Christmas decorations.

Christmas Boat Parade (☎ 949-729-4400) A parade of 150 or so brightly illuminated boats floating in Newport Beach harbor.

First Night Santa Cruz Alcohol-free New Year's Eve street festival, with dance, theatre and music, suitable for families. Santa Rosa and Monterey also have First Night celebrations. Call the respective visitors bureaus for details.

FOOD

Restaurants in coastal California run the gamut from plain and simple to fabulous and stunning. Listings are presented in three general categories: budget (entrees under $10), mid-range (entrees $10 to $18 and top-end (entrees $16+). Just as with accommodations, within each category our top pick appears first on the list. Remember, simply because a restaurant doesn't appear first on the list doesn't mean it's not good. Indeed, there are several places where everything listed is equally good. We've endeavored to write more detailed reviews to help you choose. For more on food, see p37.

GAY & LESBIAN TRAVELERS

San Francisco and Los Angeles have by far the most established gay and lesbian communities. In 2002 the *New York Times* started printing announcements of 'commitment ceremonies' on its highly prestigious Sunday Style pages. The next year, the Supreme Court overturned sodomy laws. The mayor of San Francisco marries gay couples on Gay Pride weekend at City Hall – even if the state does not currently acknowledge them. Such major advances clearly indicate a new cultural direction for America, but make no mistake, pockets of bigotry persist. Californians tend to be tolerant – especially along the coast – although there have been cases of bashings even in metropolitan areas. In small towns 'tolerance' sometimes comes down to a don't-ask-don't-tell policy.

San Francisco has its famed Castro District; San Diego's primary gay neighborhood lies in the Hillcrest area; and in LA head to West Hollywood and Silver Lake. All three cities have gay and alternative newspapers that list what's happening and provide phone numbers for local organizations.

Damron (www.damron.com) publishes the classic gay travel guides, including *Women's Traveler* and the *Men's Travel Guide*, both updated annually. Damron also publishes *Damron Accommodations*, with lists of gay-owned and gay-friendly hotels, B&Bs and guesthouses nationwide. Another established source, Ferrari Guides' *Women's Travel in Your Pocket*, provides great information for women's travel worldwide. On the web check out http://gay.com for loads of information – though some is by subscription. If you're looking for a gay mechanic or florist, see the *Gay & Lesbian Yellow Pages* (www.glyp.com).

Several important national and worldwide organizations also have a Web presence; these include the **National Gay/Lesbian Task Force** (NGLTF; www.ngltf.org), **Gay and Lesbian Alliance Against Defamation** (GLAAD; www.gladd.org) and the **Lambda Legal Defense Fund** (www.lambdalegal.org).

HOLIDAYS

Holiday travel can be very expensive and difficult, or cheap and easy. Thanksgiving weekend is America's biggest travel weekend, and you'll pay through the nose for a flight on either side of the holiday and be squeezed onto an overbooked flight – the same goes for Christmas. On the upside, people spend these holidays with their families, so city hotels stand nearly empty and consequently offer fantastic room rates.

On the following national holidays, banks, schools and government offices (including post offices) all close, and transportation, museums and other services operate on a Sunday schedule. Holidays falling on a weekend are usually observed the following Monday.

New Year's Day January 1
Martin Luther King Jr Day 3rd Monday in January
Presidents' Day 3rd Monday in February
Memorial Day last Monday in May
Independence Day July 4 (also called the Fourth of July)
Labor Day 1st Monday in September
Columbus Day 2nd Monday in October
Veterans' Day November 11
Thanksgiving Day 4th Thursday in November
Christmas Day December 25

INSURANCE

No matter how you're traveling, take out travel insurance. Read and understand your policy. Seek coverage that not only includes medical expenses and luggage theft or loss, but covers you in case of cancellations or delays in your travel arrangements. The best policies are those that also extend to the worst possible scenario, such as an accident that requires hospitalization and a return flight home. Check your medical policy at home, since some may already provide worldwide coverage.

Ask both your insurer and your ticket-issuing agency to explain the finer points, especially what supporting documentation you need to file a claim. Buy travel insurance as early as possible – if you buy it the week before you leave, for instance, you may find that you're not covered for delays to your flight caused by strikes or other industrial action that may have been in force before you took out the insurance.

Wide varieties of policies are available and your travel agent should have recommendations. Some policies specifically exclude 'dangerous activities' such as scuba diving, motorcycling and even trekking. If these activities are on your agenda, search for policies that include them.

While you may find a policy that pays doctors or hospitals directly, be aware that many healthcare professionals still demand payment at the time of service, especially from out-of-towners. Except in emergencies, call around for a doctor willing to accept your insurance. Be sure to keep all receipts and documentation. Some policies ask you to call (reverse charges) a center in your home country for an immediate assessment of your problem.

INTERNATIONAL VISITORS
Entering the Country

Since September 11, 2001, immigration into the USA has gone through major changes, with the dissolution of the Immigration and Naturalization Service (INS) and the establishment of the 'Department of Homeland Security.' Immigration now falls under the purview of the **Bureau of Citizenship and Immigration Services** (BCIS; www.bcis.gov). Getting into the United States can be a bureaucratic nightmare, depending on your country of origin, as the rules keep changing. For up-to-date information about visas and immigration, check the website of the **US State Department** (www.travel.state.gov/visa_services.html).

Passports & Visas

Canadian nationals can enter the US with proof of Canadian citizenship. Visitors from other countries must have a valid passport,

and many must also obtain a visa from a US consulate or embassy in their own country. In most countries this process can be done by mail or through a travel agent.

Under the Visa Waiver Program, citizens of certain countries may enter the USA without a visa for stays of 90 days or less. Currently these are Andorra, Austria, Australia, Belgium, Brunei, Denmark, Finland, France, Germany, Iceland, Ireland, Italy, Japan, Liechtenstein, Luxembourg, Monaco, the Netherlands, New Zealand, Norway, Portugal, San Marino, Singapore, Slovenia, Spain, Sweden, Switzerland, the United Kingdom and Uruguay. Under this program you *must* have a round-trip or onward ticket to any foreign destination, other than a territory bordering on the US (ie Mexico and Canada), that is nonrefundable in the US, and you will not be allowed to extend your stay beyond 90 days.

Your passport must be valid for at least six months longer than your intended stay. You'll need to submit a recent photo 2in square (50.8mm x 50.8mm) with the visa application (plus a fee of $65). Documents of financial stability and/or guarantees from a US resident are sometimes required, particularly for those from developing countries. In addition, it may be necessary to 'demonstrate binding obligations' that will ensure your return back home. Because of this requirement, those planning to travel through other countries before arriving in the US are generally better off applying for their US visa while they are still in their home country, rather than while on the road.

The most-common tourist visa is a Nonimmigrant Visitors Visa, type B1 (for business) or type B2 (for pleasure or medical treatment). The visa's validity period depends on your home country and specifically prohibits you from taking paid employment in the US. The actual length of time you'll be allowed to stay in the US is determined by the BCIS at the port of entry.

If you want, need or hope to stay in the US longer than the date stamped on your passport, go to the local **BCIS office** (☎ 800-375-5283 for the nearest branch) *before* the stamped date to apply for an extension. Any time after that will usually lead to a stressful conversation with an INS official who will assume you want to work illegally.

If you find yourself in that situation, it's a good idea to bring a US citizen with you to vouch for your character and to have some verification that you have enough money to support yourself. Note that if you entered the US under the Visa Waiver Program, no extensions of stay can be granted.

Customs

US customs allows each person over the age of 21 to bring 1L of liquor, 100 cigars and 200 cigarettes duty free into the country. US citizens and permanent residents are allowed to import, duty free, $400 worth of gifts from abroad, while non-US citizens are allowed to bring in $100 worth. US law permits you to bring in, or take out, up to $10,000 (cash, travelers checks, etc); amounts greater must be declared to customs.

California is an important agricultural state. To prevent the spread of pests, fungi and other diseases, most food products – especially fresh, dried and canned meat, fruit, vegetables and plants – may not be brought into the state. Bakery items or cured cheeses are admissible.

If you drive into California across the border from Mexico or the neighboring states of Oregon, Nevada or Arizona, you may have to stop for a quick inspection and questioning by officials of the California Department of Food and Agriculture.

Embassies & Consulates
US EMBASSIES & CONSULATES

Visas and other documents are usually handled by consulates, not embassies. While embassies are in a country's capital, the US also maintains consulates in many other major cities. To find the US consulate nearest to you, contact the US embassy in your country.

Australia (☎ 02-6214 5600; Moonah Pl, Yarralumla, ACT 2600)
Canada (☎ 613-238 5335; 4900 Sussex Dr, Ottawa, Ontario K1N 1G8)
France (☎ 01 43 12 22 22; 2 Ave Gabriel, 75008 Paris)
Germany (☎ 030-830 50; Neustädtische Kirchstrasse 4-5, 10117 Berlin)
Ireland (☎ 01-668 8777; 42 Elgin Rd, Dublin 4)
Israel (☎ 03-519 7575; 71 Hayarkon St, Tel Aviv)
Italy (☎ 06-467 41; Via Veneto 119/A, 00187 Rome)
Japan (☎ 03-3224 5000; 1-10-5 Akasaka, Minato-ku, Tokyo)

Netherlands (☎ 070-310 9209; Lange Voorhout 102, 2514 EJ The Hague)
New Zealand (☎ 04-462 6000; 29 Fitzherbert Tce, Thorndon, Wellington)
UK (☎ 020-7499 9000; 24 Grosvenor Sq, London W1A 1AE)

EMBASSIES & CONSULATES IN COASTAL CALIFORNIA

Most foreign embassies are in Washington, DC, but many countries, including the following, have consular offices in Los Angeles and San Francisco.

To get in touch with an embassy in Washington, DC, call that city's directory assistance (☎ 202-555-1212).

Australia Los Angeles (☎ 310-229-4800; 2049 Century Park E, 19th fl); San Francisco (☎ 415-536-1970; 625 Market St)
Canada Los Angeles (☎ 213-346-2700; 550 S Hope St, 9th fl)
France Los Angeles (☎ 310-235-3200; 10990 Wilshire Blvd, Suite 300); San Francisco (☎ 415-397-4330; 540 Bush St)
Germany Los Angeles (☎ 323-930-2703; 6222 Wilshire Blvd, Suite 500); San Francisco (☎ 415-775-1061; 1960 Jackson St)
Ireland San Francisco (☎ 415-392-4214; 44 Montgomery St, Suite 3830)
Italy Los Angeles (☎ 310-826-5998; 12400 Wilshire Blvd, Suite 300); San Francisco (☎ 415-931-4924; 2590 Webster St)
Japan Los Angeles (☎ 213-617-6700; 350 S Grand Ave, Suite 1700); San Francisco (☎ 415-777-3533; 50 Fremont St, Suite 2300)
Netherlands Los Angeles (☎ 310-268-1598; 11766 Wilshire Blvd, Suite 1150)
New Zealand Los Angeles (☎ 310-207-1605; 12400 Wilshire Blvd, 11th fl)
South Africa Los Angeles (☎ 310-651-5902; 6300 Wilshire Blvd, Suite 600)
UK Los Angeles (☎ 310-477-3322; 11766 Wilshire Blvd, Suite 400); San Francisco (☎ 415-617-1300; 1 Sansome St)

It's important to realize what the embassy of the country of which you are a citizen can and can't do. Generally speaking, it won't be much help in emergencies if the trouble you're in is remotely your own fault. Remember, you're bound by the laws of the country you're visiting and embassy officials won't be sympathetic if you've committed a crime locally, even if such actions are legal in your own country.

You might get some assistance in genuine emergencies, but only if other channels have been exhausted. For example, if you need to get home urgently, a free ticket home is exceedingly unlikely – the embassy would expect you to have insurance. If you have all your money and documents stolen, it will assist you in getting a new passport, but forget about a loan for onward travel.

INTERNET ACCESS

California leads the world in technology, so you'd think that it'd be pretty easy to check your email. It depends where you are. There are Internet cafés in cities large and small, and most hotels provide guests a place to log onto the Internet. But in smaller towns, if you must stay connected, carry a laptop, a phone cord and your Internet service provider's local dial-up numbers. Be sure you find out how to configure your modem before you leave home, and practice before you hit the road. But don't worry if you don't have a laptop: computer terminals are everywhere in the Golden State, and you'll never be too far away from your e-world.

LEGAL MATTERS

If you are stopped by the police for any reason, there is no system of paying fines on the spot. Attempting to pay the fine to the officer may lead to a charge of attempted bribery. There is usually a 30-day period to pay a fine. For traffic offenses, the police officer will explain the options to you. Most matters can be handled by mail.

If you are arrested for more serious offenses, you have the right to remain silent and are presumed innocent until proven guilty. There is no legal reason to speak to a police officer if you don't wish. Don't be cowed. All persons who are arrested are legally allowed the right to make one phone call. If you don't have a lawyer, friend or family member to help you, call your embassy. The police will give you the number upon request.

The legal drinking age is 21, and you can be asked for a photo ID to prove your age. Stiff fines, jail time and other penalties can be incurred for driving under the influence (DUI) of alcohol or drugs. A blood-alcohol content of 0.08% or higher is illegal.

Police can give roadside sobriety checks to assess if you've been drinking or using

---

MAY I SEE YOUR ID, PLEASE?

Legal Minimum Age in California to...

- Drive a car – 16
- Fly a plane – 17
- Buy a shotgun – 18
- Vote in an election – 18
- Go to war – 18
- Drink a pint of beer – 21

---

drugs. If you fail, they'll require you to take a breath, urine or blood test to determine the level of alcohol in your body. Refusing to be tested is treated the same as taking and failing the test. Penalties for DUI range from license suspension and fines to jail time. If you're in a group, choose a 'designated driver' who agrees not to consume alcohol or drugs.

It is also illegal to carry open containers of alcohol inside a vehicle, even in the passenger section, even if they are empty. Containers that are full and sealed may be carried, but if they have ever been opened, they must be stored in the trunk.

During festive holidays and special events, roadblocks are sometimes set up to deter drunk drivers.

In California, possession of under 1oz of marijuana is a misdemeanor, and though it is punishable by up to one year in jail, a fine is more likely. Possession of any other drug, including cocaine, ecstasy, LSD, heroin, hashish or more than an ounce of weed is a felony, punishable by lengthy jail sentences, depending on the circumstances. Conviction of any drug offense is grounds for deportation of a foreigner.

MAPS

Visitors centers and chambers of commerce often have good local maps, free or at low cost. For detailed state- and national-park trail and topographical maps, stop by park visitors centers or the forest ranger's station. The best are those published by the US Geological Survey (USGS), usually available at camping supply stores and travel bookshops. Many convenience stores and most gas stations sell detailed folding maps of local areas that include street name indexes for about $3.50.

MEDICAL SERVICES

You'll pay through the nose for ER care anyplace; expect bills starting anywhere from $100 to $500 – and they only go up from there.

Always check with your insurance carrier before you leave home to learn about your out-of-town coverage; or take out comprehensive travel insurance if you're traveling from overseas (see Insurance on p211).

SOLO TRAVELERS

Traveling up and down the California coast alone can be meditative and peaceful, and there are no special cautions for solo travelers. Women should not fear journeying alone, but would be wise to remain aware of their surroundings as a matter of course.

TIPPING

Gratuities are not really optional in the US, since most people in service industries receive minimum wage and rely upon tips as their primary source of income. However, if service is truly appalling, don't tip. There are customary tipping amounts:

Bartenders – 15% of the bill.
Bellhops, skycaps in airports – $1 to $2 per bag.
Concierges – nothing for simple information (like directions); $2 to $20 for securing restaurant reservations, concert tickets or providing unusual service.
Housekeeping staff – $2 daily, left on the pillow each day; more if you're very messy.

Parking valets – $1 to $2 unless posted signs call for more when you retrieve your car.
Restaurant servers – 15% to 20% of the pretax bill.
Taxi drivers – 10% to 15% of metered fare.

TOURIST INFORMATION

The **California Division of Tourism** (☎ 800-463-2543; www.visitcalifornia.com) operates an excellent website packed with useful pre-trip planning information. The office will mail you a free *Official State Visitors Guide*, but the website has just about all the same information, without all the paper.

The state government also maintains several California Welcome Centers in various regions. Staff dispense maps and brochures and can help find accommodations. Look for them at Arcata (p53) on the North Coast, Los Angeles (p146), Oceanside (p196), north of San Diego, and San Francisco (p91).

WOMEN

California is a relatively safe place to travel, even for women alone. Use the same common sense as you would at home.

If you are assaulted, call the **police** (☎ 911). In some rural areas where ☎ 911 is not active, just dial ☎ 0 for the operator. Cities and larger towns have rape crisis centers and women's shelters that provide help and support. Services include the **LA Rape Crisis Center** (☎ 310-392-8381) and the **San Francisco Rape Crisis Center** (☎ 415-647-7273).

Transport

TRANSPORT

WARNING

The information in this chapter is particularly vulnerable to change. Prices for international travel are volatile, routes get introduced and cancelled, schedules change, special deals come and go, and rules and visa requirements are amended. You should check directly with the airline or a travel agent to make sure you understand how a fare (and ticket you may buy) really works, and be aware of the security requirements for international travel.

The upshot? Get opinions, quotes and advice from as many airlines and travel agents as possible before you part with your hard-earned cash. The details in this chapter should be regarded as pointers, not as a substitute for your own careful, up-to-date research.

GETTING THERE & AWAY

AIR

Domestic airfares fluctuate hugely depending on the season, day of the week, length of stay and flexibility of the ticket for changes and refunds. Still, nothing determines fares more than demand, and when business is slow, airlines lower fares to fill seats. Airlines are competitive and at any given time any one of them could have the cheapest fare. Expect less fluctuation with international fares.

Airports & Airlines

International passengers disembark at the Tom Bradley International Terminal of the **Los Angeles International Airport** (LAX; ☎ 310-646-5252; www.lawa.org). There are several smaller area airports, mostly for domestic travel:
Burbank-Glendale-Pasadena (BUR; ☎ 818-840-8847; www.burbankairport.com)
John Wayne–Orange County (SNA; ☎ 949-252-5200; www.ocair.com)
Long Beach (LGB; ☎ 562-570-2600; www.lgb.org)
Monterey Peninsula Aiport (MRY; ☎ 831-648-7000; www.montereyairport.com)
Ontario/San Bernardino County (ONT; ☎ 909-937-2700; www.lawa.org/ont)
San Luis Obispo (SBP; ☎ 805-781-5205; www.sloairport.com)

San Diego International Airport (SAN; ☎ 619-686-6200; www.portofsandiego.org) gets mostly domestic travel as well as one British Airways flight daily from London Gatwick.

Most international flights to the Bay Area land at **San Francisco International Airport** (SFO; ☎ 650-821-8211; www.flysfo.com) on the Peninsula.

The airports in **Oakland** (OAK; ☎ 510-577-4000; www.flyoakland.com) and **San Jose** (SJC; ☎ 408-501-7600; www.sjc.org) are important domestic gateways with limited international services.

The following major domestic airlines serve California:
Alaska (☎ 800-426-0333; www.alaskaair.com)
American Airlines (☎ 800-433-7300; www.aa.com)
America West (☎ 800-235-9292; www.americawest.com)
Continental (☎ 800-525-0280; www.continental.com)
Delta (☎ 800-221-1212, ☎ 800-241-4141; www.delta.com)
Jet Blue (☎ 800-538-2583; www.jetblue.com)
Northwest (☎ 800-225-2525; www.nwa.com)
Southwest (☎ 800-435-9792; www.southwest.com)
United Airlines (☎ 800-241-6522, ☎ 800-538-2929; www.united.com)
US Airways (☎ 800-428-4322; www.usairways.com)

Major international airlines include
Aeromexico (☎ 800-237-6639; www.aeromexico.com)
Air Canada (☎ 888-247-2262; www.aircanada.com)
Air France (☎ 800-237-2747; www.airfrance.com)
Air New Zealand (☎ 800-262-1234; www.airnewzealand.com)

Alitalia (☎ 800-223-5730; www.alitaliausa.com)
British Airways (☎ 800-247-9297; www.british
airways.com)
Cathay Pacific (☎ 800-228-4297; www.cathay
pacific.com)
Japan Airlines (☎ 800-525-3663; www.japanair.com)
KLM (☎ 800-374-7747; www.klm.com)
Lufthansa (☎ 800-645-3880; www.lufthansa.com)
Mexicana (☎ 800-531-7921; www.mexicana.com)
Qantas (☎ 800-227-4500; www.qantas.com)
Singapore Airlines (☎ 800-742-3333; www.singapore
air.com)
Virgin Atlantic (☎ 800-862-8621; www.virgin.com
/atlantic)

LAND
Border Crossings
Mexico and California share a border. For
details on traveling between the US and
Mexico, see Coastal San Diego (p189).

Car & Motorcycle
For information and advice on driving, see
p219. Though each state legislates its own
rules of the road, there's little variation
from state to state.

If you're interested in driving someone
else's car to save money on transportation,
consider a drive-away car. To find an agency,
check the *Yellow Pages* under 'Automotive
Transportation & Drive-Away Companies;'
also check the website, www.movecars.com.

Bus
Greyhound (☎ 800-231-2222; passes 888-454-7277,
402-330-8552; www.greyhound.com) is the main national bus carrier and operates throughout
much of California and the rest of the USA.
See p218 for information and details about
fares and reservations.

If California is part of a wider US itiner-
ary, you might save money by purchasing
one of Greyhound's unlimited travel passes
(called a Discovery Pass or an Ameripass),
available for periods of seven, 10, 15, 21, 30,
45 or 60 consecutive days; average prices are
$229–649 per adult and $115–325 per child.
If you're coming from overseas, you can get
a slight discount by buying in your home
country; check the website for overseas offices. You can only buy tickets online from
within Canada and the United States.

On regular tickets, students and seniors
over 62 qualify for a 10% discount, and
children get 50% off.

Train
Amtrak (☎ 800-872-7245; www.amtrak.com) operates a fairly extensive rail system throughout the US. Trains are comfortable, if slow,
and equipped with dining and lounge cars
on long-distance routes. See p221 for details about intra-California routes, tickets
and reservations.

Four interstate trains pass through
California:
California Zephyr Daily service between Chicago and
Emeryville, near San Francisco, via Omaha, Denver and Salt
Lake City.
Coast Starlight Goes up the West Coast daily between
Los Angeles and Seattle, with stops in Oakland, Sacra-
mento and Portland.
Southwest Chief Daily departures between Chicago and
Los Angeles via Kansas City, Albuquerque and Flagstaff.
Sunset Limited Thrice weekly service between Los
Angeles and Orlando via Tucson, El Paso and New Orleans.

Amtrak also offers passes for exploring
other parts of the US. Children pay half
price on all passes.

The USA Rail Pass is available to non-US
or Canadian citizens only and is sold by travel
agents outside North America as well as Amtrak offices in the US (show your passport).
The pass offers unlimited coach-class travel
within a specific US region for either 15 or
30 consecutive days; price depends on the
region, number of days and season traveled.
Average prices for the West Rail Pass (good
for travel anywhere west of Chicago and
New Orleans) cost $325/405 for 15/30 day
periods between June and early September
and $200/270 the rest of the year.

Amtrak's North America Rail Pass,
available to anyone, offers unlimited travel
on Amtrak and VIA Rail (www.viarail.ca)
of Canada for 30 consecutive days. Prices
are $674 for travel between June and
mid-October and $475 at other times of
the year.

GETTING AROUND

AIR
If you have limited time and want to cover
great distances quickly, consider flying.
Depending on the departure airport, destination, time of year and booking date, air
travel can be less expensive than bus, train
or rental car.

Other than the big airports in San Francisco and Los Angeles, flights also depart from smaller regional airports, including Oakland, San Jose, San Luis Obispo, Monterey, Burbank, Ontario, Long Beach, Orange County and San Diego.

Flights between the Bay Area and Southern California take off every hour from 6am to 10pm. It's possible to show up at the airport, buy your ticket and hop on, though good fares require advance purchase. You'll get discounts for booking seven, 14 and 21 days in advance; within a week of departure you'll pay full price.

Airlines offering flights within California include America West, American Airlines, Continental, Delta, Southwest, United Airlines and US Airways (see p216 for airline contact information).

BICYCLE

Bicycling coastal California requires a high level of fitness and focused awareness. Coastal highways climb up and down wind-blown bluffs above the sea and along narrow stretches of winding road with fast-moving traffic. Nonetheless, bicyclists are fairly common. Cars pose the greatest hazard.

You can rent bikes by the hour, day, week or month. Buy them new at sporting-goods stores and discount-warehouse stores, or used at flea markets and from notice boards at hostels. Also check the newspaper classified ads or on-line bulletin boards such as www.craigslist.org. Prices vary drastically depending on what you want.

Bicycling is permitted on all roads and highways – even along freeways, if there's no suitable alternative, like a smaller parallel route; all mandatory exits are marked. It's possible to bicycle on the I-5 all the way from the Oregon border to just north of Los Angeles. With few exceptions, you may not mountain bike in wilderness areas or in national parks, but you may cycle on their main roads. Bicycles, including mountain bikes, are allowed on national forest and Bureau of Land Management (BLM) single-track trails. Inquire locally about regulations. Yield to hikers and stock animals.

The **California Department of Transportation** (Caltrans; ☎ 916-653-0036, 614-688-2597, 510-286-5598) publishes bicycle maps of Northern and Central (but not Southern) California and will mail them to you free of charge.

Also try the **Adventure Cycling Association** (☎ 406-721-1776, 800-775-2453; www.adv-cycling.org) which is an excellent source for maps, bike routes and gadgets.

If you tire of pedaling, some local bus companies operate buses equipped with bike racks; for details, call the companies' telephone numbers provided throughout this book. For more on transporting bikes on Greyhound buses, Amtrak trains and with airlines, contact the respective company for details on whether or not you need to disassemble the bike and box it.

Wear a helmet – they're mandatory for kids under 18. Ensure you have proper lights and reflective clothing if you're pedaling at night. Carry water and a repair kit for flats.

To avoid all-too-common occurrences of theft, use a heavy-duty bicycle lock; some include theft insurance. Etch your driver's license number or other ID number onto the frame of your bike. Most police stations have etching equipment on hand, and it's easy to do. Then register your bicycle with the police.

BUS

Greyhound (☎ 800-231-2222; www.greyhound.com) runs several daily buses along highways between cities, stopping at some smaller towns along the way. Frequency of service varies. Buses to more popular routes operate every hour or so, sometimes around the clock.

The cheapest way to get around, Greyhound serves the less-affluent strata of American society, but by international standards service is quite good. Sit toward the front, away from the bathroom.

Generally, buses are clean, comfortable and reliable. Amenities include onboard lavatories, air-conditioning and slightly reclining seats; smoking is not permitted. Buses break for meals every three to four hours, usually at fast-food restaurants or cafeteria-style truck stops.

Bus stations are dreary places, often in sketchy urban areas. In small towns, where there is no station, buses stop in front a specific business – know exactly where and when the bus arrives, be obvious as you flag it down and be prepared to pay with exact change.

Buy tickets either at the terminal, through an agent, over the phone (☎ 800-229-9424) or on-line with a major credit card (in the US or Canada only). You can receive tickets by mail if you order at least 10 days in advance, or show proper identification and pick them up at the ticket counter.

Children under 12 pay half price; seniors who join Greyhound's 'Seniors Club' ($5) qualify for 10% discounts; and students with a Student Advantage Card (see Discount Cards on p209) receive 15% off regular fares. Otherwise students receive 10% off by showing valid student ID.

For lower fares, buy tickets at least seven days in advance; also check the website for special promotions. For information about Greyhound's multi-day passes, see p217.

CAR & MOTORCYCLE

Roads in California are excellent, and cars provide the most effective means to reach and explore coastal California. Neither buses nor trains access large swaths of the coast, so plan on driving if you want to visit small towns, rural areas, isolated beaches or far-flung forests.

Major Routes

Three major north-south routes run the length of California. Hwy 1 is the most scenic, but it's also the slowest.

US Hwy 101, a mostly four-lane highway, and State Hwy 1 are the primary roads along California's North and Central Coast. In the Far North, Hwy 1 merges with Hwy 101 at Leggett, where Hwy 101 continues the rest of the way to Oregon.

In Southern California, Hwy 101 ends in Los Angeles; Hwy 1 merges with I-5, which hugs the coastline to San Diego.

Hwy 1, also called the Pacific Coast Highway (PCH) in Southern California, runs along high bluffs on much of its serpentine course between Los Angeles and the Far North. If winding roads make you carsick, take Hwy 101.

Los Angeles' tangled freeways can be confusing. The most important thing to note is that freeways in the LA Basin go by names *and* numbers. Hwy 101, for example, is called the Ventura Freeway northbound, but it's called the Hollywood Freeway southbound. Pay attention and take your time.

From Los Angeles to San Francisco, the trip takes nine hours via Hwy 101, but 12

hours via Hwy 1. The fastest route, inland I-5, takes six hours; if you must travel up or down California quickly, take I-5, but beware dangerous wintertime ground fog.

Road Rules

The *California Driver Handbook* explains everything you need to know about California's driving laws. It's available free at any office of the Department of Motor Vehicles (DMV), or you can access it (as well as the motorcycle handbook) on the Internet at www.dmv.ca.gov.

You must wear seatbelts at all times. Children under four years old, or those weighing less than 40lb, must ride in approved child safety seats.

In winter months along the coast, avoid high-mountain inland routes unless you have a four-wheel-drive vehicle. If it's raining on the coast in January, chances are it's snowing above 5000ft in the mountains. Chains may be required at any time. Pay attention to weather forecasts.

Unless otherwise posted, you may turn right on red after stopping, so long as you don't impede intersecting traffic, which has the right of way. You may also make a left on red at two intersecting one-way streets.

At four-way stop signs, cars proceed in the order in which they arrived. If two cars arrive simultaneously, the one on the right has the right of way. This can be an iffy situation, and it's polite to wave the other person ahead.

On freeways, you may pass slower cars on either the left or the right lane, but try to pass on the left. If two cars are trying to get into the same central lane, the one on the right has priority. Some freeways and highways have lanes marked with a diamond symbol and the words 'car pool.' These lanes are reserved for cars with multiple passengers. Fines for driving in this lane without the minimum number of people are prohibitively stiff. Read the signs.

When emergency vehicles (ie police, fire or ambulance) approach, pull over and get out of their way.

For details about penalties for drinking and driving, see Legal Matters (p214).

Speed limits range from 35mph (56km/h) on city streets to 55mph (104km/h) on two-lane highways and sometimes 65mph (112km/h) or even 75mph (120km/h) on interstates, freeways and rural highways. California has a 'Basic Speed Law' that says you may never drive faster than is safe for the present conditions, regardless of the posted speed limit. You can get a ticket for driving too slowly as well as for speeding, based on the police officer's assessment of the safe speed.

In cities and residential areas, watch for school zones, where limits can be as low as 15mph when children are present. These speeds are strictly enforced. *Never* pass a school bus from either direction when its red lights are flashing: it means that children are getting off the bus.

California has an aggressive campaign against littering. If you are seen throwing anything from a vehicle onto the roadway, such as bottles, cans, trash, a lighted cigarette, or anything else, you can be fined as much as $1000. Littering convictions are shown on your driving record the same as other driving violations. Keep any trash with you inside the vehicle until you get to a gas station to discard it.

When parking, read all posted regulations and pay attention to colored curbs, or you may be towed.

Hire

Most of the big international rental companies have desks at airports, in all major cities and most smaller towns. For rates and reservations, check the Internet or call toll-free:

Alamo (☎ 800-327-9633; www.alamo.com)
Avis (☎ 800-831-2847; www.avis.com)
Budget (☎ 800-527-0700; www.budget.com)
Dollar (☎ 800-800-4000; www.dollar.com)
Enterprise (☎ 800-325-8007; www.enterprise.com)
Hertz (☎ 800-654-3131; www.hertz.com)
National (☎ 800-328-4567; www.nationalcar.com)
Rent-A-Wreck (☎ 800-535-1391; www.rent-a-wreck.com)
Thrifty (☎ 800-367-2277; www.thrifty.com)

You must have a driver's license to rent a car; most also require you have a major credit card, *not* a debit or check card. Prices vary widely, depending on the type of car, rental location, drop-off location, number of drivers, etc. Costs are highest in summer and around major holiday periods, when demand increases. In general, expect to pay from $30 to $50 per day and $150 to $250 per week for a mid-size car, more in peak season and for larger cars. Most rental

agencies require that drivers be at least 21; drivers under 25 must normally pay a surcharge of $5 to $15 per day. Rates usually include unlimited mileage, but not sales tax or insurance.

You may be able to get better rates by prebooking from your home country. If you get a fly-drive package, local taxes may be an extra charge when you collect the car. Several on-line travel reservation networks have up-to-the-minute information on car-rental rates at all the main airports. Compare their rates with any fly-drive package you're considering.

Liability insurance is required by law, but it's not automatically included in California rental contracts because many Americans are covered for rental cars under their personal car-insurance policies. Check your own policy carefully and don't pay extra if you're already covered. If you're not, expect to pay about $12 per day. Foreign visitors should check their travel-insurance policies to see if they cover rental cars.

Insurance against damage to the car itself, called Collision Damage Waiver (CDW) or Loss Damage Waiver (LDW), costs $12 to $15 per day; it may require that you pay a $100 to $500 deductible for any repairs.

Some credit cards, such as American Express or gold and platinum MasterCard and Visa cards, cover CDW for rentals up to 15 days, provided you charge the entire cost of the rental to the card. Check with your credit card company to determine the extent of coverage. It doesn't apply to all rentals; find out in advance.

Road Conditions

Hwy 1 hugs the coastal bluffs along dramatic stretches of coastline, particularly between San Luis Obispo and Big Sur, and north of Jenner. Not for the faint of heart, Hwy 1 twists and turns on precarious cliffsides that often wash out in winter. The highway department always seems to be repairing it, and every couple of years the road closes for months at a time and you can only reach certain communities by helicopter (it's rare, but it happens).

Further north along Hwy 101, just past Leggett (where Hwy 1 ends), the road runs between the Eel River gorge and unstable hillsides that regularly slide. When you see signs that read, 'Expect long delays 40 miles ahead,' or 'Hwy 1 closed north of Jenner,' heed their warnings, but don't panic. They sometimes overstate the situation to deter unnecessary travel. If you have hotel reservations, call the innkeeper. Folks north of Leggett *always* know precisely what's happening with Hwy 101: it's their only connection to the outside world.

For road conditions statewide, check with the **California Department of Transportation** (Caltrans; ☎ 800-427-7623; www.dot.ca.gov).

Recreational Vehicles

You can drive, eat and sleep in a recreational vehicle (RV). RVs remain popular for travel in California, despite high fuel prices. It's easy to find campgrounds with hookups for electricity and water, but in big cities RVs are a nuisance, since there are few places to park or plug it in. They're cumbersome to navigate and they burn fuel at an alarming rate, but they solve transportation, accommodation and cooking needs in one fell swoop.

You can rent RVs and campervans from **Cruise America** (☎ 800-327-7799; www.cruiseamerica .com) and LA-based **Happy Travel Camper Rental & Sales** (☎ 310-675-1335, ☎ 800-370-1262; www.camperusa.com).

Motorcycles

With a heritage that predates *Easy Rider* and *The Wild One*, motorcycling in America is an almost mythic experience. When the Golden Gate Bridge opened in 1937, the San Francisco Motorcycle Club crossed it first, ahead of the cars.

If you want to ride up and down the coast, you'll need a valid motorcycle license. An International Driving Permit endorsed for motorcycles will simplify the rental process.

The free *California Motorcycle Handbook* details the road rules for motorcyclists. Pick one up free at any DMV office or on-line at www.dmv.ca.gov. Riders must wear helmets or face stiff penalties. To drive on freeways, you must have at least a 150cc engine.

Motorcycle rentals and insurance are not cheap, especially if you've got your eye on a Harley-Davidson. **Eagle Rider** (☎ 310-536-6777, 888-900-9901; www.eaglerider.com) has rental outlets in San Francisco, Los Angeles, San Diego, San Jose, Palm Springs and Las Vegas. It charges $75 to $135 per day for a Harley, depending on the rental location,

size of the bike and length of the rental. Rates include helmets, unlimited miles and liability insurance; collision insurance (CDW) costs extra. You can rent in one city and return in another for $100.

Want to ride a BMW or Triumph? Call **DubbelJu Motorcycle Rentals** (☎ 415-495-2774; www.dubbelju.com; 271 Clara St) in San Francisco.

LOCAL TRANSPORT

Cities, larger towns and counties along the coast operate local commuter-bus systems; some provide evening and weekend service. Check specific geographical chapters for coverage of local transport.

TRAIN

Amtrak (☎ 800-872-7245; www.amtrak.com) operates train services throughout California, with bus services providing connections to some rural towns. Sometimes you'll only spend an hour on the train, then four hours on a bus, but it's more civilized than Greyhound.

The sleek, double-decker *Pacific Surfliner* operates two-class service between San Luis Obispo (SLO) and San Diego. All seats have laptop computer outlets, and there's a café car. A dozen daily trains ply the San Diego–LA route (via Anaheim), with four trains continuing north to Santa Barbara and four more continuing to SLO. Tracks hug the coastline for beautiful vistas.

Coast Starlight travels daily between LA and Seattle, stopping along the coast at SLO, Paso Robles and Oakland. Despite its romantic name, it travels on inland rails north of Santa Barbara but provides a comfortable alternative to flying, driving or taking the bus between San Francisco and Los Angeles.

Check with Amtrak for fares, promotional offers, information on California rail passes and details on inland routes.

Four interstate trains (described on p217) serve California. From LA to San Francisco the *Coast Starlight* costs around $65 (11½ hours); San Diego to Santa Barbara on the *Pacific Surfliner* costs $31 (5½ hours).

Seniors (62 and up) receive a 15% discount, children (two to 15) get 50% off and students with a Student Advantage Card (see p209 for information) get a 15% discount. Fares are generally lower January through May and September to mid-December.

Reserve as far in advance as possible to ensure a seat and a good fare.

LOCAL TIME

- **Pacific time zone:** Greenwich Mean Time (GMT) minus eight hours
- **Mountain time zone:** GMT minus seven hours
- **Central time zone:** GMT minus six hours
- **Eastern time zone:** GMT minus five hours

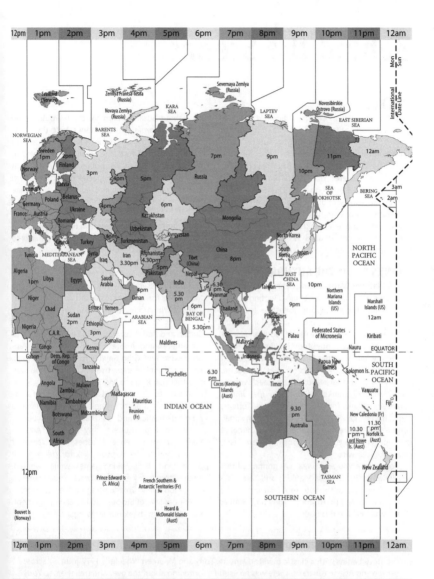

■ There are four time zones across continental USA, and California is in the Pacific Time Zone. When it's 10am in San Francisco and Los Angeles, it's 11am in Salt Lake City and Denver, noon in Chicago and Dallas, and 1pm in Miami and New York.

■ **Daylight Saving:** Daylight saving time, when clocks are moved forward one hour, runs from the first Sunday in April to the last Sunday in October in most states. Among the few exceptions are Arizona and Hawaii.

Behind the Scenes

THIS BOOK

This 1st edition of *Coastal California* was researched and written by coordinating author John A Vlahides and contributing author Tullan Spitz. John wrote the introductory chapters, the North Coast and San Francisco Bay Area chapters, while Tullan covered the Central Coast, Los Angeles Area and San Diego Area. Dirk Sutro wrote the Architecture section of The Culture chapter, Luci Yamamoto compiled 'The Hidden Coast' boxed text in the San Francisco chapter and Ryan Ver Berkmoes contributed several boxed texts throughout the book.

THANKS FROM THE AUTHORS

John A Vlahides Without Karl Soehnlein I wouldn't even have a computer, let alone a writing career; I love you. Nicole Chaison, longtime love and confidant, you inspire me; thanks for setting the fine example. To Jim Aloise, yogi and great friend, I'm forever indebted; thanks wise one. And to my fellow scribes Elizabeth Costello, David Booth and Kate Brady, thanks for cheering me on. Stanley Fuller, I adore you; please keep writing. Dan Fronczak, thanks for bringing me dinner. Putanesca, thanks for your support. Jake Torrens, sorry I haven't called. Tristy Taylor, you're an angel. Sondra Hall, you're extraordinary. Merle Oxman, I miss you. Ana Sortun, keep cooking. Brian Busta, please fix your wig.

Mom, I love you and swear I'm gonna call this weekend. Really. Barbara Vlahides and Tere Martinez, I love you both. You, too, Dad and Chris; thanks for coming to Yosemite. Tony and Norma: Please visit and use this book.

Without Susan Rimerman, there would be no *Coastal California*; Lonely Planet isn't the same without you. For her guidance and kindness, I am greatly indebted to Elaine Merrill. Thanks also to my co-author Tullan. For pointing me in the right direction on the coast, special thanks to Sherri Dobay, Debra Stegman and Jan Harris. I dedicate this work to the memory of Cap Patterson.

Tullan Spitz Numerous people at tourist offices and hotels steered me in the right direction. Thanks to Rena Ferreira for sharing memories, Jessie Singer for hikes, Devorah Herbert for wine. Special thanks to Irene Rutledge and Maui for the room, company and unsurpassed knowledge of Santa Barbara, to Mike Spitz for his generosity in LA, and to Eileen and Hal Wingard for lunch in San Diego.

Thanks to Julie Eigler and family, and Aiden Sutton and Robin, for homes in San Francisco and for entertaining Andrew. Thanks to Jenny Ambroulevich and Greg Snyder for surfing insights. For her technical expertise and calm demeanor, heartfelt thanks go to Ivy Feibelman.

Thanks to Elaine Merrill at Lonely Planet for listening to me gripe, to my co-author John Vlahides for his dedication, and to editor Susie Ashworth.

Love and gratitude to my husband Andrew Bunn for his patience, kindness and sense of humor, and to my stepson Nick for clearing the dishes (and playing video games) while I worked. Thanks, too, to my extended family and my friends at Oregon Public Broadcasting for their support.

For her love of Big Sur and her encouragement, I would like to thank Harriet Wingard.

THE LONELY PLANET STORY

The story begins with a classic travel adventure: Tony and Maureen Wheeler's 1972 journey across Europe and Asia to Australia. There was no useful information about the overland trail then, so Tony and Maureen published the first Lonely Planet guidebook to meet a growing need.

From a kitchen table, Lonely Planet has grown to become the largest independent travel publisher in the world, with offices in Melbourne (Australia), Oakland (USA), London (UK) and Paris (France).

Today Lonely Planet guidebooks cover the globe. There is an ever-growing list of books and information in a variety of media. Some things haven't changed. The main aim is still to make it possible for adventurous travellers to get out there – to explore and better understand the world.

At Lonely Planet we believe travellers can make a positive contribution to the countries they visit – if they respect their host communities and spend their money wisely.

CREDITS

Coordinating the production of this book from Lonely Planet's Melbourne office were Susie Ashworth (editorial), Birgit Jordan (cartography) and Laura Jane (layout and color).

Editorial assistance came from Imogen Bannister, Melanie Dankel, Hilary Ericksen, John Hinman and Charlotte Keown.

Mapping assistance was provided by Joelene Kowalski, Alison Lyall, Sarah Sloane, Simon Tillema, Chris Tsismetzis, Jody Whiteoak and Celia Wood. Candice Jacobus designed the cover artwork and Ruth Askevold designed the cover. Ben Handicott helped out with InDesign advice.

This title was commissioned and developed in the US office by Elaine Merrill and Graham Neale, with commissioning editor Fiona Christie in the UK picking the project up midway. Project manager Eoin Dunlevy steered the book through production.

Series publishing manager Susan Rimerman oversaw the redevelopment of the regional guides series with the help of Virginia Maxwell and Maria Donohue, who also steered the development of this title as Regional Publishing Manager.

The series was designed by James Hardy, with mapping development by Paul Piaia. The series development team included Shahara Ahmed, Jenny Blake, Anna Bolger, Erin Corrigan, Nadine Fogale, Dave McClymont, Leonie Mugavin, Lynne Preston, Rachel Peart, Howard Ralley, Valerie Sinzdak and Bart Wright.

SEND US YOUR FEEDBACK

We love to hear from travellers – your comments keep us on our toes and help make our books better. Our well-travelled team reads every word on what you loved or loathed about this book. Although we cannot reply individually to postal submissions, we always guarantee that your feedback goes straight to the appropriate authors, in time for the next edition. Each person who sends us information is thanked in the next edition – and the most useful submissions are rewarded with a free book.

To send us your updates – and find out about LP events, newsletters and travel news – visit our award-winning website: **www.lonelyplanet.com**.

Note: We may edit, reproduce and incorporate your comments in Lonely Planet products such as guidebooks, websites and digital products, so let us know if you don't want your comments reproduced or your name acknowledged. For a copy of our privacy policy, email privacy@lonelyplanet.com.au.

ACKNOWLEDGMENTS

Many thanks to the following for the use of their content.

Mountain High Maps® Copyright © 1993 Digital Wisdom, Inc.

BEHIND THE SCENES

Index

000 Map pages
000 Location of color photographs

000 Map pages
000 Location of color photographs

000 Map pages
000 Location of color photographs

INDEX

MAP LEGEND

ROUTES

Tollway	Walking Path
Freeway	Unsealed Road
Primary Road	Pedestrian Street
Secondary Road	Stepped Street
Tertiary Road	Tunnel
Lane	One Way Street
Walking Tour	Walking Trail

TRANSPORT

Ferry	Rail
Metro	Rail (Underground)
Monorail	Tram

HYDROGRAPHY

River, Creek	Mangrove
Intermittent River	Mudflats
Canal	Reef
Lake (Dry)	Swamp
Lake (Salt)	Water

BOUNDARIES

International	Ancient Wall
State, Provincial	Cliff
Regional, Suburb	Marine Park

POPULATION

CAPITAL (NATIONAL)	CAPITAL (STATE)
Large City	Medium City
Small City	Town, Village

AREA FEATURES

Airport	Forest
Area of Interest	Land
Beach, Desert	Mall
Building	Park
Campus	Reservation
Cemetery, Christian	Sports

SYMBOLS

SIGHTS/ACTIVITIES	INFORMATION	SHOPPING
Beach	Bank, ATM	Shopping
Buddhist	Embassy/Consulate	**TRANSPORT**
Castle, Fortress	Hospital, Medical	Airport, Airfield
Christian	Information	Border Crossing
Confucian	Internet Facilities	Bus Station
Diving, Snorkeling	Parking Area	Cycling, Bicycle Path
Drinking	Petrol Station	General Transport
Hindu	Police Station	Taxi Rank
Islamic	Post Office, GPO	Trail Head
Jain	Telephone	**GEOGRAPHIC**
Jewish	Toilets	Hazard
Monument	**SLEEPING**	Lighthouse
Museum, Gallery	Sleeping	Lookout
Picnic Area	Camping	Mountain, Volcano
Point of Interest	**EATING**	National Park
Ruin	Eating	Oasis
Shinto	**DRINKING**	Pass, Canyon
Sikh	Drinking	River Flow
Taoist	Café	Shelter, Hut
Winery, Vineyard	**ENTERTAINMENT**	Spot Height
Zoo, Bird Sanctuary	Entertainment	Waterfall

NOTE: Not all symbols displayed above appear in this guide.

LONELY PLANET OFFICES

Australia
Head Office
Locked Bag 1, Footscray, Victoria 3011
☎ 03 8379 8000, fax 03 8379 8111
talk2us@lonelyplanet.com.au

USA
150 Linden St, Oakland, CA 94607
☎ 510 893 8555, toll free 800 275 8555
fax 510 893 8572, info@lonelyplanet.com

UK
72–82 Rosebery Ave,
Clerkenwell, London EC1R 4RW
☎ 020 7841 9000, fax 020 7841 9001
go@lonelyplanet.co.uk

France
1 rue du Dahomey, 75011 Paris
☎ 01 55 25 33 00, fax 01 55 25 33 01
bip@lonelyplanet.fr, www.lonelyplanet.fr

Published by Lonely Planet Publications Pty Ltd
ABN 36 005 607 983

© Lonely Planet 2004

© photographers as indicated 2004

Cover photographs by APL/Corbis and Lonely Planet Images: Santa Cruz coastline, David Muench (front); brown pelican, Steve Rosenberg (back). Many of the images in this guide are available for licensing from Lonely Planet Images: www.lonelyplanetimages.com.

All rights reserved. No part of this publication may be copied, stored in a retrieval system, or transmitted in any form by any means, electronic, mechanical, recording or otherwise, except brief extracts for the purpose of review, and no part of this publication may be sold or hired, without the written permission of the publisher.

Printed by SNP SPrint (M) Sdn Bhd
Printed in Malaysia

Lonely Planet and the Lonely Planet logo are trademarks of Lonely Planet and are registered in the US Patent and Trademark Office and in other countries.

Lonely Planet does not allow its name or logo to be appropriated by commercial establishments, such as retailers, restaurants or hotels. Please let us know of any misuses: www.lonelyplanet.com/ip.

Although the authors and Lonely Planet have taken all reasonable care in preparing this book, we make no warranty about the accuracy or completeness of its content and, to the maximum extent permitted, disclaim all liability arising from its use.